Parisia

Parisian Bob Caruthers

Baseball's First Two-Way Star

DAVE HELLER

McFarland & Company, Inc., Publishers

Jefferson, North Carolina

LIBRARY OF CONGRESS CATALOGUING-IN-PUBLICATION DATA

Names: Heller, Dave, 1968– author.
Title: Parisian Bob Caruthers : baseball's first two-way star / Dave Heller.
Description: Jefferson, North Carolina : McFarland & Company, Inc., Publishers, 2024 |
Includes bibliographical references and index.
Identifiers: LCCN 2024000986 | ISBN 9781476691800 (paperback : acid free paper) ∞
ISBN 9781476651033 (ebook)
Subjects: LCSH: Caruthers, Robert Lee, 1864–1911. | Baseball players—United States—
Biography. | Pitchers—United States—Biography. | Right fielders (Baseball)—
United States—Biography. | Baseball—United States—History—19th century. |
BISAC: SPORTS & RECREATION / Baseball / History |
BIOGRAPHY & AUTOBIOGRAPHY / Sports
Classification: LCC GV865.C323 H45 2024 | DDC 796.357092 [B]—dc23/eng/20240125
LC record available at https://lccn.loc.gov/2024000986

BRITISH LIBRARY CATALOGUING DATA ARE AVAILABLE

ISBN (print) 978-1-4766-9180-0
ISBN (ebook) 978-1-4766-5103-3

Front cover: 1888 Goodwin Champion series card featuring
Brooklyn pitcher Bob Caruthers (Library of Congress)

Printed in the United States of America

*McFarland & Company, Inc., Publishers
Box 611, Jefferson, North Carolina 28640
www.mcfarlandpub.com*

For Laben and Kieran, my boys who are now men,
still and forever my champions.

Table of Contents

Acknowledgments

Easily the most oft-asked question of me with any of my books is "Why did you write about so-and-so?" To be honest, Bob Caruthers was never on my mind. I can't even recall how much I knew about him before tackling this project. Yet here we are. So, to answer the question before it is asked of me, here's the story of how I decided to write about him.

During the pandemic of 2020, when Major League Baseball went on a hiatus before restarting with a 60-game schedule beginning in July, I wanted to keep my mind active—and what better way than doing a little baseball research and writing about it?

I belong to a couple of St. Louis Browns groups on Facebook. I thought maybe people were in the same boat as me, missing baseball. Every day I went online and went through St. Louis newspapers from the Browns' existence (1902–53) and tried to find something interesting. Perhaps it was someone having a big game, a debut, or a trade. Some days were easier than others. Usually each evening after work, I'd find something and write a few words (and attach a picture from Google, if one could be found).

When baseball finally returned, it seemed like a good time to stop this exercise. I posted a note in the group thanking everyone for obliging my daily story. And oh, I'm always interested in writing another book but am out of ideas. If you have any, I'm always on the lookout.

I got a few responses, but one resonated from Craig Lammers, who wrote: "You should write about Bob Caruthers," who had an "interesting story." That spurred me to do some quick research on Caruthers, and I concurred with Craig—this seemed like an interesting story. The fact that his major league career was largely spent in St. Louis and Brooklyn—newspapers from that era being readily available online—helped clinch it. So thanks, Craig.

Of course, not everything is available online. Roughly 16 hours after emailing the Baseball Hall of Fame research department asking for any articles they might have on Caruthers, a clip file was in my inbox.

I had to fill in some gaps as well from Caruthers' time in Grand Rapids, especially in 1883, his introduction to professional baseball. For that I headed to the Grand Rapids Public Library's main branch, where the staff was incredibly helpful in getting me set up with microfilm and even brought me a folder they had on Grand Rapids baseball over the years. (I'll also note that there were a couple of good eating establishments within walking distance of the library, which was nice.)

You never know what you might encounter while doing research. I found a photo of Caruthers from his brief time coaching at the University of Indiana. I had some brief but pleasant exchanges with Bradley D. Cook, the university's curator of photographs, and that picture is now within these pages thanks to his permission.

I'd be remiss if I also didn't thank McFarland editor Gary Mitchem, who allowed me to directly pitch him this idea and, of course, ensure the book's publication. I had a chance to meet Gary in person at the 2022 SABR convention in Baltimore and had a great time chatting and getting to know him. It's hard to get to know someone through emails. Thanks, Gary, for your continued support and (hopefully) working together on more projects.

Now's the time for the obligatory family acknowledgments, no more so than my sons, Laben and Kieran. Honestly, they might never read these words (although they'll have a copy, so hey, maybe one day), but even as they grow older and move out, they do continually inspire me as they chase their dreams.

I know my parents, Mel Heller and Elaine Lyon, are proud of me authoring books, because, well, they tell me. Alas, they are not baseball fans, but that's OK. No one's perfect. My mom continually asked me, "How's the book coming along?" or "Are you done with the book yet?" Well, mom, this is proof that I indeed did finally finish it.

During the late process of writing this book I had a personal crisis going on. I appreciate my parents, my brother Steve—he *is* a baseball fan! Huzzah!—and friends John Basil, Jim Brady, John Desing, and Dave Wasserman being there when I needed it. You never know what life is going to throw your way and what twists and turns it will take.

Bob Caruthers probably never saw the direction—downward—his life was to take (how's that for a transition?). His story is vastly more interesting than mine. There's the Civil War and Brotherhood War, wealth and poverty, heroic behavior and sinning, being at the top of the baseball world and the bottom of the barrel. Caruthers didn't live a very long life, but he had an interesting journey. I hope you enjoy learning more about his experiences, much as I did.

Preface

It's no secret that baseball was different in the 19th century. As was life in America.

Bob Caruthers began his professional baseball career in 1883, 14 months after legendary outlaw Jesse James was killed. There were just 38 states at the time. Among things which couldn't be found were toothpaste in a tube—that wouldn't happen until 1889 (it came in a jar before then)—or zippers, which were invented in 1893. Karl Benz didn't secure the first patent for a gas-fueled automobile—a three-wheeled one at that—until 1886. Forget flying, of course. The first passenger flight didn't occur until 1908, and the initial commercial airline in the United States wasn't established until 1914—three years after Caruthers' death.

Yet despite all the technological and geographical differences, if you were teleported back to the late-19th century, life would still be familiar. Different, but familiar. The same goes for baseball.

The rules of the game when Caruthers played were still evolving. There was no pitcher's mound, and the distance from the flat, outlined box was just 50 feet from home instead of 60 feet, six inches. In 1884, when Caruthers first made his foray into the majors, players could ask for a high or low pitch, and if it was determined to be out of that zone, it was a ball. The number of balls for a walk also changed during Caruthers' time, before finally settling into our current four (there was also a year when four strikes were needed for an out).

When the pitcher threw to the catcher, the latter might be stationed well behind the batter, especially if no one was on base. The so-called glove the catcher wore was akin to a modern-day batting or golf glove with a little padding and cut-off fingers.

Ballparks could be smaller, and outfielders often played closer to the infield. One of Caruthers' teammates, Hugh Nicol, played a notoriously shallow right field and was known for throwing batters out at first base on hits to the outfield.

Hitters didn't swing from their hips and try to hit the ball out of the park—in some instances, a ball over the fence just meant two bases for the batter—although that's not to say there weren't power hitters or those who didn't swing for the fences (Caruthers would be chastised for doing this on occasion later in his career, when he was back in the minors).

There was also usually just one umpire, with ballplayers taking advantage of the situation by doing whatever they could get away with to win a game. Hold up or even trip a runner? Sure. Cut across the infield instead of touching third on the way home? You bet. Hiding balls by the outfield fence to assist in getting hits back to the infield quicker? Hey, that's called home-field advantage.

Even what we take for granted these days—the visitor batting first—was not the norm for quite some time. Teams would flip a coin to see who batted first (in later years, the home team had the option to decide).

But again, if you were transported back in time and could watch a game during Caruthers' time, you'd know what you were watching. It was still baseball. A pitcher trying to retire a hitter. Nine men in the field. Singles, doubles, triples, home runs. Three outs in an inning.

During this time, Bob Caruthers was one of the stars in the majors. His name was known throughout the country, despite there being no radio, television, or movies of his games and no major league team west of St. Louis.

He was perhaps the best pitcher of his era, or if not, one of the most durable. Of his 311 starts, he completed 94.2 percent. He consistently completed a higher percentage of games than his peers, owning a higher percentage in every season of his career but one, 1890, and even then he was at 90.9 percent compared to the National League average of 91.1. From 1885 through 1887, Caruthers started 116 games and finished all but one—and that was because he was hit in the stomach by a line drive. He finished the game in right field.

That's what made Caruthers different and, in part, stand out. For much of his career when he wasn't pitching, he was often put out in the field, usually the outfield. He didn't embarrass himself at the plate. He thrived.

Caruthers owned a .282 average in the majors with an OPS+ of 134. He possessed a keen batting eye with a .391 career on-base percentage, topping .400 in four seasons and leading the league in 1886.

It wasn't just his pitching and hitting which made Caruthers famous. And make no mistake, he *was* as much of a celebrity as a baseball player could be in his day. In an age when few players were quoted, Caruthers' words often appeared in newspapers. His background and eventual holdouts made for an interesting story of one of the early stars of the game.

No one is still around who played with Bob Caruthers, and there haven't been for a long time. His story is told not through voices but words. There was a lot packed into the short life of Bob Caruthers. He'd no doubt be an internet and social media sensation in today's world. But he lived in a different time, with his exploits mostly long-forgotten. With the research and writing in these pages, I hope to capture the background, career and life of truly one of baseball's most interesting characters—as well as its first two-way star.

1

History Lessons

In major league history, there have been numerous two-way players—those who pitched as well as played in the field during a season—but none quite like Bob Caruthers.

Babe Ruth, Bullet Joe Rogan, and, more recently, Shohei Ohtani might be the most notable two-way players. Others have done it, for example Johnny Cooney in 1924–1925 and Willie Smith in 1963–1964, but none could produce both pitching and hitting like Caruthers, Ohtani, and Ruth. That trio weren't just good at each, they *excelled* at both during the same season.

Only four players in MLB history have both a career offensive WAR and pitching WAR of 16 or higher: Caruthers, Rogan (who played in the Negro Leagues, for which we don't have complete statistics, unfortunately), Ruth, and John Montgomery Ward, who wasn't really much of a hitter, topping an above-average OPS+ just five times in his 17-year career. (Note: As of this writing, Ohtani is short of the pitching threshold but could reach it.) Caruthers and Ruth are the only ones to have led a league in both ERA+ and OPS+.

Yet, there are differences which put Caruthers in his own category.

Ruth, who began solely as a pitcher for the Boston Red Sox starting in 1914, saw his time on the mound greatly curtailed as the team started getting him into the lineup more often in 1918. After pitching 323⅔ and 326⅓ innings in the previous two seasons, Ruth toiled just 166⅓ innings in 1918 while playing 59 games in the outfield and 13 at first base. The following year, he was down to 133⅓ innings in just 17 appearances while being stationed in the outfield 111 times and at first base five others. By 1920, now with New York, he was a full-time outfielder, pitching in just five games the rest of his career.

In 2021, Ohtani won the MVP after a successful year at the plate and mound. However, he threw fewer innings than Ruth—130⅓ in 23 starts—while barely seeing any time in the field. Thanks to the designated hitter, Ohtani was in the outfield for all of 8⅓ innings. In 2022–23, Ohtani threw 298 innings combined, but otherwise never appeared in the field, spending all his time at DH.

There was no DH to save Caruthers' body from wear-and-tear. During his stint as a two-way player, mainly from 1886 to 1891, he split his time almost evenly between pitching and the outfield—and he was pitching in excess of 300 innings—twice going over 400—each season.

Physically, Ruth, at 6-foot-2, and Ohtani, 6–4, stood out as being bigger than their contemporaries. Not so with Caruthers. Modern references list him as being 5–7, although he could well have been taller, albeit still not more than average height.

His height was listed as 5-foot-10, 169 pounds when he broke into the majors in 1884. Three years later, in a list of measurements of him and his St. Louis teammates in *Sporting Life* (likely submitted by Browns secretary George Munson), it was given

Babe Ruth pitched just 133⅓ innings in 1919 and appeared in only five more games on the mound the rest of his career (Library of Congress).

that Caruthers was 5–10½, 150 pounds. That same year, a biographical sketch started appearing, one which would run for years in newspapers and magazines with statistical updates, and he was touted as 5–10½ "in his shoes"[1] and 152 pounds. In that same capsule two years later, his measurements were changed to 5–9½, 142 pounds. In 1908, when Caruthers was an umpire, the *Spokesman-Review* said, "He weighs not a pound over 130, and stands about 5 feet 7."[2] Included in the Baseball Hall of Fame's clip file on Caruthers is information from a "biographical research committee report" which mimics that 20th-century article, listing Caruthers at 5–7, 130 pounds (this report also incorrectly listed his year of birth, but more on that below). *The Sporting News'* contract card for Caruthers, however, has him 5–10, 150 pounds.[3]

A picture of Caruthers in the *Spokesman-Review* in 1909 at home plate, surrounded by players and managers, shows him to be of average height, at least compared to those around him, and in fact slightly taller than a couple of them.

While Caruthers might not have been as diminutive as thought, he was different from the players of his era in other ways. The majority of ballplayers associated with other players off the field. Caruthers found his company elsewhere, usually in a pool hall or with gamblers.

He also came to the game with something few in his possession had: money. Lots of it. It also gave him something else down the line which his fellow brethren didn't have: leverage.

When he broke into baseball, Caruthers was wealthy, but not self-made. His parents, specifically his mother, came from great wealth. Caruthers' paternal grandfather,

Col. James Caruthers—he was called Colonel by his friends but it's unknown if that was his actual military rank or just a nickname for having served—was given eight acres of land in Lincoln County, Tennessee—south of Nashville and west of Chattanooga—via a North Carolina military grant for fighting in the War of 1812.

At some point after 1840, James Caruthers, his wife Statira (known as Tyra) and their six children moved to Aberdeen, Mississippi. When he died in 1859, James Caruthers had accumulated a lot more than those eight acres. His will provided Tyra with "100 acres of land, houses, stock, carriages, utensils and slaves."[4]

John and Tyra's youngest child, born in 1818, was a son named John, Bob's eventual

Bob Caruthers (left in black suit and hat) is as tall as, if not taller than, players and managers before a minor-league game in Spokane in 1909 (*Spokesman-Review*).

father. John P. Caruthers attended law school in Lebanon, Tennessee, and was named Attorney General for the 11th Judicial Circuit in 1841 (he would be nominated again in 1847 but lose badly in the voting done in both the Tennessee House and Senate).

In 1846, John P. Caruthers married Elizabeth Rivers McNeill. Her father, Malcom McNeill, owned a great deal of land, including tobacco and cotton plantations in Mississippi, although he himself lived in Christian, Kentucky, where John and Elizabeth were wed.

John and Elizabeth didn't reside on as big an estate as her father, but they were living a good life. He was a lawyer, and they had their own plantation, which included at least one cow ("She is perfectly gentle and gives the richest milk Mr. Caruthers says he ever drank,"[5] Elizabeth wrote her sister, also noting a couple of Mardi Gras masquerade balls the couple attended). However, Elizabeth died on April 1, 1849. Their lone child, Malcolm, born the previous May, was sent off to live with his grandfather in Kentucky.

John continued his work as a lawyer and later as a judge at the Common Law and Chancery Court of the City of Memphis, where he earned a tidy $1,800 salary in 1857. He was solely concentrated on his work. It was noted, "He was usually to be found at the court-house. He had no residence, no family, no office at which he performed any publicly known business."[6] Caruthers was living either in the Blythe Building, where he also had his law library, or various hotels, including the Gayoso House, which was "known up and down the Mississippi River for its elegance and hospitality."[7]

In 1860, Caruthers started practicing law again while remaining a judge in Common Law and Chancery Court. He also was added to the Union Executive Committee of Shelby County. On April 21, 1861, that group issued a rebuke of Abraham Lincoln and what they felt was Northern aggression which would lead to war. After opposing secession, the group publicly sided with the other Southern states. In part, their letter, which was published in newspapers across Tennessee, read:

> We have been deceived by false and treacherous representations of what would be the policy of Mr. Lincoln's administration. Instead of peace being his purpose, a cruel coercive policy has been announced, to carry out which, he has called the hordes of Northern fanatics to rally to his standard. A Northern army is to be marched over the territory of the Southern States that have stood loyal to the Union to subdue and chastise our brethren. In view of this state of facts, believing there is no power given to the Federal Government, to coerce a sovern [sic] State, there is but one course left for Tennessee to pursue. When the flag of our common country becomes the insignia of a hostile invasion of Northern fanaticism upon our soil, WE CAN NO LONGER FOLLOW ITS GUIDANCE. We will therefore turn to the banner of our own gallant State, and with loyal and true hearts, rally around IT to resist any invasion of our soil. Mr. Lincoln's government, pursuing the course that is indicated, we will feel absolved from all obligations thereto, and acknowledge fealty ALONE to our own State.

Each member of the committee's name was printed along with the letter. A month-and-a-half later, Tennessee became the last of the 11 states to secede from the Union. Caruthers also signed petitions later that year in relation to the defense of the Mississippi River and communication to private citizens regarding the war effort.

John P. Caruthers' mind wasn't just on politics, however. In July he married again—there actually were two ceremonies. The first took place July 17, 1861, in Coahoma County, Mississippi, and the other 12 days later in Shelby County, Tennessee (likely Memphis). His new bride was 25 years his junior and also the daughter of his first wife's older brother, and thus also the granddaughter of Malcom McNeill (who had a plantation in Coahoma County), Flora Rivers McNeill.

Caruthers was still advertising as a lawyer in January 1862, but shortly thereafter the family was living in Mississippi, likely at his mother's plantation—called Oak Grove—just outside Aberdeen. John and Flora's first child, James, was born in April, although it isn't known if this occurred in Tennessee or Mississippi (the 1870 census, however, does list James as being born in Mississippi). They had certainly left Tennessee by early June, when the Union captured Memphis.

James was joined by a brother, Thomas, in November 1863. This date is important because modern sources list Bob Caruthers being born in Memphis on January 5, 1864, which, physiologically, would have been quite the feat for Flora Caruthers. He also wasn't born in Tennessee.

On January 5, 1865, Robert Lee Caruthers was born at Oak Grove. On the 1870 census as well as the 1900 document, Caruthers is recorded as being born in Mississippi. His son's death certificate lists his father being born in Jackson, Mississippi (roughly 160 miles to the southwest of Aberdeen). We'll note that the 1910 census does list Caruthers being born in Tennessee, but that was likely filled out by his in-laws. Malcolm Caruthers, now back living with his father, wrote to his aunt, Martha Rivers McNeill Boddie (she was the sister of Elizabeth Caruthers and was married to William Perry Boddie; Boddie's sister, Catherine, was Malcom McNeill's fifth and final wife, having wed in 1846) in a letter dated January 26, 1865, from Oak Grove telling her had had a new half-brother, Robert.[8]

Either way, Mississippi or Tennessee, Bob Caruthers would be just one of 13 major league players born in the Confederate States of America.[9] It would be Tennessee, however, where Caruthers got his start playing baseball.

Chicago

John Caruthers wanted to return to Memphis after the Civil War. It wouldn't be that simple. Even though he didn't fight in the war, he clearly was a Confederate sympathizer. His property in Memphis was now controlled by the United States government. Caruthers applied for a pardon, in part to get back his plantation.

He got the pardon from President Andrew Johnson, but not anything he owned. Among the things Caruthers had to agree on to get his pardon were to take a loyalty oath, never buy or use slaves, and disavow any claims to his property. Forty acres of land near Memphis was sold off in May 1866.

Caruthers settled back into Memphis quickly, once again starting up a law practice, although by 1867 he accumulated a great amount of debt which he was unable to repay and which put him "in embarrassed circumstances."[1] He was listed as Memphis Board of Reference for St. Louis Mutual Life Insurance Co. and was the Democratic nominee for the Shelby County Chancellor of Chancery Court in 1869, but finished third in voting. In 1870, he was named chairman of the Memphis bar.

While Caruthers appeared to be getting his life in order, the reverse was true. He "was addicted to the use of intoxicating liquors to the extent which seriously impaired his business ability."[2] Because of Caruthers' alcoholism, Malcom McNeill changed his will in order to, as he saw it, protect his daughter, Flora. Now, Flora's brother Malcom M. McNeill (known in the family as Malcom Jr., to avoid confusion with the grandfather) controlled the interest in her trust although Flora could "manage, do with it and by it as she may think is proper to direct."[3] The will would cause some problems later, with Flora suing her brother in 1894.

Just in case Malcom McNeill wasn't clear in his addition to the will, he had a codicil included as well, which in part read: "It is my express intention in this my last will and testament that the portion falling to Flora … is for her sole and separate use, free from all control of any husband she may at any time have or any debt or contract of said husband."[4]

That codicil likely was inserted thanks to an incident in which McNeill fronted $15,000 to John P. Caruthers to build a house in Memphis which was supposed to be put in Flora's name. However, Caruthers instead used his name on the deed and not Flora's as intended, and thus "creditors seized the property and sold it."[5]

By 1870, the Caruthers household included two more children—Elizabeth (or Lizzie, as often called), who was born in Mississippi in 1866, and another daughter, Emma, born in Memphis in 1868. The domicile also included Flora's brother, Rivers McNeill, an 11-year-old who was attending school in Memphis, Eliza Robinson, an 18-year-old listed as being half-white, who could not read or write, Lucy Narker, 14, who was Black and couldn't write but was noted as attending school, and a seven-year-old May Caruthers, perhaps a cousin.

Robert Caruthers was also attending school. In 1877, he was at the Memphis Protestant Collegiate Institute, one of 115 students. He made the Roll of Honor, having accumulated the "highest grade in G,"[6] which was equivalent to sixth grade.

When he wasn't in school, Caruthers found time to play some baseball. It has been widely written in various forms—from the time he was playing to modern days—that Caruthers was "sickly as a boy, and a doctor recommended outdoor exercise. So the boy took up baseball, over the objections of his mother,"[7] or that "The boy was slender and delicate in appearance and his father believed the exercise incident to the game would benefit him,"[8] the latter of which remained in the syndicated biographical sketch over the course of his career.

While it's true that Flora Caruthers objected to her son playing baseball *as a professional* and Robert had certain health issues as an adult (some of which were self-induced), there's no evidence otherwise that he was "sickly," that his mother objected, and/or his father pushed him into the game. This scenario likely originated in 1885, when St. Louis Browns owner Chris Von der Ahe, speaking in regard to Caruthers, was paraphrased as saying "His family did not want him to play base-ball, but he was weak, and the doctor advised out-door exercise."[9] Von der Ahe also said John Caruthers was a lawyer in Grand Rapids, so perhaps his words should not be taken as gospel.

Malcom McNeill was an early investor in Chicago property, which helped make him a very wealthy man. He did not, however, trust his daughter Flora's husband, John P. Caruthers, and tried to keep him away from his fortune (FindAGrave.com).

Robert Caruthers did get to play some baseball in Memphis in his pre-teen years. Jake Sneed, another of the baker's dozen born in the C.S.A. who made the majors, playing in the American Association in 1884 and 1890–1891, was a few years older than Caruthers, born in 1861. In 1888, he reminisced about their childhood in Memphis, saying of Caruthers, "Many a time have we chosen up rival nines. He was a rattling good hitter then."[10] However, Caruthers' formative baseball years wouldn't be spent in Memphis, but rather Chicago.

Malcom McNeill didn't just have land in Kentucky and Mississippi. In the early 1850s, he went to Chicago and bought some property (there's some evidence he might have made purchases there as early as 1842). It was a wise business decision. "He had to reach Chicago by private conveyance or horseback at great discomfort," said one biographical sketch, "which made his foresight and determination to invest in Chicago at that early date all the more remarkable."[11] According to the 1850 census, Chicago had a population of 29,963, the 24th-largest city in the country. By 1860, it was ninth with over 112,000, and in 1870 fifth at nearly 300,000 residents.[12] McNeill died in 1875, and his wife, Catherine, in 1876. It was written that his holdings were worth "about $1,000,000. A number of lots in Chicago, three five-story buildings on Clark St., estimated $100,000–$200,000."[13]

His estate was divided amongst his children and grandchildren, Flora Caruthers included. Among the items left to her in his will was property in Chicago as well as a share of his two plantations, which she eventually sold to her brother, Malcom.

In the summer of 1877, now possessing property in Chicago and with John Caruthers' alcoholism perhaps getting in the way of a prosperous career, the Caruthers family bid adieu to Memphis and headed north. They left Memphis on August 28. Youngest daughter Emma died three days into their trip at Martin's Station. John P. Caruthers sent a postcard to his hometown newspaper with the news while declaring, "Oh! Of all my great troubles, this is the saddest of my life."[14]

It's not known how the Caruthers family subsided for the first few years. It wasn't until 1880 that John Caruthers had his application to practice law in Illinois granted by the state Supreme Court. However, thanks to Flora's inheritance, the family wasn't starving—far from it. Living at 751 Segewick St. (now known as N. Sedgwick St., located less than a mile west of the Magnificent Mile), the family residence had among its members a servant, 17-year-old Laura Cook (or perhaps Coot or Coor), who was from Germany. Among the four kids, two worked as clerks—James, now 18, and Thomas, 16— while 15-year-old Robert and 13-year-old Elizabeth were in school. On the 1880 census,

Randolph Street in Chicago in 1880. The Caruthers house on Segewick Street (now known as N. Sedgwick) was only two miles away to the Northeast (Chicago Department of Transportation).

all four children were listed as having been born in Illinois, which we know not to be true.

While in school, Robert was playing baseball. In 1887, he brought with him to camp a fellow pitcher from Chicago, Thomas L. Dawson. When asked how he knew Dawson, Caruthers replied, "Dawson was a school-mate of mine in Chicago. He and I always played in the same nine at school, and we would both do the pitching."[15] While there was baseball being played in Chicago high schools when Caruthers attended, it should be noted, "some of the high school teams in the early to mid–1880s were no more than sandlot outfits. ... The predominant baseball activity in the schools was still intramural contests, typically played between two classes or two literary clubs at a picnic."[16]

Soon Caruthers graduated from playing school ball to amateur teams. William Veeck, later the president of the Chicago Cubs and father of baseball owner Bill Veeck, used the nom de plume Bill Bailey as a sportswriter in Chicago in the early 20th century. Veeck, as Bailey, told a story about how Caruthers hung around an amateur team in Chicago and eventually wormed his way into being a bat boy and water boy. One day the team was playing in Peoria, which only had eight players. Caruthers volunteered himself, and the Peoria captain acquiesced, saying, "Well, we can beat 'em with eight."[17] Peoria didn't win but was getting beaten badly, and Caruthers was inserted as pitcher. He did well enough, according to Veeck/Bailey, that Peoria used him again. It's a fun story except that William Veeck was six years old in 1882.

Baseball in Chicago took off after the Civil War with teams for both 14 or younger (in what was known as pony leagues) and for those 17 or older (juniors, which sometimes acted as a pseudo-farm team for amateur teams). In the early 1870s, "Chicago's baseball youth represented a population group somewhat high on the socio-economic scale."[18] It took a decade before Caruthers was on the Chicago amateur baseball circuit, but he qualified with his background of newfound family riches.

When he was 17, Caruthers joined the North End Club, an amateur team in Chicago. The following year, he was playing for the Lake Views as a catcher, not exactly his position of preference. A month or so into the season, Caruthers took it upon himself to work on pitching. He must have made an impression, as he was inserted into that role for a few weeks. It was good timing on his part. Good pitching has always been needed as long as baseball has been played, and Caruthers' life was about to change thanks to his new duties.

3

Grand Times

The Northwestern League's 1883 season was barely over a month old, and Grand Rapids needed another top-flight pitcher. It's not that the team wasn't doing well—its 12–6 record after the games of June 5 put it near the top of the standings. In an era when roster sizes were limited—and even more so in the minors—thus meaning fewer pitchers per club, Grand Rapids still was in good shape thanks to having two strong hurlers.

Charles "Pretzels" Getzien was born in Germany but was living, like Caruthers, in Chicago when he joined Grand Rapids for his first professional season. The two perhaps crossed paths playing amateur baseball. Getzien eventually pitched nine years in the National League, but even at age 19 and this early in the season, it was apparent he was one of the better pitchers in the league. Harry Arundel was Grand Rapids' other top-flight hurler, having started 14 games for Pittsburgh of the American Association, the other major league, in the circuit's initial season of 1882.

On the evening of Friday, June 1, Arundel attended a traveling circus which happened to be in town and became "badly intoxicated."[1] Confronted by the evidence, Arundel gave an excuse about his wife being gravely ill and her condition leading him to drink. He promised he was done with booze—and later that night was spotted drinking beer. He and outfielder Robert Ross, who "had been on a spree for two days,"[2] were released and placed on a blacklist, meaning they couldn't sign with any other organization in the league (although Ross was brought back by Grand Rapids later in the season).

Grand Rapids was hardly the only team with an issue keeping its players temperate. Just a few days before Arundel's incident, Bay City catcher Tug Thompson was suspended for 60 days for drunkenness (he appealed but the league board denied his protest, and the suspension held). Grand Rapids had just finished playing a series with Fort Wayne. Four of the Fort Wayne players went out on the town in Grand Rapids. One, shortstop Marr Phillips, "was found in a varsity dive opposite the hotel and was promptly fined ten dollars."[3] Not long after all four—Phillips, infielder Walt Kinzie, outfielder Ed Merrill, and catcher Tony Suck—were all cut by the team due to "insubordination and drunkenness. … These men have been on a protracted spree since going to Grand Rapids."[4]

Heavy drinking wasn't limited to the minors. Both the National League and American Association were affected. In looking back at the 1883 season, *Spalding's Base Ball Guide and Official League Book* had a subsection titled "Inebriety Among Players" in which it was stated, "The number of League and American matches that were lost last season by dissipation of players would surprise the fraternity were they enumerated in full. … During 1883 while many of the clubs were injured by inebriates in their teams, there was scarcely one team in the arena that did not have at least one 'weak brother' among its players."[5]

Alcohol wasn't the only issue. Arundel, in addition to his charge of drunkenness, was accused by the *Grand Rapids Daily Democrat* of throwing two games against Toledo, a team which, the paper surmised, he hoped to join after getting his release following those poor performances. On July 11, Fort Wayne's Bill Geiss, who was considered that team's top pitcher, drew a 60-day suspension for throwing a game—not to be released but "in the interest of gamblers"[6] (yet another problem the game faced)—against Toledo. The final score of that contest was 19–0, so apparently Geiss didn't exactly make a lot of effort to hide his misdoings.

This is the baseball backdrop an 18-year-old Robert Caruthers was about to join.

* * *

Grand Rapids manager Henry Monroe Jones sent one of his catchers, Len Stockwell, to Chicago in search of a pitcher. Chicago was relatively close and had already delivered him players such as Getzien, catcher Ed Gastfield, and third baseman Frank Meinke. Plus, Northwestern League secretary Sam Morton was in Chicago and was a partner in Albert Spalding's sporting goods store. If anyone had their ear to the ground when it came to baseball talent in Chicago, it would be Morton, who had a stake on finding quality talent for the league.

We don't know for certain how Stockwell located Caruthers—or how Caruthers' family felt about him leaving home to play baseball—but it wasn't soon after Stockwell arrived in Chicago that he wired back to Jones that he had his pitcher. Later reports indicate Caruthers' contract called for him to make just $75 a month (Stockwell, who had a few years of experience in pro ball, including two games with Cleveland of the National League in 1879, was making $150 a month).

Grand Rapids had a team in 1882 and paid its players but wasn't affiliated with any league. When the Northwestern League was formed the following year, it was one of eight cities to join, along with Bay City, Fort Wayne, Peoria, Quincy, Saginaw, Springfield, and Toledo. Grand Rapids played in the appropriately named Baseball Park, which had been built the previous September, could seat 1,000 spectators, and was located on the corner of Franklin Street (now called M.L.K. Jr. St.) and Jefferson Avenue. Games commenced at 3:40 p.m. with a ticket costing 25 cents—25 cents extra if you wanted to sit in the grandstand.

If there was a buzz in the Grand Rapids baseball circle, it wasn't about Caruthers but the prospect of Clarence Terwilliger pitching for the team, as reported by the *Grand Rapids Daily Democrat*. Terwilliger was a member of the Hillsdale Rowing Club, a well-known group dubbed the Four Oarsman (they won the national regatta in record-breaking time in 1879) who happened to be from Hillsdale, Michigan. Terwilliger also pitched for his local team.

Despite the report, Terwilliger never arrived. Caruthers did, with Stockwell, on the morning of June 12 and made his professional debut later that afternoon in a game against Quincy. He likely made them forget all about Terwilliger. In front of approximately 400 people, Caruthers led Grand Rapids to a 6–1 victory. He allowed just five hits while collecting three of his team's 11; no one else had more than two.

The game wasn't without some drama. With two outs in the second inning, Caruthers, batting left-handed (he switch-hit for part of his career but mostly batted from the left side), singled to left-center field. Charles Eden, Grand Rapids' best hitter, then poked a ball over the right-field fence. This was not a home run, however, under the ground rules. As Eden ran around the bases, a young boy threw the ball to a Quincy player. This was considered a "blocked ball," and under the rules of the day, the ball had to be returned to the pitcher before the baserunner could be tagged out. Quincy claimed it did just that. The umpire, John Morrisey, disagreed, and Eden had a run-scoring triple. Quincy manager Charles Overrecker was livid at this decision. When the second inning ended, he not only pulled his team from the field, but he also had them pack their bags, saying Quincy wouldn't continue to play and he'd file a protest. Morrissey declared a forfeit. Members of the Grand Rapids baseball team board of directors, seeing refunds having to be distributed and no money earned on the day, came out of the stands to try to cool down Overrecker and convince him to have his team play. Overrecker relented, although a few days later he still filed a protest on the grounds that Eden should have been limited to a double, per the rules if a ball was hit over the fence.

The incident didn't rattle Caruthers, who didn't allow a clean hit until the fifth inning and earned praise for his all-around play. "Caruthers, Grand Rapids' new pitcher, had an accurate and swift delivery, did some beautiful batting, and is more than an average baserunner. He seems to be just the man to change off with Getzien, and under the tutorship of our own inimitable Stockwell, will throw lots of dust into the eyes of the enemy,"[7] wrote the *Grand Rapids Daily Eagle*, which also said Caruthers "bats with safety and grace."[8] The *Grand Rapids Daily Times* opined: "Caruthers, the new pitcher for the home team, proved an agreeable surprise both in the box and at the bat. If his work of yesterday is kept up he will prove a valuable acquisition to the club."[9] The *Grand Rapids Daily Democrat* was the only one to supply a description of the newest pitcher for its readers, saying "Caruthers is very slim and young but he seems a ballplayer from the ground up. His delivery is very peculiar and he has good speed."[10]

Caruthers pitched again the next day, a 4–3 win over Quincy in 10 innings. In the bottom of the ninth, with runners on second and third and two outs, he struck out Clarence "Kid" Baldwin, the fifth-place hitter. It was Grand Rapids' sixth consecutive win. After not playing the next day, Caruthers was in right field for a game vs. Springfield on June 15. However, the new pitcher Grand Rapids used, called Magrady in the papers but likely McGrady (no first name was given, and he was never heard from again) didn't fare well, so Caruthers was brought in as a substitute in the sixth inning. He allowed three runs, but Grand Rapids came back to take the lead in the eighth—in part on a run-scoring hit by Caruthers, who later also scored—then pitched a 1–2–3 ninth. Grand Rapids was now tied for first place with Saginaw.

The team won its next three games as well, Caruthers pitching only the last, allowing 12 hits in an 8–6 win over Peoria. "Caruthers, who, for a new man in the club, and one who has pitched only a half dozen games so far this season, is doing splendidly in the box," observed the *Grand Rapids Evening News*. "He is also a fine general player, and if given a fair show will demonstrate himself a first-class man."[11]

The team was rewarded for winning. Players were given new uniforms, which included a red cap and stockings, and the board of directors presented each with a box of cigars and a white hat. Grand Rapids left town after a 9–5 victory over Peoria on June 21, a game won by Caruthers and stopped after five innings due to rain. One day later, Grand Rapids was flooded, with major log jams taking place—when the team returned home in late July, the logs were still jammed, and a few railroad bridges had been washed away. Things didn't go so great for Grand Rapids on its road trip, either.

Caruthers was moved to shortstop for a game in Chicago against the independent professional Unions team—the homecoming didn't draw a big crowd as only 300–400 showed up—and he stayed at that position during a four-game series at Toledo, in which Grand Rapids lost every game. An injury sidelined Caruthers in Indianapolis and Peoria, as well as the first game of a series at Springfield, Grand Rapids losing five of the six games. Caruthers returned in left field on July 18, going hitless as Grand Rapids was whitewashed, 7–0. The team was now 1–10 on its road trip. "It is alleged that the men do not keep regular hours, and are drinking,"[12] reported the *Grand Rapids Daily Eagle*. The players later said these rumors were put out there by a disgruntled John Piggott, who had played briefly with the team before being released.

The paper further eviscerated the team in the form of a poem:

> "The Grand Rapids Club think they can play ball.
> When everyone knows they can't play at all.
> But for goodness sake don't say I told you.
> There's Stockwell, Caruthers, Ross, Jones, Eden
>   Farrell, Bell, Getzien and Big Meinke,
> Step up to the bat and go out one, two, three,
>   But for goodness sake don't say I told you."[13]

More losses—and excuses—piled up. "I have private information to the effect that there is too much faro and poker connected with the club, and more or less 'stimulants,'" said local fan Darby Hull, who had been a proponent of the Northwestern League. "The club needs a first class manager, and if it had one there would be two or three vacancies immediately. It strikes me that several players are working for a release, because they have been offered more money by other clubs than they are now receiving."[14]

Jim Hillery, who had played shortstop for Grand Rapids but was released back when the team was in Peoria and since had signed with Fort Wayne, was asked about his former team by a local reporter after returning to the town to collect his belongings. He deflected when asked if the players were imbibing, but when asked about card-playing or flouting the rules, he succinctly answered, "They all know how to play poker."[15] Caruthers became adept at poker (and faro), and perhaps he already was at age 18. At the very least, he was getting an education in the game.

Caruthers lost some of his poker-playing money on July 24, when he was issued the first fine of his career. In a game at Quincy which resulted in a 6–5 Grand Rapids win in 10 innings, while running from second to third base, Caruthers tried to dislodge the ball from the hands of shortstop Tom Sexton. Throughout Caruthers' playing career, the umpire could issue fines on the field, and this was one of those cases as Edward Hengle docked the young player $5 for his interference.

Two days later, Caruthers made his first start in over a month, his last coming in Grand Rapids' last home game. Getzien and Frank Bell, the latter despite a sore arm, had been doing the pitching. But on July 23, Getzien was hit by a pitch on the wrist—Caruthers had to come in from left field and pitch the final eight innings in a 6–4 loss at Springfield—and was sidelined, not to return until August 27. Caruthers and Grand Rapids lost to Quincy, 8–7, in 11 innings but finished their long road swing with a 12–11 win two days later. Caruthers, after beginning the game at shortstop, where he made three errors, pitched the final four innings and gave up no runs and just one hit. Quincy manager Overrecker resigned after the game. His replacement? Hengle, who umpired that day's game.

Back home, Caruthers pitched the final three innings of an exhibition against Detroit of the National League, then in Grand Rapids' next game two days later. He lost despite giving up only six hits, 7–5 to Bay City against future major league team-mate Dave Foutz. Despite the loss, his effort "won nothing but praise from those witnessing it."[16] He pitched again August 3 but allowed 11 hits and six walks in once again falling to Bay City, this time 6–2. Getzien was still out, Bell was hurting as well—he left Grand Rapids' August 4 game and did not return to pitching for nine days—and now "Caruthers' arm has commended to ache a little and a few more games will cripple him."[17]

Nevertheless, Caruthers kept pitching—for the time being—including an 8–4 win over Saginaw on August 6 in which he struck out nine. Three days later he faced off against Saginaw and John Clarkson, who pitched for the NL's Worcester team in 1882 and eventually had a Hall of Fame major league career. Caruthers was not pleased by some of the calls made by umpire William Montgomery (who previously that season was the manager of Bay City), and in the seventh inning started taking his time between pitches, slowing the game down. Team captain Charlie Eden jogged in from right field and switched positions with Caruthers, much to the delight of the crowd, which "applauded greatly."[18]

The next day, Grand Rapids signed a pitcher from Cincinnati, E.C. Clark, and added another, the eccentric "The Only" Nolan, a couple of weeks later. Caruthers' days in the box, at least in 1883, were about over. He pitched in only six more regular-season games for Grand Rapids (he did go the distance in a 6–5 exhibition loss to Port Huron, which went 22–4 vs. Northwestern League teams, on August 17). In three of those, he didn't pitch a complete game. He went four innings on August 20, facing Clarkson again before being removed. On September 4, as the middle of three pitchers used in a 14–6 win over Quincy, he pitched just two frames. Exactly two weeks later at Fort Wayne in a 10-inning, 4–4 tie, he had to relieve Getzien, who pitched despite his arm hurting so much he couldn't even cut his food. Not surprisingly, Caruthers left after three innings with an injury. The next day, Caruthers again was one of three pitchers to make an appearance in yet another 4–4, 10-inning tie with Fort Wayne.

Caruthers did make two starts at the tail end of the season, likely because Nolen got shelved for the year due to an injury, going the distance in both. He won at Springfield on September 25, walking none despite a small but spirited crowd which was "one of the most disorderly ever seen at a game, howling and yelling so as to get the visitors rattled."[19] His last pitching performance was September 29 in Quincy's final home game, a 15–7 Grand Rapids win in which he allowed just five hits and one walk while striking out 10 and at the plate went 4-for-5 with a double and four runs scored while batting in the cleanup spot.

While Caruthers wasn't in the pitching rotation, he was still in the lineup nearly every day, missing only three games the rest of the way. He mainly played center field with Eden in right and manager Jones in left, making the Grand Rapids outfield "the strongest it has ever been."[20]

Caruthers moved around the batting order a bit, usually batting second, third, fourth or fifth as he established himself as one of the better hitters on the club. According to the 1884 *Spalding Guide*, Caruthers hit .288, tied for 12th in the league among those playing in at least 50 contests, the exact number of games in which Caruthers appeared, and he scored 51 runs. The secretary of the Northwestern League had him at a .284 batting average (although Caruthers was listed as having 63 hits and 277 at-bats, which is actually .227). Grand Rapids as a team was second in the league with a .254

average (Toledo was far in front at .275). Depending which source you trusted, Eden led the league with a .359 average, followed by Jones at .344, or the pair was second and third at .350 and .314. Pitching statistics, unfortunately, weren't divulged.

Grand Rapids, which finished in fourth place with a 48–36 record, saw enough of Caruthers, among others, to place him on its reserve list—meaning it controlled his rights; he couldn't sign with any other team in organized baseball. The team lost $4,500 on the season, and Elias Matter, who was the team president before being elevated to that title with the Northwestern League, saw high-priced players as the problem. He noted that catcher Les Stockwell was looking for a $100 monthly increase in his salary, while Eden claimed he had an offer of $1,200 ($200 a month), $250 to be received as an advance, from Indianapolis. "The majority of players who have been in the several clubs of the Northwestern league have been receiving on an average of $1,000 for six months' work, and it might be safely said that no one of them can earn $500 a year in any other business," Matter said. "The salaries are too high and will undoubtedly be reduced next season."[21]

Like Caruthers, both Eden and Stockwell were also reserved by Grand Rapids, and the pair eventually returned to the team in 1884. As Matter indicated, though, both prospered more in baseball than in their other work—Eden was employed as a railroad conductor in the off-season, while Stockwell in years past had been a factory worker. Matter clearly didn't know Caruthers' situation. For the first time in his professional career, but not the last, Caruthers said he wouldn't be playing baseball the following season. Also for the first but not the last time, the bluff worked.

4

The Dude

Benjamin Tuthill had no previous experience in baseball but found himself as the manager of a fledgling team in Minneapolis. He had already signed 10 players for the club's inaugural season in 1884 when he sent notice to one of the board of directors, Joseph Murch, a bartender at the Nicollet House in the city and one of the team's main investors, that their application for admittance into the Northwestern League had been approved.

The league was expanding from eight to 12 teams, with Bay City, Fort Wayne, Grand Rapids, Peoria, Quincy, and Saginaw returning (Toledo, which had dropped out of the league before the end of the 1883 season, and Springfield were gone from the previous year). In addition to Minneapolis, Milwaukee, Muskegon, St. Paul, Stillwater, and Terre Haute were added, in part because of their larger populations (which in turn the league hoped would fuel greater attendance and thus more revenue). Those six cities supposedly combined to account for 450,000 potential paying customers.[1]

With the team's fate now in place, uniforms were needed. Tuthill traveled to Chicago to Albert Spalding's sporting goods store to place an order. Tuthill ordered two color combinations. One was a "regulation suit with a narrow blue and white stripe running up and down the shift and hose, and from front to rear on the cap, with white pantaloons and belt."[2] Spalding had an idea for the other: A black shirt and belt with maroon pants and cap. There was also a maroon "M" placed on the breast of the jersey. The look garnered fashion opinions on both ends of the spectrum. The *Bay City Tribune* said Minneapolis' players were the "dudes of the base ball profession"[3]—dudes being a compliment for an "extremely well-dressed male"[4]—but the *Cincinnati Commercial Gazette* remarked the get-up was "one of the oddest ever seen on a ball field."[5]

Tuthill didn't just leave with a uniform order—he also added another player.

Robert Caruthers had been placed on Grand Rapids' reserve list despite his intentions, or at least what he told the team, of not playing baseball in 1884. Then Caruthers caught a break. Horace Phillips, the new manager of the Grand Rapids club, had a proposal which was quickly agreed upon by unanimous vote of the team's board of directors. He would send out contracts to all the reserved players, and they had 30 days to sign or be blacklisted. However, if within 10 days upon receipt of the contract, a player either in person or by registered letter notified the team and the Northwestern League secretary, who happened to be Sam Morton, Spalding's right-hand man and co-owner of his sporting goods store, that he wanted to be released, the team would comply. The deadline to do this was January 25, though getting set loose wasn't necessarily as easily accomplished as written. Charlie Eden, the team's star player, wanted his release so he could return to his job as a railroad conductor, but Grand Rapids denied his request. After meeting with the team president for a few hours, Eden re-signed.

Caruthers was more fortunate. On January 17, Grand Rapids released both Caruthers and Frank Meinke, the latter signing a couple of weeks later with Detroit of the National League. Morton, as league secretary, knew of Caruthers' new playing status. He approached the player and asked him to sign with the Chicago White Stockings' reserve team. Caruthers wanted $125 a month. Spalding, however, had a cap of $100 per month for his reserve players, thus Caruthers declined the offer. Morton did Caruthers a favor and mentioned him to Tuthill, saying he could become a good outfielder for the Minneapolis club and the manager should give him a shot. Caruthers was playing a baseball game on ice—this was a winter fad for a few years in a number of cities, including Chicago—and Tuthill liked what he saw. The two agreed to the $125 a month salary, Tuthill perhaps knowing Caruthers' demands in advance.

Tuthill had pegged Caruthers to be Minneapolis' left fielder. But circumstances quickly changed that plan. Minneapolis trained for a few days in Sedalia, Missouri, in early April, then prepared to take on the local team. However, Sedalia was in need of players, particularly a pitcher. Recalling the incident six years later, Tuthill said he had no pitchers to spare as most had sore arms. He knew Caruthers could throw fast, so he loaned him to Sedalia, along with a catcher. Minneapolis found itself trailing by a run late in the game. "I was in a sweat, for it would never do to send word to Minneapolis that we had been beaten the first game of the season by an amateur team," Tuthill remembered. "I took Bob to one side and told him he would have to let up a little and give us a show. He slowed up and our boys batted the game out in the next inning."[6] Caruthers did as he was told, but the impression was made.

Tuthill saw "good stuff in his arm"[7] and wanted to witness more of Caruthers in the box. In Minneapolis' next exhibition, played on a cold day in St. Louis against the American Association's Browns on April 15, the 19-year-old Caruthers began the game in left field before switching places in the fifth inning with Fred "Tricky" Nichols, a 33-year-old who had experience playing for teams in the National Association, National League, and American Association. Caruthers entered with Minneapolis trailing, 2–0. That ended up being the final score. Caruthers gave up just one hit—a bunt single by Arlie Latham—while walking four and striking out five. Tuthill wasn't the only one coming away impressed. Caruthers "did magnificent work and is a most promising young player,"[8] the *St. Louis Post-Dispatch* commented. Caruthers got another shot against St. Louis on April 17, but Minneapolis committed 11 errors and lost, 15–2. "Had he been well supported he would have won the game,"[9] surmised Tuthill years later.

When he wasn't pitching, Caruthers, at least early in the season, was in the lineup playing left field, where he also was getting rave reviews. "Caruthers … is one of the finest fielders in the league,"[10] said the *Quincy Daily Whig*. However, as the season progressed, his time was being spent either pitching or on the bench. After playing in left field June 10 (a game in which he also was summoned to pitch, closing out an 8–7 win at Stillwater), he didn't see the field again until July 3, when he was back in left and "made two beautiful fly catches in the ninth inning, running an unusually long distance for them"[11] in a 6–5 loss at St. Paul.

In a short period of time, Caruthers established himself as Minneapolis' best pitcher. He ended up pitching in 36 of Minneapolis' 81 games in 1884, his 30 starts—of which he completed all of them—the most on the team. As such, Caruthers was used in big situations.

On June 9 in Stillwater's home opener—the *St. Paul Daily Globe* dubbed that team the "Prison City Ball Tossers,"[12] perhaps not a nickname a town wants to be known

The 1884 Minneapolis Northwestern League team. A clean-shaven Bob Caruthers is seated on the right (Baseball Hall of Fame collection/Washington County Historical Society).

as—in front of a packed ballpark, he outdueled Bud Fowler, the first African American to play organized baseball and a 2022 Hall of Fame inductee, 3–2. Caruthers allowed just three singles while striking out, depending on the newspaper report, 13 (*St. Paul Daily Globe*), 14 (*Minneapolis Daily Tribune*) or 17 (*Quincy Daily Whig*).

Minneapolis was set to host its first game of the season in its new ballpark on June 12 against Quincy. A wagon with streamers pinned to the side rode down the streets displaying a sign reading "base ball to-day."[13] The players, adorned in their "nobby blue suits and white hats"[14] walked alongside, as did a brass band, just in case the others didn't attract your attention. Crowds gathered near the Nicollet House, where they could hop aboard a streetcar to the field. However, a downpour ruined the opener, washing it out well before the scheduled gametime. The next day it was more of the same— the Great Western Band led the way as players, now wearing white uniforms with black trim, were escorted to the park in carriages.

This time the game was played with Caruthers in the box. When the bell was rung at 4:05 p.m., signaling the start of the contest, the crowd of 3,000 erupted. "All was hushed and still until the Dudes began to assume their positions in the field. This was the signal for the second peal of applause," the *St. Paul Daily Globe* reported. "There was a large number of ladies in the audience and they too testified to their appreciation by waving their handkerchiefs and clapping their hands."[15] Caruthers gave those in attendance plenty of reasons to cheer, which were "deafening and prolonged."[16] He allowed just one hit—a two-out single in the fifth inning—while walking none and striking out four in a 2–1 victory (Quincy scored its lone run in the fourth on a walk, steal, balk and passed ball). The crowd left the stands and went to the players' tent to celebrate the victory.

Part of Caruthers' success was due to the way he was pitching—overhand. The previous season, this type of delivery was not allowed. As noted by *Spalding's Official Base Ball Guide*, in 1883 "before making the forward swing of the arm, the hand could be raised as high as the pitcher chose; but when the arm was swung forward the hand holding the ball had to pass below the line of the pitcher's shoulder, or foul balks were called."[17] This style of pitching, combined with Caruthers' "great speed, and a little curve"[18]—one report said he threw "as though fired from a cannon's mouth"[19]—was giving Northwestern League batters all sorts of fits.

Caruthers and Saginaw's John Clarkson staged a classic matchup in Minneapolis on July 12, a game called due to darkness after the 15th inning with the score tied at 4. Caruthers gave up just six hits while striking out 15. Clarkson was even better, allowing the same number of hits but fanning 26. The two faced off again three days later with Caruthers besting the future Hall of Famer 4–3, walking none and striking out seven as well as knocking in a run in the fourth inning to give Minneapolis a 4–0 lead.

Caruthers won three of his next four starts but then took ill July 26 and was sidelined until August 8 ("There is anything but a pleasant prospect ahead for the boys as long as Caruthers is absent,"[20] mused the *Minneapolis Daily Tribune*). The Northwestern League wasn't in good shape, either. Bay City had already disbanded in July, Evansville taking its place. Fort Wayne and Stillwater were gone by early August. On August 9, Grand Rapids, which was in first place, and Muskegon, which lost to Minneapolis earlier in the day, dropped out of the circuit after refusing to contribute a $500 bond to help the league stay afloat. Saginaw hosted Minneapolis for a couple of games then was kicked out of the league on August 14.

The Northwestern League reorganized with Winona joining Milwaukee, Minneapolis and St. Paul in a four-team circuit. That didn't last long. But before the league officially came to a close, Caruthers got hit by pitches, in separate games, on the wrist and head, the latter knocking him unconscious. After being carried off the field, he went back into the game 15 minutes later and finished off an 8–0 blanking of Winona. While injured, he umpired the August 25 game between St. Paul and Winona and had no complaints from players or fans. He also was behind the plate August 27 when Minneapolis hosted Milwaukee and took a foul ball off his head, "knocking him senseless."[21]

Caruthers returned to action August 28 but perhaps was not putting forth his best effort, Tuthill later saying the player told him, "I want to get released, and I don't want to play ball here."[22] In this game, in which he didn't pitch well and was removed after just three innings, he didn't run to first base after hitting a grounder in the first inning and failed to cover the bag when first baseman Charlie Isaacson went to field a ball between first and second. Tuthill fined Caruthers $50 and sat him out a game. It's easy to imagine Caruthers being displeased with that. Not just that he was fined, but because the players hadn't been paid since July 15 other than some petty cash here and there.

The team still owed over $2,000 for the stadium it had built, and $2,500 in payroll needed to be doled out to the players.

Despite all this, Caruthers pitched—and won—on September 1, going the distance in a 5–2 win over St. Paul, allowing seven hits with no walks and nine strikeouts. He also was 2-for-4 at the plate with a double and scored a run. He didn't play the next day, and when Minneapolis was set to leave for Milwaukee for one game and then to Winona, he and two other players refused. The board of directors met with Caruthers, who later estimated he was owed around $700, to try to convince him to make this road trip, as they said it would guarantee them at least $500. Caruthers wanted his money up-front. The board said it would give him $50 now and the rest when the team returned to Minneapolis. "It makes me laugh now to think of it,"[23] Caruthers said in 1888. There was no agreement. Caruthers didn't get his money ("and by the way, they owe it to me yet,"[24] he later said), and Minneapolis was out of luck—and time. That was the death knell for the team and the Northwestern League.

Because the league folded, Northwestern League statistics, other than standings, weren't included in the *Spalding Base Ball Guide*. Baseball-reference.com has Caruthers batting .218, a tad below the league average of .230, while as a pitcher allowing 144 runs in 292⅓ innings—4.43 per game, well under the league average of 5.56. Caruthers also was better than the league average in WHIP (0.968), K/9 (5.9) and strikeout-to-walk ratio (4.11).

There was no more baseball in 1884 for the Northwestern League, but Caruthers continued playing. He claimed to have "offers from a dozen different clubs"[25] when the league folded, but his preference was to play for the Chicago White Stockings. Caruthers negotiated with Albert Spalding through Sam Morton but couldn't agree on a price. Caruthers wanted $200, but Spalding went as high as $175. Cincinnati wired Caruthers, telling him to "Jump the first train for Cincinnati, we want you. Money no object."[26] Caruthers, though, didn't take it as a serious offer and wasn't about to chance arriving and having terms he couldn't accept. "It just didn't strike me as a business proposition and I tore it up,"[27] he said.

Tuthill, looking to make a little money back on his investment, wired St. Louis owner Chris Von der Ahe, saying Minneapolis might have some players he'd be interested in. Based on the recommendation of Dave Foutz, who had pitched in the Northwestern League for Saginaw in 1883 and Bay City in 1884 and signed a few months earlier with St. Louis, Von der Ahe signed Caruthers for the $200 per month salary he sought.

A German immigrant, Von der Ahe was a self-made man. He came to the United States as a teenager and eventually moved to St. Louis, where he started as a grocery store clerk but quickly climbed up the ladder to the point where he bought that store and opened a saloon. Taking an interest in baseball, as he saw that people visited his tavern after games, he co-founded the St. Louis Sportsman's Association in 1877 and in 1882 became the majority owner of a St. Louis team which joined the newly formed American Association, a competitor to the National League. The American Association offered lower ticket prices (25 cents compared to 50 cents), and, unlike the National League, played on Sundays and offered beer at their ballparks. The latter part appealed to Von der Ahe, who eventually established a beer garden on the St. Louis grounds, named Sportsman's Park.

Von der Ahe had a larger-than-life personality—he has been described as a combination of 20th-century owners Charlie Finley, George Steinbrenner, and Bill Veeck[28]—who wanted nothing more than to field a winning ball club while also being heavily involved in making that winner. Over the course of his ownership, he'd sit on the team bench, tell his manager to make moves during a game, fire managers even more often later in his tenure, (inserting himself as field boss on occasion), and become great fodder for newspapermen, who either cleaned up his German accent and gave him perfect English diction—as most St. Louis papers did—or, as often happened in the 19th and early-20th century with minorities, went with stereotypical and often cartoonish pronunciations (for the purpose of this book, when quoting Von der Ahe, we use what the source wrote). For example, there was a story written in *The Sporting News* in 1892 describing a play in a Browns game in which Von der Ahe was quoted using perfect, or close to it, English. In 1913, *Baseball Magazine* had a version of the same incident but quoted Von der Ahe speaking with heavy German phonetics.

Von der Ahe's Browns barely missed out winning the American Association pennant in 1883, but things didn't go as well the following season. The team had a decent record of 51–33 but stood well behind the pack and in fifth place when on September 4, manager Jimmy Williams abruptly quit, not happy with the drinking and brawling on the team. Perhaps not coincidentally, starting second baseman Joe Quest was released the same day as well as catcher Nin Alexander, who had a one-game tryout. Williams returned home to Columbus, at first becoming a clerk for the local Republican party and then secretary at Columbus Water Works. Politics, it seems, was easier to deal with than ballplayers—and Von der Ahe. "Williams announces himself as being thoroughly disgusted with the business of base ball management, in St. Louis, at least,"[29] reported the *St. Louis Globe-Democrat*. Added *Sporting Life*: "Jimmy Williams is of the opinion that he would rather tackle a hundred angry water works customers than a solitary St. Louis base baller especially when the slugger is drunk and possessed of an idea that it is his solemn duty to slug the manager of the nine."[30]

Looking for answers, Von der Ahe brought in three players from Minneapolis—Caruthers, infielder Walt Kinzie, and catcher Jim McCauley—along with Saginaw outfielder John Lavin. Kinzie and Lavin didn't appear in the majors again after 1884, while McCauley was done by 1886. Caruthers, though, quickly proved to be a find.

Getting off a train from Minneapolis on Sept. 7, Caruthers went right to Sportsman's Park, where 7,000 were in attendance to watch the Browns play the Philadelphia Athletics, a team much like St. Louis: Sporting a winning record (50–34) but in sixth place, well behind league-leading New York. Caruthers held Philadelphia off the scoreboard for the first eight innings, allowing just two hits, while his teammates backed him with six runs. At one point, the Athletics had runners on second and third with two outs, but Caruthers struck out the next two batters "in sharp style. His delivery is a swift, rapid down shoot in the main, which he varies with an occasional cross fire and a slow drop sneaked in from time to time."[31]

In the ninth inning, Fred Corey broke up the shutout with a run-scoring triple, then scored himself on Caruthers' wild pitch. Caruthers allowed just the two runs on four hits with two walks and seven strikeouts in his major league debut. "Caruthers created a very favorable impression and his first appearance with St. Louis as a notable triumph," said the *Globe-Democrat*. "He is but 19 years of age, and while not a phenomenal pitcher he is cool, strategic and puzzling in his work."[32]

In St. Louis' next game two days later at home against Baltimore, Caruthers, in part because Foutz was ill, was again the choice to pitch. He was almost as brilliant as in his initial foray. He again allowed just two hits in eight shutout innings—a pair of doubles by shortstop Jimmy Macullar—and held a 1–0 lead, the only run coming on his second-inning single, his first career hit. "Several times Baltimoreans reached third base, with no one out, but Caruthers showed his skill and command of the situation by retiring the side without a run," opined the *Globe-Democrat*. "His work is the best when the bases are occupied."[33] However, in the ninth inning a full-count pitch—that is, six balls and two strikes—one that "could not have been better had it been made to order,"[34] was called a ball. Baltimore first baseman Dan Stearns got the walk and scored the tying run on a Sam Trott double. St. Louis eventually lost, 2–1, in 10 innings despite some calls, at least in the eyes of the local reporters, which went again the hometown club.

With Foutz healthy, Caruthers was inserted into the lineup by Charles Comiskey, the first baseman who took over managerial duties after Williams resigned, as the team's right fielder while also being used as a change pitcher—switching positions with the pitcher during the game. Hugh Nicol, who had been the St. Louis right fielder, moved to second base in the spot vacated by the release of Quest. "The infield, strengthened by the placing of Nicol at second and Caruthers at right, will not only field like a clipper but will fill out the strongest batting force St. Louis has ever put on the emerald diamond,"[35] claimed the *St. Louis Post-Dispatch*.

In two games at home on September 17 and 18 against Richmond and Pittsburgh, Caruthers did it all. He reached base in all 10 of his plate appearances—nine hits and a hit by pitch. Against Richmond, he relieved Foutz in the fifth inning and struck out 11 while walking none, and in a 6–4 win over Pittsburgh, he robbed Ed Swartwood of extra bases, crashing into the right field fence while making a catch.

On September 23, Caruthers hit his first home run off Jim Conway in an 18–5, seven-inning win over Brooklyn in the final game of the season at Sports-

St. Louis Browns owner Chris Von der Ahe has been described as a combination of 20th century owners Charlie Finley, George Steinbrenner, and Bill Veeck—a character, promoter, and busybody who wanted nothing more than to win (Library of Congress).

man's Park. Baseball-reference categorizes it as one which bounced over the fence, but the *St. Louis Post-Dispatch* described it as "a clean home run."[36] Four days later in Richmond, in another seven-inning affair, Caruthers hit his second homer while also striking out nine in a 13–7 victory.

St. Louis finished the season, which ended with a 13–0 loss in Baltimore with St. Louis players leaving the field in the sixth inning, "refusing to play any longer"[37] after Macullar scored the final run on a passed ball, with a record of 67–40–3. After the arrival of Caruthers, the Browns were 16–6–2. Caruthers pitched 82⅔ innings over 13 games with seven starts, striking out 58 (6.3 per 9 innings). According to baseball-reference, he posted a 2.61 ERA and 0.919 WHIP, the latter the best on the team and the former behind just Foutz (2.18) among the five hurlers who toiled. He also appeared in 16 games in the outfield and had 22 hits in his 23 games played (a .268 average according to baseball-reference and .262 via the 1885 *Spalding Guide*; the league batting average was .240).

Player contracts ran until the end of October, and St. Louis played a few exhibition games after the season, including one on October 18 at Sportsman's Park against Columbus, which finished second in the American Association. Caruthers pitched and struck out 18—considered at the time a record—in a game which ended after eight innings with St. Louis winning, 11–2.

Adding Caruthers gave St. Louis a solid core, along with players such as Comiskey, Foutz, third baseman Arlie Latham, shortstop Bill Gleason, and pitcher-turned-outfielder Tip O'Neill. All except Foutz were 25 years or younger, with Caruthers one of the youngest players in the league. Comiskey's promotion to manager proved to be a smart decision. But Von der Ahe wasn't satisfied. He wanted more, and he was about to get it. The transformation of St. Louis to a baseball power was nearly complete.

Covering Himself in Glory

It didn't take long for Chris Von der Ahe to strengthen his club. The American Association was bloated with 12 teams in 1884—that number was trimmed to eight the following season. Toledo knew it was on its way out. The team arranged a meeting in St. Louis between Von der Ahe and Toledo manager Charlie Morton. The pair met on the morning of October 24 at the Laclede Hotel, then left together on a train to Toledo, where a deal was officially made the next day.

Von der Ahe paid either $1,600 or $2,500 (reports varied) for the release of five players who then would sign with St. Louis. The big catch was pitcher Tony Mullane, who got a $3,500 salary from Von der Ahe. Mullane was one of the game's top hurlers and had been on the Browns in 1883. But after that season, he signed with the St. Louis team in the Union Association, only to renege on that contract and instead join Toledo, where he went 36–26 with a league-high seven shutouts. Von der Ahe didn't object to the signing, so perhaps Toledo felt it owed the Browns owner a favor, and this was the time to repay.

St. Louis also was getting Morton, who reportedly was promised the Browns' managerial gig in return for his help securing the other four players, including second baseman Sam Barkley and outfielders Tom Poorman and Curt Welch. "It has cost me more money than I ever expended any similar venture, but I was determined not to let money stand between me and the players I needed," Von der Ahe said. "I think I have got a winning nine, and I hope the public will appreciate my earnestness in trying to give them the best that money will procure."[1]

The players officially were released November 4, and upon agreement all signed with St. Louis—with one exception. Despite appearing "before a justice of the peace and subscribed to an oath that he would sign with St. Louis as soon as he was eligible to contract,"[2] Mullane boarded a train for Cincinnati and signed a $5,000 contract with that American Association club. This time Von der Ahe objected, and Mullane eventually was suspended by the league for the entire 1885 season.

Of the four remaining players, Poorman was released a week later, and Morton not only wasn't named manager but also was cut before the start of the season. Barkley was a definite upgrade at second base in 1885, although that was his only year with the Browns. Welch, who had a lackluster year with Toledo, his first in the majors, ended up the key to the transaction—a speedy center fielder who did anything to get on base and seemingly tracked down any fly ball hit remotely in his vicinity.

Von der Ahe was happy with the additions but knew his team still needed a catcher, especially after Tom Deasley asked for his release, which he got—after paying Von der Ahe $400 in a deal negotiated by the owner and Deasley's wife. Von der Ahe signed William H. Robinson, later better known as "Yank," partly to fill that role as well as be a backup third baseman. He didn't do much catching, however, and down the line ended up as the team's second baseman and a fill-in all over the field. Another opportunity arose, however. Cleveland of the National League was disbanding. What would happen to its players was a little confusing—Henry Lucas of the Union Association was in line to get the franchise, but the UA was technically still alive (it shortly became defunct). He wanted the Cleveland players to fill his new NL team, located in St. Louis. But Charlie Hackett, Cleveland's manager in 1884, spent his off-season securing releases from seven players and having them agree to sign with Brooklyn of the American Association. Each player got some money in advance, and Hackett joined them as manager. To ensure no one could get them to change their mind, the seven players "all have been ordered to report at a town near the Canada border, to stay until contracts have been signed."[3]

Among the seven players was a catcher, Doc Bushong, who was known for his defense and baseball acumen. Instead of keeping Bushong, though, Brooklyn transferred him to St. Louis. Von der Ahe had his catcher.

The St. Louis roster for 1885 was all but set. As with any team, the players came from different backgrounds. But unlike modern times, only two—Robert Caruthers, who Von der Ahe listed as an outfielder, although that wouldn't be the case (for this season, at least), and first baseman Charles Comiskey—were baseball players from the start (Comiskey beginning his pro career at age 17). New second baseman Barkley started out making cigars in his native West Virginia. Shortstop Bill Gleason, a native of St. Louis, had been a fireman. Third baseman Arlie Latham was a shoemaker, while Bushong went to school to become a dentist, which he practiced out of season. Among the outfielders, Hugh Nicol learned to be a marble cutter at 17, Tip O'Neill was a tailor, and Welch was "by trade a molder of crockery."[4] Pitcher Dave Foutz spent time mining gold in Colorado, while fellow hurler George McGinnis was a glass blower.

"One of the chief drawbacks of the St. Louis Club," a man named Ixion wrote in the *St. Louis Post-Dispatch* near the end of the 1884 season, "has been the behavior of certain men, who labored under the opinion that they were essential to the existence of the club and could do as they pleased."[5] That behavior, it was implied, kept the team from fulfilling its promise. Even with their disparate upbringings—and eventual intra-squad squabbles—with Comiskey captaining them, the Browns didn't disappoint again.

With all the additions Von der Ahe made in the off-season, there were rumblings that Caruthers was headed to an unaffiliated team in Mobile, Alabama. However, he had signed with St. Louis—"His contract is in Mr. Von der Ahe's safe, together with the voucher for the advance money sent him."[6]—as had all the Browns. Caruthers was to make $1,500 for his first full year in the majors. By comparison, McGinnis, heading into his fourth season, would earn around $2,100. The veteran Bushong, who turned 29 in September and played in a handful of games in 1875–1876 before returning to the National League in 1880, was signed for either $2,500 (per the *Cincinnati Commercial Gazette*), $2,800 (*Sporting Life*) or $2,850 (*St. Louis Globe-Democrat*). Comiskey, as captain, received $3,000.

The latest edition of the Browns arrived in St. Louis in mid–March—Latham was the last to join, 10 days late—and quickly got into their season training: Daily gymnastics under the tutelage of Charles Muegge, an instructor of gymnastics at Washington University. After a handful of tune-up games in St. Louis and Kansas City, the Browns began their season April 18 at home against Pittsburgh on a rainy day. With Foutz pitching, St. Louis lost, 7–0. Caruthers got the nod the next day and in front of a packed house on a Sunday, he blanked Pittsburgh, 3–0, allowing just five hits and a walk while striking out eight. "Carruthers pitched a wonderful game, being very speedy, and developing more tactics than he generally uses," reported the *St. Louis Globe-Democrat*, using an extra "r" in his last name. This occurred frequently over Carruthers' lifetime, although more so later in his life. He never bothered to correct anyone. "Carruthers gave the visitors much trouble," the paper continued, "and several times he was uproariously applauded for striking out some of the big batters."[7]

Foutz and Caruthers alternated in the box nearly every day of the season. They combined to start 99 of the Browns' 112 games—every one of them a complete game. McGinnis— whose nickname, "Jumbo," was for obvious reasons; he was described as a "large, fleshy man"[8]—made his first start on April 25 and then not again until June 2. St. Louis fans wouldn't see him again until July.

Caruthers won his next three starts as well: 2–1 over Cincinnati on April 23, then back-to-back shutouts, 2–0 over Pittsburgh in another Sunday contest at Sportsman's Park on April 26—fans threw seat cushions onto the field

Doc Bushong was a practicing dentist in addition to being one of the best defensive catchers of his era, even with having to use the equivalent of cutoff batting gloves (Library of Congress).

after the win, much to the delight of the players and dismay of Von der Ahe—and three days later, 6–0 in Cincinnati. In the latter, Comiskey and Welch both homered while Caruthers limited Cincinnati to just six hits, prompting the remark that "The batting of the home team reminded one of a lot of school boys playing with professionals."[9]

The Red Stockings were also shut out by Foutz the previous day, prompting Cincinnati management to fine everyone who played against Caruthers $25. The motivation didn't work as they were blanked again a few days later by Louisville, causing the *Globe-Democrat* to wryly note, "How much the players were fined for that offense has not been reported."[10]

In his first four starts, Caruthers allowed 23 hits and one run. "Carruthers is loom-ing up as one of the best pitchers in the American Association,"[11] the *Globe-Democrat* wrote. Caruthers lost his next start, 4–2 at Louisville on May 4, but neither he nor the Browns would taste defeat for a while. St. Louis reeled off 17 consecutive victories, set-ting an American Association record which was never broken—for longest winning streak. It was snapped, ironically, in a game started by McGinnis, a 7–1 loss June 2 in Baltimore. Caruthers pitched in win No. 17, a 10–4 victory in that same city. "Caruthers pitched a strong game, and was remarkably steady," said the *Baltimore American*. "The home team played a faltering game all the way through. They seemed to be afraid of Caruthers, although that individual is not much bigger than a bar of soap."[12] St. Louis was 23–5, in first place by 5½ games—no team got closer than 4½ games the rest of the way.

It was thought by some that Caruthers would start to falter once the team was on the road in the East, but he kept plugging along, picking up believers along the way. The *Philadelphia Inquirer* called him the "strongest pitcher in the association."[13] At the end of June, the *St. Louis Post-Dispatch* listed him with a 1.21 ERA while *Sporting Life* had him at 1.31—either way, both were easily tops in the American Association.

While Caruthers was getting acclaim, the Browns were not. Even with all the vic-tories and in an era of players doing anything to win, St. Louis wasn't exactly being seen as good sports. Complaining to the umpire was being regularly reported on during road games. After a rare loss in Cincinnati, it was said that the Browns "have the bighead bad. They have come to thinking themselves invincible, and take their medicine like small boys take castor oil," complained the *Cincinnati Commercial Gazette*. "It has been so everywhere on their trip. They claim the earth and demand the most outrageous things from the umpire. When they are being squarely beaten, as they were yesterday, they act more like rowdies than ball players."[14]

Not bothered by the criticism, St. Louis went on a 12-game winning streak from July 2–16, even without hard-hitting outfielder Tip O'Neill, who injured his leg June 10 and missed nearly three months. With O'Neill out and Sam Barkley sick, Caruthers saw his first action other than as a pitcher on July 10, stationed in left field and batting fifth. Barkley returned the next day and homered as Caruthers beat Brooklyn, 5–4, receiv-ing his second $5 fine in a month for arguing a called ball, then taking his time walking back to the box.

Even when Comiskey went down with a shoulder injury in early August, the Browns kept winning. By the middle of the month, they stretched their lead to dou-ble digits. With a couple of players banged up, Caruthers got a few more chances to play in the outfield. In a 6–1 win in Cincinnati on August 23, he "played a great game in left field"[15] and made a sensational running grab of a Hick Carpenter long drive, helping quash any thoughts of a Red Stockings comeback. "[It] was a 'paralyzer,'" observed the *Cincinnati Commercial Gazette*. "It was nothing less than marvelous."[16]

O'Neill returned to action in a home game against Louisville on Sept. 3—receiv-ing a "grand ovation by the crowd"[17]—although he needed someone to run for him when he reached base. This left Caruthers to be used, with one exception, as just a pitcher the remainder of the season. But he demonstrated he could still wield the bat. In O'Neill's return, he doubled and tripled (although he was out trying to stretch it to a home run) while also tossing a six-hit shutout, striking out six and walking one. "Caruthers cov-ered himself in glory,"[18] said the *Post-Dispatch*.

Three days later, Caruthers pitched in the final home game of the season, a 2–1 win in 10 innings over Louisville. There was no score after nine innings. Caruthers led off the top of the 10th—Louisville won the coin flip and elected to go in the field first—with a single, then stole second, went to third on a passed ball, and scored on a grounder to third which couldn't be handled. St. Louis ended up with a 2–1 win, finishing with a 44–11 record at Sportsman's Park. "It was a grand and fitting termination to the Browns' remarkable work on the home diamond this season,"[19] observed the *Globe-Democrat*.

With 17 road games remaining, St. Louis had all but clinched the American Association pennant. The Browns went 12–5 on the trip, losing three of the last four. In the finale, third baseman Arlie Latham caught for seven innings while Doc Bushong played third base—his first time manning that position in five years. Finishing with a 79–33 record and 16 games in front of the closest competition, St. Louis could afford to have some fun.

According to modern calculations, Caruthers hit only .225—this would be the only time in his career he had a lower than league average OPS—but pitched 53 games, leading the American Association in wins (40), winning percentage (.755) and ERA (2.07) while finishing second in WHIP (1.010) and shutouts (6). All while toiling a career-high 482⅓ innings, and he wasn't done pitching quite yet in 1885. St. Louis headed to Cincinnati for some exhibition games. Caruthers matched up against Tony Mullane, who was allowed to pitch because the season was over, splitting two matchups as Cincinnati took two of three.

St. Louis returned home October 7, and the town greeted its returning champions with a parade. The Browns arrived at Union Station 30 minutes late, their train, adorned by streamers, stars and stripes bunting, made conspicuous with a sign boasting that the American Association champions were on board. The players were quickly ushered to horse-driven carriages, suitcases and bat cases in tow. The parade was quite the affair. Mounted police led the way, followed in part by the U.S. Calvary band and a float, which had a large globe covered with the faces of Browns players—at this point Caruthers did not have a mustache, although seven of the 13 St. Louis players did—with a young woman standing next to the glove "personating the goddess of Liberty,"[20] waving a U.S. flag, and blowing kisses to the crowd. There were two other floats, and various players from other American Association, National League and amateur teams and the local Flambeau club walked the streets, shooting off fireworks. A few people were injured by stray balls from roman candles. One, J.C. Dowd, suffered a cut from below his right eye to his chin, causing his nice white outfit to be covered in blood. Thomas Reilly lost part of his nose and suffered such a blow that his cheekbone became exposed. The parade ended at Schnaider's beer garden, where everyone enjoyed some adult refreshments before finally heading home around midnight.

The Browns continued their exhibition series the following day against Cincinnati and, not surprisingly, lost 6–1. Caruthers played right field in both the first and third games of the St. Louis contests, pitching in the second—the Browns' only win of the three, a 10–1 victory. In the finale, an 18–3 defeat, Browns players were heckled by fans who asked that the game be called so the Buffalo Bill Wild West show, which was being held at Sportsman's Park as well, could begin. "The Browns played as if they did not care whether they won or not,"[21] observed the *Globe-Democrat*. More important games lay ahead.

In 1884, the winners of the National League (Providence) and American Association (New York) had agreed to play a postseason series. While on the season-ending road sojourn in 1885, Chris Von der Ahe made a side trip to Chicago and arranged with Albert Spalding, owner of the NL champions, for a best-of-nine series, with each owner putting up $500. The White Stockings had edged out New York by two games to win the National League in what was essentially a two-team race all season—only one other team had a winning record, Philadelphia, and the Quakers finished 30 games off the pace. Chicago was led by its captain, first baseman Adrian "Cap" Anson, arguably the best player in the National League, and the most well-known ballplayer, outfielder/catcher Mike "King" Kelly, perhaps the most popular, and Caruthers' former Northwestern League rival, John Clarkson, who pitched over 600 innings in 70 starts, of which he won 53.

The first game of what the *New York Clipper* called "The Championship of America"[22] was held in Chicago on Wednesday, October 14 with top pitchers Caruthers and Clarkson dueling. Before the contest, there were two contests held—Chicago's Ed Williamson claimed the longest toss at just over 400 feet (there's no record if bouncing and rolling counted), while teammate Fred Pfeffer was the fastest to sprint around the bases, albeit on a muddy field, at 15¾ seconds. Caruthers was last among the six contestants, rounding the bags in 17¾ seconds (he was also the only St. Louis player to participate).

As for the game, St. Louis led, 5–1, after seven innings, Caruthers allowing but two hits. However, as it began to get dark—those contests pushing the start time back a bit didn't help—Chicago tallied four times in the eighth, including a home run by Pfeffer which tied the score. Umpire Dave Sullivan called the game after the eighth inning, and the 2,000 fans at West Side Park left without seeing a victor.

The scene shifted to Sportsman's Park on Thursday, with Caruthers on the bench as Foutz toiled in the box. Sullivan, who worked in the National League, was umpiring again and came under attack from St. Louis fans over several calls. Beyond the usual jeering, "Get another umpire" and "robbery" were yelled from the stands. At one point on a play at first in which Sullivan called Chicago's Kelly safe, allowing a run to score, Charles Comiskey argued vociferously and said he wanted a new umpire, a request which Anson refused. During a long argument between teams—Missouri congressman John J. O'Neill, saying he represented the Browns with Von der Ahe absent, jumped onto the field into the fray as well—Sullivan sat down on the Chicago bench and put on his coat. Eventually play resumed, but another controversy arose on a ball ruled fair which Comiskey said was foul (by American Association rules, which the game, in St. Louis, were being played under). This time there was no resolution. Comiskey pulled his team from the field, and Sullivan—later from his hotel room—declared the game a forfeit, Chicago winning 9–0. Adding to the controversy, St. Louis had led, 4–2, after five innings. It was the top of the sixth, with Chicago scoring three times, when the game was stopped. The bitterness extended to the hometown newspapers, which often openly rooted for their local team. "Comiskey, seeing that Sullivan was determined to have Chicago win, wisely determined to withdraw his men from the field," said the *Post-Dispatch*, "as forfeiting the game was much more acceptable than playing for nine innings only to be robbed."[23]

The next day at Sportsman's Park, there was a new umpire on the grounds—Harry McCaffrey, a former player for St. Louis and Louisville who umped a handful of games in the Union Association in 1884 and the National League in 1885. Caruthers faced Clarkson again and this time emerged with a 7–4 win. He allowed eight hits, walked just one (using NL rules, it was six balls for a walk) and struck out seven while going 2-for-4

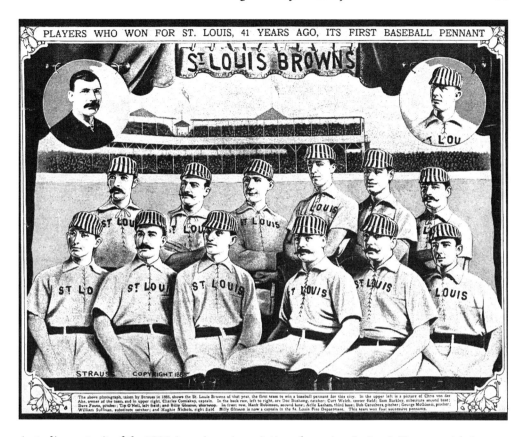

PLAYERS WHO WON FOR ST. LOUIS, 41 YEARS AGO, ITS FIRST BASEBALL PENNANT

St. LOUIS BROWNS

STRAUSS   COPYRIGHT 1885

The above photograph, taken by Strauss in 1885, shows the St. Louis Browns of that year, the first team to win a baseball pennant for this city. In the upper left is a picture of Chris von der Ahe, owner of the team, and in upper right, Charles Comiskey, captain. In the back row, left to right, are Doc Bushong, catcher; Curt Welch, center field; Sam Barkley, substitute second base; Dave Foutz, pitcher; Tip O'Neil, left field; and Billy Gleason, shortstop. In front row, Hank Robinson, second base ; Arlie Latham, third base; Bob Caruthers, pitcher; George McGinnis, pitcher; William Sullivan, substitute catcher; and Hughie Nichols, right field. Billy Gleason is now a captain in the St. Louis Fire Department. This team won four successive pennants.

A studio portrait of the 1885 American Association champion St. Louis Browns with Sportsman's Park in the background. Bob Caruthers is in the bottom row, third from left (Missouri Historical Society).

at the plate with a triple, knocking in a run on a grounder in the sixth. Caruthers punctuated the victory with a strikeout of Silver Flint to end the game. Anson wasn't distressed with the loss—Providence had won all three games the previous year vs. New York—saying, "The Browns are a good club. They are liable to beat us a game or two or more, of course; but wait until they have played ten games with us and see where they will be."[24]

McCaffrey's stint as umpire lasted all of one day. Anson didn't agree to use him again when the teams assembled at Sportsman's Park on October 17. That, of course, presented a problem: There was no one else to officiate. Both sides insisted—Charles Comiskey wanted McCaffrey, while Anson suggested one of the St. Louis National League players. When no decision could be reached, Anson's solution was to flip a coin; Comiskey demurred. Finally, an agreement was made. Out of the stands was pulled local baseball fan William Medart, who had a dry goods business in town with his brother. Forty minutes after the game was supposed to begin, the first pitch was thrown.

Caruthers didn't pitch in this contest, but he did start in right field, with Hugh Nicol benched. The move paid off as Caruthers drove in St. Louis' first run in the third inning on a grounder which tallied Arlie Latham. In the eighth, with the Browns down, 2–1, thanks to Abner Dalrymple's home run in the fifth, Caruthers' single scored Latham to tie the game. St. Louis added another run later in the inning and won, 3–2.

There was, however, more controversy. In the fifth inning, Medart called Chicago's Tom Burns out at third; even St. Louis scribes thought Burns was safe. In the ninth, Jim McCormick hit a pop to Comiskey, who dropped it. He faked a throw to third, where Burns was headed, and instead ran over and tagged McCormick, who had wandered too far off first base. Chicago's Billy Sunday took great exception to the call. "That man was not out,"[25] he yelled at Medart, who called the White Stockings outfielder "a liar" and told him to be quiet and, "If you don't do it I'll make you."[26] McCormick and Sunday prepared for a fight, but teammate Mike Kelly interfered and things cooled off. Medart said he was done with umpiring (although he did officiate two American Association games in 1887). That meant Chicago and St. Louis had to—again—find someone else. At least the next game wasn't until five days later, in Pittsburgh.

Before that contest, though, the Browns played the St. Louis National League team—known as the Maroons or Black Diamonds (because many of their players had been with the Union Association team and were blacklisted)—at Sportsman's Park. Even though this was an exhibition and there were more championship games to be played against Chicago, the Browns trotted out their starting lineup, with the exception of Yank Robinson in right field, and with Caruthers pitching. The Sunday game brought out 10,000 spectators, who witnessed a 5–2 Browns victory although "on the whole the event was neither interesting nor exciting."[27]

While the Browns-Maroons game packed the ballpark, there were fewer fans in Pittsburgh for the fifth game—including the forfeit—of the Browns-White Stockings series. Just around 500 showed up on a cold day for the latest matchup on October 22. There would be no questioning who would ump the remainder of the series. Owners Spalding and Von der Ahe agreed to use Bob Ferguson, a former player who officiated in the National League during the season. Caruthers again was in right field but went hitless in two at-bats as the Browns fell, 9–2, in a game called after seven innings.

The clubs moved to Cincinnati for the next two games, to be followed by contests in Baltimore, Philadelphia, and Brooklyn. But due to cold snap on the East Coast, Spalding and Von der Ahe decided to end the series in Cincinnati at seven games. Another frigid day in Cincinnati—and poor playing (the teams combined for 17 errors)—probably left the pair feeling good about their accord. Instead of the winner getting the full $1,000 put up prior to the series by the clubs, it would be divvied up based on how many contests each won. Chicago took Game 6, 9–2, in front of 1,000 freezing Cincinnatians. Caruthers pitched, allowed 11 hits, and didn't strike out a batter.

Before Game 7, the teams met and decided "by mutual agreement"[28] that the earlier forfeited game was wiped off the books. The series was tied at two (with the one tie), with this final game to determine the champion. Caruthers, having pitched in Game 6, didn't play. Dave Foutz started, and Robinson was in right field. John Clarkson was supposed to pitch but arrived at the park late, perhaps hungover. The following September, Detroit manager Bill Watkins accused Chicago of being drunk during the series. "When the Chicagos got off the train in Cincinnati last year only three of them were able to walk straight from the depot," Watkins claimed. "That's the condition they were in, and then they fooled around instead of playing ball."[29]

St. Louis pounded McCormick, who had to pitch for a second consecutive day, and easily won, 13–4, in a game ended after eight innings. While Caruthers didn't play, he reaped the rewards of the victory: Von der Ahe bought each player a new suit. The Browns were champions … that is, until later in the off-season, when Chicago decided it wouldn't cancel that forfeited game. History records the series as a tie, but for those Browns in October 1885, they were the best baseball team in the land.

The Browns returned to St. Louis on the morning of October 25, then went to Union Park to play the Maroons. It was another greatly anticipated game, with 10,000–15,000 in attendance. But these teams weren't even close in caliber; the Maroons finished in last place with a 36–72 record. Caruthers pitched and allowed just four hits while striking out four as the Browns won a yawner, 6–0. "The game is notable for being the biggest baseball fizzle in the history of St. Louis,"[30] declared the *Globe-Democrat*.

There were two more games left in this exhibition series. The first was postponed, and the other was another listless affair played November 1 at Sportsman's Park, the Browns winning, 1–0, when it was stopped after six innings due to darkness. During the game, Von der Ahe was presented with some gifts, including a watch and chain and a couple of flags to be displayed at the park. One said simply, "Good Luck to the Browns," the other, "Champions, 1886."[31] If it's confusing why it read 1886 instead of 1885, well, it wasn't entirely clear then, either. A letter to the editor in June the following year asked that very question. "Ella is right. Strictly speaking, the Browns are really the champions of 1885, having won the banner that year; but they are the champions of 1886 for the reason that during that year they are the champions, and remain so until some other club takes it from them,"[32] explained the *Post-Dispatch*.

The season was finally over, and Von der Ahe began signing players for 1886. He quickly inked all but two. One, Latham, affixed his name to a contract in mid–November. The other wasn't about to sign any time soon. Robert Caruthers wasn't happy, and not just about the salary being offered.

6

Parisian Bob

Chris Von der Ahe's St. Louis Browns might have beaten the Chicago White Stockings to win what the *St. Louis Globe-Democrat* dubbed "the championship of the world"[1] and the *St. Louis Post-Dispatch* called the "championship of America,"[2] but he was not in a magnanimous mood when it came to the 1886 season.

The Browns owner drew a line on salaries, deciding to pay his three outfielders $1,800 each for the season, his four infielders $1,900, and his three catchers and pitchers $2,000. First baseman Charles Comiskey received an extra $500 for managing the club on the field—he'd still be taking a $500 pay cut from the previous year—and Doc Bushong had in his contract a $10 bonus for every game beyond two he caught in a week. However, he, too, was taking a large cut, having earned $2,800 in 1885.

It's not like the players had much choice. Each was reserved by the team and couldn't sign elsewhere. Of those 12, 11 signed, plus catcher Rudy Kemmler, who had played in 18 games for Pittsburgh of the American Association in 1885 (second baseman Sam Barkley eventually had his release bought by Pittsburgh and signed with them for $2,000). Robert Caruthers was the lone unsigned player.

After the season he had, that money didn't satisfy Caruthers. He tried to make a little side cash before leaving St. Louis, though. Browns third baseman Arlie Latham was quite the character. He was known for his coaching antics—loudly yelling to encourage his teammates or rattle an opposing pitcher—and eccentric personality. He once tried to make a "fancy finish"[3] on an easy popup and, instead of catching the ball, saw it fall to the ground. Von der Ahe fined him $50—then $50 more when Latham loudly complained. "I told him that he was hired to play base ball, and not to do fancy tricks,"[4] Von der Ahe groused.

"Arlie, the clown, the best entertainer ever on the diamond," Caruthers said of his teammate decades later. "Wherever the team played he was the star attraction because of his witty sayings on the side lines."[5] In a separate interview, Caruthers also noted, "When it came to coaching I don't believe that Arlie Latham ever had a peer. He could not only jolly a pitcher to death and get his man around the circuit, but he could enliven the dullest game and the most morose crowd any time with his monkey shines."[6]

Caruthers admitted Latham was "fast on the bases,"[7] but the third baseman fancied himself quicker than anyone in the game. While in Cincinnati for their exhibition series in early October, Latham issued a challenge to every other baseball player to a 100-yard dash. He specifically had his eye on the White Stockings' Billy Sunday, who eventually agreed to race. On November 8 at St. Louis' Union Park, the two men squared off. Bets were placed, and Caruthers backed his teammate with "several hundred dollars."[8] Latham, however, was easily defeated. An angry Caruthers thought Latham threw the race and, along with Sunday, cleaned up on bets. Nearly six years later, the *Philadelphia Inquirer* noted, "Carruthers thinks till this day that Latham 'double crossed' him and allowed Sunday to win. They are still enemies, but Latham says Carruthers is known as a squealer and weakener."[9]

It wasn't long after the sprint that Carruthers got into a conflict with another teammate. Before the Browns were to embark on an exhibition trip to New Orleans, there was a poker game—Carruthers was never one to turn down a game of cards. Neither was Dave Foutz. Somewhere along the way, an argument broke out, and the one thing they agreed on was that if one headed south, the other wouldn't. Foutz ended up going to New Orleans, with Carruthers headed back home to Chicago.

Caruthers didn't need the extra few dollars being earned by going on that trip. He was starting a shoe store in Chicago with his brother, James, as well as being paid to roller skate—the activity took off in the 1880s as equipment became readily available to the masses—at an indoor rink. His family also came into some money. The beneficiaries of Malcom McNeill's will split $400,000 after selling a property to the Phenix Insurance Company.[10] It had been purchased roughly 20 years earlier for $2,003.[11] Caruthers' parents also sold two buildings on Clark Street for $96,115[12] (which amounts to over $3 million in 2023[13]).

As the calendar turned to 1886, Caruthers was still unsigned. There was a rumor afloat that the player and owner were not on good terms because Von der Ahe wouldn't advance Caruthers money so he could open his shoe store. Based on Caruthers' family fortune—and recent real-estate deals—this seems unlikely, and Von der Ahe expressed as much publicly. Still, he was confident he'd have Caruthers in the fold soon. "Carruthers will sign with us for next season," Von der Ahe said on January 12. "You can state that positively. I sent the contract out to him last night and it will come back signed."[14]

Caruthers traveled to St. Louis ostensibly to talk with Von der Ahe about the contract, but first stopped by a local pool hall. Caruthers "plays a good game of billiards"[15] and was "an expert three-ball billiard player"[16] as well as "an expert in pin pool."[17] When in town, he often could be seen playing a game with local billiards player Louis Reed or, after Reed moved, actor Berry Mitchell. There's no report of how Caruthers did at the pool hall, but it probably went better than his meeting with Von der Ahe. The two were at an impasse.

Caruthers supposedly was asking for $2,700–$2,900. Von der Ahe was sticking to his $2,000 offer—and threatened to pay less if the player didn't sign soon. Caruthers told Von der Ahe he could make more money selling shoes, to which the owner replied, "Well then, you better stick to your shoe business."[18] Caruthers countered by saying he'd pay $1,000 for his release—thus making him eligible to sign with any team in either the American Association or National League, which he couldn't do while on St. Louis' reserve list. "Oh, no, that would be foolish," Von der Ahe slyly responded. "You don't need any release to run your shoe business, and it would be only throwing the $1,000 away."[19]

With no settlement in sight and the two sides nowhere close to an agreement, Caruthers returned to Chicago. He telegraphed Von der Ahe that unless his terms were met, he'd leave on a trip to Europe and Australia—at the prodding of his mother—and would be gone for over a year, thus wouldn't play at all in the upcoming season. The *St. Louis Globe-Democrat* called it "the thinnest bluff of all."[20] In 1913 a story—and this might be a work of fiction—was told that when he heard Caruthers was headed to Paris,

Von der Ahe commented, "Why, there is no ball club over there. Bismark put that place on the 'bum.' Let him go there if he wants."[21]

A couple of weeks went by, and Von der Ahe sent Caruthers another contract calling for a $2,000 salary. It was written that Caruthers signed—reporters perhaps jumping the gun based solely on the contract being sent—but that was false. On February 9, over a week after he mailed the contract, Von der Ahe said he hadn't heard from Caruthers.

In Chicago to purchase uniforms for his team, Von der Ahe went to Albert Spalding's sporting goods store. There, the proprietor told him Caruthers had come in the other day and said his goodbyes. This was confirmed by new Browns catcher Rudy Kemmler, a Chicago native, who said he went to the train station with Caruthers as he left town. Caruthers left Chicago on February 8, taking a train to New York, where he and his younger sister, Elizabeth, checked into the Windsor Hotel on 5th Avenue. The Windsor was described as "at the time, the most luxurious and aristocratic hostelry in New York."[22] and "the most comfortable and homelike hotel in New York."[23]

Two days later, Caruthers telegraphed Charles Comiskey, who became the middleman between player and owner; Comiskey had just opened a tavern in Chicago called The Café, with a new proposal. This was no compromise. He wrote:

> "New York, February 12.—Charles Comiskey, 504 West Twelfth street, Chicago: Will stay for $5,000. If accepted, send telegraphic order for $3,000 by 6 o'clock. R.L. Caruthers, Windsor Hotel."[24]

Comiskey later recalled that Caruthers wanted $1,500 of that salary up-front. Von der Ahe happened to still be in Chicago. His response upon seeing that telegram is not known, but one can imagine his reaction, although Comiskey, speaking in 1900, claimed he offered $3,500 with $1,000 of it in advance, which Caruthers refused. The *Globe-Democrat* called it a "ridiculously extravagant proposition."[25] Von der Ahe, predictably, refused the offer and headed back to St. Louis. The next day he wired Comiskey, asking if Caruthers had left the country. Comiskey's reply: "Yes; he bid me farewell and sails for Europe to-day."[26]

Caruthers and his uncle Alexander McNeill—the son of Thomas Henry McNeill and his second wife, Ann Eliza Arthur; Flora Rivers Caruthers was the daughter of Thomas McNeill and his first wife, Martha Rivers—were among the 224 first-class passengers listed on the *Aurania*, part of the Cunard shipping line, which sailed for Liverpool, England on February 13. The boat was 470 feet long and "known as a badly rolling ship, and was never very popular."[27] It took a week for the *Aurania* to arrive on the English shore. Caruthers and McNeill hopped a train to London, reportedly bringing with them $7,000 for use at European casinos.

"The Browns will be deprived of the services of a most valuable pitcher, but there is one thing certain, Mr. Von der Ahe is deserving only of praise for his action in this matter," wrote *Sporting Life*. "It was his determination to hold down Caruthers to the salary limit, and he did it at the risk, and as it proved, at the loss, of a valuable player. There will not be a case like Caruthers' in a hundred years. It happened that he had enough means to enable him to refuse Mr. Von der Ahe's offer without inconvenience to himself."[28]

However, the publication added, "One of the Browns last Saturday was so confident to believe that Caruthers would yet bob up in St. Louis about the first of May, but this is not likely. One thing is certain, however, that when he does return, if he desires to go onto the ball field again he will do it with the St. Louis Browns and at terms dictated

The steamship *Aurania* of the Cunard line, on which Bob Caruthers sailed from New York to Liverpool.

by Mr. Von der Ahe, for the latter says he will hold him down to the limit now though the heavens fall. It is not improbable that Caruthers will not be seen again on the diamond."[29]

In the meantime, the Browns found themselves another pitcher. With Caruthers seemingly out of the picture, Von der Ahe and Comiskey got tipped off by Sam Morton to check out Nat Hudson, who had twirled a bit the year before for Keokuk and Denver. Being in Chicago, as was Hudson, Comiskey was charged with signing him to a contract. As Comiskey remembered it 14 years later, when he asked Hudson for his price, the pitcher wanted $3,500—the amount Comiskey supposedly was willing to pay Caruthers. "I tried to jolly him along by telling him he was worth it, but that Carruthers, then the best in the business, was the better player. … finally compromised on $2000."[30] *Sporting Life* reported that Hudson signed for $1,500.

Meanwhile, after eight days in London, Caruthers and his uncle headed to Paris. It was there Caruthers claimed he was wired an undisclosed offer from Comiskey, who was now in St. Louis. However, it was reported by the *Globe-Democrat* and *Post-Dispatch* that it was Caruthers who sent a cable from Paris to either Comiskey or Von der Ahe— the papers didn't agree—asking what salary could be offered to him for the 1886 season.

The Browns wired back their response—however Caruthers already had bought a train ticket to Rome. With the situation gone silent again, rumors abounded. Caruthers never actually sailed for Europe and was hiding out in New York. No, he was in St. Louis negotiating with the Browns. There was even one which had Comiskey negotiating to join Chicago. All of those were denied—by Von der Ahe, recently hired club secretary

Harry Weldon, and Comiskey. The Browns could do nothing but wait, not knowing the outcome but nevertheless optimistic. "We don't know that Caruthers will play with us next season; we only hope he will,"[31] Weldon said.

After a week in Italy, Caruthers returned to Paris, where he quickly fired off a cable to Comiskey on March 15 simply stating, "Offer accepted. Will sail Saturday, March 20."[32] Caruthers' expected 15-month journey instead lasted all of five weeks. *The Sporting News* confirmed the news on page 1 of its inaugural issue. With a Paris dateline, the new weekly reported that Caruthers told their writer "He says he has received a satisfactory answer to the cablegram he sent to the president of the Brown Stocking nine, and he will play with that team the coming season."[33]

The salary wasn't the $5,000 he demanded, but it also wasn't the $2,000 Von der Ahe had refused to budge from. The exact amount Caruthers was to receive is disputed. *Sporting Life* reported it was to be $3,000. In March 1887, *The Sporting News* said Caruthers claimed he was paid $3,200. Teammate and fellow pitcher Dave Foutz, when discussing his salary in 1887, said Caruthers "got $3,500 for the season. That's $1,500 more than I got."[34] At the time, when asked the terms of the contract, Caruthers responded, "the limit"[35] although there could have been signing and/or performance bonuses to help inflate his yearly sum.

While his teammates were gathering for practice and calisthenics at a St. Louis gymnasium, Caruthers was making his away across the Atlantic. On March 20 in Liverpool, he boarded the Cunard Line's *Gallia*, the ship making its maiden voyage of the year to New York. Caruthers arrived back in the United States on March 30 and made his way to St. Louis, getting there April 1—which as far as he was concerned was perfect timing as that was the day his contract officially began.

When Caruthers stepped off the train at St. Louis' Union Station, he looked a little different. One of the six clean-shaven players on the Browns in 1885, he was now sporting a moustache and sideburns—"A quite English looking man," observed the *Globe-Democrat*.[36] Caruthers was also adorned with some of the latest European fashions, including a "light gray overcoat and silk hat."[37] The facial hair might have been a slight surprise, but the clothes certainly were not. Caruthers always dressed well. Even in his brief time in the minor leagues, he wore a nice suit to the game and then exit wearing a different, but still dapper, set of clothes. "He was the finest dressed player I ever saw, always slick as a band box," Comiskey asserted in 1911. "And as clean-cut a young chap of eighteen you ever saw when he came to me."[38] Even in the off-season, he could "be found on any afternoon on Madison and State streets, Chicago, displaying the latest styles of clothing," noted *The Sporting News*. "Quite a dude, you know."[39] In 1893, with his playing career winding down, he was still observed as being "dressed to the height of Brummel picturesqueness."[40] Being fashionable was important to Caruthers and, William Veeck (using his Bill Bailey pseudonym) of the *Chicago American* wrote in 1911, he "was one of the few ball players who believed in wearing the latest modes. There was nothing in the dress line which came out that did not adorn the figure of the pitcher. He was a dandy and it is doubtful whether there is a man in the game today who dresses better than Carruthers did when in his heydey [sic]."[41]

But it wasn't his wardrobe that Caruthers wanted to address upon his return to St. Louis. He wasn't happy about how he was being portrayed in the newspapers or with the rumors that he never went to Europe. "This, I think, is an injustice to me, and I am surprised that there are people who would accuse of me of doing such a cowardly act. I had a good opportunity to see the country on the other side and took advantage of it, and I think that any one would have done the same under the circumstances."[42]

Asked why he cut his world trip short, Caruthers told a *Globe-Democrat* reporter, "Merely because I did not like the country as well as I imagined I would. I was greatly disappointed and, I may add, a little homesick. That was the only thing that induced me to come back. It was not a matter of salary at all that I changed the programme. The reason I went away was simply because I was tired of base ball and wanted a rest. It is true, however, that Mr. Von der Ahe did not want to pay me as large a salary as I received last season, but that had nothing to do with the matter."[43]

From the train station, Caruthers headed to the Laclede Hotel. He signed his name in the register as "Robert Caruthers, London, Eng."[44] It was another city that would attach itself to his name, however. It would take a while to gain a foothold, but the nickname "Parisian Bob" was born and remained with him throughout his life and beyond.

Fighting for a Pennant
and Each Other

Robert Caruthers' appearance wasn't the only thing which had changed. The American Association had made some rule changes for the 1886 season, some of which affected pitchers. The box in which the hurlers threw from had been increased by a foot (in the direction of second base) "while a stone slat one foot wide is to be placed across and in front of the pitcher's square."[1] The batter's box went from 3 feet by 6 feet to 4 × 6, the same dimensions the National League used, and moved from 12 inches from home plate to six inches—both measurements are used to this day. In addition, a walk now took place after six balls instead of seven.

Players could no longer wear spikes—a rule teammate Arlie Latham tried to flout during the season to no avail. Many Browns players, though, had a sliding pad sewn into their pants, an invention of Sam Morton. St. Louis was one of the most, if not the most, aggressive baserunning teams in the league. Caruthers was one of five members of the team who slid head-first, along with Latham, Hugh Nicol, Yank Robinson, and Curt Welch. "As a slider, little Nic is doubtless without a peer in the country," the *St. Louis Post-Dispatch* said of the small, speedy Nicol. "Little Nic is an artistic slider and goes forward as though he were shot out of a catapult instead of impelled by motion of his own skill. With his right hand forward to touch the bag at the earliest possible moment, his left fast against the slide, he skims along the earth as though it were a sheet of ice instead of a hard, sandy soil."[2] Chicago White Stockings second baseman Fred Pfeffer noted, "In the matter of sliding the Browns are unsurpassed, but they won't keep it up long. After they have been a little longer in the business, they'll drop that. This plunging in head foremost is dangerous work. They are liable to break their necks. … Sliding in feet first is my motto. I will take desperate chances to win a game, but I won't risk my neck."[3]

One thing the Browns did adorn was new uniforms, Chris Von der Ahe purchasing white tops with brown trim and "St. Louis" written in brown across the chest, white pants also with brown trim, and brown socks. The Browns owner also put in some of his own money, on top the $100 the American Association provided, to purchase a "dandy"[4] championship pennant.

Caruthers' teammates had already had a chance to get used to the new rules before his return from his European trip, having played a couple of exhibition games against the National League's St. Louis Maroons. After a rainout between the two teams on April 3, Caruthers sat on the bench as Dave Foutz pitched in a 2–1 loss at Sportsman's Park. Caruthers was expected to be out again the following day at the Maroons' Union Park, with Nat Hudson announced as the starter. However, amazingly just six days after stepping off a train, it was Caruthers who pitched for the Browns that day. The fans—even at the opposing ballpark—were happy to see him; "a wild yell went up from the 'gang' when Bobby stepped into the box."[5]

There weren't many cheers for Caruthers after that. Not surprisingly, he was rusty, walking five batters in the first inning—although only one run was tallied—and allowing five runs to score in the second and three in the third, his "lack of speed being noticeable."[6] The Maroons pounded him for 12 hits, including five doubles, a triple, and a home run, to go with nine walks, a wild pitch, and only one strikeout. Caruthers said his arm was weak, hardly a revelation given his off-season and lack of training.

Caruthers was back pitching four days later against the Maroons on Saturday, April 12, at Sportsman's Park, and despite a report that he had a "a very bad pain in his side during the whole of the game,"[7] he allowed only five hits and two walks in an 8–1 win, clinching the city series and earning each player a new silk hat courtesy of Von der Ahe. That wasn't the only gift the Browns got. During a parade to celebrate the opening of the season on April 17, they were presented with a floral arrangement adorned with a note: "Presented by the employees of the Famous clothing house to the champions of the world. … with the hearty wish 'winners of the pennant for '86.'"[8]

Bob Caruthers' 1886 Old Judge card used an old picture. Someone drew in a moustache on this card, reflecting Caruthers' new look upon his return from Europe.

The game, and the 1886 season, however, was delayed due to rain. There were mixed reports on who was going to start the opener for the Browns—the *Globe-Democrat* said Caruthers and the *Post-Dispatch* Hudson. They both turned out to be right, sort of. Thanks to the American Association playing on Sundays, a doubleheader was held the next day, and both ended up pitching. First, though, the pennant flag was raised—with Sam Barkley of Pittsburgh, St. Louis' opponent, joining the Browns for the ceremony— as the fans cheered and 13 firework bombs were set off.

Caruthers did get the call for the first game, although his time in the box was delayed as Pittsburgh won the coin toss and took the field at the start. The Browns won, 8–4, with Caruthers allowing nine hits and five walks while striking out five, although three of the runs were scored in the final three innings after St. Louis took a 7–1 lead. Caruthers' next outing didn't go as well.

He wasn't helped by eight errors made by the Browns, but facing Louisville at Sportsman's Park on April 21, he was racked for 18 hits and walked four batters, looking nothing like the pitcher who was the best in the American Association in 1885. "Caruthers is said to be out of condition, and no doubt he is," observed *Sporting Life*, "as he could pitch nothing but a slow drop ball, getting in a swift one only occasionally."[9] After the game, Caruthers went to Von der Ahe and asked for time to get in shape and not to be used in the box.

Von der Ahe agreed, but when shortstop Bill Gleason was ill a few days later, Caruthers was sent out to right field, with Nicol filling in for his sick teammate in the infield. In a 16–10 win over Louisville on April 25, Caruthers, batting second in the order, had three hits, including a double, drove in three runs and scored four times, once after getting into a rundown between third and home before a wild throw by catcher John Kerins allowed him to cross the plate.

Gleason was still sidelined the next day as the Browns took on Cincinnati, meaning Caruthers again played right field. He had a hit, steal, two walks, and three runs—but had perhaps the game's biggest play in the ninth inning. Cincinnati tied the game at 12—hitters thought all these recent high scores were due to the new batter's box dimensions—and had John Corkhill on third base with one out. Larry McKeon lofted a fly ball to Caruthers. Corkhill tagged, aiming to score the tying run. Caruthers, sore arm and all, threw a strike to catcher Rudy Kemmler—a "remarkable throw"[10]—in time to nail Corkhill at the plate. The crowd erupted as Caruthers "lay on the ground several moments writhing with pain."[11] With his injured arm, Caruthers then had to bat leading off the top of the 10th—St. Louis again losing the toss and batting first. He popped out, but the Browns rallied for two runs and won, 14–12.

Caruthers sat out one game but was back in right field for the final game of a homestand on April 28, a 7–3 win in 10 innings over Cincinnati, producing a hit, walk, run, and two steals. However, when the Browns hit the road for 2½ weeks, Caruthers stayed at home to recuperate and build strength back in his right arm. He spent most of his days at Sportsman's Park, throwing to Phil Powers, a catcher recently signed by Von der Ahe (Powers, however, never played for the Browns, released a little over a month later).

On May 10, Caruthers found something else to do—he umpired a National League game between St. Louis and Kansas City. Due to an error by League president Nick Young, there was no umpire present in town, John Gaffney, who had officiated the previous Maroons series, having gone to Detroit the day before. Caruthers happened to be in the stands as a spectator. There was a little hesitancy to ask an American Association player to umpire, but eventually Caruthers was asked and acquiesced. In a 5–3 game won by St. Louis, Caruthers' "decisions were excelled all around, and were met with general satisfaction from both the players and the audience."[12]

The results of Caruthers' return to pitching didn't go as well as his umpiring. He was in the box for a quick home game against Cincinnati on May 16 before hitting the road again, and allowed 12 hits, including five for extra bases (although one was a double which fell between outfielders Curt Welch and Tip O'Neill, who did an Alphonse and Gaston act) in a 7–6 loss.

But he slowly started getting into form. On May 21 against the New York Metropolitans, a game played in Staten Island at St. George Cricket Grounds—where one could see the construction of the Statue of Liberty beyond the left-field fence—he allowed just six hits and one walk while striking out eight in a 3–1 victory, with a happy Von der Ahe joining the players on the bench. Five days later, backed by the second and final home run of Doc Bushong's career, he beat the Metropolitans again, 9–4.

However, Nicol, who played both second base and center field in the win, injured his finger (*The Sporting News* reported it was "blood poison"[13]) and was sent back to St. Louis to heal. Caruthers, who had played four games in right field subbing in for absent players, now was pressed into regular duty in the field when he wasn't pitching.

Some days he did both—and performed exceptionally well at each. In a Decoration Day doubleheader at Philadelphia in front of around 12,000 fans on May 29, Caruthers started the first game and allowed one run on five hits and a walk with six strikeouts. At the plate, he had five hits, including a double and triple, adding a stolen base and scoring three runs. The Athletics tried to slow down the Browns by putting loose rocks on the basepaths. St. Louis players found brooms, brushed them away, then ran with abandon, stealing nine bases (Philadelphia had none) in an easy 18–1 win. In the second game, batting sixth (up two spots from the previous contest) Caruthers had two more hits, including another double, and scored in an 11–3 win.

Not everything worked well for the Browns, however. In a June 1, 7–2 loss in Baltimore in which Caruthers pitched, St. Louis made nine errors, including four by catcher Bushong. At times, he tried to pick a runner off third base with Latham having to do everything he could to catch the ball (and once missing, allowing a run to score). Latham didn't hide his dissatisfaction with Bushong's throws. Two days later, Baltimore's Chris Fullmer tripled, with Latham not exactly going out of his way to field a throw from center fielder Curt Welch. After the inning, it was Bushong's turn to complain. Both players took a seat on the Baltimore bench—Bushong presumably to get away from Latham for a while, Latham likely just being the rascal he often was. It didn't take long for the catcher to accuse the third baseman of not trying his hardest. Latham cursed out Bushong—"Latham's language yesterday is said to have been so vile that Manager Barnie has determined to write President Wikoff"[14]—with Bushong responding by punching Latham, who tried to return the blow, but the remaining Baltimore players and manager Bill Barnie quickly stepping in to break up the scuffle.

The Browns were rapidly gaining notice for infamous behavior. "The members of the St. Louis Base Ball Club have already achieved the unenviable reputation of being wranglers, both off and on the diamond," wrote the *Baltimore American*. "According to the statements already published, they have two cliques in the club, and occasionally there is an outburst of feeling among the players."[15]

Years later, former team secretary George Munson noted:

The intense rivalry before the shrine of individuality caused friction in the old Browns' ranks. The brilliant talents of such men as Foutz, Caruthers, Bushong, Latham, Welch and poor little Yank Robinson were such striking figures in the Browns' repeated successes that they lead to an undercurrent of want-to-do-each-other feeling that only the mast hand of a Comiskey could have successfully coped with. There was scarcely a season in their halcyon days when Welch, Foutz, and Caruthers and Latham were on speaking terms, off the ball field. In fact about six of the players were at swords points, and Comiskey's locks became tinged with gray hairs in his efforts to keep these men in line.[16]

Despite their differences off the field, the Browns played well together as a team—usually. St. Louis got into a bit of a rut, losing two of three in Louisville (having too good a time in that city might have been a factor; second baseman Yank Robinson was fined $300 "for illuminating the city of Louisville during the Browns' recent visit there."[17]) then returning home to lose three straight to the same club. On June 10, Caruthers lost, 3–2, to left-hander Toad Ramsey, who had a no-hitter for six innings and finished with 12 strikeouts. Caruthers later said Ramsey was one of the early pitchers who threw a spitball. "Tommy Ramsey, the great Louisville pitcher, used the slobber ball. The trouble was that nobody recognized just what it was and termed it a drop," Caruthers explained. "Hardly a game went by in those that that Ramsey did not fan fifteen or sixteen men. Ramsey was a southpaw and had perfect control of this ball, a wide shoot and a world of speed. I think that the continued use of the spit ball put him to the bad, as it does everybody else who uses it continuously."[18]

Caruthers might have thrown a spitter as well, at least according to Bud Fowler. Fowler played in the Northwestern League for Stillwater in 1884, the same year Caruthers toiled in the same league with Minneapolis. In 1905, Fowler recalled: "The spit ball isn't new. Nat Hudson, Bob Carruthers and John Clarkson, as well as myself, all had it and worked it during the old days in the Northwestern league. We didn't call it the 'spit ball' but an 'overhand drop.' It was a ball of most uncertain destination and slipped off two wet fingers toward the plate. All that the pitcher knew was that it was sure to drop, but where and how much was a mystery. I never could tell whether it would [drop] four inches or a foot."[19] Caruthers, however, never made any claims to throwing one.

St. Louis' final loss to Louisville put its record at 26–19 (.578), one-half game behind Brooklyn for first place in the American Association. The Browns went 67–27 (.712) the rest of the way, starting with three consecutive shutouts. Caruthers pitched two of them, a four-hitter in a 2–0 win over Pittsburgh on June 13 and a two-hitter, both singles (Caruthers had three hits himself, including a double and triple, the latter to deep center field, scoring a pair of runs), in an 11–0 whitewashing of Cincinnati on June 18. This was also when St. Louis papers started first starred referring to his offseason exploits, with the *Post-Dispatch* writing, "Two hits were all the Reds could secure off Caruthers' Parisian delivery."[20]

From June 26–July 10, the Browns won 12 of 13 games, winning four by shutout and allowing more than three runs just once (an 8–6 victory at home over New York on June 28). Jumbo McGinnis, who pitched the fourth of those shutouts on July 8, was released the next day and signed with Baltimore. With Dave Foutz and Caruthers, he wasn't needed. The pair wasn't just winning games with their right arms. According to averages calculated by the *Pittsburgh Record*, Foutz was third in the league in batting average at .326 and Caruthers was ninth at .315. Hugh Nicol was hitting just .245.

With a crisp 4–2 win at Sportsman's Park over Baltimore on July 10 played in just an hour and 20 minutes, Caruthers allowing six hits, the Browns increased their lead in the American Association to eight games over Pittsburgh and nine over Brooklyn. Not everyone was impressed, however.

Adrian Anson and his Chicago White Stockings arrived in town to open a series with the St. Louis Maroons. His team was 38–14 (.731) but trailed league-leading Detroit, which held a 40–13 (.755) record. Over the years, there had been constant rumors of the Browns moving to the National League, with the two circuits merging. Camped out at the Lindell Hotel, a *St. Louis Post-Dispatch* reporter found Anson and asked him how he thought the Browns would fare in the National League. "Well, counting the clubs now in the League with their present force of players, I should think the Browns would come in somewhere around fifth or six," Anson replied. "The Chicago's would be first, Detroit, second; New York, third; Philadelphia, fourth, and the Browns fifth."[21]

That comment, naturally, did not sit well with the Browns. "After we have beaten Anson and his club in a fair and square manner, I do not think it is just the right thing for him to do to run us down in such a manner," Charles Comiskey said.

> Anson knows that we can beat him every day of the week, and I will wager anything he may like that we can win five or more games from his club out of a series of nine. Now, if Capt. Anson is so positive that the Chicagos are a better club than the Browns, here is a chance for him to prove it. We will play him any time after the close of the championship season. On the other hand, I think that if the Windy City Pets were in the American Association this season they would be fifth at least. I will bet that the Cincinnatis, the Pittsburgs or the Louisvilles can beat his club, and without any great amount of difficulty either. Now, if Anson thinks he can beat us, and is willing to back up his opinion with money, let him trot out his club and we will meet them whenever he may say.[22]

After the Browns beat Philadelphia on July 13, Chris Von der Ahe held a dinner for his team and some guests. The event was held at the beer garden in the right-field corner. The players were feted with glowing speeches, toasts and even song. The topic of Anson's remarks was still on the mind. When it was Caruthers' turn to speak, he addressed it head-on. "I saw Anson's bluff," he said. "I don't think the Chicagos can beat us, and I have a lot of money that I will bet that way, while my friend Foutz here has also some stuff that he would like to place on our team."[23]

Perhaps—okay, likely—fueled by alcohol, at 9 p.m. Caruthers and Foutz marched from Sportsman's Park to the Lindell Hotel, where they found Anson and a bunch of Chicago players. "I'll bet you a thousand dollars that the Browns can beat your nine and I'll put this money up as a forfeit,"[24] exclaimed Caruthers as he produced $200.

Anson flashed a grin but didn't respond. "Anson simmered down, backed water and crawfished until he made Caruthers and Foutz sick. Not only Anson but Kelly, so prodigal with his money, refused to put up or offer a single nickel," reported the *Post-Dispatch*. "For two long hours did Caruthers and Foutz hang around the Lindell rotunda and at every whisper from a Chicago man, flash the roll of bills in their faces and observe that 'money talked' but without effect."[25]

The situation simmered and was soon forgotten as the summer of baseball continued. But the fuse was lit. The explosion just took a little longer to go off.

A Champion Pitcher
and Hitter

Even though Browns players partied into the night at Chris Von der Ahe's celebratory feast on July 13—while Bob Caruthers and Dave Foutz hung around the Lindell Hotel late into the evening pestering Chicago White Stockings players—it didn't affect their play on the field. The following day, they routed Philadelphia, 9–1, bursting out of the gates with six runs in the first inning. Caruthers, starting in right field, hit a two-run triple, his third consecutive game with a three-bagger.

The Browns were feeling pretty good about themselves as they embarked on their latest road trip. When Caruthers made his next start, July 17 against New York on Staten Island, St. Louis players adorned new caps. The silk white hats with brown stripes were similar to what they had worn previously, with a notable addition: A ring, made of velvet, wrapped around the visor containing the word "Champions," large enough for their opponents to see. Caruthers pitched like one in his debut donning the chapeau.

The Metropolitans didn't secure a hit off Caruthers until there was one out in the ninth inning, when four-place hitter Frank Hankinson singled. The Browns won easily, 12–2. It was Caruthers' sixth win over his last seven starts. "Caruthers is one of those pitchers who do not fizzle in one season,"[1] noted the *St. Louis Post-Dispatch*.

With Hugh Nicol now stricken with malaria—he'd lose 15 pounds and miss most of the season—Caruthers was playing every day, either pitching or in right field. He was doing both with aplomb. Caruthers put together three straight multiple-hit games from July 29–31, going 4-for-4 with a pair of doubles and a walk in the second contest. In early August, he was sixth in the American Association with a .328 batting average. At the end of July, he was also fourth in ERA (1.41 per computations at the time) and tied for fourth in opponent batting average (.206).

St. Louis kept on winning. Starting July 31, the Browns won 12 in a row, scoring 10 or more runs in nine of those victories while allowing two or fewer runs eight times. Opponents tried to do anything to slow down St. Louis, and even that didn't work.

On August 11 at Sportsman's Park, the Browns faced off against Baltimore and Jumbo McGinnis, who clearly knew his old teammates well, including some of their tricks. McGinnis complained to umpire George "Foghorn" Bradley that Caruthers was using a bat which was flat on one side. Bradley checked it out and ordered Caruthers to use a fully rounded one. The ploy didn't turn out as McGinnis intended. Caruthers had a pair of hits, including his first home run of the season, depositing a McGinnis pitch in the ninth inning far over the right-field fence. The other Browns didn't take it easy on McGinnis either, pounding him for 19 hits in an 18–7 win.

After the season, among the rule changes announced by the American Association and National League was that either a flat or round bat could be used. Caruthers approved.

> What do I think of the new rules? Well, I think most of them are decidedly sensible. This applies particularly to the flat bat arrangement. The batter is given his choice between the round and the flat bat, but I think that the great majority of them will take the latter. With a round bat you have to hit a ball squarely in the center to make a good hit; with the flat bat you have a much larger surface with which to do effective work, and, in addition, the catcher is not nearly so liable to get a crack in the jaw. A foul from a flat bat will almost invariably go up into the air, instead of flying back into the catcher's face. This not only saves the catcher, but gives him a better chance of catching the striker out.[2]

Stuck with his rounded bat, Caruthers continued to strike the ball well. He had three hits the next day in a game called after seven innings, and four hits, with two triples, on August 15. The only thing hotter than Caruthers' hitting was the temperature and, as it turned out, the St. Louis fans' emotions.

The Sporting News reported that it was 120 degrees in the shade. The *St. Louis Post-Dispatch* claimed it was 132 degrees. The official temperature was 105 degrees, the second-highest recorded in St. Louis history, although the *St. Louis Globe-Democrat* noted that at Four Courts, which housed various courthouses and police headquarters, it measured up to 110. Even the wind was warm. The Browns were hosting Brooklyn on this day, August 16, and second baseman Yank Robinson didn't make it past the first inning, pulled for what was deemed heatstroke. Meanwhile, Caruthers not only pitched but also had perhaps his best day at the plate in his career.

In his first four times at the plate, Caruthers hit a two-run home run, knocked in another run with a double, was called out on a close play at first base denying him a single, and hit another home run with nobody aboard. That latter poke occurred in the eighth inning and put the Browns up, 6–1. Caruthers was also masterful in the box, having allowed just two hits.

But in that heat, having already thrown a lot of pitches and run around the bases all day, including in the top of the inning (Brooklyn won the toss and elected to be in the field), Caruthers was more than a little fatigued. He proceeded to allow 10 runs in the bottom of the eighth on 10 hits, including a double, triple, and homer, and two walks, both of which ended up scoring.

St. Louis wasn't finished, however. The Browns scored twice in the ninth and had two outs and a runner on first, Rudy Kemmler, when Caruthers stepped up to the plate to face Brooklyn starter Henry Porter. He connected again, sending the ball to the left-center field seats. Kemmler raced around the bases with Caruthers on his heels. The throw came in, there was a play at the plate, and the umpire, Bradley, called Caruthers out. "There was not a particle of doubt that Caruthers got in safely and the decision was unfair,"[3] declared the *Globe-Democrat. Sporting Life* claimed, "it looked very much as if he called Caruthers out at the plate just for spite."[4]

The decision cost Caruthers a three-homer game—ironically, Louisville pitcher Guy Hecker hit three the previous day, the only time this was accomplished in the American Association—while the previous call at first base in effect also denied him hitting for the cycle. It also ended the game. Browns fans weren't happy—with any of it. A large contingent of displeased St. Louisans congregated around the umpire and walked with him step-for-step as he attempted to leave Sportsman's Park, yelling invectives throughout. Brooklyn owner Charles Byrne, who was in attendance, was so concerned for Bradley's well-being that he ran out onto the field and led him to the players' dressing room for his own safety. Eventually things cooled down, and Von der Ahe notified Bradley that no one would bother him and he could leave the park for his hotel.

Umpires being accosted by fans was unfortunately not that rare an occurrence in the 19th century (and one reason it has been theorized that the home team often got the benefit of decisions). When St. Louis was in Brooklyn nearly a month later, after a 5–4 win called after seven innings, a crowd formed around umpire Bill Walsh, chanting "Kill him! Lynch him!"[5] The umpire ended up on the ground, where he was kicked and punched in the face and "lower extremities."[6] Local police came to Walsh's rescue, beating off the crowd with billy clubs. Four days later in Baltimore, umpire Billy Carlin made an unpopular decision, ruling the Browns' Robinson safe at home on a close play late in the game. St. Louis ended up winning by one run, 3–2. As he exited, a fan reached out and swatted Carlin with an umbrella. "Carlin did not leave the club-house with the St. Louis players," the *Baltimore American* reported, "but waited some time for the crowd to disperse."[7]

Caruthers was peeved as well, but it had nothing to do with umpires. While playing an exhibition in Alton, Illinois, he had two hits, including a double. Talking with a reporter from the *Post-Dispatch*, Caruthers noted how Tip O'Neill was listed as leading the Browns in batting average. However, Caruthers said, according to his calculations, it was he and not O'Neill who was the team's best hitter. The account of the conversation reported that Caruthers "thinks he has found himself grossly wronged. … He figured it out himself and is sure he is right."[8]

Things otherwise were going well for Caruthers. He was reportedly seeing a young, red-headed woman who often attended Browns games ("Take my advice, Bob, get married this fall and don't take another trip to France,"[9] *Sporting Life* wryly suggested). From August 29–31 he had three straight two-hit games; his average was listed at .327 (O'Neill, probably to Caruthers' chagrin, was at .346). Caruthers did take a shot to the midsection while fielding a line drive off the bat of Cincinnati's Hick Carpenter on August 30, but he still had the wherewithal to throw to first base and double off John Corkhill (his day pitching was done, however). Things, though, were about to take a turn for the worse.

St. Louis opened a road trip in Louisville on September 3—well, it was supposed to start in Cincinnati on September 1, but the Browns' train was late and the game was postponed. The Browns were trailing, 15–7 in the eighth inning when Caruthers, who had doubled and scored twice, stepped to the plate. The game was stopped, however, and a telegram was given to Caruthers. It was notice that his father died earlier that afternoon. There was no explanation of when the telegram arrived or why it was given right at that moment, but Caruthers headed back to the bench—replaced by Nat Hudson, a rare pinch-hitter in that era—and eventually his hotel, where he made arrangements to travel to Chicago as the funeral was to be held the following day.

Caruthers returned to the team a week later in Pittsburgh—that team was so excited to have the Browns in town it had a giant poster affixed to a prominent building in town declaring "Great struggle, Von der Ahe's Champion Browns vs. Alleghenys"[10]— and he was put right back in the box, pitching a 4–3, 10-inning loss on September 9. He also incurred a $20 fine for continued arguing from umpire Al Pratt, who was officiating only because the regular ump, John Valentine, was injured in the first inning after being hit by a foul. At one point, Caruthers said to Pratt, "That it was a dirty steal,"[11] which drew his pecuniary punishment.

On September 18—the game of the Carlin incident—Caruthers doubled with two outs in the sixth inning. Bill Gleason ran for him, which was strange enough as Caruthers batted leadoff and Gleason hit third (it ended up not mattering as Gleason advanced to third on a passed ball and scored on an O'Neill single for the game's first run). No reason was given for the move, but later that night Caruthers complained of intense chest pains.

He said that in the past while pitching, sometimes he had "felt severe pains at the heart, but as they did not affect me very much and passed off soon I paid but little attention to them."[12] Caruthers had a history of ailments. Around the time he started playing professionally, his mother noted that he "had the pneumonia, and since then he has been unable to rest on his right side. We have to build up his bed so that he can lie on his left side and rest easy."[13] In 1884 with Minneapolis, he took ill and missed two weeks. This was different, though.

"I pitched a hard game that day and in the evening I was suddenly taken with a severe palpitation of the heart and a terrible pain in the heart also," Caruthers explained weeks later. "I was not prostrated, you know, but the pain was bad and the violent beating unpleasant."[14] He added that the next morning, he called for a doctor—whose name, interestingly, he could not remember—who told him, "it was heart disease induced by ball playing and told me that I would have to stop it for the future if I care for myself a little."[15] Caruthers continued, "I consulted with my friends and determined to take his advice. I will play ball no more."[16]

The rumors were again in full force. He wasn't really sick; his family was paying him off to quit the game. Or it was all a ruse to draw his release from the Browns so he could sign with his hometown Chicago White Stockings. His teammates thought it was either malaria or due to smoking, which he did even more than the average person (Caruthers did quit cigarettes after the incident). Teammate Yank Robinson, his roommate on road trips, noted that Caruthers "used to get up in the night and smoke them."[17]

Chris Von der Ahe wasn't buying what Caruthers—or others—were selling. Regarding the prospect of retirement, Von der Ahe resisted that notion. "Oh, they all say that, you know, but it doesn't make any difference," he said. "Caruthers is going to stay with me."[18] And forget about Chicago. "If he pitches ball next year, he will pitch for the Browns or he won't pitch at all,"[19] Von der Ahe affirmed.

As for Caruthers, by the end of September his tune was changing slightly. Joe Pritchard, the St. Louis correspondent for *Sporting Life*, visited Caruthers, who was back in St. Louis after recuperating in Chicago, and described him as "looking much better than I expected. His cheek bones are a little more prominent than they were a month ago, but the color in his face is good and I told him that he didn't look like a sick man. He moves around rather cautiously, being afraid to take any exercise at all just now."[20] When asked about a return to the field, Caruthers left the door open.

> I like to play ball, and if I am not stout enough to go in and pitch in any of the remaining championship games, I want to be all right for the Maroon games after the championship series at an end. If I find out that violent exercise is detrimental to my health I will do no more work this fall and will take things easy this winter. In the spring I hope to be as stout as ever, and if I am you can rest assured that I will be found right here in St. Louis with the Browns. My folks are uneasy about my present bad health, but their scare is unnecessary.[21]

Pritchard also talked with Von der Ahe, who told the writer that "he would hate to see Bobby on the shelf; that he was a first-class man in every respect,"[22] while captain

Charles Comiskey stated that "Caruthers' shoes couldn't be filled, no matter who they could get; that there wasn't a man in the country that was as valuable as Bobby."[23]

It didn't take long after his conversation with Pritchard for Caruthers to consider himself sturdy enough to play. On October 2, it was announced that not only would he pitch the following day at Sportsman's Park against New York, but he would also fling the ball when the Browns faced the St. Louis Maroons in an exhibition series and in the upcoming championship series against the Chicago White Stockings, Von der Ahe and Albert Spalding having agreed to play a seven-game set (down from the nine Spalding proposed, because Von der Ahe claimed it interfered with the already scheduled Maroons games).

By his own admission, Caruthers didn't go all-out upon his return to the field. The good news was he felt fine physically afterwards and the Browns won, 6–4, as he allowed seven hits and two walks but struck out just one. The next day, with Robinson nursing a sore hand, Caruthers played second base for the first time in his career (he appeared there just eight more times) and made one error in his five chances. He pitched two more times before the close of the season—losing 11–7 to Brooklyn on October 8, then beating the same team two days later in the season finale, 8–6, allowing a combined 24 hits.

Upon his reappearance with the Browns, Caruthers played in each of the team's final seven games and had at least one hit in each. In that above loss to Brooklyn, he had three, including a two-run home run into Sportsman's Park's right-field seats. When the American Association averages were announced in November, Caruthers was listed as hitting .342, behind just New York first baseman Dave Orr's .346 (the league's statistics were later adjusted, with Caruthers officially at .334 and .338 for Orr). "It's the best batting record ever made by a pitcher, isn't it?" Caruthers mused in 1904. "I guess it must be. I know I was mighty proud of it, but terribly disappointed that I didn't get first place."[24] Tip O'Neill was listed at the time as hitting .339—having the highest batting average on the Browns earned him a medal presented by a local jeweler. However, O'Neill is now recorded as having batted .328—meaning Caruthers lost out on a medal, which surely would have caused him further distress had he known. Caruthers did lead the American Association in on-base percentage (.448), OPS (.978) and OPS+ (201) and was second in WAR (11.4) and slugging percentage (.527), but these were statistics unknown to him, presented long after his death. He also was second in the league in ERA (2.32), WHIP (1.056) and winning percentage (.682), and fifth in wins (30). Not bad for someone who arrived at camp late after taking a trip across the ocean.

Caruthers and the other Browns, save Yank Robinson and Curt Welch, who were absent for reasons not disclosed, were feted at Furber's restaurant, whose attendees included doctors, judges, and former ballplayer Ned Cuthbert, who played for the Browns before Caruthers' arrival. Doc Bushong, Arlie Latham, and Tip O'Neill all sang, but not Caruthers even though he, along with those three, Charles Comiskey, Bill Gleason and Hugh Nicol, often belted out tunes during St. Louis' lengthy train rides from city to city. Earlier in the year, the St. Louis Globe-Democrat noted that Caruthers, Latham, O'Neill, and the since departed Jumbo McGinnis "have musical voices, and their efforts as a quartet are of no mean order."[25]

In addition to a dinner, the Browns were presented with the newly created Wiman Trophy. The brainchild of New York Metropolitans owner Erastus Wiman, it was given to the American Association champion. Made "of solid silver and ... valued at $2,000,"[26] the trophy was a statue of a ballplayer leaning back with bat in hand.

The reward Browns players were the happiest with likely occurred a couple of days earlier. In that final regular-season game, nearly 8,000 were in attendance to cheer on their team. Each time a Browns hitter went up to bat for the first time, the crowd burst out in applause. During a ceremony after the third inning, it was announced that Von der Ahe agreed to give the players half the receipts from their upcoming series with Chicago—if they won. The ovation given after that revelation was the loudest of the day, Browns players likely joining in.

9

Big Game Pitcher

Before the Browns were to play the Chicago White Stockings, there was the matter of a best-of-nine exhibition series with the rival St. Louis Maroons. Rival might be a strong word—they weren't in the class of the Browns, after all. While the Browns cruised to an American Association pennant with a 93–46 record, 12 games better than second-place Pittsburgh, the Maroons struggled to a 43–79 mark, a distant 46 games behind Chicago.

But Browns owner Chris Von der Ahe didn't like others encroaching on his territory, whether it be in the Union Association, where the Maroons got their start in 1884, or the National League, which admitted the team in 1885. It might not be a battle of league champions, but it meant something to Von der Ahe, as evidenced by him buying his players hats the previous year after the Browns won the postseason series.

The first game was played on October 14 at the Maroons' Union Park in front of around 6,000 people. Bob Caruthers—as he was now commonly referred to instead of Robert—batted third and played right field. In the seventh inning, he singled. The next batter, Charles Comiskey, appeared to follow suit but the ball went foul. Running to second base, Caruthers tried to stop suddenly, and in doing so badly turned his ankle and had to be carried off the field. He returned three days later, back in right field and now second in the order as the Browns won their fourth straight over the Maroons by a combined score of 24–5.

The Maroons series took a break until October 25 for the playing of what O.P. Caylor of the *Cincinnati Commercial Gazette* referred to as the "World's Championship Series" against the Chicago White Stockings. While there was local fervor for the meeting of the two St. Louis clubs, the Browns-White Sox rematch from a year ago garnered national attention. Henry Chadwick, the future Hall of Famer who was a great proponent of the game, purported inventor of the box score, and noted baseball writer, was impressed by what he saw from St. Louis entering the series. "In calling the St. Louis team the 'Chicagos of the American Association,' I simply express my views of them as a first-class base-ball team," he wrote in late September. "They play ball for all it is worth. There is a vim and earnestness in their work which is lacking in every other American nine I have seen play, except, perhaps, the Pittsburg team, they standing next to the champions in team work."[1]

Von der Ahe was treating the matchup as a big event as well. He brought the Wiman Trophy, which ended up displayed in a window at Albert Spalding's Madison Street sporting goods store, rented a sleeping car to be attached to the regular train which headed to Chicago, and adorned the outside with bunting, flags, and pennants made of canvas which included the phrase "St. Louis Browns-Champions 1886–87."[2]

The 1886 St. Louis Maroons—better known as the Black Diamonds—were no match for the crosstown Browns (New York Public Library Spalding collection).

Fans gathered to see the team off, sending up a loud ovation whenever Von der Ahe or a player appeared. "Bobby Caruthers was asked about the condition of that strained tendon half a hundred different times,"[3] noted the *St. Louis Globe-Democrat*, not offering if an answer was provided.

As the train was about to head to Chicago, site of the first three games—the next three were to be held in St. Louis, with Game 7 eventually scheduled for Cincinnati—"We'll meet you when you return"[4] and "Bring back two games, and we'll bring the city down here to escort you up-town"[5] were shouted from below. Some St. Louisans decided to make the trek to the Windy City to witness the games for $10 round-trip, the price all the railroads were charging.

Others saved their money for bets. The *Globe-Democrat* suggested, "$15,000 is already staked by St. Louis parties on the games"[6] while noting reports out of Chicago that "the betting has been very heavy there, $70,000, it is said, being a fair estimate of the amount that is up on the result. Large sums have also been bet in New York, Philadelphia, Pittsburg and other cities having a membership in either the League or American Association."[7] The gambling wasn't limited to fans. The *Daily Inter Ocean* of Chicago reported, "Dave Foutz, it is said, wagered considerable money on the Browns winning the series before leaving St. Louis."[8] The paper also reported that Ed S. Sheridan, *St. Louis Republican* reporter, "is a heavy plunger on base ball, and he may drop a thousand or two on the Browns,"[9] while also intimating *St. Louis Globe-Democrat* sporting editor Frank E. Schuck bet on the games.

Waiting for the Browns to arrive in his town, Chicago captain Adrian Anson was approached by a reporter at a local billiards hall. Anson's words about the Browns from earlier in the summer hung in the air, as did George Watkins' accusation, made just a month earlier, about the White Stockings' lack of sobriety the previous year. "You're going to ask me what I think about this series, aren't you? Well, I'll tell you. We're going to beat the Browns in these games just as sure as I'm going to make a point on this position."—which Anson of course did—"My men are not drunk now. They are perfectly sober; and I see no reason why anybody should intimate that we will endeavor to back out on any proposition we make. We will play the St. Louis Club on a square basis, and if we beat 'em, we beat 'em; if we don't, we don't, and that's all there is to it."[10]

Game 1 was played Monday, October 18 at Chicago's West Side Park. The stands were roughly half full—depending on the source, there were 4,000 (*Post-Dispatch*), 5,000 (*The Sporting News*) or over 5,000 (*Inter Ocean*) in attendance. After a brief ceremony which included a marching band, St. Louis lost the opening coin flip, and the White Stockings elected to take the field. Foutz, who led the team with 57 starts, a 40–16 record, and 2.11 ERA, got the nod to pitch the opener for the Browns, with Caruthers, who was 30–14 with a 2.32 ERA in 43 starts, stationed in right field and batting second. When Caruthers strode to the plate in the first inning, the game was paused as some of the friendlier locals in his hometown gifted him a silver bat fastened on a base.

It was the high point of the game for the Browns, who were heckled mercilessly by the crowd as well as Chicago newspapermen, who, according to the *Globe-Democrat*, "acted like hoodlums, and from their box directed the most abusive language at the visiting club."[11] The lone umpire officiating the game, Jack McQuaid (or McQuade as the papers called him) even kicked a fan out of the park.

John Clarkson, the ace of the Chicago staff who sported a 36–17 record in 55 starts during the season, handcuffed the Browns, allowing just five hits while striking out 10 as the White Stockings cruised to a 6–0 victory. The Browns weren't overly concerned. Taking in a production of "The Golden Goose" at the Casino Theater later that night, the players were relaxed. Catcher Doc Bushong summed up the St. Louis attitude by saying, "The fact was that the Chicagos never played a better game of ball in their lives. We certainly did not play up to our standard. It was Clarkson who won the game, and he won it by pitching in a way he seldom does."[12]

The second game was a completely different story with a larger crowd (between 6,000–8,000, again depending on the source). One change was the use of three umpires instead of one. John Kelly, termed a referee, was in the field the entire game, either standing behind the pitcher or second base, moving whether or not there was a runner on base. When St. Louis was in the field, Joe Quest was the ump at home plate. For Chicago, it was McQuaid. The new system had an immediate effect. After Chicago once again won the toss and elected for the Browns to hit first, Arlie Latham led off with a walk and was apparently picked off first base, or at least that was the call by McQuaid. Kelly, however, overruled him, saying Latham wasn't tagged.

Two batters later—Caruthers was now on first, getting on after a dropped third strike by catcher Mike Kelly, who caught Latham off second—Tip O'Neill smacked a Jim McCormick pitch where the horse carriages were parked in left field, racing around for an inside-the-park home run and the Browns' first runs of the series. There were plenty more to come. St. Louis tallied two more runs in the fourth inning, including a two-out single by Caruthers, who was thrown out going for a double. The Browns tacked on three more in the fifth, O'Neill hitting another home run, and five in the seventh. Caruthers nearly hit two home runs, but both times the ball bounced off the top of the right-field fence and he had to settle for a double and triple, the latter knocking in a run.

The best part of Caruthers' day, though, came on the other side of things, when he was pitching. George Gore led off Chicago's first inning with a single—and that was the only hit Caruthers allowed on the day. He struck out five batters and walked two. In the eighth inning, Gore reached on an error by Arlie Latham and eventually made his way to second. Chicago had a chance to spoil the shutout with Anson up, but Bushong caught his foul tip, and with darkness settling in, both teams agreed to call the game, the Browns winning, 12–0. Nearly 30 years later, Chicago syndicated writer Joseph B. Bowles claimed it was one of the best pitching performances in postseason history. "[I]t was his pitching that was making a record that was destined to stand as one of the best feats of its kind for more than a quarter of a century," Bowles wrote. "Carruthers was the first pitcher to stop the heavy batting Chicago White Stockings."[13] In April 1887, Chicago shortstop Ed Williamson reflected on the series against the Browns and offered a concurring opinion, stating, "I never faced a pitcher so hard to hit in all my life as when I faced Caruthers last fall."[14] Chicago's *Inter Ocean* had another thought as to why Caruthers was so dominant. "BEER BEATS THEM," screamed the headline on its game story, with a subhead which read, "Their Sight Sadly Impaired, and Caruthers Enhances His Reputation as a Pitcher."[15]

The boos the Browns heard the previous day turned to cheers as fans spilled out onto the field after the game, happily leading the players to their waiting carriages and then giving them "three prolonged cheers"[16] as they left. Later that evening, Caruthers was again given a present, this time a cane with a gold handle. But Caruthers wasn't fully satisfied with his performance and gift. He wanted to do it again and pitch the third game the following day.

Nat Hudson was scheduled to start Game 3 on April 20. If Caruthers was considered young, Hudson was a baby. Just 17 years old, settling in as St. Louis' third starter, he made 27 starts and finished with a 16–10 record and 3.03 ERA. He might have been a rookie teenager, but he was raring to go and ready to face Chicago. Caruthers, however, pleaded with the man on top—owner Von der Ahe—asking to pitch back-to-back games. "He would not listen to any other man going into the box and he would have pitched the whole six games if I would have let him,"[17] Charles Comiskey recalled 15 years later.

Von der Ahe acquiesced. Caruthers pitched, and Hudson took his spot in right field. St. Louis won the coin flip and elected to have Chicago hit to open the game. The White Stockings didn't need their bats often in the first inning as Caruthers walked four—remember, it took six balls; Caruthers had finished third in the American Association in fewest walks per nine innings (2.0)—and Chicago scored twice without managing a hit. Those were the only bases on balls Caruthers issued, but he allowed 12 hits—including home runs to Gore and Kelly—and struck out only one as Chicago romped, 11–4, in another game called after eight innings due to darkness. The White Stockings did most of their damage late, scoring single runs in the fourth and fifth innings, two in the sixth, three in the seventh, and two in the eighth. "No greater mistake could have possibly been made than in again allowing [Caruthers] to do the twirling. … The score tells how the experiment worked,"[18] said the *Globe-Democrat*.

If Browns players weren't exactly enamored with Caruthers as he was—he was known to be quick to leave the ballpark after a game and rarely hung out with teammates—this didn't help. O'Neill wasn't thrilled at the late maneuverings. Third baseman Latham insisted the Browns would have won if Hudson pitched. "I had counted on winning the game yesterday, and if we had that we would have had a walk-over for the rest,"[19] he said upon arrival back in St. Louis. Shortstop Bill Gleason was blunt in his assessment of the goings-on.

> It was dead wrong to put him in. We all wanted Hudson and made a special request that Hudson be pitcher. Caruthers insisted on going in, and why they put him in I don't know. Hudson was anxious to pitch and understood he was going to until the last minute. From the very

start we all knew how the thing was going, and when the Chicagos took four bases on balls, that settled it. Even then it was not too late, and I heard that Mr. Von der Ahe told Comiskey to bring Hudson in from the field, but why it wasn't done I don't know.[20]

Even Von der Ahe, who was angry at the entire team following the defeat, took ownership of his poor decision. "It was certainly wrong to put in Caruthers at Chicago that last game,"[21] he admitted the next day.

Down two games to one, the Browns returned to St. Louis in a despondent mood. The scene at the train's arrival the morning of October 21 was in stark contrast to its departure days earlier. The players exited dejected and silent. Fortunately for them, no one saw it other than a few newspapermen—no fans were there to greet them.

They turned out later in the afternoon for Game 4, though, with between 10,000–13,000 cramming into Sportsman's Park. Unlike in the National League, in the American Association the home team decided whether to hit or take the field first. Comiskey chose the latter. It didn't look like a wise move as Foutz allowed three runs in the first inning, although Caruthers helped keep the score down by making a great catch on a long fly to right hit by Ed Williamson.

Back in the box again for Chicago, Clarkson allowed runs in the second and third innings before the Browns took the lead with three runs in the fifth. However, the White Stockings quickly tied things up—and quieted a raucous crowd—with a pair of runs in the top of the sixth. In the bottom of the inning, with one out, St. Louis loaded the bases on a walk to Yank Robinson, a single by Bushong and, after reportedly fouling off 19 pitches—mostly on bunts, as the foul third-strike rule was not in effect in 1886—Latham also walked. He had done the same in an earlier game back in Chicago, fouling off 20 pitches before finally striking out. Fifteen years later, Caruthers recalled that at-bat—although in his mind it was 14 fouls.

> The trick of bunting balls foul with the idea of wearing out the pitcher had just come into vogue, and one of the first to get it down to perfection was Arlie Latham. When Latham encountered a pitcher whom he was confident he could not bat successfully, and Clarkson was one of these, he proceeded to wear him out by batting as many balls foul as possible. On this occasion he ran up a string of fourteen and concluded the performance by fanning out. That shows how great a pitcher was John Clarkson. There are not many pitchers who could have run that gauntlet with safety, I can tell you.[22]

Despite the long at-bat by Latham against Clarkson, with the bags full Caruthers could only send a pop towards second base. This is when nineteenth-century chaos took over. With no infield fly rule yet established, Fred Pfeffer decided to let the ball drop and attempt a double play. He picked it up and threw to shortstop Williamson to force Latham out at second. Caruthers, though, was hustling down the line, and with his speed wasn't going to be doubled up. Instead, Williamson threw to third baseman Tom Burns to try to nail the slower Bushong. However, Burns couldn't corral the toss, and Bushong was safe, with Robinson scoring the go-ahead run. After O'Neill was walked without being given anything to hit, Gleason stroked a two-run single, and the Browns suddenly led by three.

After Comiskey lined out to Burns, Foutz induced the 3–4–5 hitters—Anson, Pfeffer and Williamson—all to fly out. By this point, the sky had grown dark, and the game was called, St. Louis an 8–5 victor, tying the series at 2. Some Browns fans came out of the stands and lifted players upon their shoulders, leading them to their changing area. Relaxing at the

ST. LOUIS.	1	2	3	4	5	6	7	8	9	10	R	BH	E
Latham, 3b													
Caruthers, rf													
O'Neill, lf													
Gleason, ss													
Comiskey, 1b													
Welch, cf													
Foutz, P													
Robinson, 2b													
Bushong, C													
TOTAL RUNS.													

CHICAGOES,	1	2	3	4	5	6	7	8	9	10	R	BH	E
Gore, cf													
Kelly, C													
Anson, 1B													
Pfeffer, 2B													
Williamson, SS													
Burns, 3B													
Ryan, rf													
Dalrymple, lf													
Clarkson, P													
TOTAL RUNS													

A scorecard from Game 4 of the 1886 World Series (Leland Auctions).

Lindell Hotel that night, Clarkson remarked, "Yes, they got away with me to-day, without a shadow of a doubt. I can't say anything, but that they beat us all around."[23]

Clarkson was a workhorse, even in his era, having pitched over 600 innings the previous year and 466⅔ in 1886, not counting his first three appearances over this series' initial five games. But pitching three straight days was not optimal. White Stockings owner Albert Spalding had a plan, however. The previous week, he had signed right-hander Mark Baldwin, who pitched for Duluth that season. Baldwin had been practicing with the White Stockings in Chicago and made the trip to St. Louis. Anson listed Baldwin as the team's starting pitcher for the October 22 game. Von der Ahe—at the prompting of his players, at least that's the story Spalding told—strenuously objected.

There had been a rumor that Von der Ahe had tried a similar trick, wanting to sign Louisville's Tom Ramsey and have him pitch for the Browns, but Spalding interjected. Von der Ahe denied this conjecture, saying he had no intention of signing Ramsey. Spalding insisted Baldwin was signed for the 1887 season but also 1886—contracts for players ran through the end of October.

As the argument continued, the game was delayed, making the large crowd—estimated between 12,000–16,000—impatient. There was another problem causing the contest to start late, however. The umpire chosen for Game 5, Grace Pierce, was nowhere to be found. The teams reverted to the three-ump system, with John Kelly again in his place as the so-called referee and McQuaid and Quest the alternating umpires. With

Spalding and Von der Ahe unable to resolve their dispute surrounding Baldwin, the officiators were left to decide the outcome. Kelly bowed out of the process and a coin was flipped to see who'd make the verdict. McQuaid won the toss and ruled Baldwin ineligible (supposedly if Quest had made the choice, Baldwin would have pitched).

This left Chicago in a precarious position. Clarkson was unavailable. It had been announced that either Baldwin or Jack Flynn, who went 23–6 with a 2.24 ERA, would pitch Game 5. Flynn, though, hadn't twirled since October 5 and had a sore arm, hence him not having been in the box for the White Stockings in the series. Anson felt McCormick had lost his effectiveness, evidenced by his getting pasted in Game 2, and it was said he also was sick.

Instead, Anson decided to shuffle his lineup. Shortstop Williamson, who had a little pitching experience, having 11 appearances and 33 innings over the past six seasons (18 of those innings occurred in 1881) and had relieved McCormick for the final inning in Game 2, was tabbed to start. Catcher Mike Kelly was moved to shortstop, with Silver King coming off the bench to backstop. With Baldwin not able to play and Flynn obviously disabled despite the pronouncement he'd pitch or play the outfield, Jimmy Ryan went from left field to right field, and Abner Dalrymple, who was to sit out, went to left. As one might expect, the plan didn't work out well.

Williamson allowed two runs on three hits—including one to Caruthers, who was thrown out trying for a double—and a walk. That experiment ended, with Williamson headed back to shortstop. Ryan, who pitched in 23 innings over five games for Chicago that season, was called to the box, third baseman Burns taking his place and Kelly sliding over to third. Ryan fared no better.

The Browns tallied a run in the second inning and four in the third off the outfielder-turned-emergency pitcher before putting the game away with three runs in the sixth. Caruthers scored twice, as did Latham, and led the team with three hits. In the third inning, he tripled to the center field bulletin board, behind which teammate Curt Welch was known to hide "a stock of beer,"[24] then scored on a passed ball, and in the sixth inning, he knocked home a run with a single. Hudson allowed just three hits as St. Louis cruised to a 10–3 win—the game, which started late, was again called due to darkness after Chicago batted in the top of the seventh—and a 3–2 series lead.

Spalding was still fuming later that night in regard to the decision on Baldwin, who he still felt should have been allowed to pitch. "I am not at all satisfied with the result of to-day's business, and I think that the action of Mr. Von der Ahe in the matter was unsportsmanlike and wrong, and if the loss of this game interferes with our winning the series, I think it would be only right to make some kind of protest against it,"[25] he said. He had calmed some the next morning and remained optimistic. "I am sure we will win it," Spalding answered when asked what he thought would be the result of the series. "We pitch Clarkson to-day and will pitch him also next Tuesday [for Game 7]. He is in good condition and I am confident of winning both games."[26]

Facing Clarkson in Game 6 was Caruthers. For all the issues his teammates had with him, including earlier in the series, there was no other pitcher they wanted in the box in a big game. "We don't like him personally, but he is the nerviest boy that ever stood between those four corners of the pitcher's box, and we can't help admiring him and doing our best behind him,"[27] an anonymous former Browns teammate said in 1902.

The anticipation for Game 6 and a potential Browns championship was high. "Betting was very heavy last night and this forenoon," reported the *Inter Ocean* from St.

Louis, "both on to-day's game and the series. Fully $10,000 was sent here from Chicago last night, and everything offered was taken."[28] While it was even money on the winner for this contest, Chicago was still a 10–8 favorite to win the series.

Fans once again filled Sportsman's Park, an estimated 10,000, as St. Louis and Chicago faced off for the sixth consecutive day. This time, however, the game was starting an hour earlier—at 2:30 p.m.—to ensure it wouldn't be called due to darkness. There was no umpire delay either as Pierce had re-emerged and umpired the game by himself.

After a scoreless first inning, Pfeffer singled off Caruthers to open the second. A steal and passed ball set him up on third base with none down. Caruthers bore down and struck out both Williamson and Burns, his first two of the game. With Ryan stepping up, Latham cheered on his teammate, yelling loudly for all to hear, "That's right, Bobby, strike him out, too."[29] However, Ryan dumped one over the third baseman's head to score the game's first run.

In the fourth inning, it was Pfeffer again; this time the Chicago second baseman sent one into the beer garden in right field and circled the bases before Dave Foutz could find the ball beneath the seats. The White Stockings made it 3–0 in the sixth when that guy Pfeffer reached third base after his grounder went through the legs of second baseman Yank Robinson, then eluded Foutz as well. He scored on Williamson's fly to Foutz.

Caruthers wasn't pitching poorly, he just wasn't doing as well as Clarkson, who didn't allow a hit until O'Neill tripled in the seventh inning, but to the Browns' misfortune, the outfielder overran the base and was tagged out. In the eighth, St. Louis finally got something going. Comiskey singled and Welch followed with a bunt hit, reaching first base as Anson couldn't handle Burns' bounce throw. A passed ball moved Comiskey to third, where he scored on a Foutz fly out. After Robinson popped out to Anson, Clarkson walked No. 9 hitter Bushong. The White Stockings' pitcher was one strike away from getting out of the inning, having a 3–2 count on Latham, but the Browns' third baseman—who had been challenged by Kelly to Pierce for using a flat bat and had to switch to a round one—laced a pitch into left field over Dalrymple's head for a triple (the White Stockings' outfielder got plenty of blame from a number of teammates and owner Spalding, for what the detractors determined was a misplay). The game was tied and "the behavior of the crowd was more like that of a tribe of Comanches than of civilized people,"[30] reported the *Inter Ocean*. Earlier in the contest, Spalding remarked to Von der Ahe that perhaps they should send a wire to O.P. Caylor in Cincinnati to begin preparations for Tuesday's Game 7. "When we began to count," Von der Ahe said, referring to the three-run eighth inning, "you ought to see how his face dropped."[31]

Caruthers failed to get in the go-ahead run, grounding out to Burns to end the inning. While he couldn't get his bat going, Caruthers still had some juice left in his right arm. Williamson led off the ninth inning and spurred on by the incessant cheering of Latham ("Now, Bobby, you got him. There's Williamson; he can't hit a balloon; strike him out; that's the way, Bobby"[32]) he fanned the Chicago shortstop. Burns followed with a double to center and went to third as Ryan sacrificed. With the leading run 90 feet from home, Caruthers whiffed Dalrymple. Clarkson set down the order in the bottom of the ninth, Ryan making a great catch on an O'Neill fly, Gleason fouling out to catcher Kelly, and Comiskey bouncing to third. Caruthers did the same in the 10th, striking out Clarkson before inducing a pair of fly outs to left.

Curt Welch led off the bottom of the 10th for the Browns. A great fielder and heavy drinker, as evidenced by his outfield beer shenanigans (Von der Ahe continually fined

Welch for imbibing but instead of keeping the money gave it to Welch's wife on the sly), Welch would do anything to win a baseball game. He often cut across the field while an ump wasn't looking, eschewing touching third base for a faster path to home. Welch also tried to get on base when needed at all costs, intentionally trying to be hit by a pitch. "He was continually allowing the ball to hit him in order to get on base when a run was needed," Von der Ahe recalled years later. "He'd let the ball hit him on the head if the occasion demanded. I frequently cautioned him against taking such desperate changes, but he would only say: 'If I get killed, you'll have to take care of the family.'"[33] A tie game in the bottom of the 10th where a run meant a Browns championship was one of those times.

Welch leaned into a Clarkson pitch, was plunked, and took his base. Anson was irate, an argument ensued, and Pierce eventually concurred, calling Welch back to hit. On the next pitch, Welch stung one to center for a single. Foutz grounded one up the middle which Williamson couldn't handle, and Robinson bunted the pair over. Bushong stepped in with the winning run on third. What happened next might never truly be known except for the most important part: Clarkson's pitch ended up behind Kelly, who didn't chase after it, and Welch ran home to give St. Louis the championship.

No one seemed to know what occurred. Was it a passed ball? A wild pitch? Something else entirely? After the game, Kelly gave his version: "I signaled Clarkson for a low ball on one side and when it came it was high up on the other. It struck my hand as I tried to get to it, and I would say it was a passed ball. You can give it to me if you want to. Clarkson told me that it slipped from his hands."[34] The *Chicago News'* theory was that Kelly called for (using modern terminology) a pitchout, as Welch was taking a nice lead, but the toss, instead of going wide, was over the dish with Kelly unable to grab it. Comiskey offered another story in 1899. "Clarkson was giving some sort of a signal to Kelly, and shot the ball shoulder high to Mike and close to Bushong's breast bone," he said. "Bushong dodged. Mike swung his arm for a throw to third, but dropped the ball behind him as he swung. All I could see was a streak and Welch slid over the plate. I was there, too, and took a slide for the ball and got it. A man jumped out of the grand stand and offered me $20 for it, but I still own that ball."[35]

The play is remembered as the $15,000 slide, although only Comiskey said Welch slid (there's no mention in any of the newspaper game reports), and the total game receipts totaled $13,994.94 (originally reported as $13,920.10, but Spalding and Von der Ahe later agreed the former was the correct calculation), of which the players split with Von der Ahe (Spalding had also promised the White Stockings half of the receipts if they had won). It was reported that the Browns received $580 a man—that was based on the $13,920.10 total, however. (*The Sporting News* gave the total at exactly $580.50, with shares also given to Hugh Nicol and Rudy Kemmler, neither of whom played in the series.) A few months later, Von der Ahe put the amount at $610. In 1900, Comiskey said each Browns player "got about $800 as his share of the receipts."[36] The umpires received $100 plus expenses.

When the game ended, fans rushed out onto the field, lifted the players up, and carried them to the locker room. Williamson made his way through the crowd to the dressing area to congratulate the Browns players, the only Chicago player reported to have done so. Other reports mentioned the White Stockings leaving the grounds quickly. It was estimated that 3,000 stuck around, enjoying the moment, and cheered each player as he exited after getting dressed, some even extending the celebration by following the

THE MONARCHS OF THE SPHERE.

The 1886 St. Louis Browns—"The monarchs of the sphere" (Library of Congress).

carriages as they headed downtown. "It was long after dark before Sportsman's Park and vicinity had settled down to its usually quiet state,"[37] reported the *Globe-Democrat*.

Von der Ahe suggested to Spalding that the teams keep their meeting in Cincinnati on Tuesday—with the Browns winning the series four games to two, there was no need for a Game 7—but played just as an exhibition. In a letter back to Von der Ahe, Spalding penned, "Friend Von der Ahe: We must decline with our compliments. We know when we have had enough. Yours truly, A.G. Spaulding [sic]. P.S. Anson joins me in the above message."[38]

> "Furl that Pennant, oh, 'tis weary!
> Round its staff it's drooping dreary,
> And the batting men feel sweary,
> While all Chicago darkly frowns!
> Fold it gently and consign it
> To Mound City—we resign it!
> Spalding's champions now assign it
> To Von der A-he's howling Browns!"[39]

10

Holding Out—Again

Bob Caruthers, for one, was not about to complain that a Game 7 wasn't needed and the proposed exhibition game against Chicago in Cincinnati for October 27 was called off. Beginning with the series against the St. Louis Maroons, the Browns hadn't had a day off since October 13, and Caruthers had not only pitched 10 innings in the World Series Game 6 clincher, but also relieved Dave Foutz in the eighth inning the next day as the Browns topped the Maroons, 6–5. "And I sorter drew an easy breath when it was declared off, for I had been in two straights and Clarkson had had a rest,"[1] Caruthers relayed years later.

Earlier in the day before that victory over the Maroons, the team, as well as White Stockings players Mike Kelly and Ed Williamson, appeared at the Merchants Exchange Hall, presented to the throng after morning trading was complete. Before descending to the floor to talk to the members, each player was introduced and asked to speak. "Caruthers said he was sorry they called on him, as he thought he was no speaker,"[2] reported *The Sporting News*. Even the Chicago players were asked to speak. Williamson was gracious in defeat. "Gentlemen, all I have to say is that it was a very fair contest," he said. "They beat us, and now I propose three cheers and three hearty cheers for the champions of the world."[3]

At the event, Chris Von der Ahe made plans for the team to be feted at the Hall, with tickets to be sold and the players sharing in the profits. It was reported each would receive in excess of $500. The banquet wasn't the only thing on their agenda. After the latest game against the Maroons on October 26 was called off because it was too cold, nine of the Browns—catcher Doc Bushong, shortstop Bill Gleason, and second baseman Yank Robinson excluded, the latter two due to injuries—Von der Ahe and Williamson (who acted as umpire) hopped on a train for Arkansas to play a pair of games, and pick up a little extra cash, against the Little Rock team.

The champion Browns playing in Little Rock was a big occasion. When the team arrived at the train depot on the morning of October 28, they were greeted by officials from the baseball team and given a carriage ride to the hotel. That night, the Browns were given box seats at Hyde's Opera House, where the "Vassar Beauty," Blanche Curtisse, headlined in her 200th performance as Zozo the magic queen. It was a production worthy of the distinguished guests, with numerous set designs painted by noted artist Henry E. Hoyt and having been "originally produced at a cost of $30,000."[4]

The games were also an event. The park was packed—the local paper estimated over 1,000 people, not bad for a small town such as Little Rock, which had a population of just 13,138 in 1880, growing to 25,874 by 1890.[5] "Banks, factories, stores and offices closed to permit employees to take in the game,"[6] which began at 3 p.m. The mayor and state treasurer attended, as did a couple of local judges from nearby towns. The makeshift St. Louis lineup—right fielder Hugh Nicol played shortstop, little-used Russ Kemmler caught, and first baseman Charles Comiskey played second base—easily won, 10–6, with Foutz and Nat Hudson sharing pitching duties. Batting third and splitting his time between first base and right field, Caruthers went 2-for-4 with a run scored and a double which plated another. The only downside for the fans in attendance was that Caruthers didn't get a turn in the box. "Caruthers must pitch in a portion of the game today," the *Daily Arkansas Gazette* said in its next-day recap of the game. "The public demand it and he is too accommodating a gentleman to disappoint them."[7]

The fans got their wish. "A large crowd was in attendance and when Caruthers took his place in the box the spectators cheered until the great pitcher acknowledged the compliment by lifting his cap," reported the *Gazette*.[8] A couple of errors by his teammates helped Caruthers allow four runs in the second inning, but otherwise Little Rock couldn't do much against the Browns' hurler, totaling just five hits (three of those coming in the second) and just one man left on base. Caruthers had three of St. Louis' 15 hits, including another double, as the Browns romped, 15–4. Tip O'Neill went 5-for-5 with two doubles but failed in his promise to knock a ball over the fence. That night, the Browns were given a reception at the Capital Hotel where "good things in the solid and liquid lines were provided in abundance, and songs, toasts and speeches were the order of the evening."[9]

The Browns returned home, although delayed long enough in Little Rock that their entry into St. Louis was too late to play a scheduled game against the Maroons. On Sunday, October 31 the two teams squared off for the final time, with the Maroons prevailing, 2–1, Hudson doing the pitching for the Browns. Because they lost the series, per a deal made prior to the series, the loser had to present the winner "an elegant pennant."[10] However, that gift likely never materialized as Maroons owner Henry Lucas was so frustrated with baseball he sold the team to the National League, which in turn found a buyer in John T. Brush, who moved the team to Indianapolis. St. Louis wouldn't be a two-team town again until 1902.

Caruthers played right field and had a hit in that game against the Maroons, then went to Schneider's pool parlor, where he engaged in a billiards match with Frank Maggioli, a professional player. With Browns teammate Kemmler acting as judge, Caruthers took an early lead, but Maggioli was strong at the finish and won, 100–78, costing the St. Louis pitcher $50. Before leaving town, Caruthers also played Arlie Latham in some 15-ball at $1 per game. There's no account who came out on top, but at last report Latham was in the lead. Even with his losses, Caruthers made out well. *The Sporting News* reported that he, Foutz, and Robinson each headed home with "something like $2,000 in their pockets,"[11] while Tip O'Neill boarded his train with $1,800.

Most of the players left before another celebration for the team, this one held at the Elks Club on November 3. There, each player received a stickpin from the Mermod-Jaccard Jewelry Company. Another reward was coming as well. A fund had been collected to present each player with a medallion. The *St. Louis Post-Dispatch* described the medal, also made by Mermod-Jaccard:

> They consist of a background of a diamond. The top piece, a crown, is set with nine diamonds, surmounted with a hand in white gold holding a ball of the same metal. Suspended from this is a medallion head representing the coat of arms of the city. On the medal proper is a golden hemisphere on which are the words "The World." The hemisphere is supported by two female

figures in white gold, and entwined by a wreath of green gold. The enameling on the medal consists of the words, "St. Louis Browns, Champions of the World." On the smooth back an inscription is engraved, reading: "Presented to ____ by the Citizens of St. Louis."[12]

Caruthers received his gifts in December. Of course, what he really wanted was a raise. He was coming off a season in which he won 30 games, and in his first three seasons was 77–29. Also, according to the records of the day, he finished tied for second in batting average at .342 (if Caruthers had known he led the American Association in on-base percentage, OPS and OPS+, he likely would have wanted even more money). In addition, Caruthers was coming off a World Series in which he won two of St. Louis' four games, including the clincher, was 7-for-24 (although this has since been changed to 6-for-24) with a double, two triples (tied for the team high), and six runs scored (one behind team leader Curt Welch). He also drove in five runs, although RBI was not tracked officially until 1920.

As was the norm, Caruthers wasn't the only one wanting more money. Von der Ahe, as was *his* norm, wasn't amused by the requests.

> Some of them have [asked for raises] but with them I have done nothing. They will come around at the right time. I have signed others at a rate similar to that of last year. Comiskey is one of the few I have signed. … They will all play here or nowhere. It may happen that one or two men will quit the business but they will not be missed. The success of the Brown Stocking team does not depend on any one man. It is the dash and the playing for the side that wins and that will remain even should one or two of the old team drop out.[13]

Even without a contract in hand, Caruthers was living the life of a champion. Wealthy (thanks to his mother), attired with the best clothes, well-known around the country as one of the best ballplayers, and coming off a most successful season, it's hard not to imagine the 21-year-old feeling good about the way his life was going. Back in Chicago, he eyed a horse he thought was a good, fast one and made a prudent deal for its purchase. As it turned out, a friend of Caruthers' who was also a big baseball fan, Louis Powell, also owned a horse. The two agreed to a race to determine the faster steed and decided a two-mile stretch of Grand Boulevard in south Chicago was just the place to do it.

Caruthers and Powell acted as drivers with Otto Floto, a former boxing manager and later circus owner and sportswriter, operating the whip for Caruthers with baseball and theatrical manager Billy Harrington doing the same for Powell. Wisely, Caruthers attached a lighter buggy to his horse, while Powell stuck with his heavier cart. Caruthers, often toying with Powell, got off to a fast start and easily won. Powell wanted a rematch and off they went again, this time a closer race. However, Powell, trailing by a small margin, happened to hear the sounds of another horse. He turned around in time to see an approaching Chicago park policeman and quickly veered off to his right, turning onto Oakland Boulevard and out of sight.

Caruthers had no idea his opponent was no longer on the same road nor was he aware of the impending cop, who, not encumbered with a carriage, caught up to the unsuspecting pair. Caruthers and Floto were determined to talk their way out of it and, with the former convincing the policeman he was from St. Louis and was "not aware that any rules existed in this city which forbade the exercising of a horse on the streets."[14] The policeman bought it. He gave the two a warning and let them on their way, with Caruthers probably laughing all the way to his mother's house on the other side of town.

Boxer James J. Jeffries and promoter Otto Floto. Bob Caruthers and Floto went on a wild horse race down the streets of Chicago. Caruthers later crossed paths with Jeffries on the baseball diamond (Amon Carter Museum of American Art, Fort Worth, Texas).

When he wasn't racing horses or showing off the latest style while walking about town, Caruthers was gambling—more on that in a bit—and letting people know he wasn't about to sign with the Browns. After reporting that he got a clean bill of health after a doctor's appointment, the heart disease scare behind him, Caruthers said he wanted $4,000 in 1887. Told of the demand by a reporter, Von der Ahe replied, "Only $4,000, eh? Well that's $1,000 less than he wanted last year, and if he starts out that well he'll end better. When I want Mr. Caruthers I'll send for him."[15] But after the previous year's fiasco, Von der Ahe was also well aware of the special circumstances surrounding Caruthers compared to other players. "I know Caruthers offered to bet [Detroit manager Bill] Watkins $400 to $500 that he would not play with the Browns next season for less than $4,500, but he will not be betting that way when the spring comes. His case, however, is an exceptional one," Von der Ahe explained. "Both he and his relatives are well off, and I happen to know that several of the latter object to his playing professionally."[16]

Von der Ahe didn't take this tack with other players. Arlie Latham said he wouldn't sign for the $2,000 the Browns owner offered, claiming Pittsburgh, which was jumping from the American Association to the National League, would give him $1,500 more. "I'm tired of working myself to death for any little $2,000," Latham said. "I'm offered a little raise, but it ain't enough."[17] Von der Ahe wasn't moved by Latham's proclamation. "If 'Lathe' wants to go to Pittsburg, let him,"[18] he said. Of course, Latham couldn't just sign with Pittsburgh, nor could Caruthers seek a deal elsewhere, because of the reserve clause, which kept the players bound to the Browns and Von der Ahe unless he released them.

A depiction of a man taking an electric bath from an 1886 catalog (Welcome Collection).

As with a year earlier, Caruthers and Von der Ahe were at an impasse. Also like 1886, Von der Ahe made a trek to Chicago to see Caruthers a couple of weeks later, this time after the pitcher's 22nd birthday. Unlike the prior year, Caruthers was in town, but Von der Ahe was taken aback by what he saw. Visiting the home of Flora Caruthers on the north side of Chicago just a couple blocks west of Lake Michigan at 2 Burton Place (Flora Caruthers had recently purchased a residence on LaSalle Street as well, but the family wouldn't move there until a little later), Von der Ahe found Bob Caruthers in terrible condition. He was "pretty bad off physically, a heavy cold having settled in his lungs"—it was the onset of pneumonia, which was the second-leading cause of death in the United States in 1890[19]—"and he looked very haggard and forlorn."[20] Caruthers couldn't leave the house and for a time was bed-ridden. When he finally could get out of the house, Caruthers headed downtown every day and took an electric bath. (According to a 2015 article on the Institute of Electrical and Electronics Engineers Insight website, "Electric baths gained popularity in France in the 1870s, where a low current was administered to the patient while in a bathtub, purporting to help rheumatism.... Electrotherapy treatments like these were so popular that in 1887 the U.S. Congress had a device attached to the Capitol Building's electrical system, allowing congressmen to easily receive treatments during congressional sessions."[21])

Von der Ahe went to Chicago with the intention of signing Caruthers and, according to the owner, the ballplayer's mother and two older brothers encouraged him to do so. Despite talk about Caruthers potentially quitting, Von der Ahe remained optimistic he'd have the stellar pitcher/outfielder in the fold for 1887.

> If he is in good condition, I feel pretty certain he will be again found with the Browns. He feels pretty blue at present, and says he intends giving up base ball entirely. I know he don't have to play for a living, as his mother has a splendid home, surrounded by all the luxuries of life, and is very wealthy. But when the invigorating spring weather comes and the season opens up again, Bobby's old-time enthusiasm and love for the game will return with it, and he'll want to play as badly as ever.[22]

Von der Ahe didn't leave Chicago empty-handed, however. Caruthers recommended an amateur pitcher named Thomas Dawson, a postal clerk who also happened to be Caruthers' former high school teammate. "He did not at first like professional pitching, but after I joined the Minneapolis Club and then came to St. Louis, he began to take a good deal of interest in twirling," Caruthers later explained of his find. "He soon began to show good command of the ball, and has won many a game for the semi-professional clubs of Chicago and through Illinois and Michigan. We have practiced a good deal together, and I know he is capable of doing creditable work. ... He has a powerful physique, is a fine gymnast, and will, I think, prove himself a valuable man for our club."[23] Von der Ahe gave Caruthers permission to sign Dawson for the Browns, which he did. Dawson did report to training with the Browns but otherwise never pitched professionally. Caruthers had better luck later in life in suggesting prospects.

Even with Dawson, who was a project at best, the Browns lacked signed players. Besides Caruthers, pitchers Dave Foutz and Nat Hudson (there were rumors the three were acting in concert, holding out so each could get a better salary—similar to Don Drysdale and Sandy Koufax in 1966—although Foutz later denied this, saying he hadn't even been in contact with the others during the off-season), catcher Doc Bushong, shortstop Bill Gleason, third baseman Latham, and center fielder Curt Welch had yet to ink their contracts. Von der Ahe blamed the $610 the players got for winning the World Series, saying "they made too much money last season."[24] A couple weeks after visiting Caruthers, and with the pitcher still unsigned, Von der Ahe nevertheless retained his confidence. "Caruthers will certainly sign in spite of all the talk," he declared. "His family is not opposed to his playing base ball, since he can make more money at that than at anything else and has no capital invested. His health is also improved by the work."[25]

Things changed over the coming weeks, and not just with Caruthers' condition getting better. His mother and brother Thomas, second oldest of the three sons, were hoping Bob would join his sibling in starting a hardware store. "Bobby is old enough to go into business," said Flora Caruthers, who added that she would provide the seed money to get venture started, "but he wants to pitch, and pitch I suppose he will."[26] Starting to feel like his old self again, the only hardware Caruthers had his mind on was a bat and ball. "I am willing to play in St. Louis for a slight advance over last year, as I would rather play there than anywhere else," he told a visiting *Post-Dispatch* reporter. "I have many friends there and like the people. Indirectly I have received offers from three or four clubs of more money than Von der Ahe is willing to pay, but he asks such a colossal sum for my release that no club can afford to pay it. On the whole I think I will play in St. Louis this year."[27]

An 1887 portrait card of Bob Caruthers sans facial hair from Gold Coin Chewing Tobacco (Library of Congress).

While Caruthers was ambivalent, Foutz was angry. "I see they are going around now and saying I got $2,500 as salary last year. That's a lie. I never got a cent more than the limit, $2,000, and what's more I'm not going to play ball for another season at that salary," said Foutz, who was headed to Hot Springs, Arkansas, instead of St. Louis. "I'm not going to come back until they come after me. I notice they find no trouble in going up to Chicago after Caruthers and if he's worth going after, I think that I am. ... I'm blessed if I ain't worth as much to the club as he is."[28]

Von der Ahe wasn't the only owner having problems signing his players. Louisville's Zach Phelps was having similar issues. In fact, the Browns boss offered to purchase the release of pitcher Tom Ramsey—reportedly up to $5,000. "A quartette of first-class pitchers is better than a trio, as it entails less work on each, and it keeps them in better condition," Von der Ahe explained. "The Browns have always been patronized liberally and we propose to show the people of St. Louis that we appreciate their liberality. With Foutz, Caruthers, Hudson and Ramsey, the Browns would be better equipped in pitching talent than any club in the country—bar none."[29] Ramsey, however, remained with Louisville.

On March 7, during the American Association's scheduling meeting in Cleveland, the league—mainly due to the situations with St. Louis and Louisville—amended its constitution to deal with these pesky players who were taking holdouts oh too close to the start of the season and allowing the league (with prompting of the owner, surely) to place them on a blacklist, thus keeping the player out of organized baseball as long as they were on it. The new rule adopted read thusly:

> And in case any player under reserve shall willfully hold off and refuse to sign a regular contract with the club which has served him, for the purpose of harassing the club or compelling such club to increase his salary, or who shall by any means, directly or indirectly, endeavor to attempt willful extortion from the club which has him reserved, he shall, upon complaint and satisfactory evidence being furnished from the club so aggrieved, be placed up on the black list by the President and Secretary and notices issues to all clubs as provided by this constitution and the national agreement.[30]

Players were already peeved by the reserve clause, and this didn't exactly temper their anger. Yank Robinson was a member of the slowly rising baseball union established in 1885, the Brotherhood of Professional Base Ball Players, and was quick to give his reaction to the new measure.

> It is time that ballplayers were treated other than like slaves. Ball-players have grown tired of being driven around like so many dogs, and they will not stand it any longer. ... That was a fine rule that was passed at the Cleveland meeting which permits the blacklisting of players for not signing with the club by which they are reserved whenever the Manager or President says so. The rule was passed for the benefit of Von der Ahe and a few others who anticipate some trouble in obtaining the signatures of a few of their players. Such a rule is a disgrace to the American Association, and the first thing the Ball-Players' Association will do will be to break it up. We may be obliged to slave this season, but you can bet we won't be driven about with a lash next year.[31]

In Chicago, Caruthers found out about the amendment via a letter sent to him by Von der Ahe, supposedly. One report was that Von der Ahe sent Caruthers a copy of the new rule; another claimed the owner included in his missive that the blacklist would be used if Caruthers didn't sign by March 21. Both Von der Ahe and club secretary George Munson denied the owner sent any ultimatum. It's likely Von der Ahe did send Caruthers the amendment as an implied threat, and a newspaper merely wrote it as fact. Either way, Caruthers let his feelings be known by hiring a lawyer and threatening to sue if placed on the blacklist. He would, however, come to St. Louis to discuss a deal. Writing an acquaintance in St. Louis, Caruthers proffered that "Chris has threatened to blacklist me unless I sign before March 21. The new rules give him the power to carry out his threat, but I have consulted an attorney and am sure the rule will not stand in law. Blacklisting will hurt Von der Ahe more than it will me. I will get my contract Friday, and cannot determine on my future conduct until I see it."[32]

As was the case in 1886, Charles Comiskey was the go-between. It was at his request that Caruthers come to St. Louis to discuss a contract (he made the same ask of Foutz, who acquiesced and signed on March 19). On March 21, Caruthers signed, reportedly for the same amount as Foutz—$3,000 (although later reports also put the figure at $3,250 and $3,500). "I've had a pretty tough time of it and though badly off at one stage of my sickness, am now feeling all right again," he said after inking the new deal. "I don't think I'll have any difficulty this season from any sickness of the past year or so, as I did the last season, as I'm feeling very much better than I have felt for a year. I intend to go in and do my full share of the work, and more, too, if necessary."[33] Caruthers didn't mention why he suddenly had a change of heart and accepted less than his original request. It might have had to do with his gambling. Caruthers was not having a good winter—and it was about to get even worse.

11

Green Baize Bob

There was a myriad of places to gamble in Chicago, and Bob Caruthers probably hit most of them. Some of the illegal parlors he frequented were located relatively close together at 70 Adams Street, 119 Dearborn Street, 98 Randolph Street, and 178 State Street. Three were right next to each other between 123–125 S. Clark Street.

When he came home after the 1886 season, Caruthers was faring well at these illegal gambling houses, both on his own—his usual game was faro—and by investing in other gamblers and taking a portion of their earnings. One report had him winning in excess of $10,000. But his luck would turn. After signing his contract with the Browns in St. Louis, Caruthers returned to his familiar haunts and quickly squandered away his previous winnings and much more. March 25, just days after agreeing to his deal with Chris Von der Ahe, was a particularly bad night, one which extended into the morning of March 26.

Caruthers lost $2,000 at 123 Clark Street, went across the street, and went down another $1,000. He then moved to the gambling outfits on Adams and Randolph Streets and dropped another $4,000. At his last stop, on Adams Street, he went bust and asked one of the proprietors, Jim Crawford, for $200, using a diamond stud and ring as collateral. Crawford gave him $150, which Caruthers took. That loan didn't last long. Less than 30 minutes later, Caruthers went back to Crawford and offered up his watch for the same purpose, which netted him $100. This time Caruthers started winning at the tables, but he was betting in low amounts, $2.50 and $5. Buoyed by his newfound luck, he upped his ante and was putting up the $50 limit per hand. Soon, he'd lost all his money.

Daybreak had come, and Caruthers had nothing in his pockets. He went to Crawford to try to retrieve his baubles. "I should have given it to him … but some of the boys made the remark that he was ahead of the house on the winter's playing about $3,000, and he had not offered to turn any of it in, and so I've got the stuff yet,"[1] Crawford told the *Chicago Daily News*. Caruthers had an idea how to get more money. He reportedly said, "I can make $1,500 if I can get released"[2] and supposedly had a lawyer contact Von der Ahe to get that process moving along.

The Browns owner didn't speak of any such arrangement, and when asked about the details of Caruthers' gambling, told the *St. Louis Post-Dispatch* "I was greatly surprised when I read about the way that Caruthers is carrying on in Chicago, and I telegraphed him this morning to come immediately to the city. I do not know whether he will be in condition to pitch good ball or not, but from the way things look now he cannot be in a very good form. As soon as he gets here, however, I will put the screws on him and make him work hard."[3]

Caruthers did hire a lawyer, of sorts, for another purpose, however. His uncle, Alexander McNeill, with whom Caruthers went on his journey to Europe, was a real estate agent—there's no indication he practiced any type of law, but he undertook this role for his nephew. McNeill, likely with the help of his attorney, Player Martin, petitioned for warrants to be issued and gambling materials seized. He also swore out affidavits for the arrests of a number of those who ran the illegal houses. To top it off, McNeill filed two suits against trios of them—Crawford, Kirk Gunn, and Frank Tiernan in one and John Condon, Sam Dahl, and Jeff Hankins in another—asking for Caruthers to be repaid his gambling losses.

Not much amounted from any of it. It took McNeill awhile to find someone to issue a warrant to find the equipment, and by that time the gambling houses were empty other than "four roulette tables and one faro table and some checks,"[4] although everything taken was reobtained after the gamblers went to Superior Court and filed a motion for their return. Arrests were made and bonds issued, but none (including Cy Jaynes, who quickly departed Chicago for Hot Springs, Arkansas) were even brought to trial. A year later, Caruthers' lawsuit against Condon, Dahl, and Hankins was thrown out "for want of prosecution,"[5] this coming after Caruthers tried to arrange a settlement, which the gamblers' lawyer, Perry Hull, was having none of. Six months later, Caruthers gave up on the other lawsuit, dismissing it. While McNeill had made a promise to try to shut down these gambling operations, he was fighting a losing battle. Tiernan died by suicide via poison in July 1889, but the others kept going on. As late as 1894, Gunn and Jaynes were served multiple indictments for running gambling establishments. Condon, later known by his nickname, "Blind John," operated racetracks and handbooks into the early 20th century.

The gambling losses did not sit well with Caruthers' family, who, for obvious reasons, preferred not to discuss it. A minor league catcher named Duke Jantzen happened to be in Chicago on March 26, when Caruthers' escapade ended in the early morning. Jantzen had heard that Caruthers was headed to St. Louis the following night and went to look him up. There's no indication how Jantzen knew Caruthers, as little is known of the catcher who never played in the majors, but Jantzen was also headed to St. Louis as his team, Syracuse, was to play a series of exhibition games with the Browns. Why not have a traveling companion? Calling on the Caruthers abode, Jantzen talked with Thomas Caruthers, who relayed that his brother was ill and wasn't going to leave St. Louis that Saturday or any time in the near future. This caused a slight panic in St. Louis, although a couple days later the truth—Caruthers' gambling escapades—was revealed.

Caruthers' contract began April 1, and while he wasn't in St. Louis by that date, he arrived two days later. He'd have to quickly adopt to a host of new rules, which were made in both the American Association and National League as the two leagues agreed to abide by the same guidelines, many of which affected pitchers. Among the actions taken for the 1887 season: The pitcher's box was shortened to 5½ feet long and 4 feet wide, while pitchers could no longer gain momentum with hops or skips before throwing; they had to keep their foot on the back line (55½ feet with the new dimensions) and take just one step. The pitcher also could no longer try to fool a batter by hiding the ball, stand with his back to the hitter, quick pitch, or other such deceptions. In addition, it now took only five balls for a walk, but the number of strikes for a strikeout was increased from three to four (walks also counted as hits, although this quickly came under scrutiny and was abandoned after one season; strikeouts also reverted to three strikes in 1888, although four balls for a walk didn't take place until 1889). On the flip side, hitters could no longer call for a high or low pitch. A strike zone was established between the shoulder and knee. "What do I think of the new rules?" asked Caruthers after arriving in St. Louis. "Well, I think most of them are decidedly sensible."[6]

Browns manager Charles Comiskey wasn't worried about his pitching staff—Caruthers, Dave Foutz and Nat Hudson—when speaking about the subject in mid–March. "Do I think the rule will affect Caruthers and Foutz? No, I do not," he said. "They do not resort to any of these tricks to fool the batter. They don't need to. ... Caruthers, Foutz and Hudson are not tricky pitchers in any sense of the word, and as the rule was made to cover that point mainly, they will not be affected by it."[7]

Comiskey was right. While walks increased across the board in both leagues—from 2.4 per game in the National League in 1886 to 2.7 in 1887 and 2.9 to 3.0 in the American Association—Caruthers *decreased* his bases on balls. He averaged 2.0 BB/9 in 1886 but lowered that to 1.6 in 1887. While his hits allowed were up—from 7.5/9 to 8.9/9—he was well below the league average of 12.7 per game and would lead the AA in WHIP (1.167).

Rules weren't the only changes. The Browns' roster was slightly different. Von der Ahe wasn't about to make any wholesale changes, but after seeing his team win the championship with Hugh Nicol sidelined, he determined that the diminutive outfielder was expendable. Nicol was traded to Cincinnati for $400 (to procure his release) and catcher Jack Boyle, the first player-for-player trade in major league history. "Again, he has not batted in good form for two years past, and in that respect was a weak spot in the team," explained Von der Ahe for his reasoning in dispatching Nicol, a popular player in St. Louis, especially with kids. "Under the new rules, I think, his batting will be very light, as he can only hit a low ball, and the pitchers will know enough to put it at his shoulders every time. Nicol is a great fielder, however, and threw more men out at first base than any one I ever saw, yet he was a short distance thrower, and could not cut a man off home plate."[8] The trade also helped Von der Ahe rid himself of a higher-priced contract and one he didn't necessarily have to fill, with Caruthers and Foutz able to play the outfield (which they did a combined 104 times in 1887). In addition to Nicol, Hudson wasn't with the team, having stayed in Chicago due to the death of his father, followed by a serious illness contracted by his mother.

Right field is where Caruthers made his 1887 debut for the Browns on April 3 in the third and final meeting against Syracuse at Sportsman's Park. As he had just arrived in town earlier that day, he wasn't intending to play although he told a reporter that morning, "You needn't be a bit alarmed about me or my condition. You'll see that I'll come out on the top and pitch as good ball as I ever pitched in my life."[9] However, his pitching find, Thomas Dawson, was hit by a line drive in the first inning and forced to exit the contest. Foutz, who had been in right field, replaced him, with Caruthers taking over in the outfield. Caruthers, who was "warmly received"[10] by the hometown crowd of around 5,000 when he batted, had a pair of hits, including a double, and scored twice as St. Louis won, 19–13, although the Browns had to score 12 runs in the ninth inning to put the game away.

Caruthers kept playing right field in a two-game exhibition series at Sportsman's Park against new American Association foe Indianapolis. The Browns also debuted a new uniform used just for non-regular season games: blue with brown socks. "The new blue costumes which the Browns wore yesterday were the subject of general condemnation," critiqued the *St. Louis Post-Dispatch*. "Blue suits with brown hose are far from forming a happy combination."[11]

Chicago came to town next as St. Louis and the White Stockings played a rematch of their championship series. In November, when Caruthers was supposedly considering giving up baseball, he remarked that the Browns shouldn't participate.

> Von der Ahe is a fool if he plays it. If I expected to be with the Browns next year I would kick against it. Suppose we win such a series? We only beat a club that we have already beaten, and don't improve our reputation a particle. Besides, a great many people would say that the Chicago team is not as strong as it was last fall, and, as a fact, we would be given very little if any credit. Suppose we lose? Then everybody will say our victory last fall was all luck, and our reputation will be lowered considerably. Von der Ahe may make some money by such a series, but he can't afford to take the chances of playing it. If he don't play it, it's a sure thing that the Browns will be the champions of the world until the close of next season, and will be a big card all through the season, and will make plenty of money. If I could see the boys I would tell them to kick against playing the Chicagos and not to play them unless compelled to. The boys ought to insist on the right to go through next season with their title of champions of the world undisputed.[12]

Caruthers' words proved to be prophetic. Arriving in St. Louis at the Lindell Hotel for the spring meeting, Chicago first baseman and team captain Adrian Anson commented, "If we hadn't been crippled last year we would have won for sure, and, bad as we are, these fellows only won from us by a scratch."[13]

In the opener, played April 7, the first of three contests in St. Louis, Foutz pitched and Caruthers was in right field as Chicago won, 6–3. The next day, just five days after arriving in town, Caruthers hurled for the first time and won, 7–4, striking out four while allowing just seven hits and one walk—considered eight hits under the new rules. (Walks as hits were already drawing ire. The *St. Louis Globe-Democrat* noted, "[Tip]

A nicely coifed, nattily attired, mustachioed Bob Caruthers is pictured on an 1887 card from Allen & Ginter's cigarettes (Library of Congress).

O'Neill made three base hits yesterday before he had touched the ball at all, going to base the first three times on balls. Another sample of the absurdity of the new rules."[14])

Caruthers' performance cost Anson $1,000—he'd bet on a number of these games (later winning $300)—but also gained him respect. "In Caruthers and Foutz the Browns have two of what I consider the way-uppest, crackest pitchers in the country," said White Stockings shortstop Ed Williamson. "They are both speedy, both have good control of the ball and both are prime batters. I did not think that Bobby would be in the good trim he is in and did not think that he would show up as well as he has. Of the two though I think that Caruthers pitches harder and swifter ball against us than Foutz does. He is not pitching as effectively against us now as he did last spring, but that I think is due more to the new rules, which militate against his speed, than to any other cause."[15]

After a 9–7 win over the White Stockings on April 9 with Foutz back in the box and Caruthers in the field, followed by two games at home against Topeka of the Western League (Caruthers sat out both, with subs Dawson and Ed Keas doing the pitching), the team boarded a train for Louisville for the next matchup with Chicago. In typical Von der Ahe fashion—and bluster—he hung two banners on each side of the car, one reading "The St. Louis Browns"[16] and the other "Champions of the world."[17]

Caruthers—or "Faro Bob" as some papers were taken to call him (his teammates referred to him as "Green Baize Bob,"[18] likely a reference to the color of the coverings on billiards, faro and poker tables)—got the nod in that contest, but in the sixth inning, while he tried to catch a liner off the bat of Fred Pfeffer, the ball tore through his hand, specifically his middle finger, which had the fingernail dislodged and skin ripped off. Caruthers finished the game, which Chicago won, 16–15, in right field, with Foutz taking over as pitcher. Afterwards, he found a local doctor to patch him up, but he was expected to miss roughly one week's time.

With Caruthers sidelined, the Browns tried to save Foutz for another day and had catcher Jack Boyle pitch—it was claimed he'd done this before, although in his 13-year major-league career this was his only pitching performance—and that experiment lasted all of one inning, in which he allowed two runs, before being replaced by Foutz.

The next game between the Browns and White Stockings was in Indianapolis, but St. Louis had a conundrum on who would pitch. Von der Ahe had intended to bring along Joe Murphy, a native of St. Louis who pitched in one game for the Browns in 1886 as well a handful for the Maroons and Cincinnati. But he didn't show up or make the trip. Hudson was still in Chicago tending to his mother. Foutz, having to pitch back-to-back days, was in no shape to go again. Von der Ahe felt he had no choice: He went to Caruthers and asked him to pitch. Caruthers said he would but noted he was hurting, and any excessive work could cause further damage to his finger. Clearly not pitching at full strength—or effort—he did well early, allowing five runs through six innings, but then gave up 14 over the final three, Chicago winning, 19–9, and taking the series, four games to two. Caruthers was battered for 21 hits, with Pfeffer doubling and homering twice while Anson also circled the bases. "Caruthers's pitching permitted the Chicagos to send the ball wherever they pleased,"[19] observed the *Indianapolis Journal*. Despite Caruthers' ineffectiveness, Von der Ahe lay the blame for the loss elsewhere. "The game at Indianapolis was evidently fixed. The umpire gave us the worst deal that a ball club ever received on the diamond," he claimed. "I never expect again to see such criminal umpiring as Doescher indulged in that day."[20]

Caruthers sat out the next two days—an exhibition against Indianapolis and the regular-season opener at Louisville. A rainout on April 17 and a scheduled day off gave him more time for his finger to heal. Even though Von der Ahe declared Caruthers now fit to pitch, with Hudson still not with the team, that same day the Browns' game was wiped out he was pitching in an amateur league for the Chicago Whitneys (and not even lasting two innings). St. Louis signed Silver King (real name Charles Koenig, but his hair color led to his nickname, while King was roughly the English translation of his last name). King had pitched for Kansas City at the tail end of the 1886 season, and when that franchise was removed from the National League, the NL held onto his reserve rights, which Von der Ahe purchased, reportedly outbidding a handful of clubs.

Caruthers returned to the rotation April 19 and pitched four times in eight days, winning three games and improving with each start. He gave up 12 actual hits plus three walks (recorded as 15 hits at the time, though for our purposes, walks and hits are separated) in a 9–7 win over Louisville on April 19, 10 hits in a 5–2 loss at home to Cincinnati three days later, but just four hits and a walk in a 6–1 victory over Cincinnati on April 24, and no walks and seven hits in 19–3 plastering of Cleveland on April 27.

He was doing well at bat, too. In that April 27 game, he had a couple of run-scoring singles—both times then stealing second—before depositing a George Pechiney pitch into the right-field seats in the eighth inning with the bases full. The next game he played, as the Browns' right fielder in a 28–11 win over Cleveland (called after eight innings), he nearly repeated the feat, this time clearing the bases with a triple.

The victory put the Browns into a tie for first place after 10 games. After some brief jostling at the top, when Caruthers beat Louisville, 12–7, at Sportsman's Park on May 7, the Browns were alone in first place—and they never relinquished that spot. St. Louis was gliding to another easy American Association pennant, its third straight, but the path to the championship would still be filled with plenty of bumps and bruises.

12

Powerhouse

The St. Louis Browns opened the 1887 season by losing three of their first five games but then reeled off a 15-game winning streak. After losing, 4–3, in 10 innings to Philadelphia to drop their record to 17–4, the Browns won 14 of their next 15. By June 2, they were already nine games in front of the closest competition.

St. Louis was clearly a powerhouse. This wasn't great news for the other American Association teams, all of whom were already vying for second place yet again. "There is no use talking further about the matter, the St. Louis Browns are the greatest players on earth," Baltimore manager Bill Barnie said. "They outclass all rivals, in either the Association or the League. The team will win the championship again in good style, simply because they can't be downed. Individually and collectively, they are the best ball-tossers on the diamond."[1]

The *St. Louis Globe-Democrat* posited that the Browns might move players to other teams to make it a more challenging pennant race. "It has become such a steady thing for the Browns to win that the interest in the fight for the pennant has already begun to lag," said the paper, "and the Eastern clubs are complaining that it is impossible for them to work up interest in the fight while the Browns are so strong."[2] St. Louis owner Chris Von der Ahe snickered at the suggestion, but seven months later it wouldn't seem as funny.

Also taking a hit were gamblers. "There is no money to be made by betting on the Browns nowadays," observed the *St. Louis Post-Dispatch* in mid–May. "In the pool rooms odds of 10 to 5 or 2 to 1 are freely offered and there are no takers."[3] Bob Caruthers made a long-term bet, however. He staked money that Baltimore would have a better record than both Cincinnati and Louisville. When Caruthers made his bet, Baltimore was 11–3 and the others 8–6. However, this gamble was not to be a winner—Cincinnati ended up in second place in the American Association, four games ahead of Baltimore, which finished with a slightly better record than fourth-place Louisville.

Things were going well for the Browns otherwise, off the field, too. In mid–June, players were showing up in advertisements for Merrell's Penetrating Oil in *The Sporting News*, with a different player highlighted each week with a quote about the product. Caruthers' turn came in the July 30 issue. His caption read: "Pitchers are most liable to catch cold of any of the players—by reason of the heavy strain they undergo while in the box. I have been troubled considerably by stiffness in the arm, by reasons of taking cold. Since using MERRELL'S PENETRATING OIL, the stiffness has disappeared. I think all pitchers, especially, should use it. R.L. Caruthers."[4] St. Louis players, Caruthers included, were also listed in an ad in *Sporting Life* for baseball shoes made by Philadelphian Waldo M. Claflin.

A view of Brooklyn's Washington Park from a May 30 game against the St. Louis Browns. The teams played a doubleheader that day, with Bob Caruthers in left field for the opener and pitching the second contest. The Browns won both games, 8–7 and 9–3, with Caruthers going 7-for-9 with two walks. This photograph is likely from Game 2, which had an estimated Decoration Day crowd of 20,000.

On the field, though, the team was slowly coming apart at the seams. In a June 10 game in Philadelphia, Charles Comiskey swore at fans (according to the official report, he said, "I do not care a goddamn for any of them"[5]), as did center fielder Curt Welch, who was also accused of punching Athletics pitcher Gus Weyhing while trying to stop Weyhing from getting to second base by intentionally interfering with him. Six days later in Baltimore, Welch was the center of conflict again. Attempting to steal second base in the ninth inning, he reportedly went out of his way to take out second baseman Bill Greenwood, who dropped the throw from the catcher and ended up on the ground as Welch made his way safely to the base. A melee quickly ensued—a fan even ran out of the stands to confront Welch but was cut off and taken away by a policeman. Welch was arrested on the charge of assault (he was given a $200 bond) and escorted out of the park, with Comiskey, by two policemen. The game was called off (an 8–8 tie after eight innings). When the Browns left the field in their carriages, people threw rocks at them. "Yes, the boys had a lucky escape and by a miraculous dispensation of Providence, were permitted to leave the worst ball town in America, alive," said outfielder Lon Sylvester a couple of days after he was sent back to St. Louis.

It was a severe ordeal, and in the darkest hours of the exciting period on June 17, it was a time when men's souls were tried, and we all had great reason to feel thankful that we escaped the clutches of an angry mob. … They not only threw rocks at us, but threatened to shoot King. Bob Caruthers was struck on the head by a well-aimed rock, and not a pebble as the papers of Baltimore stated. It was thrown at him in the carriage while on the way to the hotel, and Bob has it as a momento of Baltimore mob spirit. Latham was also struck with a rock behind the ear and had I not guarded my face, I would have been hit with a rock. The Baltimore patrons of ball are the worst gang of hoodlums and ruffians in America."[6]

Welch was in court the next day but was released with a $1 fine plus $3.25 in court costs as Greenwood testified that he didn't think the Browns outfielder tried to intentionally injure him. Welch, for obvious reasons, not only didn't play the next day but also wasn't even at the ballpark. Tensions were still high as Caruthers, nursing another

sore finger, pitched for the first time since May 30. With a large crowd on hand and unseasonably warm temperatures, the Browns did everything they could to keep the peace. Baltimore first baseman Tommy Tucker tried to goad St. Louis players by continually pushing players off the bag. The Browns, normally an aggressive team on the basepaths, for the first time all season, didn't try to steal. That seemed to soothe most of the crowd—well, that and twice as many police than usual being at the game. Caruthers didn't give the hometown fans much to cheer about either. He allowed two runs in the first inning but only one run and two hits after that as the Browns won, 7–3, with Caruthers allowing just four hits and two walks. "He seemed to know the weakness of all the Baltimore players, and repeatedly fooled them on a slow drop ball," observed the *Baltimore American*.

"Occasionally he used his speed, but mostly depended on a high ball, and out-shoot or a curve."[7]

Caruthers wasn't so masterful his next time out, an 8–4 loss at Cincinnati on June 20, but he homered in Cleveland off George Pechiney on June 24 as the Browns swept a three-game set. The team returned home to face Louisville on June 28—the

WELSH, C. F. Athletics
COPYRIGHTED BY GOODWIN & CO., 1888.
OLD JUDGE
CIGARETTES.
GOODWIN & CO., New York.

Outfielder Curt Welch would do anything to win a game, whether trying to get hit by a pitch, hiding balls in the outfield, or socking an opponent who got in his way (Library of Congress).

first game at Sportsman's Park in exactly a month—to great fanfare. "As each of the team stepped up to the bat he was greeted with prolonged applause,"[8] reported the *Globe-Democrat*. Welch was given an especially big cheer and was gifted a diamond stud. Caruthers was in prime form, tossing a five-hit shutout with no walks and five strike-outs. No Louisville runner got past second base. The *Globe-Democrat* said that "Bobby seems to have struck his gait, and is now pitching a great game,"[9] while *Sporting Life* said of Caruthers, "Combined with perfect command of the ball he had lightning speed."[10]

The pitcher, however, wasn't in the mood to talk about his performance. Rather he was peeved over a recent rule passed in which the reserve list was made to be in effect all year—in other words, players couldn't sign with teams which played during the winter. The ruling got Caruthers to beat an old drum—talking of retirement.

> It may sound like a chestnut, but I'm pretty certain that I won't play ball any more. They can blacklist me if they want to, but I've got a good chance to go into business next year and make some money for myself, and I'm going to take it. People may make think that ball players get more money for their work than it is worth, but when you come to consider things you'll notice that a ball player is not treated like other employees are. As soon as he gets a little old, say about 35, or whenever he gets badly hurt, and that can happen any day in the year, he's thrown overboard as though he were an old carcass and that's the last that's ever heard of him. No sir; I'm going into business next year and they can pass all the rules they want afterward.[11]

Whatever his mindset, it didn't affect him on the field, as evidenced by the game he just pitched as well as the following day at the plate. Batting fifth and playing right field, Caruthers doubled in Tip O'Neill in the first inning, singled and scored in the sixth, homered off Guy Hecker over the right-field fence with a runner aboard in the seventh, and led off the eighth with another shot into the seats in right.

The only downside to Caruthers' game that day was in the sixth inning, when he and Welch collided while chasing a fly ball. Caruthers left after the eighth inning and missed the next two games—but not because of injury. He headed back to Chicago to see his sister off on a European trip of her own. Rejoining the team in Louisville, he pitched a 10–3 win while collecting another four hits. At one point in the game, Caruthers was on second base and tried to score on a single. Charles Comiskey was coaching third and could see Caruthers was going to be easily out, so he ran down the line and crossed home. Louisville catcher John Kerins tagged Comiskey but not Caruthers, who was following quickly behind. The ruse didn't work, however, as umpire Al Bauer wasn't fooled and ruled Caruthers out.

The Browns, like every other team, did anything to win. For example, they cut across the field and avoided third base to score. In a July 24 game at Brooklyn in which St. Louis won, 4–3, the Browns' Yank Robinson did just that with the umpire's attention diverted elsewhere. An infuriated Brooklyn owner, Charles Byrne, went to the Browns' bench to chastise the player, saying, "That was a damn dirty trick of you, Robinson, to try to win a game that way."[12] Von der Ahe was sitting with his players, as he often did, and yelled back, "Now look here, Byrne, you manage your men and I'll attend to mine," he said. "If the umpire didn't see the play that was his fault, not ours. Your men would cut a base, too. Now, you get off our bench and leave us alone, or I'll see that you do."[13] The Brooklyn fans were upset as well and, after the game, threw rocks and bricks as carriages left the park. One hit another umpire, Jack McQuaid, who just happened to be at the game, in the head, causing significant damage. Thus was the baseball experience in 1887.

At the New York Metropolitans' home at St. George Park on Staten Island, baseball in 1887 also presented an interesting obstacle. Beginning June 25, the play "Fall of Babylon" was performed at the park. To accommodate the stage and structures, the baseball diamond was shifted slightly. But because of the expanse of the sets, they weren't moved and remained in play. On July 20, Caruthers hit a "terrific drive to the left of the Babylon stand and scored a home run."[14]

Not that Caruthers or St. Louis for that matter needed any help on offense. In late July, eight American Association batters were hitting .400 or better—remember, walks were counted as hits—and four of those were Browns. Foutz was listed at .482, O'Neill .480, and Caruthers .469—those were the top three averages in the league. Robinson was the fourth Brown over .400, at .420.

However, once again, Caruthers' season hit a speed bump. Facing the Athletics in Philadelphia on August 2, Caruthers drew a walk and scored during a five-run Browns second inning. But he wasn't feeling well—he didn't play the two previous games and had the chills the day before—and was removed from the game. With his teammates heading back to St. Louis after the game, Caruthers remained in Philadelphia at the Continental Hotel. Von der Ahe hired a doctor to look after him, and the initial report was "typhoid-pneumonia,"[15] although some reports thought it was another bout with the heart disease which sidelined him for part of 1886 (Yank Robinson dismissed those reports, saying cigarette smoking had caused his earlier issues and Caruthers quit that habit). A few days later, it was reported that Caruthers was struck with malaria.

The Browns remained optimistic. "He'll be down here in a few days and shut out some nine on only one hit,"[16] said team secretary George Munson. Robinson, standing nearby, heard the comment and added, "That's just what he'll do."[17] But Caruthers wasn't headed to St. Louis, rather back home to Chicago to recuperate. He was expected to be gone a week. But that time period came and went, and no Caruthers.

Reports started trickling in that Caruthers was seen about town, specifically at a Chicago White Stockings game and the racetrack, which didn't please Von der Ahe, who telegrammed the pitcher asking when he'd be back. Caruthers didn't reply but did send a note to Comiskey indicating that his health had only slightly improved. Von der Ahe sent an ultimatum: Caruthers was to report to the Browns by August 19 or he'd stop paying him. It didn't help that Foutz sprained his thumb and Hudson, who briefly joined the team, was also back in Chicago tending to his sick mother. That left Silver King as the Browns' only pitcher. Robinson had to be used in relief in an 11–4 win at Cleveland on August 16. (Pitcher wasn't the only position where the Browns were banged up; Doc Bushong had been sidelined for a while, causing Jack Boyle to catch over 40 consecutive games.)

Caruthers beat Von der Ahe's deadline by two days, although his absence remained a point of contention for the owner, one which he was not soon to forget. "I was all broken up and if I remained in St. Louis with the club and attempted to indulge in any hard athletic exercise, I think it would have been the worse for me," explained Caruthers. "I merely went home to get a sniff of the lake breeze and to brace up on the cold weather up there. I'm in first-class trim now and will be able to do as good work pitching as I ever did. I do not think I am in danger of another attack of typhoid fever very soon, or at least I hope that I am not."[18]

Caruthers was back but due to a rainout and day off, he wasn't on the field again until August 19, when he was in right field with Joe Murphy pitching (Murphy's only appearance of the season and final major league game). When Caruthers took the field, the Sportsman's Park faithful erupted in "prolonged applause."[19] It turned out to be quite the return. Facing the Athletics' 35-year-old hurler, Bobby Mathews, he reached base six times—four hits and two walks—and clubbed his sixth home run of the season in the eighth inning, a two-run shot which cleared the right-field fence.

With a month and a half to go in the season, the Browns didn't have much to play for. After beating the Athletics, 22–8, in Caruthers' return, St. Louis was 17 games in front of the competition (of course, the Browns still went on a 12-game winning streak from August 23-September 3). It was a given that the Browns would be in that year's World's Series—as it was now often called—and Von der Ahe was already making scheduling plans for the event as early as August 24, with different scenarios for playing either Detroit or Chicago, who were in first and second place in the National League. There were other ways to motivate the players, however.

The musical "Our Jennie" was opening at St. Louis' Poe Theater on Saturday, August 27. Perhaps looking to stir up some advance notice, J.J. Rosenthal, a self-described fan of baseball and manager of lead actress Jennie Yeamans, wrote to Von der Ahe and Munson with a proposal. His client, Yeamans, would supply a gold medal to the Browns player who recorded the most steals in their game that Saturday against the New York Metropolitans, with the winner receiving the award at the theater on opening night, presented by comedian Gus Williams. Both teams, of course, were also invited to attend the entire performance. Von der Ahe wrote back with his approval.

To no surprise, the gambling element seized upon this opportunity as well, with Charles Comiskey, Arlie Latham, and Curt Welch made the favorites (and for good reason; modern tabulations show Latham, Comiskey and Welch as the top three stealers on the team, in that order). "Considerable money was wagered on the result,"[20] wrote the *Globe-Democrat*, which noted that Caruthers was "a rank outsider in the betting."[21] Already well in front of the American Association pennant race, the Browns had won their previous four games by scores of 8–1, 24–6, 14–8 and 15–6, the latter against the Mets. Thus, this contest also enlivened the fans. "Some life was infused into yesterday's game between the Browns and Mets by the contest for base running," noted the *Globe-Democrat*. "The large crowd present paid more attention to the contest in base stealing than they did to the game, however."[22]

It's not as if the Browns needed more reason to run the bases—they led the league in steals in 1886 and repeated in 1887. "Yes, you talk of base running. I never saw so many games won with as few hits in my life as that old team used to win,"[23] Caruthers said in 1904.

Caruthers might not have been a prodigious base stealer like Comiskey, Latham, Welch, and former teammate Hugh Nicol, but he was "considered the best base runner of any pitcher in the American Association"[24] and was thought of as one of the "principal examples of the great long-legged base runners."[25] Against New York, Caruthers reached base three times and stole four bases. Two of those came in the sixth inning after second baseman Joe Gerhardt booted his grounder. No one else on the Browns had more than Comiskey's two stolen bases. Catcher Jack Boyle, who had only seven steals in 88 games, was clearly motivated and had one, as did Bill Gleason, O'Neill, Latham, and Robinson. Only pitcher King and Welch ("although he had several chances"[26]) didn't record a theft. That night, Caruthers was brought up on the stage of Pope's Theater and given the gold medal. Over 15 years later, he still considered it one of his prized possessions.

There were other ways to persuade players. In early September, the Browns were

Jennie Yeamans, depicted here in an 1887 theatrical poster, provided a medal which Bob Caruthers considered one of his most prized possessions (Library of Congress).

playing a series against the Metropolitans with the third of the four games taking place in Weehawken, New Jersey, on Sunday, September 4. Comiskey put a curfew on the team, but Yank Robinson got drunk that night, and when the manager made the rounds the next day to gather everyone for an early train, the Browns' second baseman was passed out. Comiskey woke Robinson by dousing him with water. Slow to dress, Comiskey then threatened Robinson with a $100 fine if he missed the train and another $100 if he was late to the game (this on top of the $100 he levied for the morning incident). Robinson not only made it, but he also made the "only brilliant play"[27] of the game and finished with two hits and two runs. "He stayed sober the rest of the season, trying to win back that fine, but I did not remit it,"[28] relayed Comiskey in telling the story years later.

Comiskey had other problems to deal with besides an inebriated second baseman. In that game at Molitor Park in Weehawken, in the fourth inning O'Neill swung and missed, with the bat flying out of his hand and hitting Welch flush in the nose. Already shorthanded—Bushong and Foutz both were injured—the Browns used only eight players the rest of the game (and still won, 16–6). With Welch out, St. Louis had to use recently signed pitcher Ed Knouff in the outfield. Caruthers and Silver King also played outfield when they weren't pitching. Six days later, in a game at Philadelphia, Comiskey tripped over the first-base bag and, as he landed, broke his thumb. Welch—with his broken nose not healed and puffy eyes—played for the first time since he was hurt because there was no one else left on the bench.

The next day, September 11, Von der Ahe had scheduled an exhibition against the Cuban Giants, made of up Black players, in West Farms, New York. The players had other ideas. Eating dinner at the Continental Hotel in Philadelphia after his team's 5–4 loss earlier that day, and ruminating over the expected one-month loss of his first baseman and manager, Von der Ahe was startled when Tip O'Neill emerged and dropped a letter on the table. It read:

PHILADELPHIA, September 10.

CHRIS VON DER AHE, ESQ.

DEAR SIR: We, the undersigned members of the St. Loui Base Ball Club, do not agree to play against negroes to-morrow. We will cheerfully play against white people at any time, and think by refusing to play we are only doing what is right, taking everything into consideration and the shape the team is in at present. Signed, W.A. Latham, John Boyle, J.E. O'Neil, R.L. Caruthers, W. Gleason, W.H. Robinson, Charles King, Curt Welch[29]

The wire report categorized this as "For the first time in the history of base ball the color line has been drawn."[30] Von der Ahe was miffed. Not due to the racial implications but because he figured this was going to cost him around $1,000 in revenue, not to mention the train tickets he had already purchased for his team's travel. He quickly confronted the players—all but Comiskey and Knouff, who didn't sign (Comiskey didn't know anything about the movement, and Knouff was too new to either be asked or want to create any waves)—but none spoke up. It was reported that Boyle, Latham, and O'Neill headed this effort, and while "they had considerable trouble in securing the signatures of some of the men,"[31] on this, the team stuck together. A ticked-off Von der Ahe called off the contest against the Giants.

If it was a question of principle with any of my players I would not say a word: but it isn't. Two or three of them had made arrangements to spend Sunday in Philadelphia, and this scheme was devised so they would not be disappointed. There are no players in the profession who receive as large salaries as my men, and who are accorded so many privileges or are so well treated, but it has been my experience that a base ball player is the most unappreciative of any class. Of course, there are exceptions, but there are very few.[32]

Comiskey naturally backed his players. "I think some of the boys wanted a day to themselves," he said. "They have played against colored clubs before without a murmur, and I think they are sorry for their hasty action already."[33]

While the team was banged-up and surely was looking forward to a day off, it's hard to dismiss race being a factor, especially when hearing what Latham told A.J. Reach, president of the National League's Philadelphia Phillies, who also chastised the Browns for their action. "Why, you don't know all, Mr. Reach," Latham responded. "We played every day last week, and one day we played two games, and had to get up at 3 o'clock in the morning to catch a train. And then look at the team we've got. It's like a third-class amateur club. We did not want to go over there on a Sunday, especially, to play a nigger club, and we didn't go."[34]

Von der Ahe got some slight revenge after the series finale at the Jefferson Street Grounds in Philadelphia. The park had opened in 1883, and in that time only two players hit a ball over the right-field fence (and one of those didn't count as a home run). We don't know the distance of that fence, but center field was 500 feet and left field between just 225–250,[35] which likely made for an odd-looking field. In the fourth inning of the Browns' game against the Athletics, Caruthers showed off his power by knocking one over that fence, "the longest hit of the season"[36] at the park. The Athletics played

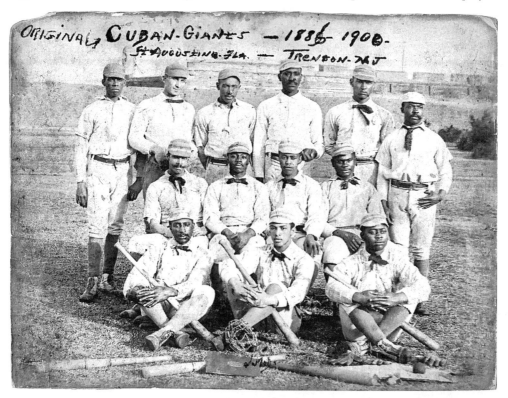

The Cuban Giants, circa 1886. St. Louis Browns players created a firestorm with owner Chris Von der Ahe when they refused to play the team, citing, in part, injuries to the team.

at Jefferson Street Grounds until 1890, and no one else managed to clear the right-field fence.

Despite the long homer, the Browns ended up losing, 10–8, in a game called due to darkness after eight innings. With the road trip continuing to Baltimore, a few players decided to take in a play before their overnight train departed. However, here's where Von der Ahe exacted a small amount of vengeance. Instead of the usual late-night trip, he put the Browns on the 6:57 p.m. train to Baltimore. That meant the players had to change at the park and hustle to the train depot. "We will get to Baltimore about 11 o'clock, and have to go without our supper,"[37] complained one unnamed player. Latham, who reportedly was fined $100 for the Cuban Giants affair, remarked, "The old man's beginning to squeeze us. Never mind, boys, we will have to stand it."[38] Ironically, the game in Baltimore the next day got rained out.

The next day, September 14, perhaps still peeved at their quick exit from Philadelphia, the Browns were lethargic. The team wasn't making simple plays and committed seven errors (in a game which lasted only seven innings). Caruthers was angered by the lack of support from his teammates, who claimed they had trouble seeing the baseball due to a dark and cloudy day—and asked to be removed from the game following the third inning, trailing 5–0. Shortstop Bill Gleason, filling in as captain in Comiskey's absence, denied Caruthers and had him continue to pitch. Caruthers did settle down, not allowing a hit over the final three innings, but after he plunked second baseman Bill Greenwood, the ump called the game. In addition to losing, 9–4, Caruthers failed to get on base, ending a 25-game streak. The Browns also lost another player as Robinson was spiked in the hand while stealing second base in the sixth inning. He wouldn't return until October 1.

Upon returning to St. Louis, the Browns had an exhibition game September 19— this one they played—in which the Kansas City team was promised $10 by their manager for any run it could score. They managed two (the Browns had 12). Watching the game that day was a young William B. Hanna, later a sportswriter for several New York newspapers for nearly four decades. In 1928, he recalled being at that game and his impression of Caruthers:

> Through all these years I've never seen a pitcher except Herbert Pennock, who so appealed to me as the embodiment of graceful skill. Many a pitcher I've seen come and go since then with fully as much and more skill than Parisian Bob, so many there isn't room to mention them all here … but none who was at once the equal, as painted by the brush of youthful fancy, of Bob Caruthers. Jaunty, all the assurance in the world, a moustache the equal of which no stage villain ever had, handsome and a craftsman to his finger tips. … There wasn't anything flamboyant about Carruthers, but his personality, as I recall it, was a wee bit more obtrusive than Pennock's yet none the less he was an agreeable, pleasant-mannered man. … Every move Carruthers made was of unstudied grace, and he still holds first place in my mind as the most graceful dexter-hand pitcher I ever saw. Were I picking an all-graceful team I should name him as my pitcher.[39]

With the season winding down, things weren't getting much better for the Browns. Using a makeshift lineup with Welch at second base, Knouff and King in the outfield, and Caruthers and Foutz splitting time at first base, the Browns played seven games against Cincinnati—six on the road with one, on September 25, back in St. Louis since that city didn't object to Sunday games—and lost six. Playing center field, Caruthers split a finger in the lone home game, but at least it was on his left hand and he could still pitch. After one of the defeats, Munson sounded off. "They are playing wretched ball," he wrote. "Whatever the cause may be, and not even Comiskey's return [he played September 29 but in right field before moving back to first base in the next game, October 1] to the team has helped matters. They played against Cincinnati with no more vim or enthusiasm than a lot of wooden men, and the 10,000 people who witnessed the game were thoroughly disgusted with the exhibition."[40]

Things weren't going well internally either. It was reported that there were several factions on the team. Bushong and Latham were already at odds. Caruthers had issues in the past with Latham and Foutz. Robinson and Welch were at it as well, and no one got along with Gleason other than Comiskey and O'Neill. St. Louis finished with a 95–40 record in easily winning their third consecutive pennant. But the Browns were just 16–14 over September and October. The indifferent play plus discord among teammates meant the Browns weren't exactly at their peak for the World's Series.

13

The Last Straw

Back in early September, St. Louis Browns owner Chris Von der Ahe remarked that he would rather have his team face Detroit in the World's Series than Chicago. "I would rather play them because I think they are an easier team to beat than the Chicagos," he explained. "Besides that, St. Louisians have never seen the Browns play the Detroits, so that the games would be more of a novelty than those with Chicago."[1] Von der Ahe got his wish as the Wolverines, unlike the Browns, had a good September, going 18–6 to pull away from the pack and win the National League pennant.

The two teams were set to play a 15-game series beginning October 10 in St. Louis, where tickets ranged from 50 cents to $1.25, although the majority of the games were to be played at neutral sites. Both teams had decent pitching but in a year of offense each led their respective leagues in batting average, on-base percentage and slugging percentage. Detroit would be without one of its top sluggers, first baseman Dan Brouthers, who sprained an ankle in a game two days prior to the start of the series. Caruthers was getting the call in Game 1, but Wolverines outfielder Ned Hanlon wasn't worried. Asked if he feared the Browns' pitcher, Hanlon responded, "Oh, no, we generally find that we can hit a pitcher pretty hard after we bat against him two or three games. There's no telling what you're going to do with a pitcher when you tackle him for the first time. After we get accustomed to Caruthers' delivery I suppose we can do something with him if we fail to do it in the opening game."[2]

Hanlon slightly changed his tune after the opener, in which Caruthers allowed just four hits and a walk as the Browns won, 6–1. "Caruthers pitched like a catapult from the jump to the finish," said the *St. Louis Post-Dispatch*. "His curves were wide, his command was almost magical, and his speed was all that could be desired."[3] Only one runner reached second base—pitcher Pretzels Getzien led off the ninth inning with a double and eventually came around to score. "Caruthers is a mighty fine pitcher," said Hanlon, who went 0-for-3. "He has good curves and his command of the ball is superb. There are plenty of pitchers as speedy as he, but there are few who are as graceful in their movements."[4] Charlie Snyder, a catcher for Cleveland, was at Detroit's hotel and told the players assembled in the lobby that night, "Boys, St. Louis has you Buffaloed. They'll win easily, for they have the class."[5]

The Wolverines rebounded in the second game at Sportsman's Park, beating Dave Foutz, 5–3. On October 12, the teams took a train to Detroit. It was a 15-hour ride, which forced the players to put on their uniforms on the train, get picked up by carriages, and taken to the field. Caruthers held a 1–0 lead into the bottom of the eighth, when after striking out the first two batters, he made a poor toss to first base with catcher Charlie Ganzel ruled safe (the *St. Louis Globe-Democrat* noted "the decision being very questionable"[6]). Jack Rowe beat out a bunt, with Ganzel not stopping. Browns first base-man Charlie Comiskey's throw to third base was off-target, and the tying run scored. St. Louis had chances to score in the 11th and 12th innings but couldn't push across a run. In the bottom of the 13th, Getzien blooped a hit between Comiskey and right fielder Foutz. Caruthers got three straight grounders hit to Yank Robinson, who made the play on the first two, but Comiskey couldn't handle the throw on the third, and Getzien ran home with the winning run. The *Globe-Democrat* called it "one of the greatest ball games ever played in the United States."[7]

The Browns looked to change their luck and brought out their blue uniforms for Game 4—they'd done the same during a long winning streak earlier in the year—but there was no magic left in them with Detroit shutting out St. Louis, 8–0. Caruthers didn't play; Silver King pitched and Foutz was in right. But Caruthers was involved in some card playing on the train. While the Wolverines eschewed poker, the Browns, Comiskey included, had no issue passing the time with a little gambling. With the poker also came drinking, and it led to a fight between a couple of intoxicated players, Yank Robinson and Curt Welch, the former punching the latter in his not-yet-healed bro-ken nose. Caruthers reportedly lost $50 in one of the card games (with the team trav-eling city to city after the third game, there was a lot of time to kill). The local papers were split on their coverage of the extra-curricular activities. "The late stories recently published concerning dissipation, poker-playing and fighting among the Browns have been exaggerated beyond all measure," reported the *Globe-Democrat*. "It is true that the Browns played poker, but every game was stopped before 11 o'clock at night, and by mid-night all in the car were in bed. ... Then, too, no player has been drinking to excess."[8] The *Post-Dispatch* countered with "Some of the players have been making fools of them-selves with strong drink. Club rules are stringent. They absolutely forbid gambling of any kind or drinking of any kind."[9]

All the goings-on didn't affect Caruthers. He was back in the box on October 14 in Brooklyn and downed Detroit, 5–2. "Finer pitching than that of Caruthers' in the Brooklyn game of Friday.... I have never seen,"[10] noted baseball writer Henry Chadwick opined. The Wolverines hitters were impressed, too. "He's got as nice a curve as I ever saw and he can put the ball just where he wants it every time,"[11] said slugging outfielder Sam Thompson. Said Hanlon: "I wouldn't mind it if he didn't seem to take it so awful easy."[12] Third baseman Deacon White added, "It's funny we don't hit him, but he hands 'em over pretty smooth."[13] "I'll pitch every game in the series," Caruthers said, "and win all of 'em, too. I feel so much like pitching that I don't want to do anything else."[14]

St. Louis' good feelings were fleeting. Getzien blanked the Browns, 9–0, at New York's Polo Grounds the following day, St. Louis managing just two hits and three walks. At dinner that night at the Grand Central Hotel, the players complained to each other that Von der Ahe was "not doing the 'right thing' by them,"[15] followed by grum-bling concerning their salaries. The Browns likely found out that Detroit's owner, Fred-erick Stearns, was going to give each Wolverines player $500 if they won the series. After giving the Browns a bonus in 1885 and a share of the receipts in 1886, Von der Ahe made no such pecuniary promises for this World's Series.

The teams resumed play on October 17 (of course, the Browns played an exhibition against Brooklyn on the day off) but without their shortstop, as Bill Gleason requested to be taken out of the lineup. "Bill has lost his nerve and asked for a few days' rest until he could recover his confidence,"[16] reported the *Globe-Democrat*. Confidence was never a problem Caruthers suffered from, and in Game 7, played in the park of Philadelphia's National League team, he was once again stellar, allowing six hits and a walk. But the Browns tallied just once, on Tip O'Neill's homer in the ninth inning, falling 3–1. "I do not think that Caruthers ever pitched as he has pitched in these games,"[17] Comiskey said afterwards.

Foutz hadn't been effective, and neither Nat Hudson nor Silver King were trusted. With Game 8 in Boston, hours before the game, Von der Ahe felt he had no choice. "I will put in Caruthers to-day and to-morrow and the next day, and the day after that and every day until he can't pitch any more, and after that I don't know what I'm going to do."[18] But pitching in back-to-back games and for the third time in five days, Caruthers didn't have his best stuff and was pounded for 13 hits, including two home runs by Thompson. St. Louis' offense was again dormant in a 9–2 loss. "That was no game we played to-day," third baseman Arlie Latham said. "The men were like a lot of amateurs in a vacant lot. I never saw them go on like that before. It made me sick. It disgusted me. It made me wish I was dead. We were a regular custard pudding for Detroit and they ate us without any sauce. We are not ball-players, we are chumps."[19]

With two days of strenuous work, Caruthers' arm was bent at a right angle. Unfortunately for him, this was not a rare occurrence for his elbow. He had his own healing method—submersing it in boiling water for two hours. "It thaws out like butter,"[20] he said. Caruthers also announced that he would no longer pitch on back-to-back days. "I can win from them every other day, but I'm not made of iron," he said. "I'm a man and I can't do the work."[21]

The next day in Philadelphia, St. Louis turned to King, with Foutz in right field and Caruthers sitting out, nursing his arm. Detroit won that one as well, 4–2. "You have one ball player on your team, Caruthers," Stearns said. "I want Caruthers and will pay any price for him if I can get him. If I was in the Association, Caruthers would be wearing a Detroit uniform."[22]

Even not fully healthy, Caruthers was St. Louis' best option, and he won again the morning of October 21 in Washington, D.C., 11–4. He allowed two runs in the first inning, including a leadoff homer by Hardy Richardson, but only eight hits total with one walk. The Browns' defense backed him with a triple play in the third inning when, with runners on second and third in motion, Gleason, back at shortstop, made a diving catch on a Thompson liner, then threw the ball around to nail the runners who were caught off base. The teams played again later that afternoon with Foutz getting pasted once again, Detroit winning, 13–3, and clinching the series with its eighth win.

The teams finished out the series largely in front of small crowds—the attendance listed for the final two games in Chicago and St. Louis was 378 and 659. Caruthers pitched twice more, losing in Detroit on October 24, 6–3, then winning the finale at Sportsman's Park, 6–2, on October 26 in a game called after six innings. A mostly bored crowd cheered just one of the hometown players: Caruthers. For good reason—he started eight of the 15 games and, in a year of offensive explosion, allowed just 29 runs (3.6 per game) and 64 hits in 71 innings (8.1 per nine innings). He also went 4–4; Foutz and King combined to go 1–6, allowing 15 more runs than Caruthers in 14 fewer innings.

"We were in no condition to play ball with any club, much less the Detroits. We only had one pitcher, Caruthers, and they knocked the life out of him every time he went in the box," said Von der Ahe in assessing the series.

The Detroit Wolverines easily disposed of the St. Louis Browns to claim the 1887 World's Series championship (New York Public Library Spalding collection).

Foutz's thumb was hurt, and he could not curve a ball to save his life. Gleason was no good; he was sick and broke up, and he lost three of the games for us. Besides that the Detroits had great luck. We outplayed them in several games, and still we were beaten. They played the best games of their lives—they admit that themselves—and the men individually wanted to win the series, both for the glory and the money. Our boys wanted to have the same arrangements as last year made with then, that I should give them half the receipts, but once is enough to do that. I pay them double salary, and that is enough. I don't think they tried quite as hard as they might to win. Just wait till next year. We will have a new shortstop and a couple of pitchers that will make things hum.[23]

A few days after the conclusion of the World's Series, the players went to Von der Ahe to collect their final paycheck, their contracts running out at the end of the month. When Caruthers got his, it wasn't for the full amount. The Browns owner deducted some money—reported over the years between $100–$125—in part for arriving late to St. Louis in the spring and out of shape, but also for the incident over the summer when Caruthers was seen cavorting around Chicago after heading there to convalesce following getting sick. "I told him to go home and take good care of himself and to come to St. Louis as soon as he was able," Von der Ahe related. "This he did not do, but he remained up there and attended the ball games and the races, and had a good time, while we were without pitchers here. I heard that he was going to the games and the races, and I notified him to report here within a specified time (and I gave him plenty of time) or his pay would be stopped. He did not report time as I had asked him to, and I took out of his salary the amount I said I would, and that is all there is to it."[24]

"He coolly told me when I asked him for the cheque that he didn't think I deserved it and he would not give it to me," Caruthers recalled months later. "That's the kind of man he is. If any man had talked to me the way I talked to him that day, I would have soiled the linen for him, sure, but Von der Ahe—he sat there with a grin on his mug and took it all. He could *afford* to take it, you see."[25]

Caruthers wasn't the only one not happy about the fine. "Whatever cause Mr. Von der Ahe may have had to direct [deduct] from Caruthers' wages, it is certain that Bob more than merited the paltry amount by his magnificent work in the World's championship series with Detroit," said the *Globe-Democrat*. "Had it not been for Parisian Bob, the Wolverines would have made a show of the ex-champions, and appreciation for this should have been shown."[26] Even Caruthers' mother spoke up, saying, "Von der Ahe called here a few times, and we treated him very nicely, and after all he took $100 out of Bobby's salary because he didn't stay in bed all the time when he was sent home from Philadelphia. That provoked me, for I coaxed Bob to get up and move around in the fresh air. Why, he knows Bob is not well at any time."[27]

For Caruthers, this was the last straw. He took his check, but before leaving Von der Ahe's office, he told the Browns owner, "Remember this will be the last chance you will ever have to dock me. This will cost you about $8000."[28]

14

A Bridge to Brooklyn

Bob Caruthers wasn't happy with Chris Von der Ahe deducting money from his final paycheck, but Caruthers' displeasure with the St. Louis Browns owner and the team didn't begin on that October day. Rumors of his discontent started early in the season. At some point when the Browns were in Brooklyn, that team's owner, Charles Byrne, disclosed that Caruthers had told him that "he wanted to get away from St. Louis and that he would like to play in Brooklyn if I could get his release."[1]

The complaints from Caruthers continued all season, at least behind the scenes. In Cincinnati late in the year, Doc Bushong got into an argument with Von der Ahe. The owner wanted Bushong in the field, but the player said he was still too injured to catch. The prospect of Bushong being jettisoned from the team in the off-season was broached—along with a potential departure of Caruthers. Asked directly if his plan was to peddle Caruthers, Von der Ahe answered in the affirmative. "If Brooklyn is anxious to get Caruthers they haven't sent me any word about it yet, but I'm open for propositions,"[2] said Von der Ahe while noting that he would wait until the season was over to think about or discuss about making such a move. However, he also thought Caruthers, even if he obtained his release, wouldn't sign elsewhere.

> Caruthers has been talking a great deal about wanting to get away from the club, and I've heard more about him on this question from more sources than one. Not long ago I was speaking to him about this sort of talk and told him plainly that if he was so very anxious to get out of the club I'd accommodate him and let him go. He then replied to me that if I would release him he would go, but he would not play with any other club.[3]

A couple of weeks later, during the middle of the World's Series with Detroit, Caruthers intimated he had other suitors. "I'll do my best in this series, but I'm going to quit playing ball after this year; that is, with St. Louis. I've been offered $4,000 a year, and $7,000 for my release by one of the best clubs in the country, and a club where I'll get better support than I get with his club,"[4] he said. Reports of offers kept trickling in as the month neared its end. One had Brooklyn proposing $10,000 for Bushong and Caruthers. Another report had Cincinnati wanting Caruthers or Louisville's Toad Ramsey, with an offer of $7,000 for either.

While on a southern trip with many of his teammates (plus Cincinnati's Bid McPhee, helping fill out the roster), Caruthers tried to douse some of the talk, saying—once again—he was going to retire from the game. "On November 10, I will quit the base-ball profession forever," he told a reporter in Memphis, where the Browns contingent played Chicago, which was touring with them.

> No doubt there are many persons who will say that this is only a bluff of mine, for the reason that on other occasions I have made the same assertion; but this time I am in earnest,

and nothing on earth will deter me from doing just what I now state. On the day named my brother and I will open an iron house on Lake Street, Chicago. My brother has been in the heavy hardware business for the past ten years. He wants to quit the firm he is with, and will do so providing I will go with him. I am perfectly aware that it will be hard work for me to quit the diamond, as I not only like the game, but the salary offered to me is very large and tempting, but, at the same time, my people want me to go into business, and I will follow their wishes.[5]

Reporters took whatever Caruthers said with a grain of salt, for good reason. A couple of days later, while still saying he had "enough of Von der Ahe,"[6] in the next breath he intimated he'd play again unless "I can't make a deal to suit me."[7] Also, November 10 came and went, and Caruthers was still with his Browns teammates, playing in New Orleans, where he stayed for a few days before heading home while the others made their way to California. Earlier, Caruthers said he wasn't going to make the leg of that trip, but his mother later relayed a story that Bob "telegraphed me from New Orleans asking permission to go to California, and I answered that I wanted him to come home."[8]

Of course, Caruthers wasn't the only one who made conflicting statements. Von der Ahe was in Philadelphia on November 12, where that team made a reported $5,000 bid for Caruthers—Von der Ahe said he'd received $8,000 offers from two other clubs (Baltimore and Brooklyn), but he refused all of them as he tried to sort things out. "All the managers seem to have an idea that I am anxious to get rid of all my players, while the contrary is the case," he said. "I will not deny that I have been tempted by several big offers and that one or two of my men may play in other clubs next season, but I have not yet made up my mind who they will be."[9]

But Von der Ahe suddenly came to the realization that it was better for parity to exist in the American Association than have his team run away with the flag every year, and thus, yes, he'd sell many players to help the league (and his wallet). "I have come to the conclusion that it does not pay to have a club far superior to every other in your association," Von der Ahe explained.

> Our games are nearly all one-sided, and as a result the attendance has diminished to a marked degree. By playing all the teams on a level, I think that interest in the game will be increased, we will make more money, and the contests will give better satisfaction to the patrons. Of course, the St. Louis Club will try and win the championship again, but there is nothing in glory; we must do something to swell the attendance. Winning championships is one thing and losing money is another.[10]

Caruthers returned to St. Louis before heading back to Chicago, and when he found time between gambling (he won $150 at billiards and another $400 playing poker), he briefly visited Von der Ahe. Nothing was solved as Caruthers insisted he was going to retire and work with his brother, and Von der Ahe wouldn't let Caruthers pay for his own release. "I think he is simply playing last year's gag over again," Von der Ahe said. "If he was going into business in Chicago, do you think he would be loafing around the Laclede Hotel in this city?"[11]

The unofficial bidding had already begun, but now things began to heat up. Joseph Doyle, one of Brooklyn's owners and Byrne's brother-in-law, stated in early November that his team would acquire at minimum three Browns—and the team had inquired about six (but the price was too steep). As Von der Ahe was now more motivated to sell, Byrne proposed giving St. Louis shortstop George Smith and $5,000 for Bushong and Caruthers. Von der Ahe, though, thought Caruthers was worth more money. The

Athletics reportedly kept their offer at $5,000 for Caruthers, while Baltimore went to $8,000. Brooklyn offered $10,000 for Bushong and Caruthers. Cincinnati made overtures as well and had promised the pitcher a $4,000 salary if it obtained him. It was a busy time for Caruthers, who "within the past few days has done some extensive telegraphing from the Western Union station at the Laclede Hotel."[12]

However, Von der Ahe set his sights elsewhere to start. He made two separate deals with the Athletics, neither of which involved Caruthers. Shortstop Bill Gleason was traded for three players—outfielder Fred Mann, shortstop James McGarr, and catcher John Milligan—while center fielder Curt Welch was sold for $3,000. Both the owner and outfielder were equally pleased. Von der Ahe said Welch's "conduct was of the Fred Lewis order,"[13] bringing up the name of a noted drinker who was out of the game by 1886, while Welch said, "I have played ball under Von der Ahe for the past three seasons, and I am satisfied that he does not know when he has a good thing."[14]

Meanwhile, Von der Ahe was setting the fee high for Caruthers. "I regard him as the best pitcher and best general player in the Association, and the club that gets him will have to pay a big price. ... this much I will say, I can get more for him than Boston paid for Mike Kelly,"[15] he said, referring to the $10,000 Chicago obtained for selling the catcher to Boston the previous February. Caruthers, hearing high dollar amounts for his release thrown back and forth, figured he deserved a piece of the pie as well. "I do not propose to stand by and let these people buy and sell me without a word," Caruthers said. "I'm not that kind of man. If any money is to be made out of me or my value as a player or base ball, I propose to get some of it myself. ... If $8,000 is paid for my release I want $2,000 out of it, or else I want a salary of $5,000 for the season. If my purchase is worth $8,000 my services are worth $5,000."[16]

Brooklyn and Cincinnati were emerging as the contenders for Caruthers, who preferred to play for the latter, all things being equal. "I was dead anxious to go to Cincinnati, as I had always been stuck on the town,"[17] he said years later. But the Red Stockings finished in second place in 1887 and Brooklyn sixth. It's easy to see why Von der Ahe's preference was Brooklyn due to the strength of the team, but there was another reason. "I haven't forgotten that [Tony] Mullane deal,"[18] said Von der Ahe, recounting the trouble he had with the pitcher, who reneged on a deal with St. Louis and signed with Cincinnati in 1885. But it's not like Cincinnati—or Caruthers—stopped trying.

Like any good gambler, Caruthers was trying to hedge his bets on all sides. On November 18, he sent a telegram to Byrne to see if Brooklyn would pay for his release (Von der Ahe also later claimed Caruthers borrowed $200 from him on this day and never repaid it). Three days later, Caruthers sent a similar note to Cincinnati owner Aaron Stern, saying he could buy his way out of the Browns contract for $8,500, but with that came a demand of a $4,500 salary. Owners from both clubs sent envoys to St. Louis to try to seal a deal.

St. Louis sportswriter Joe Pritchard was acting on behalf of Byrne and Brooklyn. He thought everything had been decided and agreed upon, so he was taken by surprise when, heading to meet with Caruthers at the Laclede Hotel and hammer out a deal, he saw the pitcher talking with Cincinnati manager Gus Schmelz, sent by Stern with the same task of getting a contract signed. Schmelz, via Stern, was reportedly prepared to offer $10,000 to Von der Ahe and give Caruthers $4,500 for the 1888 season. Schmelz sent a telegram to Von der Ahe, who was in New York, and waited for an answer. Meanwhile, he and Caruthers ate, played billiards, and saw a play.

At 11 p.m. the pair, along with Pritchard and a reporter from the *St. Louis Globe-Democrat*, congregated at the hotel. Brooklyn reportedly had a deal to pay $9,000 to Von der Ahe for Caruthers' release. "I have closed negotiations with Von der Ahe regarding the Caruthers deal," Byrne said. "The figure that he named has been accepted, and as soon as Mr. Caruthers is willing to sign a contract at a price agreeable to me he can do so."[19] Pritchard tried to get him to sign a contract for $4,500. Caruthers, seeing his price increase, wanted the $4,500 plus a $500 signing bonus. Pritchard could offer only what he was told and telegraphed Byrne with the new demand.

Stern sent a number of wires to the Browns owner as well and told Schmelz he'd be willing to go to $15,000 for Caruthers' release. Schmelz waited and waited and waited for a response from Von der Ahe concerning Cincinnati's offer. None was forthcoming. "I think that you can announce positively that Caruthers will play with Brooklyn next year," an exasperated Schmelz relayed. "The Cincinnati club will give a great deal more than $8,000 for his release but Von der Ahe will not sell him to us. He is dead set on giving him to Brooklyn, and Brooklyn will get him a great deal cheaper than we could possibly hope for. I would like to secure Bob, but I've lost all hope."[20]

The next day, November 26, Schmelz headed back to Cincinnati, having never heard from Von der Ahe. He should have waited a few more hours. Von der Ahe returned in St. Louis sooner than expected with the news of his deals with the Athletics as well as Brooklyn having paid $4,500 for the release of Bushong. Von der Ahe didn't discuss the Caruthers negotiations but said, "I have no more players for sale."[21] When asked about Dave Foutz, he replied, "I will retain him on the team."[22]

Meanwhile, Pritchard set out again to sign Caruthers. He found the pitcher playing pool, naturally, at Schaefer's Billiard Parlor. Caruthers seemed willing, and Pritchard offered $4,500 with $1,500 paid in advance. Caruthers declined, saying he wanted $4,500 with $1,000 in advance plus that $500 bonus. Further discussion was futile, but Pritchard remained optimistic—if only because the player had no other choice. "You can say that there is now no doubt whatever that he will play with Brooklyn next year," Pritchard said. "In fact, he cannot play elsewhere and he will not. He now belongs to Byrne, and it is only the question of one word that stands between him and a contract. That word will be spoken, never fear."[23]

Caruthers wasn't exactly dismissing the notion that he'd be in Brooklyn.

I am perfectly satisfied to go there, and I think, with [pitcher Adonis] Terry and myself, we ought to come pretty near winning the championship. The Brooklyn boys are all nice fellows. I regret going away from St. Louis for one reason. I never knew how many friends I had in this city until this week. Why, would you believe it, about half a dozen men have called on me during the week and offered to make up the difference to me for the $5,000 if I would agree to remain here. But I couldn't do it. I have more reason for leaving than most people imagine, and my reasons are very good ones, too. I know that a good many people think I'm only bluffing when I say that my friends want me to go into business, but I assure you that such is the case, and the only thing that keeps me from going it is the enormous salary I'm getting for playing ball. I could never hope to make $5,000 in the first, or second, or third year I would be in business, and it is only a question of business with me. Nothing else."[24]

Of course, what Caruthers said today might not be true tomorrow. The next day, his tone changed dramatically. Now not only was a return to St. Louis off the table, but also was signing with Brooklyn. He once again set his eyes on Cincinnati. "Upon my word of honor I will, under no circumstances, play in either St. Louis or Brooklyn next season,"[25] he told a visiting reporter from the *New York Sun*, adding that he was angry Von der Ahe was trying to dictate where he could or could not play. Caruthers' brother (not mentioned which but likely the eldest sibling, James) was in town and added, "As far as money is concerned, Bob can have as much money at home as he can make playing ball. If he plays professionally next year, you can say he will certainly play with Cincinnati."[26]

Byrne remained adamant. "I am positive the young man will come to his senses when he sees we will not relinquish one single iota of our rights and will abide by his own agreement," the Brooklyn owner said. "We were already acquainted with Mr. Caruthers and knew enough not to make any mistake in arranging with him exactly according to our rules. We have his release and know our rights."[27] Byrne did, however, approve the $500 bonus Caruthers was seeking.

Upon hearing that news, Pritchard rushed back to the Laclede Hotel on November 28 and presented Caruthers with the $4,500 contract, a $1,000 advance (already commissioned by American Express) and the promise of the $500. Caruthers said he had to hear from his family first and telegraphed the news. While the two waited for a reply, they went to the Olympic Theater to watch the opening of "Fritz, Our Cousin German." Upon returning, the wires were awaiting Caruthers—his mother writing not to sign and to return to Chicago, and a brother, again unidentified, saying listen to mother. Showing Pritchard the telegrams, Caruthers told the agent for Brooklyn, "Well, Joe, I can not sign now. I leave for home to-morrow night. I am satisfied with my salary and all that, but will not go against my mother's wish. I may never play ball again."[28]

Commenting to the *St. Louis Post-Dispatch*, an obviously frustrated Pritchard said, "I will send back the money to Byrne to-morrow and bid good-bye to Caruthers. The jig is up. Bob has made a big mistake and he will realize it before the spring time comes."[29]

The next day, Brooklyn had a new pitcher—Foutz. This time it was Von der Ahe bluffing. He started a bidding war with the Athletics, Baltimore, Cleveland, and Louisville involved, and ended up getting $5,000 for a pitcher he felt had nothing left in his right arm. "You and everyone who watched the game last year knew that Foutz appeared to have lost his effectiveness," Von der Ahe said. "On several occasions he was hit very hard. In the world's series with the Detroits he seemed to have lost all control of the ball. His brother members lost all confidence in him, and it was the general opinion that his arm was gone."[30]

Getting Foutz didn't mean Brooklyn was giving up on Caruthers. But neither was Cincinnati. Third baseman Hick Carpenter, a friend of Caruthers, was sent to St. Louis to convince him not to sign with Brooklyn and instead join him as a teammate. Caruthers relented a bit on his stand—as far as St. Louis was concerned. Perhaps because of the Foutz sale, he said he'd play with the Browns next season for $5,000. But his preference was for Von der Ahe to take $9,000 from Cincinnati, which would then pay Caruthers a $5,000 salary. "Now, if he refuses to do that I will go to the courts, prove that he prevents me from earning my living and get judgment against him, too," Caruthers said. "I know I can do this, because I have inquired into it and find that any court in America will give a judgement in favor in the case. If I do not get $5,000 from St. Louis, or if I am not released to Cincinnati, Mr. Von der Ahe will be out just $14,000."[31] Even though Caruthers made this threat out of selfishness and not the good of all ballplayers, it would have made an interesting court case, one that was well ahead of its time. He was backed by Ren Mulford, Jr., who in *Sporting Life* wrote, "this forcing a man into a club against his inclinations I looked upon as a rule just a degree removed from slavery."[32] It would never get to that in Caruthers' time, but with no resolution in sight, Caruthers returned to Chicago.

Arriving home on the afternoon train, Caruthers was a popular man—at least with reporters. He told one he would have signed with Brooklyn if not for his mother's objections. "I think Brooklyn's chances for a winning club for 1888 are excellent, and a man would always prefer to cast his lot with a probable winner than with a probable loser. I should prefer to go to Cincinnati, though," he said, adding Von der Ahe told him he wouldn't accept even $20,000 from Stern for his release, that's how much the Mullane situation stuck in his craw.

At Mussey's Billiard Hall, another reporter bumped into Caruthers, whereupon the pitcher showed off a business card which read "J.P. CARUTHERS & CO. Iron and Steel, Carriage and Heavy Hardware, Wood Material and Farriers' Supplies, 136 E. Kinzie Street, Chicago."[33] Of course, he was playing pool, not selling hardware, which was a tip to his intentions. "If Byrne sticks to the $5,000, Von der Ahe sticks to his expressed determinations not to let me play in Cincinnati, and my mother gives her consent to my going East, I will put my name to a Brooklyn contract before many hours," he declared.[34]

The next day, a *Chicago Tribune* reporter ventured over to Flora Caruthers' house on LaSalle Avenue. The matriarch of the family wasn't budging from her stance.

> I have got my son home and I want to keep him here. I don't want him to play ball, and don't care for the salary he gets or is offered. He does not need the salary, and the only reason he plays is because he likes the game. What I dislike most is that it keeps him away from home through the whole season. I sent him to Europe to keep him from playing ball, and he came back, and now I have induced him to go into business with his brother James, and I hope he will stick to business and let ball alone. I have never seen a game of base-ball, and will not go to see one as long as he is connected with the game. ... During the last two weeks I have received telegrams from base-ball presidents and their agents, but paid no attention to any of them. I don't want a single one of them near this house, and will not let them in if I find out their business before they get inside the door.[35]

It was reported that a reason for Flora Caruthers' objection to her son playing for Brooklyn was the gambling element associated with that team. Byrne and Doyle had a gambling parlor in Manhattan, and another co-owner, Ferdinand "Gus" Abell, owned a casino in Newport, Rhode Island. With the ongoing stalemate, other teams tried to get involved. The Athletics were again showing interest, while Cleveland went a different route, trying to buy Caruthers' release from Brooklyn for $8,550.

In limbo, Caruthers, as he did during a previous holdout, started threatening to sue.

> I don't care what they do; I am perfectly easy. Von der Ahe said every man in his team was for sale, and gave me his word that I could have my release for a certain amount, and then went back on his word, I have in my pocket a written agreement signed by a certain responsible party well known in the association, and it says I will be paid $5,000 a year if I can get my release and sign a contract with him. Now if Von der Ahe don't give me my release and I want to play ball next season he will have to pay me $5,000 a year. I have shown the agreement I hold to good lawyers, and they say if Von der Ahe interferes with my getting that money I can sue him for the amount and damages besides. The reserve rule can have no standing in a court of justice; there was a limit to my contract with Von der Ahe, and when that limit expired his legal claims on my services ended, and if he don't think so I'm just the boy that will prove it to him. If I didn't have this agreement I couldn't go into court and prove what I could get; but I've got it and that's why I've got Von der Ahe.[36]

Those words might have hastened the approach by Brooklyn. At the American Association meeting in Cincinnati on December 7, Byrne and Pritchard huddled for a prolonged discussion. A plan was hatched—a telegram was sent to Caruthers making sure he'd sign with Brooklyn, pending his mother's approval. He wired back that that was the case. Now, Byrne would go to Chicago to try to put an end to it all.

On Sunday, December 11, Byrne and Pritchard arrived at 530 LaSalle Ave. The purpose wasn't to talk to Bob but to Flora. Byrne did the talking. He later relayed the experience to the *Brooklyn Eagle*:

> I found his mother a most charming lady of much cultivation. She had always been opposed to her son playing professional ball and was still prepared to continue her very natural objections for the reason that she wanted him to enter some inexhaustible business, knowing that the longer he postponed his step the harder it would be for him to catch up with those who would be his competitors. She had already invested considerable capital in the hardware business in giving her eldest son a start and she was prepared to invest a still larger amount whenever her youngest son was willing to enter into partnership with his brother. It took me a long time to overcome her objections, especially as she has ample means and as the base ball playing keeps her son away from her for some months of the year. She admitted that the compensation offered was very liberal and much larger than he could hope to obtain in any other profession present. After considerable persuasion I succeeded in having Mrs. Carruthers [sic] waive several of her principal objections and she gave a quasi consent to let her son go with us.[37]

The deal wasn't signed right then and there, however, and Byrne and Pritchard retreated to their hotel. Bob Caruthers wanted time to think and discuss it with his family. His brother, James, was now in the camp of Bob joining Brooklyn. The next day at noon, Caruthers showed up at the hotel and signed his contract. His salary was only $2,000—as per American Association limit—but there were ways of giving players more money through bonuses or buying image rights to use their likeness on promotional material or advertisements. Byrne, who in the end gave Von der Ahe $8,250 for Caruthers' release, wouldn't comment on the amount the pitcher would receive other than to say, "it exceeds $5,000. We are perhaps crazy in going so far as we did in the matter, but we had gone too far to stop, but we have got Caruthers, and in him the best player in the country. We will gain our money back by charging an increased price of admission and in the larger crowds the Brooklyn club will draw."[38]

Caruthers, for once, wasn't discussing the details of the deal, but it was reported that he got $5,500, although decades later $6,000 was the figure given. The *Cincinnati Commercial Gazette* calculated that Caruthers would earn $39.28 per day if he appeared in every contest (the average daily wage for unskilled labor in 1888 was $1.85[39]). Caruthers did have one clause added to the contract—if he were to miss time due to injury or, perhaps more importantly, illness, he wouldn't lose any pay. Pritchard, who received $1,000 for his help—in case you were wondering why he was so dogged in his pursuit—gave Caruthers a diamond pin worth $200. Caruthers in turn gifted Pritchard a "handsome umbrella."[40]

Byrne was well satisfied with his off-season—in addition to Bushong, Caruthers and Foutz, he also had bought out the New York Metropolitans and kept a few of their players, including slugging first baseman Dave Orr, outfielder Darby O'Brien, and pitcher Al Mays. But the cost, he'd live to regret. "Bob figured that if we were willing to pay $8,500 for his release that we needed him bad enough to give a princely salary. His conclusions were correct," Byrne said years later. "That deal will always be a sore subject with me."[41]

For all his hemming and hawing, back-and-forth statements, and holding out for over a month, Caruthers got exactly what he was looking for, much to his surprise. "I had pitched four seasons for Von der Ahe and always did question if I really was worth that much to Byrne," he said in 1904, before adding with a chuckle, "but I was in a position to get it."[42]

15

Brooklyn Bumps

Bob Caruthers' trade from St. Louis didn't exactly go over well in that city. The *St. Louis Post-Dispatch* summed up the feeling around town when it succinctly said, "St. Louis loses the best ball player in the country.[1]" Owner Chris Von der Ahe, who rid the Browns of five key players from the three-time defending champions in short order, had a tinge of misgivings in dealing just one of those. "Well, the only man I regret losing is Caruthers. He is a great ball player, but very stubborn and hard to manage."[2]

Across the country in Brooklyn, Charles Byrne couldn't be more ecstatic. The owner had completely remade a team which finished sixth in the American Association in 1887 with a 60–74 record, Caruthers being the crown jewel of his overhaul. "If we do not have a winning team now," he said, "I do not think there is any use of our trying further."[3]

Caruthers was coming off a standout year, having hit—according to the statistics of the day, which counted walks as hits—.460, good for fourth in the American Association. Modern recalculations put Caruthers at .357, fifth in the league, but also second in slugging percentage (.547), third in on-base percentage (.463) and third in OPS (1.010). In addition, he finished fourth in ERA (3.30) and led the AA in WHIP (1.167). Knowing the package he was getting in Caruthers, Byrne implied to the 23-year-old that he wanted him to be team captain, but the player demurred. "Mr. Byrne and myself talked it over informally when I last saw him, but I told him I would prefer not to fill the position, as I did not want to take the chance of creating any ill-feeling in the club," Caruthers said. "Besides, I do not think it does a pitcher any good to play a championship game every day. … Oh, I do not think it will come to a point where I shall have to refuse or accept it. I think I convinced the club that it would better for me not to undertake it."[4]

Now with a new team and big contract, while eschewing any talk of captaincy, Caruthers could focus on things other than baseball. Namely, marriage. The *Inter Ocean* of Chicago printed this note in its March 4 edition: "There is an able-bodied rumor in the East that Bobby Caruthers contemplates matrimony. No cards have been issued here, however."[5] This turned out to be more than gossip as three days later, Caruthers wed 22-year-old Mary Burton Danks—known as Mamie (the name was even used on census forms)—at the home of the father of the bride at 592 Cleveland Avenue. The coupling was interesting in that Caruthers was the son of a Confederate sympathizer while William Newton Danks, Mamie's father, fought in the Civil War for the Union, rising to the rank of captain with "Ellsworth's Avengers" in the 44th infantry regiment of New York after having begun his service with the United States Zouave Cadets out of Chicago. Unlike the marriage of Bob's parents, this doesn't seem like the joining of two well-off families, as William Danks worked as an inspector for the Internal Revenue

Service. The ceremony was described as "unostentatious"[6] but they were nevertheless inundated with presents, reportedly receiving in excess of $4,000 in gifts, including "a solid silver tea service and a solid silver dinner service."[7]

The couple left immediately for a honeymoon—Caruthers had to report for training in Brooklyn in just a few short weeks—which took them to Niagara Falls, New York (where a heavy snow forced them to stay longer than anticipated), Philadelphia, and Washington, D.C. While in D.C., the couple stayed at Ebbitt House, which was located blocks from the White House and was "the favorite resort for bridal parties visiting Washington."[8]

The Caruthers arrived in Brooklyn on March 22, checking into the Hotel St. George. On March 24, Bob gathered with his new teammates at Casey's Court. Like Caruthers, several of the Brooklyn players had been married that off-season. In addition to Caruthers, pitcher Al Mays, outfielder Darby O'Brien, third baseman George Pinkney, outfielder Ed Silch, shortstop George Smith, and pitcher Adonis Terry all tied the knot, and 11 in total were married (Dave Orr was said to be engaged, which he denied). The proliferation of so many newly wedded players led *Sporting Life* to wonder, "Now, isn't this a 'bridegroom team?'"[9] The name stuck and soon Brooklyn, as early as April 7 in the *Brooklyn Citizen*, were referred to as the Bridegrooms. The nickname stuck until 1899.

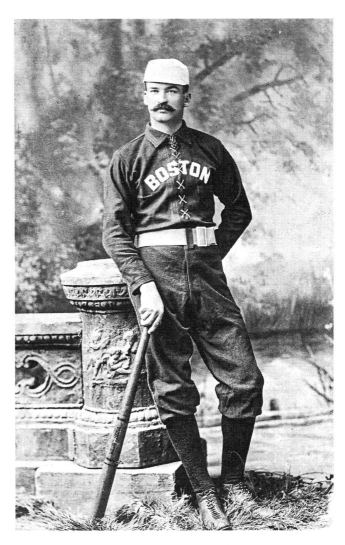

Mike Kelly set the bar for the sale price of superstar players when Boston paid $10,000 to Chicago for him in 1887 (Michael T. "Nuf Ced" McGreevy Collection, Boston Public Library).

Training at Casey's consisting of handball and some light pitching. Caruthers was one of eight to play handball, teaming up with his former Browns teammates, Doc Bushong and Dave Foutz, as well as newcomer Silch, a St. Louis native who played with Denver in the Western League the previous season. The quartet faced off against second baseman Hub Collins, catcher Bill Holbert, manager Bill McGunnigle, and Terry, with each team winning one game.

Later in the week, Silch volunteered to catch Caruthers—but did so with no protection for his hands. He found out that the pitcher had some life in his fastball even in late March, and he had to quit the game of catch after several painful snags which left his hands bloodied. "When the ball hit the palms of his hands," it was said of Silch, "the report in the high-walled Court was louder than an ordinary pistol shot."[10]

While Curt Welch didn't think much of his former teammate's prospects in 1888 with his new club, the outfielder saying, "Caruthers will not be near as good a pitcher next season as he was last year,"[11] there was obviously great anticipation for the player in his new home. Playing an exhibition against the Newark Little Giants in Queens at Ridgewood Park—Brooklyn's home for Sunday games—on April 1, over 5,200 turned out to watch despite it being a frigid day and heavy rains having left "a pond of water in deep right field."[12] Caruthers, one of three pitchers used by Brooklyn, pitched five hitless innings while striking out three—with the three-strike rule returning, 15 batters fanned in the game, which Brooklyn won, 3–2, in 11 innings.

Three days later, despite a cold day, around 8,000 spectators showed up at Washington Park to watch in intrasquad scrimmage (it helped that no admission was charged). Caruthers captained the Grays against the Whites, pitched five scoreless innings (allowing two hits, both to Orr) and had two hits himself, including a double, in a 3–2 win. He also was plunked on the thigh, which hurt for a couple of days, but he was still able to play, and pitch three innings, against Yale and young pitcher Amos Alonzo Stagg, who also played football at the school.

After more exhibitions against Newark, Williams College, Worcester, Lowell, and Troy, plus an intrasquad game, Brooklyn was finally ready for its opener at Washington Park. Located in the Red Hook section of Brooklyn, the field and stands were built adjacent to the Gowanus House, where George Washington quartered during the Battle of Long Island in 1776 and which the Bridegrooms used as a de facto locker room. According to the Ballpark Database on Seamheads.com, the dimensions of Washington Park were 335 feet in left field, 445 in center, and 215 in right.[13] Despite the big off-season for the club and six new players in the starting lineup, the announced attendance was 2,586 for the first game—a disappointing figure especially considering that Brooklyn, not yet a borough, was the fourth-largest city in the country (according to the 1890 census), behind just New York, Chicago, and Philadelphia.[14] A rainy day and a boost in ticket prices—in part due to the league now demanding 15 cents per admission but also because the team looked to recoup some of its off-season expenditures; Brooklyn carried 16 players into its first game, which was more than any St. Louis team Caruthers played on ever had—didn't help the cause.

Pitching and batting fourth, Caruthers cruised to a 10–1 victory. He allowed eight hits—no runner reached third base after the fifth inning—didn't walk a batter, and struck out five, while getting on base twice (hit, walk), stealing a base, and scoring twice. The toast of the town, at least on this day, Caruthers and the rest of the players on both teams then enjoyed an evening at the Brooklyn Theatre for a production of *Lost in New York*.

Caruthers didn't take the field again until April 22 in a Sunday game at Ridgewood Park. Center fielder Paul Radford, being a Sabbatarian, refused to play on that day—not a problem from 1883 to 1886, when he was in the National League, which didn't allow Sunday games—so Caruthers took his spot and "captured everything that went within a mile of him,"[15] including a running catch in right-center off the bat of Cleveland's Ed McKean for the final out in a 6–1 win.

Brooklyn took a quick trip to Baltimore for a four-game set, and in the April 23 opener, Caruthers was knocked around for 11 hits and 11 runs and had to leave the game in the ninth inning after taking a line drive off his finger. A couple of days later, Byrne, on the trip with his team, reported back to the local paper that "Caruthers' finger is still bad,"[16] yet there was Caruthers in the box on April 26 for the finale. Mickey Hughes had been slated to pitch, but Caruthers, as he had done in the past, wanted to atone for his poor play and convinced Byrne and manager Bill McGunnigle to let him start. The Bridegrooms lost again, 5–3, with Caruthers allowing 13 hits. The most interesting part of the game occurred in the eighth inning. Down by the eventual final score, Brooklyn had two runners on and two out when Caruthers stepped to the plate. He didn't have a hit but was still considered a dangerous hitter. Jack Farrell, the shortstop and team captain, ordered pitcher Bert Cunningham to walk Caruthers, who was so displeased with losing his opportunity to hit that he "threw his bat down in disgust."[17] The move worked, though, as Doc Bushong sent an easy grounder to Farrell, who forced Caruthers at second to end the inning.

Caruthers' hitting prowess wasn't the story in Brooklyn, however, it was his pitching. At least with one fan. While he won his next start, 9–3 over Baltimore in a six-inning affair, he lost his next, again to the Orioles, 7–3. In a letter to an editor, a fan calling himself "A Base Ball Crank" went on a small diatribe. He wrote, "Our expensive Mr. Caruthers goes to Baltimore and drops two games out of four. Why, poor crippled Cleveland did as well in Baltimore as did our $40,000 aggregation,"[18] and "Why not let Caruthers take a holiday until he can play and let Foutz pitch once in a while? But, no; manager McGunnigle insists on putting in Caruthers. In four games he has pitched against Baltimore he has lost three. Yesterday's game could have been won if Mr. Caruthers had played ball."[19] In a reply a few days later, another fan—"Fair Play"—defended Caruthers and the other former St. Louis players, putting much of the blame on their teammates. "Instead of the activity and sharp field work they were accustomed to see in the St. Louis Club," he wrote, "they find a jolly, fat, good natured lot of fellows who seem to take to defeat even more kindly than to victory."[20] Fair Play concluded his retort with "Messers. Bushong, Foutz and Caruthers are worth all that was paid for them, and with one-half the support they received from their old club would make a far better showing."[21] In a letter dated May 15, A Base Ball Crank softened his tone a bit.

> I agree with "Fair Play" that some of our players are a little more "boofy" than the St. Louis Club and, as he claims, Caruthers was accustomed to such fine assistance. … I do not expect Foutz, Bushong and Caruthers to win all the games they play and I, too, believe they are worth all that was paid for them. But as they have been used more since the season opened than any of the other batteries, and as their work was not near what it should be, I think it is only fair to give them notice that they are in Brooklyn now and with a people that will appreciate good work.[22]

It probably didn't hurt Caruthers' image in the eye of this critical fan that in the two games he pitched while the letters were being exchanged, he beat the Athletics, 3–2, and Cleveland, 7–3, over a three-day span. A Base Ball Crank was surely satisfied when Caruthers went out and pitched back-to-back shutouts over Cleveland (15–0 on May 17), also getting three hits and his first homer, and Kansas City (9–0 on May 20). In the latter, he allowed two hits—with no walks and five strikeouts—and faced the minimum 27 batters as one runner was erased on a double play and another was thrown out by Bushong trying to advance to third base on a wild pitch.

With Caruthers pitching well despite also playing center field on occasion, a move lamented by the *Brooklyn Daily Eagle*, which opined, "It may be questioned, however, whether it is good policy to send Caruthers to center field, for throwing him from that position may tend to impair his accuracy as a pitcher,"[23] as aided by Hughes and Terry, who no-hit Louisville on May 27, Brooklyn overcame a sluggish start to the season and by the end of May took over first place. The team was on an eight-game winning streak when Caruthers' old mates, St. Louis, came to town.

Over 10,500 fans turned out to Ridgewood Park for the opener. Caruthers was stationed in center field, having pitched the day before, and Foutz was in right (although he later pitched). Browns third baseman Arlie Latham gave them the business all day and had boasting rights as St. Louis won, 6–4. Caruthers tripled and scored twice in the loss. "I think the old St. Louis contingent now in the Brooklyn club are on their mettle to defeat the St. Louis aggregation," said Byrne said the following day at the Polo Grounds where, with no game scheduled, the team watched the New York Giants beat Indianapolis, 3–2. "We must have the next three, and I rather think we will get them."[24]

Byrne was prescient as Brooklyn took the next three contests. Caruthers only played in one of those, pitching in the June 5 game. He had a shutout for six innings before allowing one run in the seventh and three in the eighth, the latter due in part to a couple of errors. With the score tied at 4, Caruthers retired St. Louis in order in the ninth, two by strikeout, and the Bridegrooms won it in their half as Pinkney tripled with one out and scored on a Nat Hudson wild pitch.

Brooklyn kept things going against Cleveland, winning three straight with Caruthers playing a hand in all three. He pitched the Bridegrooms to a 9–5 win June 9, homered the following day in a 10–2 rout on a deep fly past center fielder Pete Hotaling, and on June 12 not only pitched—getting out of two bases-loaded jams—but also hit two home runs, both to the park's Fourth Street entrance in right field, the second rolling under a carriage, in an 8–5 victory. "Caruthers demonstrates very forcibly that it is only a fallacy that pitchers can't bat well,"[25] proclaimed the *Brooklyn Standard Union*. After his second homer, "the cranks emitted any number of ear-splitting shrieks, while pretty Mrs. Caruthers"—who attended all the home games—"on the grand stand clapped her hands with glee."[26]

The team started slumping, however, and Caruthers supposedly was not making friends in Brooklyn thanks to his comments about his teammates. He reportedly told Louisville's Jack Kerins, "I like Brooklyn well enough, but I would give anything if I had that old gang of hustlers at my back. I think with those Browns behind me this season I would be pitching a better ball; the best ball, in fact, of any pitcher in the American Association. There is a feature of the Browns' play that no other team on earth possesses. The players are not on the field for records. They play to win, and to win, changes and risks of all kinds must be taken. At any rate, I am sorry I am not with the old gang this season."[27] Nothing else came of these comments, which Caruthers denied making, at least publicly, although *Sporting Life* noted, "there is no doubt that there is considerable feeling against him in the team."[28]

Among the issues for Brooklyn was health. Terry missed a couple of weeks, second baseman Bill McClellan was hurt, and first baseman Orr came down with what was reported as rheumatism and missed a couple of months. With McClellan out, Radford was moved to the infield, which meant more outfield time for Caruthers. In a June 28 game at Louisville, Caruthers stepped up with two men on and one out against right-hander Scott Stratton. During the middle of his at-bat, Caruthers moved to the other side of the plate—a wire report in the *Brooklyn Citizen* said, "Bobby shifted the stick from right to left."[29]

Caruthers normally batted left-handed—no reason was ever proffered as to how or why the right-handed thrower hit from the other side—although early in his career, as in this instance, he was known to switch-hit. The 1887 profile of Caruthers confirmed this was not an isolated incident, noting he "bats either left-handed or right-handed, so that 'south-paw' or 'north-paw' twirlers are all alike to him."[30] However, he probably picked his spots, as in February 1888, Cincinnati manager Gus Schmelz said, "I don't think there's a better left-handed batter against a left-handed pitcher in the whole country than he is."[31] His decision to move in the batter's box paid off as he singled to left field to tie the game. The Bridegrooms scored twice more in the inning and won, 9–7.

Brooklyn still wasn't playing its best baseball. The Bridegrooms split a pair with Louisville and did the same at Cincinnati. Still, after momentarily dropping out of first place, Brooklyn was back on top with a 41–20 record. In second place, a scant half-game back, were the Browns—and St. Louis just happened to be Brooklyn's next stop. The standings were not the big storyline, however. The

Bob Caruthers' 1888 baseball card denoted he was now on Brooklyn. The way things started out for Caruthers with the Bridegrooms, he might have wished he were back in St. Louis (Library of Congress).

boys—Bushong, Caruthers and Foutz—were back in town. In case you didn't think this was a big deal, the Browns' ad for the game in the local papers highlighted the trio. Included with the details of the venue, opponent, time, and price was "The Far-Famed $13,250 Pitcher, BOB CARUTHERS!"[32]—with Caruthers' name in the largest print on the page. The other former Browns were mentioned, but in the line below and in smaller text—"with Doc Bushong and Dave Foutz"[33]—which made it known who the headliner was. Those were the only players mentioned in the ad. At one point, the Browns handed out pieces of paper on which was written a simple question: "$13,250; what was it for?"[34] No, this was not going to be any ordinary series.

16

The Returning Hero

Fans turned out in droves in and around the Lindell Hotel, the lodging of choice for American Association teams playing in St. Louis. It wasn't the Brooklyn team, per se, who were the subject of such attention but three of its members: former Browns Doc Bushong, Bob Caruthers, and Dave Foutz. "The lobby of the hotel presented a scene that completely threw into shade the excitement attendant on the National Democratic Convention," reported the *St. Louis Post-Dispatch*, comparing the throng to an event which occurred one month earlier at the St. Louis Exposition and Music Hall. "It was literally packed with male citizens including all of the seven ages of man from the squawking baby up to the patriarch bowed down with age. The street, too, was lined on either side with men, who, to judge from the expectant expression on their faces, were awaiting some important event."[1]

While glad-handers tried vainly to reach their idols, Caruthers was asked to defend himself by reporters. Not only had it been written that Caruthers wasn't satisfied with his Brooklyn teammates and wished he were on the Browns, but also former teammate Curt Welch, now on the Athletics, on a recent stay at the Lindell said similar things: Bridegrooms players were "sore on Caruthers,"[2] who also wasn't fond of the town or people of Brooklyn and wanted to play for the Browns. "I want to say that I never liked anything better in my life than I do Brooklyn," Caruthers said. "It has been stated that I said that the Brooklyns were no good and that with the Browns behind me I could win five out of six games against them. Now this is all wrong. I never made any such statement and I have never spoken a word against the club or its players or managers since I joined. ... We have the strongest club in the country."[3]

Browns owner Chris Von der Ahe was never one to miss an opportunity. Promoting the first game as the return of Caruthers was one example. Another was arranging a parade to the ballpark for the first game. The St. Louis team arrived at the Lindell Hotel in carriages, fighting their way through the crowd in doing so. A band led the way to Sportsman's Park with team officials and players following, four to a man in carriages. Bushong, Caruthers, and Foutz rode with, ironically, Browns captain, manager, and first baseman Charles Comiskey. He harbored no ill-will toward the trio. Later that summer, he proclaimed, "We allowed too many of our good men to go, but it could not be helped very well. The people in St. Louis will not patronize the club, and we do well to pay 12 men. Such men as Nicol, Welch and Caruthers should never have been parted with."[4]

Despite all the hubbub, there was only a modest crowd at Sportsman's Park, likely between 4,000–4,500, although the *Brooklyn Citizen's* report had it as high as 6,000. Home teams in the American Association decided which team batted first and, on this occasion, perhaps thinking Caruthers might be nervous (although they should have known better), the Browns had the Bridegrooms take the field to start the game. St. Louis third baseman Arlie Latham tried to throw Caruthers off his game with his usual rants in the coaching box, but, the *Brooklyn Daily Eagle* reported, "he might as well have tried to move a stone wall."[5] Caruthers pitched the Bridegrooms to a 6–2 win with Foutz tallying three hits.

It was hot the next day, with temperatures hitting 90 degrees. Caruthers was in left field—regular Darby O'Brien had broken a knuckle in the opener on a play at home—and had two hits, while he, Bushong, and Foutz all drove in runs to back Mickey Hughes in a 6–3 victory. Caruthers was back in the box July 8 as Brooklyn won, 4–3, with Foutz hitting a two-out, two-run triple to win it in the bottom of the ninth. The teams rested the following day, and before the July 10 game Caruthers, as was his wont, argued to pitch once again and, as usual, he got his way. Tied at 1— Caruthers drove in Brooklyn's run with a run-scoring single in the third inning—both teams scored three runs in the ninth. In the bottom of the 10th—St. Louis kept insisting on batting first (Brooklyn manager Bill McGunnigle preferred hitting second, so he was surely happy with the Browns' strategy)—Caruthers hit one into the right-field seats to score George Pinkney from first

FOUTZ, P., Brooklyns
Copyrighted by GOODWIN & CO. 1888
OLD JUDGE
CIGARETTES.
GOODWIN & CO., New York.

Dave Foutz, who had trouble growing facial hair, moved from St. Louis to Brooklyn as well. He and Caruthers claimed to be friends, but reports of friction between the two surfaced over the years.

(it was considered a triple by some papers, but after cruising into second base, Caruthers headed to the bench).

Brooklyn swept St. Louis, on the road no less, with Caruthers winning three of the four games. In 28 innings, he allowed nine runs on 23 hits with four walks and seven strikeouts and also had several key hits. "Bobby Caruthers is a ball player," wrote the *Brooklyn Citizen*, "and he impressed the people of St. Louis with that fact yesterday."[6]

With the four wins, the Bridegrooms led the American Association by 4½ games, its largest lead in a month, and were set to play the two worst teams in the league, Kansas City and Cleveland. But Brooklyn split a four-game set in scorching hot K.C.—players wore cabbage leaves and sponges in their caps to keep cool—in a strange series. Caruthers was purposely walked in the eighth inning of the opener to fill the bases (the plan again worked, Brooklyn losing, 3–1, and making just two hits), and in the July 14 game, the Bridegrooms walked off the field in protest after Bill McClellan was picked off first base (it was considered a forfeit although Kansas City was leading, 5–4, at the time). Then Brooklyn lost three straight against Cleveland, after entering having won 10 of 11 matchups.

When the Bridegrooms returned home after a long road trip, over 6,000 turned out to Washington Park on Saturday, July 21, to greet the team. Before taking its turn at bat against the Athletics, the team was given a floral arrangement shaped like a horseshoe (the nickname of each player was attached to a card, with "Parisian Bob" used for Caruthers) for good luck. It worked for one day, at least, with Caruthers scoring twice while allowing only two hits in a 7–1 win. It was his league-high 23rd win; Brooklyn was 48–25.

The next day, however, the Bridegrooms lost and were overtaken for first place—they never returned. St. Louis, now in front, came to town and got some revenge a week later, winning two games and tying another in a series played August 4–6. Caruthers pitched just once, losing 7–6 in 10 innings. "To tell the truth, I never believed Brooklyn would be in the race at the finish," Von der Ahe said. "I feared Cincinnati and the Athletics. Why, every game that we lost to Brooklyn was won by our old boys, Foutz, Caruthers and Bushong."[7]

Brooklyn owner Charles Byrne did, however, try to improve the team. Back in July, he signed second baseman Jack Burdock, who had been released from Boston of the National League due to incessant drinking and signed a contract with the Bridegrooms pledging he wouldn't imbibe (he failed on this promise and while he finished the season with the team he wasn't reserved). On August 10, McGunnigle arranged for the release and signing of Tom "Oyster" Burns, who had been the captain for Baltimore, which just finished a series in Cincinnati, where Brooklyn had just arrived. Burns, a .300 career hitter, displaced light-hitting Paul Radford in center field (Caruthers was now playing right field on most days when he wasn't pitching). Burns might have been a good batsman, but he was what might nowadays be called a clubhouse cancer. "Personally I like Burns; but it was a good thing that he was released," said an anonymous Baltimore player. "He was a disturber, and one of the worst that ever played ball. His disposition was very bad, and he made it unpleasant for any of the boys that crossed him. He is what you would call a bulldozer."[8]

Burns was in the lineup that day, a 5–2 loss in 10 innings in which Caruthers pitched. The next day, before the contest with the Red Stockings, a throwing competition was held. Among the four Brooklyn outfielders, Burns had the longest toss at 364 feet, 6 inches. Caruthers was last at 339 feet and, making matters worse, strained his shoulder in the process—yet still went out and pitched for the second straight day. He lost, 6–5, in 11 innings. In his next start at Louisville, Caruthers allowed 12 hits and was defeated, 7–2, then got pasted by woeful Kansas City, 11–6, on August 18, allowing 15 hits and three walks while also hitting two batters. His arm was clearly hurting as evidenced by him not pitching once in a three-game series in St. Louis. He never would have passed up such an opportunity to face his old team (and Brooklyn lost all three games, 1–0, 7–0, and 4–2). Caruthers tested his arm in an exhibition at Rochester and allowed nine runs. He played in just two of the next six games, both times in right field.

The cure, at least temporarily, was the Browns—with perhaps a little prodding by Chris Von der Ahe. Before the start of a four-game series at Washington Park beginning with a September 3 doubleheader, the St. Louis owner took a shot at his former player. "I would not advise ball pitchers to get married. It breaks them all up. Look at Bobby Caruthers," he said. "He was the best pitcher in the country last season, but he got married and is all broken up. There are hundreds of cases I could point out just like his."[9]

An overflow crowd turned out to see the second contest, in which Caruthers started. It was estimated that between 12,000–15,000 spectators showed up, many standing in the outfield, prompting a rule that any ball hit into or over the crowd would be a double (it happened only once, to Burns, who lost a potential home run to center field). Trees and telegraph poles were occupied by those willing to climb. A boy propped on the fence serenaded the players and crowd with a kazoo. Caruthers and his opposing pitcher, Silver King, both thrived in the atmosphere.

Scoreless after seven innings, Brooklyn, which won the first game 4–1, got a one-out walk to Radford, who was sacrificed to second by Burdock. Bushong hit a slow grounder to Comiskey, and there was a close play at first. Comiskey was so sure Bushong was out, he rolled the ball back to the pitcher's box, thinking the inning was over. But umpire Fred Goldsmith, who performed his duties behind the pitcher instead of the catcher, which, in theory, gave him a better vantage point for calls on the bases (Caruthers used the same tactic in his days as an umpire), ruled Bushong safe, and a heads-up Radford steamed home with the game's first—and only—run. Caruthers tossed a two-hit shutout, didn't walk a batter, and struck out six. King, in a losing cause, allowed just three hits. The game was played in a tidy one hour, 25 minutes.

Caruthers, naturally, wanted the ball again two days later when the teams met. He didn't fare as well, losing 7–2, but it was more because of his defense failing him, committing nine errors, rather than his performance. Caruthers allowed just six hits, with a walk and hit by pitch, and fanned five. With his arm healing and Byrne trying to motivate the team by saying he'd give every player $500 if they took the American Association pennant (it made good copy, but with just over a month left, the Bridegrooms were 7½ games off the pace), Caruthers blanked Cleveland, 2–0, on September 11, then in Philadelphia four days later beat the Athletics, 4–2. He nearly didn't make it past the first inning of that latter game.

Four batters into the bottom of the first, Athletics first baseman Henry Larkin sent a shot right back where it came. One of the underrated facets of Caruthers' game was his fielding ability—especially as a pitcher. He was a good outfielder—with ample speed and a strong enough arm to play the position well—but he was fearless in the box. Even when fielders started using gloves, pitchers were the last holdouts (although Athletics hurlers had begun to use them). While pitchers didn't throw as hard as modern-day twirlers, they were stationed closer to the batter. Many did their best to avoid the ball. Not Caruthers, who tried to make a play on anything hit near him. "He never shirks a hard hit," *Sporting Life* noted in 1887, "and as a result he gets bruised up quite frequently."[10]

Such was the case with Larkin's hit. The *Philadelphia Times* described the play in its entirety: "Larkin hit a line ball directly at Caruthers. The latter never flinched, but tried to field the ball. It struck him with terrific force upon the calf of the right leg and he fell down. The ball rolled ten feet away. Caruthers made two springs on his left leg, picked the ball up, threw Larkin out at first and then fell in a heap. His leg was badly hurt, and he limped painfully and could not run to first base, but he pluckily finished the game."[11]

The injury kept Caruthers out of Brooklyn's next game in Philadelphia, but he suddenly had bigger concerns. Traveling to Louisville for the next series, Caruthers started experiencing the chills. It was so bad he was left in Cincinnati, where the team changed trains. It was initially thought that he could pitch when the team returned to Cincinnati a few days later for a series there, but he was bed-ridden at the Grand Hotel, with Mamie at his side trying to nurse him back to health.

Caruthers returned to action on September 29 in, of course, St. Louis, playing right field in a 7–4 loss, going 0–2 with two walks. He was supposed to pitch against the Browns the next day but wasn't up to it, and Mickey Hughes twirled instead (and lost, 13–4). Caruthers pitched two more times—an 8–5 win at Cincinnati on October 1 and a 10–8 home victory over Baltimore which lasted seven innings.

Caruthers didn't play in Brooklyn's final 11 regular-season games or five postseason exhibitions. Thanks in part to an 11–1–1 October, the Bridegrooms finished 88–52 and in second place. That was good news for Caruthers, who back in August placed a bet that Brooklyn would finish ahead of Philadelphia (which ended up third at 81–52).

Despite missing time at the end of the season, Caruthers led Brooklyn in games pitched (44), starts (43), innings (391⅔), wins (29, third in the American Association), winning percentage (.659, fourth in the league), and WHIP (0.996, third in the AA).

Without Bob Caruthers, Doc Bushong, and Dave Foutz, St. Louis still won the 1888 American Association pennant with a 92–43 record, 6½ games ahead of Brooklyn. It was the end of the Browns' 19th century dynasty, however (Library of Congress).

However, he was third on the team in ERA (2.39), behind Adonis Terry (2.03) and Mickey Hughes (2.13).

Hughes also won 25 games, causing the *Brooklyn Standard Union* to opine, "Mickey Hughes pitched again and marked himself down a star of the first magnitude. He cost $500; Caruthers cost $8,250, a diamond pin and $5,000 a year. Mickey does the work; Bob draws the salary."[12]

Caruthers hit just .230 (although his OPS+ was still above average at 112) and struck out 40 times, a career high (his 10.4 strikeout percentage also was a career worst). Newspapers roundly criticized his newfound slugging approach. Caruthers clearly was not satisfied with his season, as he relayed months later.

> Last season I did not do as well as I should have done in pitching or batting either. I was not in the best of condition so far as pitching was concerned, and I can't account for my poor batting. I was accounted a good batter all along and I think that I did fairly well with the stick, but last year I seemed to lose my grip. I am convinced that scientific batting is the only successful kind. Don't hit at all kinds of balls. Experiment until you are sure of the kind of a ball you are able to hit and then hit it. Stick to that kind of a ball and take no other. That was the way I worked up my ability. … I would wait for the ball I wanted and the belt away at it, but I couldn't touch them. I am satisfied that it is all in the eye.[13]

Caruthers was still a big name, though, considered one of the game's great players. Chicago White Stockings owner Albert Spalding was planning a trip around the world to show off the game of baseball and inquired to Caruthers about joining the group. In early September, it was reported that negotiations were under way between Caruthers and Spalding, although that appears not to have been the case. In mid–October, Chicago writer Harry Palmer reported that Caruthers never responded to Spalding, and he wouldn't be making the sojourn (the players, mostly White Stockings and a variety of players from both American Association and National League teams, toured across the Western United States before heading to Hawaii, Australia, Ceylon, Egypt, Italy, France, England, Scotland, and Ireland, finally playing in various Eastern and Midwest U.S. cities).

> The young man's gall and conceit is monumental. It is a cold day when Bobby Caruthers' place upon any team ever organized can not be filled. I myself strongly urged both Lynch [business manager Leigh Lynch] and Spalding to secure Caruthers if they could. He is bright, a good dresser and a good ballplayer, and those are the sort of men wanted for the trip. For one, however, I am heartily glad Mr. Caruthers is not going. I do like to see a man act *square*, and Caruthers has not acted so to A.G. Spalding. What is more, *he knows it.*[14]

Palmer wasn't the only person displeased with Caruthers. Before heading back to Chicago to work for his brother's hardware business in the off-season while also resting his arm, Caruthers signed a $5,000 contract for the 1889 season. Some of his teammates took notice.

Pitcher Al Mays (9–9, 2.80 ERA) wanted more money for the 1889 season, as ballplayers were wont to do. Brooklyn acquired Tom Lovett from Omaha, making Mays expendable. Byrne avoided any potential headache by selling Mays, as well as first baseman Dave Orr, who had fallen out of favor, to a new American Association franchise located in Columbus, Ohio. That was fine with Mays, who took a parting shot at Bob Caruthers and Dave Foutz on his way out. "I like Brooklyn and I like the Brooklyn Club and people, but the money is what I'm after more than glory," Mays said. "I'd rather be the best pitcher for Columbus than have to play second fiddle for broken-down stars, who do little and draw big pay for it, while the heft of the work falls on others."[15]

Hughes was offered a $2,000 contract plus a $600 bonus. Hughes wanted more and was quoted as saying, "I'm worth as much as Caruthers, and if don't get it I don't play,"[16] although he later denied asking for Caruthers money—he just wanted more than was offered. "Hughes is not the ball player that Caruthers is by any means," said the *New York Sun*. "He may be just as good a pitcher, but his ability to play ball does not go beyond that. He cannot play in the field and is not so good a batter as Caruthers. Every ball player is entitled to all he can get, but there is such a thing as overdoing it."[17] It didn't take long for Hughes to see the light, agreeing to the terms a week later.

For the first time in years, salary issues weren't an off-season story surrounding Caruthers. But being the high-profile player that he was, there was still plenty to talk about, whether accurate or not (or somewhere in between).

Father of the Bridegrooms

As much as Bob Caruthers might have wanted a normal off-season, reporters kept finding him. When he attended a wedding in November or was a pallbearer in January at the funeral of former Western League umpire Steve Hagan, it made the papers.

At its November winter meetings, National League owners agreed to a contract limit for players, who would earn between $1,500–$2,500 based on a tiered system of the league's own creation, the top level ("A") keeping players on their clubs for the entirety of their careers. There were already rumblings among players regarding the reserve rule and selling of players, and this didn't help. While this was an NL dictum, nevertheless a reporter headed to the family hardware store in Chicago, where Caruthers was putting in some time working, to get his reaction. For once, Caruthers wasn't about to make waves. "It wouldn't look well for me to come out in the Herald to-morrow morning and criticise [sic] the action the League people have taken," he said. "Of course, I know it is said the League managers want to get rid of the expense of paying big prices for men and prevent big deals like that with me and other players, and that is one reason I don't care to be in a hurry to talk."[1]

Caruthers did have an interesting take when asked about the rule change making it four balls for a walk instead of five. "Well, the pitchers will not use curve balls as much; consequently they will use the straight ball the most, and as you know, all batters wait for a straight ball to come over the plate to lace it out. Mark my word and watch how the heavy hitters of last year will keep the fielders chasing leather as they never have done before."[2] That rule ended up helping Caruthers on both sides of things. While his walks allowed went up in 1889—naturally, he'd still end up leading the American Association with 2.1 per nine innings—the next-closest pitcher was at 2.4 BB/9. As a batter, Caruthers always had a good eye throughout his career, and his eventual .408 on-base percentage would have finished sixth in the league if he had enough qualifying plate appearances.

There wouldn't be as many hitting opportunities for Caruthers in the upcoming season, however. Manager Bill McGunnigle, who spent his winter as a traveling cigar salesman, decided in December to use his starting pitchers as just that—pitchers, except when absolutely needed. He was true to his word: Caruthers ended up playing just five games in the field, Adonis Terry 10, Mickey Hughes one, and Tom Lovett none. Dave Foutz was in a career transition and was used mainly as a first baseman.

Caruthers did get some licks in during the off-season, though. He appeared briefly on the Arctics, a team which played baseball on ice at Chicago's Lincoln Park. Caruthers played first base and pitched a little. When in the field, "His jacket was buttoned about his willowy form too tight, and every time the crack tried to scoop up the ball he would lose his equilibrium."[3] When Caruthers pitched, Harry Decker, a catcher who played briefly in the majors, put his chest protector on the other side of his body because the fast pitches, combined with the conditions, caused him to fall backwards onto the ice. In the two known games in which Caruthers played, the Arctics, which had a bevy of professional players, lost 11–5 and 15–5, the latter to the Jenney Graham Gun Company. The Arctics "'struck a snag' when it met the Jenneys, who are all excellent skaters and good ball-players," reported the *Chicago Tribune*. "The game was witnessed by a large crowd, which found much merriment in the ludicrous attempts made by the ball-ballists to capture the sphere."[4] Caruthers had a hit, a run scored, two putouts, an assist, and an error. No report was given on how many times he fell.

Not long after those games, Caruthers forsook the cold for the warmth heading to Hot Springs, Arkansas, which was becoming a destination for ballplayers to heal and/or practice before the start of the season. Before departing, he placed some wagers: $25 at 4–1 odds that Brooklyn would win the American Association pennant, $50 at 2–1 odds that the Bridegrooms would finish at least in second place, $75 to win $100 at third place or higher, and $100 at even odds for fourth or better. In St. Louis, where he stopped along the way, he told a reporter for *The Sporting News* "his team would win the pennant, barring accident, and that the club was never so strong as now."[5]

While in Hot Springs, Caruthers took both a steam bath and electrical bath every day. It was reported that he sent a letter to a friend in Chicago, worried "whether his arm will be in condition to pitch this season," the blame being put on the throwing contest the previous August in Cincinnati.[6] Adding to the concern, Caruthers stayed a few days extra in Hot Springs, reporting late to training in Brooklyn. He didn't pitch in Brooklyn's first three exhibitions—Hughes, Lovett and Terry split the duties in each—finally getting in the box on April 5 against Fordham, going five innings and allowing two hits. Two more preseason appearances didn't shed light on his condition other than that he could go a full nine innings. The New York Giants pounded him for 15 hits in beating Brooklyn, 8–7, in 10 innings on April 11, while Caruthers blanked Newark on six hits, 9–0, on April 15.

Caruthers got his first start four games into the season, losing 6–1 to the Athletics on April 21 in a game played at Gloucester, New Jersey. Philadelphia touched him for 12 hits, and Caruthers also walked three batters. "The new rules compel pitchers to send in balls over the plate, and that is what I propose to do," Caruthers reiterated, "depending upon the excellent field behind me to catch the hit balls."[7] Four days later, donning a new gray uniform with red stripes and socks, he pitched the home opener against Columbus and was hit hard again, allowing nine runs and 11 hits in five innings before being replaced by Terry (Caruthers stayed in to play right field and was hitless).

Lending credence to his arm not being at full capacity, Caruthers pitched just four times in Brooklyn's first 21 games. Over his first five starts, he allowed 30 runs, yet somehow the Bridegrooms were 3–1–1 in those games but 14–10 in the others. Things turned around, at least temporarily, in, of course, St. Louis. On May 19 at Sportsman's Park, he bested the Browns, 2–1, allowing six hits. Back in Brooklyn, the grandstand at Washington Park caught fire and burned to the ground. The blaze, with an estimated damage set at $18,000, was likely caused by amateur teams which had been using the park earlier in the day. A lit cigar or kerosene lamp were among the likely culprits as to igniting the fence. When the team returned to town on May 29, they headed to the park and saw 50 men helping rebuild the seats. It was reported that Caruthers, with his hardware experience, helped.

As the calendar turned to June, Caruthers was starting to get regular work as Hughes was largely ineffective and benched. There was no questioning his arm now as Caruthers got into a groove. It started with a loss. In front of over 11,000 fans at Ridgewood Park on June 2, he pitched his best game to date—and also caught a wayward goat which made its way onto the field—allowing six hits to St. Louis. However, Silver King gave up just one hit as the Browns won, 2–1. But Caruthers won his next five starts, culminating in a three-hit shutout of Baltimore at Washington Park on June 19. The Bridegrooms were now 30–19, trailing St. Louis (35–16) and Philadelphia (32–16) in the standings.

Brooklyn got a boost—to attendance, at least—when the elevated train started to provide just one fare to its stop at Fifth Avenue and Third Street, which was the station for Washington Park. The next day, June 22, over 6,000 fans came out to see the Bridegrooms lose to Baltimore, 9–5, Caruthers relieving Terry and allowing one run in four innings, and over 7,000 were in attendance the following game, with Caruthers beating Columbus, 8–2, and knocking a two-run homer in the ninth inning (while manager McGunnigle liked to bat last, team captain Darby O'Brien preferred to hit first).

The Bridegrooms went on a road trip starting June 29 slotted 4½ games out of first place. When they returned to Brooklyn in mid–July, despite going 10–4 on their five-city tour, they were five games back. There was, however, a Union Elevated train now headed to Ridgewood Park, meaning Sunday games would be better attended.

Brooklyn continued its stellar play back home. After splitting the first two games with the Athletics, Caruthers won a game over Philadelphia at Ridgewood Park on July 21, 8–6, in front of over 8,000 fans. Two days later back at Washington Park against Kansas City, Dave Foutz got a rare pitching appearance in relief of an ineffective Terry, but in the seventh inning he was spiked on a play at home trying to score the tying run, and he couldn't continue. Trailing 3–2, Caruthers was inserted and pitched two perfect innings. Down 3–2 in the bottom of the ninth, he came up with two down and two on. After fouling two pitches off (a new ball was needed after one foul was lost in the stands, which caused Oyster Burns to exclaim, "Now we'll win the game!"[8]), Caruthers hit a hot grounder into right field which ended up in the crowd. This was considered a blocked ball, meaning it had to be thrown back to the pitcher before a play could be made on any runner. Kansas City failed to do this, and when Hub Collins, a second baseman picked up late in the 1888 season who was on first base, was tagged near home it didn't matter—he was safe because of the rule. Some fans were confused, while others poured out of the stands to congratulate Caruthers on his game-winning hit.

The rules of the day gave Foutz the pitching win. However, in 1942 research by the *Brooklyn Daily Eagle* discovered that, by modern rules, Caruthers should have been given the victory. Thus, instead of the 39 wins he was thought to have earned in 1889, Caruthers had 40. This made Caruthers one of just 10 pitchers to have two seasons of 40+ wins in a career (all of whom pitched in the 19th century). Only he and Tommy Bond did it twice while pitching in fewer than 60 games in both seasons (Bond did it in 59 and 58 appearances; Caruthers 58 and 53).

Despite the recent wins and overall decent play of the team, the players reportedly had an issue with the hometown fans—they were cheering too hard for the other team. That's what was written in a letter to the editor in the *Brooklyn Daily Eagle* by someone claiming to be a Bridegroom. The letter in part read:

> It was very evident that half the People present didn't care who won. There's where the Whole trouble lies. In every other city Where base ball is played the citizens Root just as hard as they Know for the home Team. they Root all together from the Beginning to the end of the game.

Here half of them are Rooting for the Visitors. This does not apply to the bleaching Boards, the men & Boys there do their Duty to the whole Team but to the Silk Stocking brigade in the grand stand. … How can the Brooklyns win the pennant with Half their own people Rooting against them.[9]

Owner Charles Byrne defended his players, saying "The boys are only human"[10] and in part blaming it on people from New York City coming to the park and rooting against his team. Team secretary Charles Ebbets tried to deflect trouble, saying "I know the handwriting of every man, and there is not one of them who writes like that."[11] However, the players, manager McGunnigle, and trainer Jack McMasters concurred with the letter's contents. "It is a good thing to have this thing well ventilated. There is no doubt that the man who wrote the letter to the *Eagle* knew just what he was talking about," said Caruthers, who was one of a few members of the team, including Foutz and O'Brien, who publicly criticized fans.

If the folks on the grand stand had rooted right we would have had the pennant last year, and the only reason we are not in the lead now is that they are not rooting for us the way they should. The people ought to do one thing or the other—either back us up or drop us entirely. Some people are so ignorant that they don't know how to root right. The way to do it is to just sit still and wish as hard as you can for the success of our team and disaster to the enemy. Fat Dutchmen of middle age root the hardest because they're so solid and hard to disturb. It's easy enough to win games when the people are with you, but when they are against you it's very uphill. I've felt the crowd rooting so hard against me when I've been in the pitcher's box in some other city that I couldn't get a curve on the ball to save my life.[12]

The 1889 Brooklyn Bridegrooms, with Bob Caruthers seated second from left. Many members of the team weren't thrilled with the actions of the hometown fans (Library of Congress).

The day after the letter to the editor, Caruthers beat Kansas City, 7–5, and hit a solo home run to the carriages in right field as part of a two-run ninth inning. How the 4,000 people in attendance, including 1,000 women, reacted was not recorded.

If people were put off by the comments from players, anonymous or otherwise, they kept coming out to the games. On August 2, St. Louis, in first place by two games over Brooklyn, was in town for a three-game series. It was a big enough matchup that the American Association had two umpires officiate the game. Caruthers pitched the opener in front of 7,000 spectators at Washington Park and lost, 6–2. Behind Terry, Brooklyn took the next game, 13–6. At Ridgewood Park on Sunday, August 4, 17,000 were in attendance—the *Brooklyn Standard Union* reported 16,974 in the ballpark and another 500 seated on the top of the fence (the *Brooklyn Citizen* claimed it was over 1,000). Caruthers, with one day's rest, got the ball again and allowed just three hits as the Bridegrooms won, 7–2 (in a quick one hour, 25 minutes), to get within one game of first place. "Caruthers was at his best yesterday," reported the *Brooklyn Daily Eagle*. "The St. Louis batsmen were at his mercy."[13]

It was back on the road after that final win, with a stop in St. Louis a week later. It didn't go as well for Caruthers and Brooklyn, swept 4–2, 14–4, and 11–0 (Caruthers pitching the first and third games). A seven-game win streak followed with wins in Kansas City and Louisville. The Bridegrooms took two of three at Cincinnati to get back within a game and a half of first place. But on August 25, in what was supposed to be the finale, Brooklyn lost a potential win. It was a Sunday—Cincinnati not allowing ballgames on that day—but the teams played in nearby Hamilton, assured there'd be no issues, as had been the case in previous games that season. Brooklyn was leading 4–2 in the fourth inning when Caruthers, the pitcher, stepped up to bat with a man on first. At that moment, the police crashed through the gates and arrested the players on the "charge of violating the Sabbath."[14] Players were fined—the Cincinnati team paid the entire bill of $159.30—and the game moved to Brooklyn on September 5.

After losing two of three in Baltimore, Brooklyn returned home and took three straight from Kansas City. Meanwhile, St. Louis fell three times in Columbus. After winning both games of a doubleheader on Saturday, August 31, putting the Bridegrooms and Browns in a tie for first, Byrne said, "If we secure the lead on Monday, we will retain it."[15] St. Louis' loss Sunday—with the Bridegrooms off—put Brooklyn atop the standings for the first time all season.

Following a 13–8 win over Cincinnati on September 3 in which Caruthers got the win and contributed with a pair of hits—he also was hit by a pitch in the head, which momentarily dazed him—the *Brooklyn Citizen* praised him as being "first in all-round actual play. The difference between Caruthers and an hourglass is that the sand in one runs out, while in the other it doesn't."[16] Caruthers didn't play in the final two games of the series—both Brooklyn wins—or in an exhibition in Worcester. He was being saved for St. Louis, which was coming to town in what was obviously a big series. Brooklyn led the American Association by two games, and this was the last time these teams were to meet. Tensions were indeed high.

The series opened at Washington Park on September 17 with 15,443 reported in attendance, many cordoned off in the outfield both by a rope and a throng of police. Brooklyn scored two runs in the first inning, but St. Louis got one in the fifth off Caruthers and two in the sixth to take the lead. Then the Browns tried to slow down the game. In the seventh, St. Louis engaged in three arguments with umpire Fred

Goldsmith. In the top of the eighth, Browns right fielder Tommy McCarthy "tried to soak the ball in a bucket of water,"[17] thereby giving the Bridegrooms less of a chance to get solid hits. However, the ruse was discovered, and a new ball was brought in as a replacement. After the eighth inning was completed—and St. Louis engaged in another long delay—Browns third baseman Arlie Latham lit three candles on the bench, a not-so-subtle signal that it was too dark to play. When Brooklyn batted in the ninth inning, trailing 4–2, it was 6:18 p.m. Bob Clark led off with a walk and reached second base. That brought up Caruthers, who fouled one out of play and out of sight. St. Louis' Charles Comiskey had seen enough (or rather couldn't see enough) and pulled his players off the field.

Brooklyn fans weren't rooting for St. Louis in this instance. Some fans jumped onto the field—McCarthy was punched in the jaw, and Browns owner Chris Von der Ahe said Comiskey and Latham were also struck. "Caruthers, with great coolness, went at the crowd with his bat, and they fled in all directions," reported the *Brooklyn Citizen*.[18] The Browns refused to play, so Goldsmith forfeited the game to Brooklyn. "When Comiskey first began to delay the play, I warned him distinctly to go on and play ball, as I would compel him to play as long as there was light enough," Goldsmith later explained. "I repeated that warning time and again, and was fully justified in my course. I see that Von der Ahe accuses me of being afraid to call the game. Tell him that fear is an entire stranger to me, and the right is what I strive to maintain."[19]

Von der Ahe wanted the forfeit and subsequent fine (teams were docked $1,500 if they forfeited) erased. Byrne wasn't about to give away a win (although the American Association did it for him, overturning the forfeit and giving St. Louis a 4–2 win in a ruling handed out on September 23). Citing a fear of attacks on his players, Von der Ahe telegraphed Byrne "I refuse to allow my club to play any more games in Brooklyn."[20] While the Bridegrooms and 15,000 fans turned out to Ridgewood Park on Sunday, September 8, Von der Ahe was true to his word, and the Browns didn't show up. Brooklyn played an exhibition for those who stuck around, about 8,000 in number (Caruthers didn't play, but umped; Goldsmith and old-time player Lip Pike were on a team headed by O'Brien, whose team lost to one captained by Foutz). This time the game was forfeited to Brooklyn—and it stuck.

The Browns did appear at Washington Park on Monday, as did a throng of fans and police, but rain wiped out the game and the following day as well. Nevertheless, the past two days were the talk of the town. "Never in the history of the diamond field has such food been furnished for gossip among admirers of the National game as has been caused by the Brooklyn-St. Louis controversy," said the *Brooklyn Standard Union*. "At home, in the theatres, in barrooms, on the sidewalk, in the cars, on the elevated railways, on the ferryboats, in offices, stores, in fact everywhere men congregate, it is the theme of conversation."[21]

Due to rain, Brooklyn didn't play again until September 14, when the Bridegrooms swept doubleheaders on back-to-back days against Louisville. They were now six games up on St. Louis (although in actuality five as the forfeit reversal was still a week away). A store in downtown Brooklyn displayed a diorama of a funeral procession, with a coffin reading "St. Louis B.B. Club" and six Bridegrooms as pallbearers, Darby O'Brien leading the way with a pickaxe and other players following with shovels. "This attracts a considerable crowd,"[22] reported the *Brooklyn Standard Union*. The Browns, though, wouldn't die.

From September 24-October 10, Brooklyn went 9–2 with a tie—but St. Louis didn't lose a game. The Browns put together their longest winning streak of the season, 14 in a row, extending from September 23-October 14 despite Von der Ahe fining and benching for the season pitcher Silver King and third baseman Arlie Latham. Brooklyn was nearly without Caruthers but for happier reasons. On October 9, Mamie gave birth to their first child, Robert Lee Caruthers, Jr. The new father was in Baltimore when he got word by telegram that morning, and Bryne not only expected him to leave but also encouraged Caruthers to do so. "The telegram says that my wife is doing well, and I know that in case I should go home and the club should then lose games she as well as I would be worried, and that might do more harm than if I remained away," Caruthers said. "I will therefore stay with the club until the season closes."[23] He went out and beat the Orioles, 17–9, contributing three hits on offense.

The New York Giants of the National League finished their schedule on October 5—winning on the final day to secure the pennant by one game—and then had to wait, with the American Association season ending a week and a half later. Even though Brooklyn hadn't clinched, the Giants began preparations to play the Bridegrooms. St. Louis had a thing or two to say about that.

Brooklyn's season was over, but St. Louis had five games remaining, a doubleheader in Cincinnati and three in Philadelphia. The Bridegrooms led by two games, meaning the Browns had to win all five—which would force Brooklyn to play an earlier postponed game against Baltimore to force a three-game playoff. St. Louis' pennant hopes ended quickly, losing the first game, 8–3. Brooklyn's Doc Bushong and "Pop" Corkhill were in attendance to cheer on Cincinnati and give the Game 1 battery of pitcher Jesse Duryea and catcher Jim Keenan $100 if they won, which they did with Bushong paying them off (the two Bridegrooms consistently reminded the Red Stockings players of their potential reward during the game). With the hopes of a championship lost, Von der Ahe canceled the trip to Philadelphia, but he had these parting words upon arriving home in St. Louis: "We have lost, but it was scheming and not ball-playing which beat us."[24]

Brooklyn was on its way home from Columbus and didn't find out the pennant was theirs until arriving in Jersey City, where they were met by a few local fans, including Lip Pike. They took a ferry—where cigars were handed out—and went to Washington Park for a celebration with around 2,000 fans. The toast of the town, the team sat in boxes at the Criterion Theatre the following night, invited to watch "Cheek," with star Charles Bowser incorporating some baseball jokes in the play.

The series with the Giants was scheduled for October 18–30, with Game 1 in Brooklyn at Washington Park. Caruthers had been listed as the probable starter, but instead Adonis Terry pitched. Interestingly, despite leading the American Association in wins (40), winning percentage (.784), and shutouts (7), plus finishing third in WHIP (1.231) and seventh in ERA (3.13)—all of which were best among Brooklyn pitchers—McGunnigle started Terry five times against New York and Caruthers just twice. It was likely the start—or at least near the beginning—of bad blood between the two which would come to a head later.

Caruthers started Game 2, also at Washington Park with over 16,000 in attendance, which Brooklyn lost, 6–2. The Bridegrooms committed 10 errors, with shortstop George Smith the main culprit (the *Brooklyn Daily Eagle* credited him with five miscues, and the *Brooklyn Citizen* three). It got so bad that catcher Joe Visner stopped making throws to second base, he was so frustrated by Smith's miscues. It wasn't just on fielding throws, either. "Just what got into George Smith yesterday no one knows. A man with a wooden arm would have thrown better to first base,"[25] said the *Citizen*.

On October 22 at the Polo Grounds, where far fewer spectators showed up, between 5,000–6,000—"there were plenty of seats to be had,"[26] reported the *Daily Eagle*— Caruthers relieved starter Mickey Hughes in the eighth, and what turned out to be final, inning, getting the 2–3–4 hitters out to preserve an 8–7 win. Brooklyn tied the series at two games each the next day with a 10–7, six-inning win, but Caruthers got pounded in Game 5, giving up 11 hits for 23 total bases plus four walks in an 11–3 defeat at Washington Park. He got in next in Game 7 for Tom Lovett, who was making his only start and allowed nine runs in three innings. Brooklyn lost that one, too, 11–7, and fell in the next two games, 16–7 and 3–2—Terry starting both—as New York clinched the series on October 29. Terry allowed 34 runs (25 earned), a 6.08 ERA, on 47 hits and 18 walks in his five games. Caruthers pitched 24 innings, giving up 19 runs (10 earned), a 3.75 ERA, with 28 hits and six walks.

Brooklyn players gathered at Washington Park on October 30, collecting their final paychecks and bidding each other goodbye. Caruthers was planning on sticking around awhile. Big things were afoot in baseball, and he wanted to hear what was said.

18

Is It a Championship
If Nobody Sees It?

Baseball players' discontent with owners was nothing new. In 1885, spearheaded by New York Giants shortstop John Montgomery Ward, who had recently earned his law degree, the Brotherhood of Professional Base Ball Players was formed. The reserve clause was always in the union's crosshairs, but the establishment of salary tiers, among other grievances, put the players at the tipping point.

Before the start of the World Series, Giants pitcher Tim Keefe, who was the secretary of the Brotherhood, reiterated, "We want the abolition of the classification of the players, and we want the sale of players entirely done away with."[1] The rumors of a new players-backed league were already afoot with reports that Brooklyn would have a team with Ward as its manager. Days after the final World's Series game between New York and Brooklyn, the Players' League was officially consummated.

While Keefe claimed, "We will not interfere with the American Association,"[2] a team was put in Brooklyn ("In fact, the city of Brooklyn is big enough for the champion club of the American Association and our club, too,"[3] Keefe said), and in no short order overtures were being made to players. St. Louis first baseman Charles Comiskey committed to the league's Chicago franchise to be its manager. Browns catcher Jack Boyle, pitcher Silver King, third baseman Arlie Latham, and outfielder Tip O'Neill followed his lead, while second baseman Yank Robinson headed to Pittsburgh.

Caruthers and Brooklyn teammates second baseman Hub Collins and pitcher Adonis Terry were desired by the startup. The Players' League held a meeting at New York's Fifth Avenue Hotel, and Caruthers was among those who attended. Caruthers didn't join the new league—for if it's one thing he knew, even at his young age, was leverage, as proven by his contracts and his actions surrounding them.

The mere appearance of Caruthers at the meeting, combined with a rumor that he was considering signing, might have been all that was needed for Brooklyn owner Charles Byrne. He started signing up his players, including Collins and Terry. Caruthers got a new deal as well for $6,000, the most he'd earn in any year of his career. Byrne went one step further, snagging catcher Tom Daly, who played for Washington of the National League in 1889 and was a member of the Brotherhood. He had been slated to go to the league's franchise in Buffalo, but players were told not to sign yet (only managers had contracts, while the money for everyone else was figured out), and Daly decided he needed the security so he reneged and instead signed with Brooklyn.

Charles Byrne said:

When the Brotherhood first started they said: "We do not intend to interfere with the American Association if the American Association does not interfere with us." This was all right as far as it went, but the first thing they did was to put a club in Brooklyn. We did not even mind this, but when it came to their saying that they would secure such men as Collins, Caruthers, and Terry of the Brooklyns, and several other players from other clubs, I thought it about time to act, and not only did I have the Brooklyn players mentioned by the Brotherhood under contract, but I made a break in the ranks of the Brotherhood by signing Tom Daly of last year's Washington team, one of the strongest of Brotherhood players. The action on my part, outside of strengthening the Brooklyn Club, was forced on me by the action of the Brotherhood.[4]

Ironically, Byrne's protests regarding the American Association soon became moot. The league was trying to find a new president, and Byrne was aching for a compromise. But whenever a vote was undertaken, the owners were deadlocked, 4–4. On November 15, the American Association no longer had a team in Brooklyn—the National League did. Both Brooklyn and Cincinnati, by unanimous consent, joined the NL, with Byrne named to the board of directors.

Whether Caruthers seriously considered the Players' League or just used it as a pawn in his contractual chess game is not known. But he did speak out against the circuit before year's end. In discussing the development of young pitchers and the advancement in that area of the game, he noted, "There are many young players to-day whose fame is limited to a single town, or, at best, a string of small towns, but who in a few years will be occupying the positions of the present king twirlers. In base ball, as in everything else, there is no man so valuable that he can not be replaced. The Brotherhood players would do well to consider these words of advice before they proceed further in their wild and ruinous course."[5]

Following the Players' League meeting and eventual signing of his 1890 contract, Caruthers stuck around Brooklyn for a few weeks. It allowed him to attend a local Thanksgiving tradition which started in 1885: the Bachelors vs. Benedicts baseball game—with players dressing in costume—at Washington Park. Caruthers pitched for the Benedicts, wearing an outfit reminiscent of "Sinbad the Sailor"[6] as his team won a three-inning affair, 8–5. Other attire worn by those participating included a clown, cowboy, farmer, old woman, policeman, schoolboy, and tramp, as well as some extremely non-politically correct outfits such as Bridegrooms secretary Charles Ebbets, who played first base dressed as a "Chinaman."[7]

The day's events finished with a greased pig contest with Caruthers once again demonstrating his ability to commandeer farm animals by capturing the swine. At the Thanksgiving dinner that followed, which consisted of turkey—not pork—and cranberry pie, Caruthers celebrated his accomplishment by buying a round of champagne for the 27 people in attendance. It was then back to Chicago for another uneventful off-season, although this time he spent it with his wife and newborn son.

Spring brought something different, however. For the first time, Caruthers was headed south with his team for preseason training. Brooklyn made arrangements to play in St. Augustine, Florida, heading there by ship (with a brief stop in Charleston, South Carolina). As a gift in anticipation of the new season, each player was presented with a leather handbag with their initials on it, designed by Ebbets. "Bobby Caruthers pronounces them one of the neatest and most useful articles he ever saw,"[8] said the *Brooklyn Citizen*. Caruthers brought something which he perhaps put in his satchel—a white rat, intended to be the team's good luck charm.

The Bridegrooms arrived in St. Augustine on March 8. Three days later, with little practice, they played their first game, facing the Chicago White Stockings, who had been in Florida since early February. Brooklyn management didn't do good reconnaissance on the playing conditions, however. The field was mainly sand, except for the basepaths, pitcher's and catcher's areas which were concrete. Needless to say, there wasn't any sliding into bases. Caruthers was one of three who pitched for Brooklyn, going three innings and allowing four runs. His control was understandably not yet in form, walking five and striking out none.

The next day, Caruthers' arm stiffened up. While he played right field and had a "beautiful hit,"[9] he couldn't throw the ball to the infield, and second baseman Hub Collins had to race to the outfield to retrieve the ball. Adonis Terry also suffered from a sore arm, while Mickey Hughes had leg and shoulder ailments. At times, Brooklyn was forced to use Dave Foutz, who was no longer considered a pitcher, manager Bill McGunnigle, and a resident named Lawson in the box. Unsurprisingly, the Bridegrooms lost every game they played against Chicago and another with Philadelphia which took place in Jacksonville. Caruthers didn't pitch again until March 24, when he (and Hughes, who had returned a couple days earlier) faced the local St. Augustine club. That one Brooklyn won handily, 28–1.

The team returned home to Brooklyn, reaching there March 31, greeted by snow flurries and only a few fans and reporters since their ship, the *Yemassee,* was hours late. McGunnigle wasn't worried about his team's performance in the south.

> Our defeat by Chicago and Philadelphia does not discourage us in the least, because we were not in good fighting condition when the games took place. Our pitchers all went lame after one day's work, then [shortstop George] Smith got laid up and [third baseman George] Pinkney followed suit, but we have all had a good chance to recuperate during our trip up from the South, and you may take my word for it we will give a good account of ourselves when the season opens. The Brooklyn leaguers are a good team and don't you forget it.[10]

Despite all the defections to the Players' League from both American Association and National League teams, Brooklyn had no one jump to the new circuit. The Bridegrooms had the same ballclub in 1890 that they had the previous year except for the addition of Tom Daly. Now in the National League, Brooklyn nevertheless celebrated its accomplishment from 1889 by raising its pennant flag before an April 3 exhibition against Yale. Measuring 17½ feet by 33 feet, the banner was adorned with the sentiment of the time: "Champions, American Association, 1890."[11] The first look at the Brooklyn team drew only 1,800 fans even though it was a ladies' day. In Boston, 20,000 turned out to see a Players' League exhibition against Brooklyn. The American Association put a team in Brooklyn as well, nicknamed the Guardians—in fact, that was the Bridegrooms' next preseason opponent—but even in the fourth-largest city in the United States, three clubs proved too many.

The Bridegrooms continued to play exhibitions against a variety of minor league teams—and also a local department store's nine—with Caruthers getting his work in, but the most interesting event before the start of the season occurred April 5. Tom "Oyster" Burns thought he was in good shape after a visit to Hot Springs plus the training in St. Augustine and felt he was a faster runner than Caruthers, who while not the speediest of players was still plenty quick. The two bet $10 on a 100-yard race, and Burns even gave Caruthers a five-yard head start. He didn't need it, outpacing Burns by 10 yards.

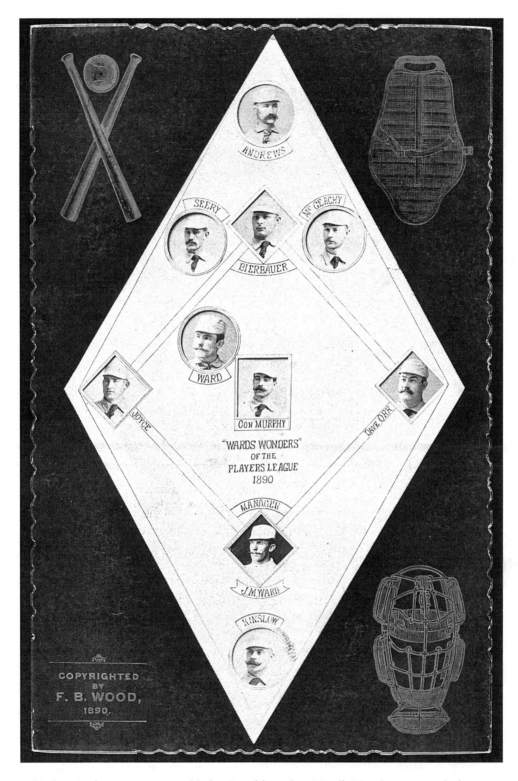

A third major-league team was added to Brooklyn when Ward's Wonders—named after manager John Montgomery Ward—of the Players' League debuted in 1890 (Library of Congress).

Brooklyn opened its season in Boston on April 19 with Caruthers getting the nod to pitch. He was off to a fine start, allowing just one hit and no runs over the first two innings. In the bottom of the second, he doubled but was hit on the shoulder by the ball when Beaneaters pitcher John Clarkson tried to pick him off. It was a hard enough throw, not to mention painful, to cause Caruthers to fall to the ground in agony for a few minutes. He remained in the game—perhaps stubbornly—and lost his effectiveness, giving up eight hits and 12 runs while walking four and hitting a batter over the next two innings before mercifully being replaced by Terry. "Caruthers is one of those men who never know they are beaten," remarked a *Sporting Life* correspondent, "and he undoubtedly believed that his confidence would give the strength to the arm that the passing injury had robbed him of."[12]

Just under 4,000 turned out in Boston to watch that first game. In Brooklyn, the Players' League's Ward's Wonders hosted the Boston Reds in front of 10,000 spectators. But attendance in every league suffered sharp drop-offs—the Bridegrooms played in front of 1,000 at their next game in Boston, while the Ward's Wonders had 2,500 at their park. "The attendance at the games of both the league and the brotherhood clubs since the season began has been dwindling perceptibly," said National League president Nick Young, "and it has clearly demonstrated the impossibility of two big base ball organizations making money."[13]

When the Bridegrooms played their first game at Washington Park on April 28 after three consecutive rainouts—there would be no more contests on Sundays at Ridgewood Park due to the National League forbidding play on that day—just 2,870 turned out to see Brooklyn in its new white uniforms. Even the mayor didn't show up until halfway through the contest, while over at Eastern Park, 4,000 congregated to watch the Players' League game. Caruthers, pitching for the first time since his injury, was magnificent, tossing a four-hit shutout over Philadelphia. "The crowd, however, was not as large as was anticipated or equaled the opening of other years,"[14] noted the *Brooklyn Times Union*.

Brooklyn didn't present a lot of reasons for fans to turn out. The Bridegrooms couldn't get going early in the season, getting off to an 8–8 start. Of course, there could be other factors in attendance as well. On May 16, a rainy day left Washington Park soaked and muddied, yet the teams played on despite fewer than 400 people in the stands (listed as 379). Behind Caruthers, the Bridegrooms won a sloppily played game over Pittsburgh, 6–3. Three days later with Caruthers pitching again, this time topping the Alleghenys, 18–2, the attendance was slightly larger—by 10. That was accounted for by the American Association's Toledo team, which refused to play against the Guardians due to a lack of fans. The *Brooklyn Times Union* said, "It is getting to be a very evident fact that 50-cent ball will not pay at Washington Park, especially with an opposition club,"[15] however Ward's Wonders drew just 483 for their game the same day.

Regardless of the number of people witnessing him, Caruthers kept winning. In a span of a week between May 22–26, he beat Cincinnati and Cleveland twice, all at home. In the finale, played during a light rain all game, only 178 turned out, the lowest turnout for any Brooklyn game played to date at Washington Park, the team's home since 1884. The other two Brooklyn teams also played that day, and the combined attendance of those two contests was under 400.

After a loss to Cincinnati on May 23, Brooklyn players decided everyone needed to shave off their facial hair. Most did, except Doc Bushong, Caruthers, Tom Daly, and manager McGunnigle. Clean-shaven Dave Foutz decided to shave his head in a moment of solidarity. Daly was very protective of his moustache, brandishing a razor to anyone who dared try to remove it. Eventually Caruthers gave in—then lost his next two starts, getting bounced after allowing seven runs in two innings against Chicago on Decoration Day (over 7,000 turned out for that game) and 6–4 to Amos Rusie and New York, giving up 22 total bases on 13 hits in the process. "Did the taking of Bobby Caruthers' mustache have anything to do with his ineffective pitching at present?"[16] wondered the *Brooklyn Standard Union*.

Caruthers started getting a little time in left field due to an injury to John "Pop" Corkhill, but his return to the box coincided with an eight-game Brooklyn winning streak, Caruthers pitching in three of those. Still, the Bridegrooms gained just one game on first-place Cincinnati, which had its 13-game winning streak snapped on the day Brooklyn won its eighth straight.

A serious injury to Darby O'Brien in Chicago further weakened Brooklyn's outfield—and meant more playing time in the field for Caruthers, who, after a loss to the White Stockings in his hometown, also reeled off four straight victories in the box. Brooklyn needed that right arm.

After beating Cleveland, 4–2, on July 7 for that fourth win in a row, Caruthers had to pitch again the next day. Mickey Hughes was suspended—and eventually released—for drunkenness (he latched on to Philadelphia of the American Association for a few days but by September was playing on Brooklyn sandlots, his career over; in 1892 he was arrested for grand larceny and imprisoned), Tom Lovett rushed off to his hometown of Providence to be with his wife, who had taken ill, and Adonis Terry was bedridden from the intense summer heat (it was reported to be over 100 degrees in the shade and 120 degrees on the field at Washington Park). Caruthers won that game, 7–1. over Cleveland and pitched two more times over the next three days against Cincinnati—making it four starts in six days, winning them all to help the Bridegrooms, winners of 11 straight, move atop the standings, at least temporarily.

Philadelphia, however, was on a 16-game winning streak and took over first place. On July 28, Caruthers lost to Cleveland, 8–4, in Indianapolis—there was a Grand Circuit harness racing convention being held in Cleveland, precipitating a change in venue—but that wasn't the worst thing which happened to the ballplayer that day. His learned that his uncle, Alexander McNeill, was suing him for $4,000.

Better times were ahead, at least on the field. After that loss, Brooklyn reeled off nine straight wins to vault back into first place. Caruthers, after saving a depleted pitching staff in early July, pitched only once during that streak—in a 14–5 win over Boston on August 7 in relief of Lovett, who had to leave in the fourth inning after being hit in the hand by a hard grounder. He was helping in other ways, though, playing in left field in five of those contests and scoring the winning run in the bottom of the ninth to beat the Beaneaters 6–5 on August 6.

Since entering the majors in 1884, Caruthers was often garnered with praise of his hitting ability. In 1886, *Sporting Life* wrote of Caruthers: "His position at the bat is remarkably easy, he hits extremely hard, is a good waiter and almost never strikes out."[17] He was known to "like a medium weight bat. He has a great knack of waiting for his base on balls. He has a great way of stepping back from the plate when the pitcher delivers the ball."[18] Al Spink, a St. Louis baseball writer and founder of *The Sporting News*, said in 1918 that on those pennant-winning Browns teams "There was only one man on the team who could hit the ball harder than Caruthers, and that O'Neil (sic), their left fielder."[19] Caruthers' batting style was said to be reminiscent of Dan Brouthers, an eventual Hall of Famer and career .342 hitter who led the league in hitting five times, on-base percentage on five occasions and had the best slugging percentage in seven seasons. The *Buffalo Sunday Morning News*—Brouthers played five years with Buffalo in the National League—described the first baseman's approach: "Dan Brouthers stands almost at the corner of the box closest to the catcher, and, being lefthanded, his left foot is placed ahead of the right one. He steps back when he strikes at the ball, moving the foot closest to the pitcher. Bobby Caruthers takes the same position."[20]

Caruthers wasn't a top power hitter like Brouthers, although he did slug over .500 in both 1886 and '87 and hit one of the balls over the right-field fence in the history of Philadelphia's Jefferson Street Grounds. On August 15 at Boston's South End

OLD JUDGE CIGARETTES Goodwin & Co., New York.

Bob Caruthers strikes a pose at home plate. Notice his batting stance, with his front foot near the base (a square, not like the modern-day plate) and his back foot behind and pointed away (Library of Congress).

Grounds he had another notable swat. Facing the Beaneaters' Kid Nichols in the seventh inning, Caruthers tried to bunt, but failed. Reverting to swinging away he sent a Nichols pitch far over the right-field fence. The *Boston Globe* and *Boston Post* both wrote no ball had traveled a longer distance at South End Grounds on the year (the *Brooklyn Citizen's* wire report went further, claiming it was the "longest ever made at the ground"[21]).

In the last two weeks of August, Caruthers was nearly exclusively playing left field. He pitched once, coming in from the outfield to relieve Terry in an 8–1 blowout loss to Cincinnati on August 27. Brooklyn couldn't pull away from Boston, though, and at the end of the month led the Beaneaters by three games. Then came September 1.

At Washington Park, Brooklyn and Pittsburgh played the first tripleheader in major league history—there have been only two since, Baltimore-Louisville on September 7, 1896, and Pittsburgh-Cincinnati on October 2, 1920—with the first game at 10:30 a.m., the teams eating dinner, then playing again at 2:30

p.m. and 4 p.m. Caruthers pitched the opener, his first start since August 16, and led, 10–0, heading into the ninth inning when the wheels fell off. With two on and two out a series of hits, hit batters, and errors got Pittsburgh back in the game. Third baseman George Miller, representing the tying run, hit one over left fielder O'Brien's head. As Miller circled the bases, O'Brien tossed the ball to Terry, playing center field, who threw it to shortstop George Smith, whose heave home to catcher Bob Clark easily nailed Miller to end the game. Lovett won the second contest, 3–2, and Terry the third, 8–4, with Caruthers stationed in left field in the finale. Coupled with Boston losing a doubleheader at home to Chicago, the Bridegrooms now led the National League by 5½ games.

It was another close game for Brooklyn against Pittsburgh the next day, and this time it was Caruthers providing the heroics. Pitching on back-to-back days, Caruthers kept the Bridegrooms in the game, allowing nine hits with a walk, strikeout, hit batter, and wild pitch but trailing, 4–2, with Brooklyn due up in the bottom of the ninth. With two men on, Caruthers ripped a Bill Day offering to the right-field fence, which it ricocheted off, allowing Caruthers to get a triple. When right fielder Bill Wilson uncorked a wild throw—it was reported as thrown home, but the ball ended up between there and third base—Caruthers scampered home with the winning run. "'Bobby' Caruthers can hit the ball at the right time," said the *Brooklyn Standard Union*. "It isn't the first time that Bobby's timely hitting has won the game for his team as in yesterday's game."22

If Caruthers was on the outs with his teammates his first year in Brooklyn, that didn't seem to be the case in 1890. He had a suit stolen from his apartment at 105 Berkeley Place, located a block or so from Prospect Park, and the other players pitched in so he could buy a

Bob Caruthers was said to have a similar hitting style to that of Dan Brouthers. Brouthers was on the Boston Reds team which won the 1890 Players' League. Caruthers' Brooklyn team tried to arrange a postseason series with the Reds, to no avail (Library of Congress).

replacement (they probably knew how important fashion was to Caruthers). Caruthers' loyalty to Brooklyn, however, was coming into question. While rumors were already floating about that John Montgomery Ward would join forces with Bridegrooms owner Charles Byrne in 1891, reports started emanating that Caruthers—as well as Doc Bushong, Hub Collins, Bob Clark, Tom Daly, Dave Foutz, Darby O'Brien, and George Pinkney—were considering moving over to the Players' League. "We are perfectly aware of whom they mean," an anonymous member of the Bridegrooms board told *The Sporting News* regarding a report of unnamed Brooklyn players looking to leave, "and have a personal denial from each that any of them intend deserting the club. There is not a man on our team who is dissatisfied … mark my predictions, there will be no Brotherhood or Players' League next season."[23] Three of the named players—Daly, O'Brien and Pinkney—signed 1891 contracts with the Bridegrooms before the end of the regular season, and by mid–October all but Oyster Burns, Caruthers, and Foutz were in the fold for the following year.

Despite the distractions of the robbery and gossip, Brooklyn clinched the National League pennant in front of 275 fans in Cleveland on September 27. Caruthers had a couple of appearances in left field and didn't start in the box again until September 30, his first start since September 2, a span of 16 games (he beat Cleveland, 4–3, in 10 innings).

The team returned to Brooklyn after that game, and a big reception, complete with a brass band, was organized at the Jersey City train station. But an accident at Greenville, Pennsylvania, delayed the arrival, and by the time they reached the destination, it was past midnight and the crowd had dispersed.

The Bridegrooms finished their season on October 4 with a win over Pittsburgh—Dave Foutz making one of his handful of pitching appearances—in front of a typically small crowd. In 1889, the team was feted after finishing atop the American Association. Winning the National League in 1890 was met with malaise. The *Brooklyn Citizen* declared:

> The champion season of both the Players and the National League closed yesterday after one of the most disastrous seasons ever known in baseball. Both organizations are heavy losers, but one will not give in to the other. Baseball has lost public favor in Brooklyn, and though the National League pennant was brought to this city by the "Bridegrooms," there was no demonstration of any kind by the people to show their appreciation of the club's work during the season. The closing games were poorly attended, and the boys seemed to be slighted all around.[24]

Brooklyn finished 86–43, 6½ games ahead of Chicago. "The American Association last year was a much stronger organization than the National League this year. Why we have walked away with the pennant this year and have had a crippled team all season,"[25] claimed Darby O'Brien, which seemed a strange assertion since the Bridegrooms didn't secure first place until late in the year.

Brooklyn was set to play Louisville, winners of the American Association, in the World's Series (Daly had tried unsuccessfully to have a series arranged with Players' League champion Boston). But first, Byrne scheduled some exhibitions—a doubleheader in Kansas City against the Western Association's Blues and a contest in St. Louis with the American Association's Browns.

Caruthers pitched in the second game against Kansas City lost 10–8, and was in left field in St. Louis when he badly twisted his ankle. Instead of heading to Louisville for the start of that series—the first four games were played there—he was bound to Brooklyn to heal.

Game 5 was played on October 25 at Washington Park. Two days of rain in Brooklyn made the field very soggy, and while sawdust was put on the basepaths, that didn't help other parts, such as the outfield, where Caruthers and his bad ankle were stationed. O'Brien and Pinkney were both sick, which caused Burns to move from the outfield to third base, with Terry positioned in center field and Patsy Donovan, who was signed in July after being released by Boston and hit just .218 in 28 games with Brooklyn, in right. Out of subs—catcher Bob Clark was injured in the opener and was done for the series— Caruthers had to play. He had neither a hit nor a putout. Caruthers "discovered that damp grounds and frosty weather are not particularly beneficial to a bad ankle,"[26] said *Sporting Life.*

Caruthers got into one more contest—Game 7, which turned out to be the finale of the series with both teams agreeing to cancel on account of bad weather and poor attendance; each winning three games with one tie. Still hobbled, he again didn't get a hit and committed an error, dropping a fly ball in his only chance in left field.

Caruthers was displeased with manager Bill McGunnigle. It was later reported that he drew a $100 fine during the World's Series for "insubordination," which could mean almost anything, but likely he argued with McGunnigle or ignored instructions. If it were because of drinking, the papers would either flat-out say that or use a euphemism such as dissipation. Either way, Caruthers wanted McGunnigle gone. He found out soon enough, however, that the grass isn't always greener on the other side.

Manager Trouble

All seemed well for Bob Caruthers, at least publicly, after the cancellation of the 1890 World's Series. Even with a bum ankle, he pitched in a benefit game for his neighbor, Brooklyn secretary Charles Ebbets, on November 1. The next night, the Bridegrooms were feted, while wearing their uniforms, at Brooklyn's Grand Old Opera House. Later, Caruthers, George Pinkney, Adonis Terry, and trainer Jack McMasters went duck hunting at Great South Bay in Long Island, while Caruthers and Ebbets bought a horse with the intent of starting a stable of harness racers.

But then Caruthers broke through the tranquility with a jarring statement: He wanted Bill McGunnigle gone as Brooklyn manager. Huddled at a "well known resort"[1] with some other players and fans, Caruthers was queried about a potential return to the Bridegrooms in 1891. The *Brooklyn Citizen* quoted him as replying, "I don't know, it depends on who has charge of the team. If McGunnigle manages the team next season I will not play on it, if a new manager takes hold I will play and play the game of my life. I like Mr. Byrne and the rest of the Brooklyn people, but I don't want any part of McGunnigle."[2] Asked over the coming weeks to comment on that report, Caruthers stayed true to those words.

At face value, Caruthers had a reasonably fine season with Brooklyn in 1890. As a pitcher he went 23–11—his .676 winning percentage was fourth-highest in the National League—with a 3.09 ERA and 1.263 WHIP (ninth-best; he also was sixth in the league with 2.6 BB/9) in 37 appearances with 30 starts, toiling exactly 300 innings. But he had periods of inactivity and felt he could have had a better season if McGunnigle used him properly. He finished well behind Tom Lovett and Adonis Terry in usage, with Lovett pitching in 44 games with 372 innings and Terry 46 and 370. Caruthers also appeared in the outfield nearly 40 times and hit a respectable .265/.397/.340 with a 114 OPS+.

McGunnigle claimed surprise at Caruthers' remarks. More importantly, owner Charles Byrne remained non-committal. "I have said nothing to Mr. McGunnigle or any one else on the subject of leaving, and as these reports are likely to prove harmful to his prospects I wish to say in his behalf that I could not have had a more honest or trustworthy man," Byrne said. "He told me at the end of last season that he thought he would retire from Brooklyn and enter some business nearer home, so that he could devote more time to his family."[3]

Back in October, there were whispers that John Montgomery Ward would leave the Brooklyn Players' League team to join—and manage—the National League one. When the Players' League disbanded in January, that became a reality, and with Ward investing in the Bridegrooms, his being placed in charge of the team on the field became a formality. "We have got something we never had before. I refer to a capable leader," Byrne said. "I do not wish to cast any slur upon the past captains and managers of my club, but I feel that in Ward I have secured the best manager-captain in the country."[4]

Ward brought with him some of his Ward's Wonders players, signing catchers Con Daily and Tom Kinslow—this signaled the end of Doc Bushong, who eventually was released—and young pitcher George Hemming. Several Bridegrooms remained unsigned, including Caruthers, who was living in Brooklyn in a rented apartment—now filled with four, with second son David Newton Caruthers born February 3—near Eastern Park, the club's new home grounds located on the edge of Brooklyn and where Ward's Wonders played the previous year.

McGUNNIGLE, Manager, Brookly

OLD JUDGE
CIGARETTE FACTORY,
GOODWIN & CO., New York.

Bill McGunnigle went 267–139 (.658) in three years as Brooklyn manager but was replaced after the 1890 season.

"Robert Lee Caruthers, called 'Costly Bob,'" said The Sporting News, "may not get the princely income he has been wont to collect semi-monthly. 'Costly Bob's' work last year was hardly up to the $6,000 notch, and nobody is aware of the fact more than Bob himself."[5] Caruthers signed March 18, along with Tom "Oyster" Burns, Dave Foutz, and Adonis Terry. He took a cut in salary—to $5,000—but was still among the highest-paid players and making more than pitcher Tim Keefe and first baseman Dan Brouthers, who were in the Players' League and received $4,000.

Living in Brooklyn, Caruthers got together catcher Tom Daly and Terry, who also lived nearby, for some off-season throwing and riding of bicycles to stay in shape. As other players started to congregate in town in late March, the workouts moved to the Prospect Heights gymnasium. As the weather started turning, the team took to practicing at its old haunt, Washington Park. "There is nothing new to be said of Bob Caruthers, except that he is the same old Parisian, wiry and full of grit," reported Sporting Life. "Somebody told him he was getting fat a couple of weeks ago, and only the coming of his new baby banished the effect. Bob has shown his old form in practice, and means to do something for the glory of his fact increasing family this season."[6]

As the team traveled to Boston for an exhibition game to be played April 2, two players were missing: George Smith, who was tending to his sick wife in Altoona, Pennsylvania, and had yet to sign his contract, and John Ward, who had been on a European trip but was delayed (likely not ingratiating himself to his new teammates). Both players were shortstops; Smith signed with Cincinnati (for $500 more than Brooklyn offered) a week and a half later.

After 10 days of practices and games, Ward was liking what he saw from his club.

> We have a first class team, and they are an intelligent lot of men who will be able to play the finer points of the game. The strength of a ball team in a pennant race is not the strength of the individual members, but it lies in the playing ball in all games as a unit. The men are good players; most of them better than average. We have not a weak player on the team. ... We are strong in batting, and I do not know of any club that is stronger in the pitcher's box than we are. ... I am confident that during the championship season the pitchers of the Brooklyn team will prove that they are equal to those of New York or any other league team.[7]

Ward used his four pitchers fairly evenly during preseason play, mostly using two in each game, but when the season opened on April 22 in Philadelphia, it was his former Players' League teammate, George Hemming who got the call. However, with Burns having injured his heel, Caruthers played in right field and batted fourth. Brooklyn won, 14–8, with Caruthers walking three times, scoring twice, and making "two good catches."[8]

Caruthers was in right field again the next day, and in the ninth inning, with his team trailing, 3–1, and two runners on, he laid down, as Ward called it, a "pretty bunt"[9] to load the bases. Darby O'Brien then hit the ball hard but right at third baseman Billy Shindle, who snared it, stepped on third to retire George Pinkney, who was off the bag, and threw to second, where Foutz was scrambling back, to complete a game-ending triple play. It was a harbinger of Brooklyn's 1891 season.

After winning the opener, the Bridegrooms lost their next six games. Caruthers played one more game in right field before Burns returned. He lost his first pitching start on April 28, when New York's Lew Whistler, whom Caruthers had fanned three times, singled to score George Gore with two outs in the bottom of the ninth (this game was at Brooklyn, with Ward, unlike McGunnigle, preferring to bat first) to give the Giants a 5–4 win.

In his next start three days later at Eastern Park, Caruthers was lifted after five innings after allowing a pair of home runs and trailing, 6–5. Burns hit a grand slam in the sixth to put the Bridegrooms back on top in an eventual 13–6 win. The *Brooklyn Citizen* theorized that there would be more home runs this season not because Eastern Park's fences were shorter in distance but further out. With slightly odd dimensions, straightaway right field was 425 feet, as was right center, but center field dipped in to 413 while left center went back to 425 before jutting in to 350 in straightaway left. With out-fielders playing shallower than they do in modern baseball, there was plenty of space for balls to travel if they were hit over a player's head, allowing batters time to circle the bases. (This was, of course, just theorizing. Brooklyn hit only 23 homers in 1891, third-fewest in the NL although they allowed the third-most, 40.)

There was more conjecture coming from the *Boston Globe* regarding the roster construction. Byrne commented that once the players started getting in shape, he'd retain just three pitchers. With Hemming and Lovett receiving most of the early work, the *Globe* said, "It looks like Carruthers for release."[10]

Making his first start in a week, Caruthers picked up his first win on May 8, 12–10 over Philadelphia, in which he pitched better than the final score indicated. A host of errors led to eight unearned runs, and he held the Phillies hitless over the final three frames. Later that night, Thomas Edison was in town, visiting his Pearl Street Station power plant. Six thousand Brooklynites were asked to attend, see the workings of electricity, and meet Edison himself. No guests were named, but perhaps Caruthers, being a rather notable name not just in Brooklyn but in the country, was among the lucky 6,000.

Brooklyn had a brief jolt starting with that May 8 game, winning five straight, but quickly fizzled, dropping seven straight and 11 of 12. Ward tried to bolster the pitching staff by acquiring Harry Staley from Pittsburgh, but they couldn't come to a financial agreement and Staley instead signed with Boston, where he went 20–5 with a 2.50 ERA. Caruthers, who had struggled in his two previous starts before Ward's near-deal for Staley, went out and pitched a two-hitter in Cleveland against a rookie "cyclone pitcher"[11] named Denton Young but lost, 4–3. He relieved Terry, who injured his arm, on June 3 at home against Chicago. Over an 11-game span, those were his only two appearances, leaving the *Brooklyn Citizen* to assert, "It is surprising that Caruthers is not put in to pitch oftener. He has clearly shown his ability to hold his end up and is in perfect condition."[12]

Caruthers backed up the paper's words the next day, getting the start and allowing six hits in beating Chicago, 6–2, while knocking two hits and scoring twice. "It was up to his old St. Louis work, and he had batting opponents worthy of his best efforts," said the *Brooklyn Daily Eagle*. "Robert is so fine a pitcher in his position, and handles the bat with such good effect, that he ranks high as an all round occupant of the box."[13]

Caruthers wasn't as strong in his next start—at first—at Eastern Park against Cleveland on June 9. He allowed nine runs in six innings, including seven runs in the fifth. In the bottom of the sixth, Young replaced starter Lee Viau, but Brooklyn quickly put two men on for Caruthers, who launched a pitch over the head of Spiders right fielder James "Spud" Johnson, with the ball settling in the carriage lot. Johnson eventually retrieved the ball, but his throw home was a tad too late, Caruthers' inside-the-park home run tying the game (note: modern references inaccurately have this home run being hit off Viau). "There were 1,570 people present at the game, but they made enough noise for 15,000," reported the *Brooklyn Citizen*. "The din and shouting lasted fully five minutes."[14] Caruthers tipped his cap to the small but enthusiastic and appreciative crowd several times during the long ovation. A Young wild pitch later in the inning put Brooklyn up, 10–9, and Caruthers settled down, pitching a scoreless final three innings for a Bridegrooms victory.

Caruthers won his next two starts as well, both against Cincinnati, allowing eight hits in a 7–2 win over Old Hoss Radbourn on June 12—extending Brooklyn's winning streak to seven games; it ended at eight—and five hits over seven innings in a rain-shortened, 6–3 victory June 16. Former Browns teammate Arlie Latham was the Red Stockings' third baseman and noted that Caruthers "has not speed enough to break an egg."[15] It wasn't the first time Latham was perplexed by Caruthers' pitching, and he was on the other end of it as well, having caught him a few times in 1885 and '87. "I don't see why Caruthers is not killed," said Latham in 1888.

> He puts a straight, speedy ball, one right after the other, right over the plate, only using an out-curve now and then, and still the opposing batsmen never punish him with any effect. The only reason I can ascribe for it is that he must put some kind of a jump on the ball. He is

a very swift pitcher, and the ball in coming to the bat seems to gather a second flight of speed that makes it very difficult to judge. I do not say this to detract from his ability, because his great record shows him to be one of the best, if not the best, pitchers in the country. Still, I cannot tell what makes him effective.[16]

When he was younger, Caruthers relied a lot on his fastball, which was one of the best in the game. He was also known to have a "very short, sharp curve … when it leaves the hand, seems as if it would never get near the plate, but suddenly curves over it."[17] He also always had pinpoint control. With Brooklyn, he learned how to put movement on his fastball, perhaps an early version of a two-seamer. Caruthers called the pitch the glide because "It waltzes up towards the batsman with a smile on its countenance, but when he attempts to smote it, it 'glides' away."[18]

But with a lot of wear and tear on his arm, he admittedly stopped trying to strike batters out and relied instead on his defense. Caruthers pitched strategically. "Bob Caruthers had more pitching sense in his head than two of the younger generation have in these days,"[19] Charles Comiskey said in 1928. Jack Rowe, who played in the National League from 1878 to 1889 and in the Players' League in 1890, regarded Caruthers as one of the few pitchers of his era who were "men of brains. They made a study of pitching, which was with them an art as well as a science. They knew the values of curves, speed, change of pace and were never forgetful of the personal equation. By the latter, I mean they diagrammed in their mind the weak and strong point of every batter in the league, and governed their delivery accordingly."[20] George Pinkney, who was a teammate on the Bridegrooms and later in the minors, said in 1911, "Carruthers was a clever pitcher, not remarkably fast, but possessing control. He could hit a quarter at the pitching distance."[21]

Caruthers continued his winning ways June 19 in Boston, allowing one hit over the last seven innings in an 11-inning, 6–5 win, then in New York on June 24 he bested the Giants and Tim Keefe, 7–3, serving up just seven hits and a lone walk. "Last season when Manager McGunnigle was 'sore' on him for some reason or other, Caruthers was kept idle for weeks at a time. When he did go in to pitch he was not equal to the task," noted the *Brooklyn Citizen*. "His reputation was all but ruined in consequence. This year he is taking his regular turn in the box, and has not pitched a losing game in almost two months."[22]

Brooklyn wasn't winning much when Caruthers wasn't in the box, however, and his luck ran out as well. The Bridegrooms were 23–23 on June 16 but after losing the next day couldn't get back to .500 as getting consecutive wins became rare. There were some injuries, too. Caruthers was back in the outfield on occasion—and even had to play an inning at second base, his first time since 1886—but in late July, the *Boston Globe* listed him as fifth in the National League with a .327 batting average. "Bob Caruthers is the hardest hitting pitcher in the League,"[23] said *The Sporting News*. On August 10 in an 8–6 loss at Eastern Park to Cincinnati, he also had a 19th-century rarity—he pinch hit for Adonis Terry, who "was evidently overcome by the intense heat,"[24] and flied out to right field (when Caruthers stepped up, Latham exclaimed, "Well, well, well! The idea of sending such as that out! Now, boys, we have got a pudding."[25]) The first pinch hitter in major league history, according to *Baseball Almanac*, occurred in 1889, and no one had a hit in that role until Tom Daly in 1892.

There weren't many more highlights. Caruthers, playing center field, hit a long home run in Philadelphia on August 17, beat Pittsburgh and his former manager McGunnigle,

4–3, in Brooklyn on September 10, making several good fielding plays to help his own cause, and tossed a five-hit shutout at Eastern Park over Cleveland on September 18.

The Bridegrooms kept falling further out of the race—after August 15, they were at least 10 games back the rest of the season; 2½ weeks later, it increased to 20 games out. As the losing piled up, so did the tumult. Caruthers and Ward, however, had been at odds most of the season. There was an instance when Caruthers was pitching with a man on base—this story was relayed after the season, and the game wasn't specified—and Ward, playing shortstop, instead of playing an easy grounder for a double play, tried to make it look spectacular and booted it, both runners being safe. "Say, Ward, what's the use of me throwing my arm off and you allowing men to gain their bases while you are endeavoring to attract the attention of the occupants of the grand stand,"[26] said Caruthers, who added, "You are paid the same as I am to do your best, so quit your grand stand plays."[27] Ward responded, "Shut up; I'm running this club. You go and pitch ball."[28] To which Caruthers quipped, "Yes, you are running it—into the ground"[29]—a retort which cost him a $50 fine, levied by the Brooklyn captain. Later, on a trip to Boston, Caruthers fought Ward in the team hotel, which got him docked another $200.

During a six-game losing streak in late August, four players—Caruthers, catcher Tom Kinslow, Darby O'Brien, and Adonis Terry, who were fined $100—played cards until the wee hours of the morning, with Kinslow and O'Brien continuing the party, not returning to the team hotel in Cincinnati until 10 a.m. When Ward went knocking on their door early in the morning, he found it devoid of players but full of beer bottles. O'Brien, supposedly the ringleader of the anti–Ward bunch, was eventually benched and suspended. Terry was hurt, and the team stopped paying him. Adding insult to injury, the team wouldn't grant him a release. When the team headed to Boston towards the end of September, Caruthers was nowhere to be found. He later claimed he was ill but never told Ward. His final paycheck was docked $125 for the four games he ended up missing (Brooklyn lost all four).

Rumors persisted that veteran players—especially the four named above—were going to be released. Ward deferred all player moves to Byrne, who did not exactly refute the story.

> All that I will say is that it has been decided to make a radical change in the personnel of the club, and infuse some young blood into the team. Several of the older players will be released, but which ones I have not yet decided. The two new men [shortstop Bones Ely and pitcher Bert Inks] we have playing now have done well, so far, and the experiment having proved a success, I see no reason for not getting a few more young players.[30]

As the season neared an end, Byrne ruminated, "One lesson I have learned this season to my cost, and that is that it does not pay to any longer condone the drinking habits of players. Another point experience has taught me is that star players in a team are played out. … Hereafter, like Anson, I shall place my faith more in the colt element of a team than in the too pampered stars of the fraternity."[31]

Caruthers was barely used in the stretch run. He was put in relief of Inks in the first game of a doubleheader loss at home to New York, going seven innings and allowing three runs, and started in the opener of a September 30 doubleheader at Eastern Park against Philadelphia—his first start in 12 days—winning 7–6 as the Bridegrooms scored two runs in the eighth inning and three in the ninth. Brooklyn won two of its final three games without Caruthers to finish 61–76 and in sixth place in the National League.

Caruthers finished the year pitching 297 innings over 38 appearances with 32 starts—all of which were second on the team behind Tom Lovett. He topped Brooklyn in winning percentage (18–14, .563) and ERA (3.12, the only one on the staff better than the league average). It was easily his worst season as a pitcher—and his fewest innings other than 1884, when he was up for only a couple of months—albeit for most pitchers those would have been good numbers. And Caruthers did it all with a dead arm, as he later claimed. While on more than one occasion he blamed Chris Von der Ahe for over-using him—saying in 1904, for example, "I really believe that if I hadn't been compelled to work so hard for a year or two I was with the Browns I would have lasted much longer than I did."[32]—he also later noted that his situation was inevitable. "What made my arm go back on me? I had just pitched it out I suppose," Caruthers said in 1907.

> Eleven years consecutive work in the box and working like we did in those days was surely enough to put a man out of business so far as his salary arm was concerned. I noticed it first in my shoulder and thought that a little rest would bring it around, but it had gone back on me so badly that nothing but a very long rest would do it any good. The needed time was of course too long. I never noticed that throwing any particular style of ball was especially damaging. All I knew was that was all in so far as pitching was concerned.[33]

Whether or not he knew his pitching days were about numbered after the 1891 season, Caruthers wasn't saying. But the bad feeling between him and Ward still existed, and one had to leave Brooklyn. It seemed as though the shine had worn out on Caruthers' time there, especially since Ward was the team captain, and he asked Byrne for his release. However, Brooklyn wasn't sure it was done with Caruthers, and Byrne—and Ward—kept him on the team. At least for the time being.

A Career Crossroads

As 1891 turned to 1892, Bob Caruthers was still a member of the Brooklyn Bridegrooms. There was no thawing of the frozen relationship between him and captain John Ward, with the divide merely growing. In December, the American Association folded. Brooklyn was eventually awarded a few players from the dissolved Boston Reds, including first baseman Dan Brouthers, pitcher George Haddock, and third baseman Bill Joyce. Also added were shortstop Tommy Corcoran, from the AA's Philadelphia Athletics, and pitcher Bill Hart, acquired from Sioux City of the Western Association.

Brooklyn's bulging roster had to be trimmed. Even with all the additions, the *Philadelphia Inquirer* posited that Caruthers would stick around the Bridegrooms "as a general utility man."[1] But Brooklyn was already trying to rid itself of Caruthers. Philadelphia was looking to add a pitcher and was interested in Hart. Brooklyn owner Charles Byrne told Phillies owner and team president A.J. Reach the team wasn't going to deal Hart, but perhaps they'd be interested in acquiring Caruthers. No transaction was forthcoming.

Caruthers continued to ask for his release from Brooklyn. Eventually, the team acquiesced. Caruthers, shortstop Bones Ely, catcher Tom Kinslow, and outfielder Darby O'Brien were taken off Brooklyn's reserve list and released. Ward left open a window for a return, saying "It is a fact that Caruthers and Darby O'Brien are not reserved, but if either one shows up in championship form before the season begins the Brooklyn team wants him."[2] Ironically, O'Brien, the ringleader of the anti-faction Ward group in 1891 who was suspended for much of the second half of the season, did re-sign and played in 122 games.

Finally, after all these years, a free agent and able to sign with any club, Caruthers found himself with no suitors. The *New York World* reported that Washington was in talks with him but the *Washington Evening Star* confirmed that "The local club is not after Bobby."[3] The Western League was a rumored destination—National League president Nick Young had sent that circuit a notice of veteran players not under reserve who could be signed, which included not only Caruthers but also such former stars as pitcher Old Hoss Radbourn and longtime Cincinnati first baseman John Reilly. "Truly these are not golden days for the old-timers,"[4] concluded the *Chicago Tribune*.

Unlike those other players, who were in their mid-to-late 30s, Caruthers was just 27 years old in 1892. With the National League holding its March meeting at New York's Fifth Avenue Hotel—not far from Caruthers' home in Brooklyn—an opportunity presented itself with 12 teams in attendance. He found perhaps the most unexpected taker.

The St. Louis Browns had moved from the disbanded American Association to the National League. The Browns weren't the powerhouse they presented when Caruthers played there, but were a strong team in the former league, finishing in second place in 1891. However, several players jumped to the National League before the American Association vanished, most notably first baseman and captain Charles Comiskey, who one year after returning from the Players' League to St. Louis, signed with Cincinnati. Outfielder Tip O'Neill joined Comiskey, while another heavy-hitting outfielder, Tommy McCarthy, and the team's top pitcher, Jack Stivetts, bolted for Boston. In addition, catcher Jack Boyle and shortstop Shorty Fuller signed with New York.

St. Louis owner Chris Von der Ahe added replacements, such as shortstop Jack Glasscock, pitcher Kid Gleason, and slugging first baseman Perry Werden, but still needed to fill out his roster. It had been rumored for months that the Browns would acquire third baseman George Pinkney, who appeared in 135 games for Brooklyn in 1891. They finally signed him—as well as his recent teammate, Caruthers—

George Pinkney played with Bob Caruthers in Brooklyn and followed him to St. Louis. The pair would be teammates again in Grand Rapids. Interestingly, despite his uniform, Pinkney never played for Philadelphia (New York Public Library Spalding collection).

March 1. After years of receiving one of the top salaries in all of baseball, Caruthers settled for $2,500 from St. Louis as well as a possible $200 bonus, to be paid if he were deemed to have played well at season's end. The conflict—and hostile words spoken—following his leaving the team before the 1888 season were all but forgotten. "Caruthers is as good to-day as he ever was," said Von der Ahe, who implied that he beat out Chicago and Washington for his services, "but Ward and he are on the outs, and Bob asked for his release and got it. The Brooklyn officials concede this; so do his associates on the Brooklyn club, who regret to see him leave. … Caruthers looks better than I have seen him in years, and he is stronger and in better health than when he distinguished himself with the old Browns."[5]

Byrne paid big money to acquire Caruthers (not to mention other players), and while his Brooklyn teams won two pennants, it never claimed a world championship in those four years. Caruthers wasn't the same hurler he was in St. Louis, but still ended his time with the Bridegrooms sporting a 110–51 record (.683 winning percentage) and 2.92

ERA, and was one of the top pitchers, if not the best, in the league during his first three seasons in Brooklyn. While he later called the signing a mistake, at the time of the parting Byrne was magnanimous, saying "Caruthers will prove his worth the coming season. He was given his release because Mr. Ward and he could not agree."[6]

After finishing a coaching stint at Princeton, Caruthers arrived in St. Louis on March 30. Von der Ahe penciled him in as one of the team's starters. Surprisingly, that's the role Caruthers saw for himself as well. "I was glad to get away from Brooklyn, as Ward and I could not agree, and one of us had to walk the plank. I believe I can pitch just as good ball as often as I did when with the Browns,"[7] Caruthers said.

Playing in his first games in his second go-round for the Browns in a pair of exhibitions against Milwaukee on April 2–3, Caruthers was greeted enthusiastically by St. Louis fans, who gave him prolonged, and loud, ovations on both days. He played right field in the first and pitched in relief in the second. "I never saw Bob Caruthers when he had more speed,"[8] said Milwaukee manager Charles Cushman.

When the season began, Caruthers was in the starting rotation. He made his initial appearance in St. Louis' fourth game on April 17, which happened to be Easter and was the first game in National League history to be played on a Sunday. In front of 14,000 fans at Sportsman's Park, he lost to Cincinnati, 5–1, allowing three home runs.

This was not the Browns team of Caruthers' heyday. Comiskey and O'Neill were the last holdouts from the glory years when the team won four consecutive American Association pennants. This St. Louis team lost nine of its first 10 games and were out of the pennant hunt by mid–May. Never one to sit idly, Von der Ahe made a host of changes.

Right fielder Bill Van Dyke, another pickup from Sioux City, lasted just four games—going 2-for-16 with an error—before being released. Von der Ahe chased after Pete Browning, a .341 lifetime hitter, but the two couldn't agree on terms. Browning was asking for $3,500, while Von der Ahe, noting that the outfielder had no leverage with just one major league, offered $2,200. Browning eventually signed with Louisville (which released him weeks later). The Browns owner also contacted Hardy Richardson after he was let go by Washington, but the second baseman/outfielder instead signed with New York.

This left Caruthers to take over as the main right fielder, to which he hardly objected. He had recently told a reporter, "I would like to play permanently in the outfield, but you cannot induce managers to assign you for outfield work when they know you can pitch."[9] The thought of Caruthers playing every day wasn't an outlandish one. Before the season, Boston second baseman Joe Quinn quipped that "Bob can be depended upon to hit a .300 clip if he is played regularly."[10]

Caruthers pitched again in Cincinnati on April 25 and lost, 8–2. After the defeat, St. Louis' seventh in a row, Von der Ahe made the first of several managerial changes on the season, replacing Jack Glasscock with second baseman Cub Stricker (it was a pattern over the years; he had five managers in 1890 and continued to rotate them while owner, even putting himself in that role).

In right field, Caruthers was flourishing. He homered off Tony Mullane in Cincinnati on April 26, knocking one to the center-field fence and circling the bases. When the Browns returned to St. Louis, fans started sitting in the right-field bleachers just to cheer him on. "With the possible exception of Little Nicol and Arlie Latham, Bob is the most popular player that has ever worn a St. Louis uniform,"[11] said the *St. Louis Post-Dispatch*.

After a 14–2 win at home over Brooklyn on May 6—"Bob Caruthers would rather defeat John Ward and his club than any other two clubs in the League,"[12] noted the *Post-Dispatch*—in which he had two hits and made a fantastic catch which drew a huge ovation, Caruthers, who said he was 20 pounds heavier than his previous normal playing weight, said he'd like to remain in his current role.

> I would prefer to play exclusively in the outfield and I guess if I can only continue to line them out as regularly as I have done lately, Mr. Von der Ahe will permit me to quit pitching. I am, however, in good condition, and can if necessary go in to-morrow and, I think, pitch well as ever. Pitching, however, is hard work, and there is nothing attached to it that one can admire after one has been at it for several years. Of course there is more money in it, and that is the rule ball players act under nowadays.[13]

On May 11, Caruthers pitched for the first time since April 25, losing at home to Baltimore, 5–3. Taking his place in right field was Frank Genins, a player Von der Ahe was anxious to see. Making his major league debut, Genins had a pair of hits but drew the ire of the Browns owner for not going after a home run hit over the fence and throwing it back into the field of play even though, as Stricker told him, that act wouldn't have changed the result. Genins was sent back to the minors. Stricker was next to go, booted as manager on May 20 and replaced by infielder Jack Crooks. Stricker was benched and eventually traded on June 14 to Pittsburgh for pitcher, and St. Louis native, Pud Galvin. Pittsburgh flipped Stricker to Baltimore a few days later for Adonis Terry. Von der Ahe also wanted Terry and sent Caruthers to Brooklyn to acquire him—perhaps not the best person to do business with Ward, who instead of releasing the pitcher dealt him to his friend Ned Hanlon, Baltimore's manager.

Ward's feelings notwithstanding, Caruthers was feted by Brooklyn fans upon his return to that city in late May. Beyond the applause—"Bob Caruthers was cheered to the echo every time he came to bat"[14] and tipped his cap on each occasion—before the start of the first game of the series, Caruthers was presented with a diamond ring (Pinkney was given a silver water pitcher, cup and bowl). Likely pleasing Caruthers most was the Browns sweeping the three-game set, 5–1, 13–1, and 10–9, with him getting at least one hit in each while scoring three runs in the finale and setting up the game-winning run with a sacrifice bunt.

Pitching was no longer part of Caruthers' regimen. In June he toiled just twice—as the third of three to pitch in Philadelphia in a 15–7 loss on June 6 and tossing a complete game in a 13–5 exhibition win against Toledo. But on May 29, he was in the box for a benefit game played for the wife and child of his former Brooklyn teammate Hub Collins, who died eight days earlier at age 28 due to typhoid fever. Playing on a team labeled the Old St. Louis Browns—it included not only Caruthers but also such players as Charles Comiskey, Dave Foutz, Silver King, Arlie Latham, and Tip O'Neill—he went five innings, allowing just one run against the current Brooklyn team—"Caruthers pleased his many old friends by pitching in great style"[15]—before giving way to King. The game raised over $3,000.

Von der Ahe signed Pretzels Getzien and acquired Galvin (although as soon as Galvin arrived in St. Louis, he had to go back to Pittsburgh as his nine-year-old son died after falling in a hot salt vat; Von der Ahe deducted $70 from Galvin's pay for the time missed) to go with Theodore Breitenstein and Kid Gleason. Caruthers wasn't needed as a pitcher, leaving him a regular to prance about the outfield where needed (and he still was fast and could cover ground, as evidenced by beating Glasscock in a 100-yard dash after a June 27 game), while being one of the best hitters in the lineup. His .304 average in early July was tops on the club and 14th in the league.

The moves provided a brief respite from losing—the Browns did have a winning record in June, going 13–11. But Von der Ahe wasn't satisfied. The National League was playing a split season in 1892, with the second half beginning July 15 and the winners of each half to meet in a championship series. "There will be a general shaking up on this team by the first of the month," the St. Louis owner said in mid–June. "I want a team of winners for the fall championship contest, which begins in July. Every man who wants to stay on the team will have to show his mettle during this coming home series."[16]

The team responded, or at least played better, winning nine and losing four with a tie from June 17–July 1. But with teams losing money, it was decided to cut the salaries of players by 20 percent. Any player who refused to take the reduction would be released. Glasscock lost out on $500 and outfielder Cliff Carroll $400. Caruthers wasn't cut, but Von der Ahe told him he wouldn't receive his $200 bonus. Browns players didn't comment publicly other than to "to say that the cut was unjust; that they had signed contracts for stipulated sums for the season's work, and that they considered themselves entitled to the full amount, but under the existing circumstances they could not protect themselves but were compelled of necessity to accept the new contract."[17]

While their salaries were being reduced, Von der Ahe did go out and buy his team new all-brown uniforms, which they debuted in the second-half opening game in Boston, a rare St. Louis blowout, winning 20–3 (Caruthers had two hits, two runs, and a stolen base). But the outfits didn't bring the Browns much luck after that. After finishing the first half with a 31–42 record (20½ games behind first-place Boston), St. Louis began the second half on the road for 17 games, going 3–13 with a tie. The team did win an exhibition at Providence on July 17, but Caruthers missed that game as his wife gave birth to a daughter, Dorothy, that day.

Two days later, after being shut out in both games of a doubleheader in Brooklyn, Von der Ahe released Getzien. He never pitched in the majors again. With Breitenstein left in St. Louis, Von der Ahe had Caruthers pitch in New York on July 22—he had originally been scheduled to play right field. It was Caruthers' first time in the box in nearly a month, and while he allowed just nine hits and three walks, the Giants made the most of it, scoring six times in the fourth inning, including an Eddie Burke inside-the-park, two-run home run, in winning, 9–1. The next day, Caruthers replaced an injured Gleason (who had relieved Galvin) and tossed three scoreless innings in a 12–4 loss to the Giants.

After missing a few games following a freak injury in Baltimore, where he put his left hand through a clubhouse window while trying to open it, Caruthers was back in the box on July 31 in Cincinnati. He didn't fare well. He allowed 15 hits and three walks while striking out no one in losing, 6–0. After the contest at the team hotel, Caruthers went to Von der Ahe's room and once again requested that he not be used as a pitcher as "he had lost his pitching powers"[18] and had nothing left on his fastball.

Von der Ahe had other things on his mind. He made another change at manager, this time installing outfielder George Gore—who had been signed a week earlier—to take over for Crooks. On August 2 in Cleveland, Galvin was staked to a 7–0 lead but allowed four runs in the third inning. With Breitenstein and Gleason having been sent home due to sore arms, Caruthers was put in, and he allowed four runs in the fourth inning. Bill Hawke, who was signed days earlier from Reading, replaced Caruthers and finished the 12–10 loss.

The *St. Louis Globe-Democrat* was critical of replacing Galvin with Caruthers and the team itself (its headline rang out, "THESE BROWNS ARE QUITTERS"[19]), writing, "If Mr. Von der Ahe was responsible for the change of pitchers he should let somebody else manage his team on the field hereafter. If Capt. Gore was responsible for the change then Gore does not deserve to be captain any longer."[20] Von der Ahe was at the game, and it was reported that it was indeed he who called for both Galvin and Caruthers to be taken out. Galvin was subsequently released, his Hall of Fame career over, while Caruthers appeared done pitching as well.

"I don't think Caruthers will be pitched any more. His performance at Cleveland yesterday demonstrates pretty conclusively that he was correct when he informed Mr. Von der Ahe at Cincinnati … that his days as a pitcher were over," Browns secretary George Munson said.

> Mr. Von der Ahe also came to that conclusion after Sunday's game, and I think he was put in yesterday simply because it was absolute necessity. Then, again, Bob in his palmy days was very effective against the "Spiders" and that in all probability also had a good deal to do with his going in yesterday. Caruthers, however, is a valuable man and he will be retained as utility player, providing, of course, the present outfield continues to realize expectations. Otherwise Bob will be played again regularly in the outfield. He can, if necessary, cover first base as Werden has not been in condition. Mr. Von der Ahe, as soon as he returns home, may conclude to rest Perry for a while and play Bob on first.[21]

Caruthers started the next nine games in right field, but a rumor was floated about that he and Von der Ahe were on the outs and Caruthers might be released. Fueling fire to that report was the signing of Ed Haigh, a third baseman for Reading who was put in right field for the August 14 game at Louisville. He went 1-for-4, striking out twice, and looked lost in the outfield in what turned out to be his only major league game.

Von der Ahe kept trying to find pieces to the puzzle, signing outfielder Steve Brodie, pitcher Pink Hawley, and infielder Jimmy "Chicken" Wolf, the latter lasting all of three games, while renewing his interest in Pete Browning, who had been released again, this time by Cincinnati. "I must strengthen my club," Von der Ahe said. "The men can not win games if they can not bat. I wish also to be ready for any emergency if a player should get hurt or any other unforeseen mishaps occur."[22] As if on cue, the day after Von der Ahe made this comment, Caruthers was hit by a pitch in the ninth inning of an 11–3 loss at home to Brooklyn and had to exit. St. Louis made 12 errors in the defeat, which dropped its second-half mark to 8–20. "My patience is exhausted," the Browns owner said after the loss. "It is bad enough for the club to lose games on its poor batting, but such fielding as was done to-day is discouraging and ridiculous."[23]

A clearly frustrated Von der Ahe sent an emissary, Harry Means, to West Baden, Indiana, where Browning was holing up after being let go. "Wait till Browning comes," said Von der Ahe. "I tell you, I am getting gray-haired over this situation. I've put my money into base ball here and tried my best to get a team of good players together, but I have been deceived. I acknowledge that some of them have been miserable failures. I will not put up with their play any longer. I will keep trying new men until I strike good ones."[24]

Von der Ahe never signed the elusive Browning, who went back to Cincinnati for a second stint, but he did make a major decision: Another managerial change. Gore was out as captain and Caruthers in. The move went over well with the local scribes. "Bobby is a man who both in manner and mental equipment is capable of controlling a team on the field,"[25] said the *Post-Dispatch*. The *St. Louis Chronicle* declared, "Caruthers is the most popular player in the team and a man of far more than ordinary intelligence."[26]

Still smarting from the pitch he took off his arm, Caruthers didn't play in the first game he managed. Four of the players in his lineup at Baltimore on August 20 were recently signed—center fielder Steve Brodie, third baseman Bill Kuehne, left fielder Gene Moriarty, and right fielder Chicken Wolf—but the Browns still prevailed, 8–4. A few days later, he surprisingly put himself in as pitcher in the second game of an August 23 doubleheader against Boston and, perhaps even more shockingly, allowed just six hits against one of the top teams in the league to win, 6–3.

Caruthers' stint as manager nearly didn't last the week, however. During an August 26 game at Sportsman's Park against New York, which the Browns lost, 3–0, Caruthers was in the lineup, batting fourth and playing right field. One of his duties was to coach at third base when St. Louis was hitting, but he couldn't do that when it was his turn at bat. In filling that role, some players didn't listen when Caruthers told them to coach. After the game, Caruthers went to Von der Ahe and said he wanted to quit. Having seen the previous four managers that season—Glasscock, Stricker, Crooks and Gore—all have to bend to Von der Ahe's wishes, it's little wonder Browns players didn't follow Caruthers' orders. They knew who was really in charge. Noted baseball writer Harry Chadwick wrote that Caruthers told the Browns owner, "Either I am to have entire control of the team and have it understood that every man must obey me, or I won't act either as captain, or manager."[27] Von der Ahe refused Caruthers' resignation request and instituted a $50 fine for anyone declining a Caruthers' directive.

Von der Ahe, though, couldn't keep out of his meddling. After a 4–3 loss to Washington on August 28, he decided his captain should play the infield, not outfield, and thus benched—and suspended—Percy Werden (that plan lasted all of two games). In his initial game playing first base, Caruthers made eight putouts and turned a double play but also made a couple of errors in the eighth inning which, combined with three singles, helped Washington score three times.

While his fielding "was a little rusty,"[28] Caruthers remained an experienced hitter. He had three hits, and his one out was a deep fly ball on which Washington right fielder Charlie Duffee robbed him of a home run. In the eighth inning, he was intentionally walked, in a fashion made popular in the 20th century. As described by the *St. Louis Globe-Democrat*, "(Washington pitcher Jesse Duryea) was so much afraid of Caruthers' batting that he made Catcher McGuire step about 10 feet to one side of home plate and deliberately sent Caruthers to his base on balls, thus filling the bases, rather than to take chances on his making another hit."[29] St. Louis didn't score but managed to hang on to win, 6–5, with Washington scoring twice in the ninth inning.

The following day a similar strategy was employed. He walked four times as "Washington pitchers were afraid of Caruthers and refused to let him hit the ball."[30] The Browns won again, 12–9, and made it three straight and seven victories in Caruthers' first 12 games as manager with a 4–1 victory over Philadelphia at Sportsman's Park on September 1.

The boost was temporary. In the final six weeks of the season, the Browns won back-to-back games just once (September 30–October 1) as turmoil and turnover once again took the reins. In an 11–3 home loss to Brooklyn on August 17, outfielder Cliff Carroll had a ball bounce into his jersey pocket, whereupon he had trouble digging it out, allowing the batter, Darby O'Brien, to reach third base. Weeks later when getting his paycheck, Carroll found $50 taken out by Von der Ahe because of that play ("It looks mighty queer that a great big ball weighing over one-half a pound could get lost in a man's shirt," he said. "I can't account for it only on the ground that Carroll must have been asleep, and that is not what St. Louis is paying for."[31]) An argument between the two ensued, and the result was that Carroll was the latest to be fed up with the Browns, or rather Von der Ahe, and refused to play the rest of the season.

A week and a half later, pitcher Bill Hawke and second baseman Jim McCormick both abruptly left the team. Hawke went to the Browns owner and said he no longer wanted to pitch. When Von der Ahe refused the request, Hawke packed his bags. No one seemed to know why McCormick took off, but his wasn't deemed a big deal. "McCormack's [sic] loss does not amount to anything beyond the fact that his release cost President Von der Ahe some cold cash, and in addition I believe he secured some advance money,"[32] Caruthers said.

McCormick leaving did have one effect on the Browns: It left them without a second baseman, at least temporarily, because Crooks was recovering from an arm injury. Caruthers took over the position for six straight games and did admirably until his last two games, when he committed a combined five errors. One of those came during an 8–1 loss in Philadelphia on September 17 when shortstop Jack Glasscock let a hard toss from Caruthers, in an attempt to force out a runner, sail by him without trying to catch it. Glasscock hadn't gotten along with Caruthers since the latter was named captain, perhaps some jealousy from having been the first manager when the season opened. While Von der Ahe wasn't pleased when he heard of the incident from Caruthers, the tipping point came when the owner found Glasscock drinking at the Washington Hotel in Philadelphia and subsequently released him. Glasscock was the second-highest-paid player on the team, having signed a two-year deal for $4,000 per annum. In true Von der Ahe fashion, Glasscock returned to the Browns in 1893 before being traded in late June.

The highest-paid player on the team was Kid Gleason, and soon he was gone, too. He was suspended for the remainder of the year following a 9–3 loss to Pittsburgh in which he pitched and his teammates made 10 errors (Caruthers, playing right field, was the only fielder not to have a miscue). The lineup Caruthers put on the field for the Browns' September 28 game vs. Pittsburgh featured six players who weren't with the team at the start of the season (St. Louis lost, 10–3).

Down to two pitchers—Breitenstein, who returned in mid–September after a month-long suspension, and 19-year-old rookie Pink Hawley—Caruthers put himself in the box on September 30 at Sportsman's Park against Cleveland and won, 7–5, allowing nine hits and one walk while striking out four. The next day, Hawley was injured in the seventh inning but remained in the game, only to load the bases on walks. He was replaced by Breitenstein, who allowed all three runs to score. Caruthers relieved with one out and two on and the skies growing dark—he wanted the game called, saying he couldn't see home plate, but umpire John Gaffney refuted the claim and had them play on. An unhappy Caruthers "used excellent headwork"[33] in getting Jesse Burkett to foul out, then saw Breitenstein, in right field, chase down a long fly off the bat of Ed McKean for the final out. Gaffney then called the game, the Browns winning 12–11.

Caruthers wasn't done pitching. He toiled in both games of an October 2 doubleheader in Cincinnati, relieving Breitenstein in the first. Caruthers allowed four runs in the ninth inning to lose, 12–10, the game-winning blow a two-run home run by none other than Pete Browning. Caruthers started the second contest, which was called after five innings due to darkness, losing that one as well, 4–1. St. Louis played an exhibition against the Red Stockings in Indianapolis—a test of sorts to see if that city was major league worthy (it wasn't, as only between 600–1,000 spectators showed up) on October 4, and Caruthers pitched in that one, too, going the distance in a 9–8 win. He pitched one more time, a six-inning, 8–3 loss in Cleveland against his old adversary, John Clarkson. It would be his final time pitching in the major leagues.

The Browns finished the season with three games in St. Louis and the finale, against Chicago, played in Kansas City (in that game, the Browns lost, 1–0, with Caruthers getting three of the five hits allowed by Bill Hutchison). In his final game at Sportsman's Park, the Browns, of course, lost (they dropped nine of their final 10), but playing right field, "Caruthers made two wonderful fielding catches, which reminded old patrons of Sportsman's Park of the days when St. Louis had a champion ball team."[34]

But the Browns were hardly a superior club, finishing the second half with a 25–52 (.325) record and 56–94 (.373) overall, both figures second-worst in the National League. St. Louis used 37 players, and no other team had more (Baltimore also used 37), nine of whom appeared in just one game, while two played in three games, one in four, one in five and one in seven. This was not an easy team to follow—or manage.

Caruthers was no longer a winning hurler either. In 16 games, with 10 starts, modern tabulations have him going 2–10—his only losing season—with a 5.84 ERA and 1.554 WHIP (interestingly, the official stats in Spalding's 1893 guide had him pitching just five games). He could still swing a stick, though. Caruthers' .277 average (as recorded both then and now) was the best on the team and was listed by the *Spalding Guide* as 11th-highest in the National League (baseball-reference has him tied for 26th). His .386 on-base percentage also was tops on the Browns and eighth in the league, while his .742 OPS (120 OPS+) ranked 23rd. No longer the player he once was and with pitching *finally* seemingly no longer an option, but now with managerial experience, Caruthers' career was at a crossroads.

The Cincinnati Kid

Bob Caruthers left St. Louis after the 1892 season a little lighter in his wallet, having dropped $1,000 at the racetrack, but seemingly with the Browns captainship in his pocket. It wouldn't be long before he lost that, too.

On November 26, Browns owner Chris Von der Ahe signed Bill Watkins to be his manager, claiming he was handing over all aspects of the team's operation. Watkins had led Detroit over St. Louis in the 1887 World's Series, which was followed by an unsuccessful tenure with Kansas City of the American Association and most recently minor league stints in St. Paul and Rochester. Watkins, though, was like Bill McGunnigle when he helmed Brooklyn: strictly a manager, not a player. An on-field captain was still needed.

Von der Ahe was making noise that Caruthers would remain captain, but again, he was leaving those decisions to his new man in charge. Watkins saw Caruthers as potentially part of his outfield mix but eyed second baseman Joe Quinn as his next captain (Quinn signed on February 11 and officially was tabbed captain just over a month later).

Caruthers moved his family from Brooklyn to Chicago, where he was helping his brother and his hardware business. If this all sounds familiar, then what Caruthers did next won't surprise you. Visiting St. Louis in early February, dressed in the latest fashions, of course—"to the height of Brummel picturesqueness"[1]—Caruthers made a familiar refrain to anyone who listened, including former ballplayer and current bartender Ned (although he was called Ed) Cuthbert, that he was done with playing baseball. "Ed, I am out of base ball," Caruthers told Cuthbert. "There is much, if not more, money for me in business with my brother, and as it's a surer game I am going to accept it. I have had my best day on the diamond, and there is no prospect of my ever making again as much as I made when I was at my best. I have many good friends in St. Louis, but my interest calls me to Chicago and other pastures."[2] Cuthbert believed Caruthers, but others raised an eyebrow at the declaration.

Watkins wasn't satisfied, for one. Later in the month, he traveled to Chicago to sign Caruthers as well as catcher Dick Buckley. Watkins got to town just in time. Caruthers had signed on to coach baseball during the winter at the University of Illinois and was at the train station when Watkins caught up with him. The two quickly agreed to terms, although nothing was signed (Buckley signed, so it was a productive trip).

Caruthers arrived in St. Louis on March 14 after his stint at Illinois (which went 14–8 that season), ready to work and train down south. The next day, the Browns released him and named Quinn captain. Earlier, Watkins indicated that Caruthers agreed to pitch—off-season rule changes had the distance moved to 60 feet, 6 inches, and a mound and pitching rubber would be used instead of a box—but when he was let go, it was reported that such wasn't the case. Browns secretary George Munson remarked, "Bob Caruthers told me that his pitching days are over, and I fully believe him."[3] Watkins felt his team had too many outfielders, and Caruthers became expendable.

There were other rumors as to Caruthers' demise with the Browns. He asked for his release after St. Louis wanted him to pitch. One had him pulling some chicanery on the train and an angry Von der Ahe and Watkins getting rid of him, which wasn't true as he was released before the team left St. Louis. Another claimed Von der Ahe cut Caruthers due to a squabble over, what else, money.

WILMOT, L. F., Washington
Copyrighted by GOODWIN & CO. 1887

OLD JUDGE
CIGARETTES.
GOODWIN & CO., New York.

Walt Wilmot said over the years that he was often mistaken for Bob Caruthers. In 1893, Caruthers replaced Wilmot in the Chicago outfield, albeit temporarily (Library of Congress).

Freed from St. Louis, Caruthers went looking for work. Chicago needed an outfielder as one of their starters, Walt Wilmot, decided to remain at his job as cashier at a bank in St. Paul. Ironically, over the years Wilmot was told that he looked like Caruthers, with people often talking to him in a case of mistaken identity. With Wilmot confirming his plan, the Colts, as they were now referred, signed Caruthers. Cleveland had also been trying to sign Caruthers, and Bill Barnie, now managing Louisville, thought he had a deal for Caruthers to join his team.

Chicago, under the guidance of Adrian Anson, played various teams in Chattanooga and Atlanta, with Caruthers appearing in every game in center field and batting leadoff. However, in a letter to team president Jim Hart, Anson ominously wrote, "Caruthers' arm is still sore, but otherwise he is all right. I have quite a job on my hands in picking the outfield. I have only six outfielders to select from."[4]

On Opening Day in Cincinnati on April 27, Caruthers led off for Chicago in right field, with Jimmy Ryan in center. He went 0-for-3 with a walk as the Colts were crushed, 10–1. The next day, he was out of the lineup with Ryan leading off and, as players who weren't going to play did to earn their keep, worked as a ticket-taker. When asked if Chicago was going to drop Caruthers, Anson told a reporter, "No, sir. If I don't use him in the outfield, he'll come in handy as a pitcher."[5] Two days later, Caruthers was released, as well as a second baseman named Taylor.

"Caruthers' arm is in bad shape," said Hart, who paid Caruthers $50 for his short service and not the $100 the player thought he deserved. "But for this fact I would not have released him."[6] Anson was more succinct about the men let go: "They were no good."[7]

Caruthers must have known this was coming. His release was conducted at the Gibson House in Cincinnati. The *Cincinnati Enquirer* reported that 10 minutes later, Charles Comiskey signed him to play for the Red Stockings, reuniting him not only with his one-time St. Louis captain but also former Browns teammates Silver King and Arlie Latham. "One thing in his favor is the fact that he is a winner," said the *Enquirer* of Caruthers. "He knows something about playing championship ball."[8]

Before playing for his new team, Caruthers went back to Chicago for a few days to settle some affairs, perhaps to pay off a lawsuit he lost a couple of weeks earlier—the plaintiff was his uncle, William McNeill. Caruthers had occasion, after nights of unsuccessful gambling, to borrow $100 from time to time (and time and time again) from McNeill in order to retrieve collateral, such as a watch or a diamond pin, he had put up to secure money from the house to keep playing.

Caruthers returned to Cincinnati in time for the Red Stockings' series opener on May 5 against, of all teams, St. Louis. He had three singles against his former team and on his lone out, "drove one that almost tore off one of Kid Gleason's hands."[9] In the 10th inning, Caruthers picked up an assist, relaying a hit to shortstop George "Germany" Smith, his former Brooklyn teammate, who threw to third baseman Arlie Latham, who tagged Steve Brodie out trying for a triple. Cincinnati won, 3–2, in 11 innings. "Bobby Carruthers felt very much elated over yesterday's victory,"[10] wrote the *Cincinnati Enquirer.*

Over the next two games, Caruthers went 2-for-5 with a run and steal in a 3–1, 13-inning win over the Browns and 4-for-6 with two runs and another steal (note: modern-day stats list Caruthers with just one stolen base with the Red Stockings, but box scores of the day had him with four) in a 16–7 victory over Louisville. "One of the few prizes that Dame Fortune has dropped in the lap of Cincinnati is the way of base-ball finds Bob Carruthers, so far, has shown ear-marks of being the best," the *Enquirer* effused.

Caruthers tailed off, going 1-for-10 with two walks as Pittsburgh came into Cincinnati and took three games. More important was some off-the-field news. May 12 was the failure of the Columbia Bank of Chicago, a week after the collapse of the New York Stock Exchange, with numerous branches closing. The Caruthers family had money in the Columbia Bank, and Bob was considered "a heavy loser"[11] with the closures. The so-called "Panic of 1893" was the beginning of the downfall of the Caruthers' wealth. Flora Caruthers wasn't listed in the 1900 census, hardly a good sign for someone who at one point was affluent and had various real estate holdings, and by 1910 she was living with her daughter, who ran a boarding house.

Caruthers didn't let the news affect him on the field, as the next day he walked four times and delivered a run-scoring single in the fifth inning as Cincinnati beat Chicago, 10–8. The following afternoon, May 14, the first contest played at Chicago's new West Side Grounds, he came up in a 12-all tie in the ninth inning, the Reds having scored three times, with two runners on and two out. He hit a sharp grounder to Colts second baseman George Decker, the ball bouncing, hitting Decker in the leg, and rolling away as Charles Comiskey came home with the winning run.

On May 15 in St. Louis, a game was marred by a fight between Cincinnati catcher Henry Vaughn and the Browns' Steve Brodie. After a collision at home, Vaughn went after Brodie with a bat, throwing it at him and hitting Brodie near the head, and eventually Vaughn had to be escorted from the park by police. Caruthers hit his 29th and final major league home run, a two-run shot off Kid Gleason in the second inning.

Over his next four games, Caruthers had only two hits but did walk twice, was hit by a pitch, stole a base, and scored five runs. However, at some point during a series in Cleveland, he injured his thumb and had difficulty throwing. He was listed in the lineup for the May 20 finale against the Spiders, but Vaughn ended up playing right field.

Cincinnati owner and president John T. Brush fancied a player named Jud "Spokane" Smith (he was from Michigan, with no reason given for his nickname, which appeared in the May 22, 1893, *Cincinnati Enquirer*), a speedy infielder who had been signed in the off-season from Butte of the Montana State League but had yet to play in a game. Once again, Caruthers was supposed to play May 21—he was in the lineup and warming up before the game—but Smith was a late substitute and made his major league debut in a 9–8 home loss to St. Louis. Later that night, Caruthers was released by Cincinnati. Comiskey didn't want to let Caruthers go, but Brush wasn't happy with his play and thought Smith deserved a longer look (Smith lasted all of 17 games, nine of those in the outfield, where he committed four errors, a .750 fielding percentage, before he, too, was released).

This time, no offers from big-league clubs were forthcoming, although Caruthers was holding out hope for an offer from Washington—the worst team in the league, which had a couple of older light hitters, including his former doesn't-play-on-Sundays Brooklyn teammate, Paul Radford, and 42-year-old Jim O'Rourke in the outfield. However, no proposal from the Senators was forthcoming. At just 28 years old, his major-league career was over. Caruthers indicated he was headed to Atlanta, with the Southern Association team of that city—George Darby, a pitcher released by Cincinnati the same day as Caruthers, signed there—but he never made it. It's likely that troubles at home interceded. His daughter, Dorothy, born the previous July, died June 24. No cause of death was given, but it's likely she became quite ill, with Caruthers staying in Chicago to be with her and his family.

Cincinnati owner John T. Brush wasn't happy with the play of Bob Caruthers and released him despite the objection of manager Charles Comiskey.

An opportunity did arise in early July. When no umpire was at Chicago's game against Washington on July 9, Caruthers stepped in. "His work was fair,"[12] said the *Chicago Tribune*. Later that summer, National League president Nick Young was looking for an official and signed Caruthers as a substitute umpire, which wasn't that much of a surprise as the league official had an affection for the former player. When Caruthers signed with Chicago back in March, Young wired Colts team president Jim Hart: "He is a huckleberry; fire along his contract; Caruthers is a good man."[13]

Caruthers ended up umpiring only a week or so of games, all in Chicago from August 12–20—ironically, his first series was the Colts playing Cincinnati, the two teams for which he played that season. He was praised early but by the end of his run, "the Chicago papers have with absolute unanimity condemned Bobby Caruthers as an umpire."[14] Reported *Sporting Life*: "Bobby Caruthers has been guessing balls and strikes for Nick Young with about as much success as he guessed horses in the past few years."[15]

While Caruthers was said to lament his decision to take on the job, he nevertheless applied to be an umpire in the Western League for 1894. Caruthers ended up in the Western League that year—but not as an officiator.

Back to Where It All Began

It's hard to pinpoint when Bob Caruthers started to lack the financial wherewithal he had earlier in his baseball career. We know he was sued for $4,000 by his uncle, Alexander McNeill, in 1890, was ruled to owe another uncle, William McNeill (both Alexander and William were half-brothers of Flora Caruthers) $1,500, and in late 1894, he lost another judgement to Alexander, this for $300.

Of course, Caruthers was bankrolled by his mother, thanks to the will of his grandfather. That money started to dry up as well beginning with the Panic of 1893, which led to a depression in the United States which lasted for a few years. Suddenly, it wasn't just uncles suing nephews for borrowed money due to gambling losses. The Caruthers and McNeill families started going after each other even more. In addition to the suits against Bob Caruthers, his brother James sued an uncle, Malcom McNeill, for $2,000 in 1890. In March 1894, Flora filed fraud charges against her brother, Malcom, alleging that he converted property which belonged to her and invested it elsewhere under his wife's name, costing Flora $50,000. (The point would be moot; upon his death in 1917, it was noted that McNeill "was quite successful in business until the financial depression of 1893–95 caused him to lose all his previous gains."[1])

Weeks later, Flora Caruthers turned her sights on her oldest son, James, who, according to Flora, had borrowed $75,000 to open his hardware business, which just recently had gone belly-up. She looked to recoup and was represented by a former county attorney named Edward Terhune, who happened to be the husband of Flora's daughter, Elizabeth. Things got heated during a deposition at which James took offense at some of the hardline questioning surrounding the money and subsequently accused Terhune and his sister of living the high life at the Lexington Hotel on money provided by his mother. A nasty fight broke out between several participants in the room, with James throwing a spittoon at Terhune's head and the meeting coming to an abrupt end.

The following year, Flora headed to Circuit Court to try to fend off a $6,500 trust deed from being foreclosed. She said the deed was actually James', which he forced her to sign under duress with, as the *Chicago Tribune* reported, "threats of death and by repeated acts of cruelty. She further says her son has extorted from her and squandered thousands of dollars."[2] In October 1895, James Caruthers was arrested for embezzling $5,000 from Kelly, Maus & Co., a hardware company which employed him as a salesman (that figure was later lowered to $1,172, and he was acquitted in January), while his sister, Elizabeth Terhune, added him to a fraud lawsuit on a note of debt, which she said was assigned to her by her mother, for $42,000. James Caruthers declared bankruptcy in 1902, although Elizabeth still had some holdings (it's little wonder why she didn't share with her brother), but she saw that taken from under her by two of her uncles, Flora's brothers, Thomas and Rivers McNeill, who sold a property which was then to be torn down even though Elizabeth's name was on the lease and she didn't sign the deed.

All that being said, we can see why Bob Caruthers was quick to find work. It all came full circle for him. His first professional team was in Grand Rapids, and that's where he signed in December 1893, one of the first players to affix his name to a contract. Grand Rapids was in the Western League, which played for roughly five weeks in 1893 before disbanding. It was reorganized in 1894 with Ban Johnson hired as league president. The circuit flourished under his reign, evolving into the American League.

The Western League was not the major leagues, however. A $1,700 salary limit per month—for the entire team—was in effect. Caruthers signed for $175 per month. The other four early signees amounted to $635 combined, or just under $160 a month. While Caruthers was a long way from the thousands he earned in the American Association and National League, he was still commanding a premium price, albeit on a much smaller scale. Upon learning of Caruthers' signing, Johnson wrote George Ellis, who founded the club, "I am pleased to note that you have signed Carruthers. He will come mighty near leading the Western League in batting."[3]

Before he headed to Grand Rapids, Caruthers supplemented his income by coaching baseball at the Indiana University (a job he'd partake in each of the next four years). While there, he was taken with the strong throwing by center fielder Lee Streaker, who turned his attention to the mound, eventually pitching for Birmingham of the Southern League in 1898. "Much to the credit of Bob's coaching, I soon acquired those elements necessary for a good pitcher," Streaker said, "namely control and a good head."[4] Looking back at his tenure in an alumni magazine in 1922, Dr. C.E. Harris wrote, "'Bobby' knew baseball from all angles, having the ability to teach all he knew, a gentleman with much refinement and dearly loved by all the fellows."[5]

After his assignment at Indiana was over, Caruthers went to Grand Rapids, where he saw at least one recognizable face on his new team, known as the Rippers: George Pinkney, who played with him in Brooklyn and St. Louis. There were several other former major leaguers on the roster, including infielder Bobby Wheelock and outfielders Fred Carroll, Bill George, and Rasty Wright, the latter of whom served as team captain (at least to start). Another was pitcher Jocko Schmit—better known as Crazy Schmit during his time in the big leagues (1890, 1892–1893, 1899, and 1901), and for good reason. After winning a game on May 14, Schmit, who was never one to turn down a drink, went on a bender and didn't show up at the next day's game. He was later found passed out near the Grand River and then picked a fight with Wright. He was put on a train back to his home in Chicago the next day.

That incident paled in comparison to that of Edgar McNabb, who pitched for Baltimore in 1893 and was considered a jewel of a signing for Grand Rapids, scheduled to be the team's ace. But in February, he committed a murder-suicide in a Pittsburgh hotel room, killing his girlfriend, an actress who happened to be the wife (although she left him to be with McNabb, they were not divorced) of the president of the Pacific Northwest League.

Grand Rapids could have used McNabb, a sober, effective Schmit, or any good pitching for that matter. Offense exploded in 1894. In the National League, teams averaged over seven runs per game. Philadelphia hit .350—and finished in fourth place. The moving of the pitching distance to 60 feet, 6 inches in 1893 was surely a factor. In the NL the league batting average jumped from .280 to .309 the first year of the new distance to the plate.

The Western League saw similar results. Double-digit scoring was common-place, and often both teams tallied 10 or more runs in the same game. "There was never such a slaughter of base ball pitchers in the United States as there has been this season," observed the *Grand Rapids Herald* at the end of June. "The extra ten feet added to the pitcher's distance is killing them off every day and before the season ends it is safe to predict that the associations will find it necessary to shorten the distance at least five feet another year."[6] The *Grand Rapids Democrat* had another theory. "The Reach ball is largely responsible for the high scores made in the Western League so far," the paper postulated in early May. "It is so lively that a square bit sends it a long distance."[7] Caruthers wasn't too pleased with all the runs, a view which he expressed in a January 1895 interview: "The public does not like the big scores. The smaller the score the better the game is almost the universal opinion. Personally I care nothing about the subject, but I believe the game was more attractive when there was not so much batting."[8]

On June 9, Sioux City, led by Bill Watkins, the manager who replaced Caruthers in St. Louis, won at Grand Rapids, 31–10 (it didn't help that the Rippers made 10 errors). On July 24 in Kansas City, Grand Rapids fell, 39–10, with Harley Parker pitching a complete game and allowing 38 hits (the Rippers made 12 errors in this one). Grand Rapids could score runs, too. In the first game of an August 19 doubleheader at home vs. Detroit, the Rippers won, 36–10, with Bill George going 8-for-8 (he went 13-for-13 in the two games), Carroll scoring seven times, Wheelock stealing five bases, and Grand Rapids hitting five home runs, with Caruthers, who had four hits and scored five runs, getting the final one in the ninth inning.

Minneapolis, taking advantage of short fences, hit an unheard-of (for that time period) 196 home runs, with five players having 20+ and three 30+ (Caruthers' former Browns teammate, Perry Werden, cranked 43). The Millers batted .363 as a team and averaged 9.1 runs per game, but like the NL's Phillies, finished fourth in the Western League.

Caruthers, playing mostly first base, hit .331—which sounds very good, but that put him fifth on the team (among players with at least 120 at-bats). Both George and Wright batted .423, which left them short of league leader Hunkey Hines of Minneapolis, who came in at .427. Upon Caruthers' suggestion, Brooklyn obtained Hines in February 1895, although his major-league career would consist of just two games.

In early June, Caruthers took over as captain from Wheelock, who had replaced Wright a couple of weeks earlier. His management style was lauded by the local papers. "Grand Rapids has made a great spurt out in the field. They have got down to playing what seems to be good unison team ball. Keep up this kind of work, Captain Caruthers,"[9] enthused the *Grand Rapids Herald*. The *Democrat* said of Caruthers, "As a captain he is teaching the Rustlers to sacrifice and play the points of the game."[10]

From July 5–13, he captained the team to a season-high nine-game winning streak while proving he was still valuable with the stick, too. During the streak, he hit in each game, five times had three or four hits, and in another game had two. "The boys have all fattened their averages in the last few games," said the *Grand Rapids Herald*. "Every player asks Capt. Caruthers advice when men are on bases. The best of feeling prevails among the players and all seem equally anxious to win."[11] A couple of weeks earlier, on June 23 in a 9–6 home win over Indianapolis, he socked "as pretty a home run drive as has been seen here this year."[12]

Caruthers was also showing off his toughness. On July 20, a throw to first from catcher Harry Spies broke his right index finger, the damage bad enough that his bone broke through the skin. He came out of the game for the final three innings—but it was the only time he missed all season. Caruthers was back in the lineup the next day, but in right field. On July 23, he was stationed back at first base.

He displayed his veteran wiles in a game at Sioux City on August 3. In the first inning, after Cornhuskers pitcher Bumpus Jones started him off with two balls, Caruthers did a 180 in the batter's box. It was a ploy to mess with the mind of Jones, and it worked as the next two pitches were balls as well.

An incident in Toledo on August 7 hinted at another side of Caruthers, one which was common knowledge but often just referred to: his drinking. Caruthers showed up late to Grand Rapids' game that day, often a sign he'd be out drinking the night before, or perhaps got an early start to his day. These instances would occur more often as time passed. Caruthers imbibed, as the majority of ballplayers did, throughout his career (we know he got drunk at the St. Louis Browns banquet in 1886, for example). Boozing was an issue throughout baseball, one which fans noticed, too. "The cranks have been continually complaining because certain players were drinking," Ellis said in mid–September.

"That was the reason Killeen [pitcher Harvey Killeen, who pitched for three Western League teams in 1894 and none effectively] was dropped and the weeding out will continue until not a boozer is left. Taken as a whole we have less drinking in the club than any team in the league."[13]

In addition to the drinking atmosphere present among his contemporaries, Caruthers' father apparently was an alcoholic, or enough of a heavy drinker that he was chastised by the Illinois Supreme Court. Alcohol would be Caruthers' eventual downfall. This episode might have been the beginning of his journey down that road.

Overall, the 1894 season went well enough for Caruthers. He got good notice as a captain and hit well. The team finished in fifth place at 62–64 but were 41–22 at home, winning eight of its final 12 games, which had to leave the home faithful at least somewhat pleased.

Grand Rapids reserved Caruthers, and there was talk of him returning as the first baseman or in the outfield. Of course, Caruthers, as usual, made other claims, once again saying he might stay in Chicago and work in the hardware business and, according to *Sporting Life*, "does not care much whether he plays ball or not next year."[14] And again, Caruthers' talk wasn't taken seriously, especially by a couple of his former teammates. "In the heyday of Bob's success he threatened to retire into the hardware business," said Dave Foutz, who was still playing in Brooklyn, "but he still sticks to the diamond, and even a four and a half months' contract does not scare him into retirement."[15]

John Montgomery Ward, Caruthers' nemesis for one year in Brooklyn who retired following the 1894 season to practice law, took a shot at his old teammate, even if some of the evidence he presented wouldn't hold up in a court.

The very players who when in the zenith of their playing glory were accustomed to talk about getting out of the game and taking up other lines of business about signing time every year, in order to squeeze more salary out of their clubs, are the very last to get out of harness. Parisian Bob Caruthers and Orator James O'Rourke are two cases in sight. Parisian Bobby, who, by the way, is of a wealthy and influential family, and who used to spring the business gag every year about signing time, is now signed to a $1000 contract with the Bay City team. There was a time when Bob wanted about twice that amount as a bonus for signing a contract.[16]

But, true to form, after another stint coaching at Indiana University, Caruthers was in Grand Rapids in April with the team now known as the Gold Bugs. From April

13–16, he umpired a three-game series in Grand Rapids between the Gold Bugs and Page Fence Giants, an all–Black team formed by Bud Fowler in the off-season which had just begun play a week earlier. After the finale, Caruthers was given his release by Ellis, who was happy with the practices of new first baseman Pete Cassidy. Caruthers had been kept around as insurance and now was no longer needed.

He wasn't out of work long, quickly signing with the Jacksonville (Illinois) Jacks in the Western Association. After playing in an exhibition, Caruthers didn't travel with the team to St. Joseph—perhaps moving his family to the Dunlap House, a three-story hotel where Mark Twain stayed in 1869—and when he joined the team in Des Moines, it already had a new manager, shortstop Bill Deveney having replaced Jake Aydelott after just three games. A couple of weeks later, after a 3–10 start, Caruthers was put in charge. His salary for the season, which now included these extra duties, was $1,200. In his first game as manager, May 18, Deveney didn't show up and one of Jacksonville's best players, Bill Zeis, was injured. The Jacks lost, 11–1.

Jacksonville was not a good team. Caruthers tried all spring and summer to have a better roster, but it wasn't easy. "Manager Caruthers says the Jacksonville boys are outclassed," reported the *Quincy Daily Herald*. "He is trying to find new men and is after them hard. However, he finds it uphill work."[17] Caruthers even pitched a few times, something he hadn't done since 1892, and for the first time it was on a mound and from

The Page Fence Giants circa 1896. In 1895, Bob Caruthers umpired exhibition games involving the Giants shortly after their founding.

a further distance than he was used to. On May 31, he was the third of three Jacksonville pitchers in a 22–7 loss at Quincy. The *Quincy Daily Whig*'s report of Caruthers' effort was that "his arm was not what it was in the days when Brooklyn paid St. Louis $6,000 for him, and the boys batted him all over the field."[18] He pitched the final four innings, allowing eight runs. He was better in relief on July 30 in a 10–1 loss to Des Moines, giving up three runs in six innings. His last appearance on the mound was August 6, when he started and pitched a complete game at home, falling to Lincoln, 6–5. Depending on the report, he allowed six, seven or eight hits but walked six and wasn't helped by six Jacks errors. "Had he had good support, he certainly would have won the game, and considering that he has had but little practice he did wonderfully well,"[19] said the *Jacksonville Daily Journal.*

The losses kept piling up, and Caruthers was under pressure to win. Looking for players of his own in the Midwest, Pittsburgh manager Connie Mack ran into Caruthers in Peoria. "He showed me a telegram from his employers," Mack said, "in which they roasted him for having lost a few games, winding up by telling him that the team would have to win oftener, or they would know the reason why."[20]

The stress of losing, only magnified by Jacksonville management, was enough to drive a man to drink. For Caruthers, that was a short trip. "Word comes from Jacksonville, Ill., that the Western association team there is leading a hard life under Capt. Bobby Caruthers," read a wire report in the *Indianapolis Sun.* "He will, it is said, go off on one of his still boozes, come on to the grounds the next day, play rotten himself and fine everybody in sight unless they are angelic."[21]

Making matters worse, even when he had good players, he lost them. Jacksonville signed "Happy Joe" Katz, a veteran of a few minor league seasons, in the off-season to a relatively higher-priced contract. The board of directors wanted him to take a pay cut. Katz refused and was released. He finished the year with St. Joseph and in 82 combined games between the two clubs, he batted .338 and scored 121 runs.

Caruthers had to resort to nearly anything to field a competitive team. On August 17 in Lincoln, he gave an amateur pitcher named Doc Cronley a chance—and he won, 8–7. Caruthers quickly offered him a contract for the remainder of the season, but Cronley passed; he had just wanted to see how he'd fare. He never played another game of professional ball.

Fans stopped turning out to games in Jacksonville, with the count regularly under 100. The team also played some games in Springfield, which drew better crowds. While the team was playing in St. Joseph, it was announced that the franchise was being shifted to Springfield. It was a change in team name only as the newly tabbed Springfield lost, 9–3, to drop its record to 32–62, last in the eight-team league.

Springfield won its next game—but that would be the last. After an 8–3 victory, a wire was sent to bring the team back home. On August 22, the Jacksonville/Springfield team was disbanded. Denver, which had financial issues—players were owed more than $300, and only $20 had been paid out since the beginning of August—dropped out of the Western Association. To make it an even six teams in the league, Springfield was sacrificed.

The players gathered at Cassell Bros. cigars in Jacksonville for their final paycheck. Already not pleased at losing out on a month's pay due to the team folding, players' tempers flared often. Knowing he'd likely see few of his teammates again, Caruthers approached catcher Frank Belt, to obtain money the manager said Belt owed him. After the catcher said he wouldn't pay, the two fought, with Caruthers striking Belt in the face, causing a nasty cut with a copious amount of blood spilling forth.

Opportunities opened for several players, who signed with other teams in the Western. Caruthers, whose .321 average was best among the remaining Springfield players (he also scored 100 runs in just 92 games), played in a couple of amateur games but turned his eye back to umpiring, hired by the Western Association—which was back to eight teams after adding two teams from the Eastern Iowa League, Burlington and Dubuque—on September 1.

His first assignment was in Burlington, and he was received favorably, the *Burlington Gazette* commenting, "Bobby Carruthers makes an ideal umpire. He shows no favoritism, and his decisions are invariably accompanied by wisdom and good judgment."[22] The *Dubuque Daily Times* said Caruthers "is the best umpire that has been sent here this season, and all things considered he has been very fair."[23] It wasn't just the newspapers. Jay Andrews, who played for Des Moines, in a letter to a friend wrote of Caruthers: "I can say he is head and shoulders over any minor league umpire I ever saw. He is fine on balls and strikes and base decisions. If the National League is looking for good, first-class material, they need not expect to find a better man than Caruthers."[24]

In 1889, Caruthers mused about life after baseball. He wondered, "Why does not some entertaining genius ascertain from prominent ball players why they play ball and what they propose doing when their connection with the diamond ceases?"[25] In his experience, he said, he'd seen several different outcomes.

> To some ball-playing is strictly a business, and a very unpleasant one. Their idea is to make enough money out of playing to set up in business and talk ball to their customers. Others live right up to their incomes, never save a cent, and commence borrowing a week after the season is over. There are also quite a number who play ball rather from choice than from necessity, and who never have ample means outside their baseball salaries. These last look at the game as a pastime, none the less enjoyable because it is profitable, and regard a season or two's work as good training and conducive to health.[26]

Caruthers clearly didn't listen to his own words. As the 1895 offseason commenced and the new year approached, he had several ideas about what he could do but no concrete plan. After all the talk about going into business in Chicago, though, it was fairly obvious by now that Caruthers was a baseball lifer. What life he'd lead next, however, was unclear.

Resignations of an Umpire

Pitcher, player, manager, umpire—Bob Caruthers hoped to add another title to his resume: magnate. Caruthers had his eyes on operating a team in Cedar Rapids, which had been in the Eastern Iowa League in 1895, but the town hoped to join the Western Association. He talked a good game and was said to have the backing of local fans—with his (and his mother's) financial situation, he was in no position to front a franchise with money of his own.

Cedar Rapids did end up joining the Western Association in 1896, although it was not Caruthers leading the franchise but a local businessman, Al Franchere, who owned a department store with his brother and had the finances to back the team.

In November 1895, there was a rumor that Caruthers was going to take over managing Sioux City, but that franchise ended up being ousted from the Western Association.

While waiting for his next move, Caruthers acted upon his other experience: gambler. On November 1, still in Jacksonville, where he lived with his family throughout the winter, Caruthers went to see a man named James Browner. The two played craps, and eventually a discrepancy led to a fight, which spilled out of the room and outside onto the street. Caruthers extricated himself from the tussle, but a drunken Browner followed—there was no report of Caruthers being intoxicated, but he made his way towards a bar, where Browner caught up with him and the fight resumed. Browner took out a knife and slashed Caruthers on the arm while slicing his own hand in the process. Browner was charged with attempted murder but posted a $100 bond eight days later. There is no record of the result of the arrest, but apparently there was no punishment as eight months later Browner was arrested again, this time for disturbing the peace (on this he pled guilty and paid $3 plus court costs).

That type of incident probably served Caruthers well as preparation for becoming an umpire—not only did players try to intimidate umps, but also fans would come out of the stands and brandish weapons if they were especially displeased with how things were going for the home club—which was the gig he eventually landed, signing on to officiate in the Western Association (after another stint coaching at the Indiana University for a few weeks).

Caruthers' opening assignment was in Quincy, and neither the team nor the fans appreciated his work. On Opening Day, he fined three Quincy players $10 each and quickly drew the ire of the local papers, which blamed him for several losses. One, the *Quincy Journal*, called for his firing. Things were better for Caruthers in Burlington. "With Caruthers umpiring the landscape from the grand stand seems brighter and there is an air of dignity pervading a game that is absolutely refreshing after having been obliged to be in the presence of Allen the strongarm,"[1] observed the *Burlington Hawk*

Bob Caruthers (middle top row) coached at Indiana University during a few off seasons. This is the 1896 Hoosiers team, with Odie Porter to the left of Caruthers. Porter pitched one game for the Philadelphia Athletics in 1902, making him the first Indiana alum to appear in the majors (courtesy Indiana University Archives).

Eye. The *Burlington Gazette* was flattering, saying, "Carruthers umpires all right, and is the best that ever came over the plank,"[2] but also noted "the 'rooters' didn't enjoy his decisions at all times."[3]

If the fans weren't happy with Caruthers as an umpire, they soon were pleased that he was the team's manager. While umpiring in Burlington, Caruthers agreed to take over as a player-manager for the Colts and oversee all personnel decisions. He'd be paid $200 a month, a $75 raise over his salary as an umpire. Caruthers was quick to release three players, including former manager Paul Hines—perhaps learning his lesson from previous stops, when managers were fired but remained on the team—who had led Burlington to a 9–17 record, in sixth place. He also acquired five players, including second baseman Harry Scholler, whom Caruthers coached at Indiana, and shortstop Wallace Hollingsworth, obtained from St. Paul, which was owned by Caruthers' former teammate and manager, Charles Comiskey.

Caruthers, still wearing his blue umpire cap, put himself at first base—Hines' position—and batted third in his debut, May 28 at home against St. Joseph. He showed off some veteran wiles on a steal of second. Taking advantage of a billowing of dirt, Caruthers got control of the baseball and chucked into the outfield, then raced around the bases for a run. Burlington, however, lost, 9–8, in extra innings. "A noticeable improvement could be plainly seen in the team work, and the coaching, which was never heard in the grand stand before, sounded like two fog horns," said the *Burlington*

Gazette. "He was in the game every minute and ready to take advantage of every play that would help the Colts to win. Caruthers is just the man we have been looking for, and under his leadership Burlington will land some place among the bunch on top."[4]

However, much like the previous year in Jacksonville, this was not a strong team. Caruthers kept trying to change the roster, even signing another college protégé in catcher George Huff out of the University of Illinois, but after losing five straight to Des Moines (which at 34–7 was running away with the Western Association), Burlington was 17–32 and in seventh place. Caruthers remained upbeat, however. "If you will look at the standing of the clubs you will find that the club occupying second place, has won but twelve more games than Burlington [Peoria was 28–17]," said Caruthers, who was 8–15 since taking over as manager. "If it had not been for Burlington's unfortunate start in the race, losing nearly a dozen games out of the first fifteen, we would be high up in the list. I have several new men coming that will add strength to the team and put us on equal terms with the best clubs in the league. When we leave Des Moines, if I can get the men I expect, we should take fifteen out of the next twenty games."[5]

On May 23, Caruthers added another description to his growing biography: hero. After Burlington's 9–7 win at St. Joseph, the team was headed back to its hotel on an electric streetcar. On the other side of the tracks, another trolley had stopped to let off a Mrs. Dalhoff, who started to cross over to her destination when she tripped and fell— right in the path of the oncoming car carrying the Burlington team. The trolley conductor attempted to stop, but the car was going too fast and barreling down on the woman. Caruthers, sitting in a front seat, quickly hopped down onto the tracks, picked up Dalhoff and moved them both out of the way. "A second later she would have been crushed to death," reported the *St. Joseph Gazette.* "Caruthers assisted her to the sidewalk, tipped his hat and sprang back on the car, paying no more attention to the congratulations bestowed upon him than if the risking of his life to save others was an hourly occurrence."[6] "The car was already so close to her that but for Carruthers' presence of mind in springing from his seat on the front end and jerking her off the track, she would doubtless have been seriously hurt and possibly killed outright,"[7] concurred the *St. Joseph News-Press.* "Robert Caruthers … is a hero in every sense of the word,"[8] espoused the *Gazette.*

Back on the ballfield, Burlington kept losing, dropping seven of eight after the trolley incident. On July 2, adding injury to insult, Caruthers was run into while playing first base and broke his collarbone. There happened to be a doctor at the ballpark, who came down and snapped it back into place. Caruthers passed out. It was reported that he would miss at least three weeks. Burlington didn't play again until a July 4 doubleheader, and after sitting out the opening game, Caruthers played in the second contest, to the delight of the home crowd, which gave him a nice ovation. "I know when I am able to play better than the doctor does,"[9] Caruthers said afterwards. Ten days later, he hit his first home run of the season, a three-run shot in the ninth inning of yet another Burlington loss, 10–8 at Cedar Rapids.

The Western Association was crumbling, however. Quincy dropped out of the league on July 16, and St. Joseph was kicked out—guilty of being located too far from the remaining teams. The circuit declared Des Moines the winner of the first half—Burlington was last at 25–48—with the now-six-team league embarking on a new second half. The Colts started out 3–2, tied for first place, with Caruthers hitting a three-run homer over the right-field fence in Dubuque in an 8–3 victory.

However, days later Peoria folded, followed by Des Moines. Burlington was willing to stick it out in a four-team league, but the Western Association saw the writing on the wall and disbanded completely. In the official statistics disseminated by the league, Caruthers hit .291, good for 21st in the league and fifth on the team (fourth if Hines' .324 in his limited time with the club is excluded). He scored 45 runs and had 23 steals, third on the Colts. "No ball player has been more popular in the city of Burlington than Bob Caruthers,"[10] said the *Burlington Evening Gazette.*

A little over a week after collecting his last paycheck from the Burlington Colts, Caruthers had a new job—back in Ban Johnson's Western League but this time as an umpire. Four games into his tenure, he officiated a game between St. Paul and Minneapolis, which featured seven of his former teammates. Perry Werden was on Minneapolis, while St. Paul was owned and managed by Charles Comiskey, who had on his roster Jack Glasscock, Bill George, Wallace Hollingsworth, Tony Mullane, and Harry Spies, all of whom played with Caruthers at some point along his baseball trail. Caruthers didn't play favorites, ejecting Werden (of course, Werden *had* threatened to decapitate pitcher Roger Denver with his bat after being hit in the head).

Caruthers rapidly got the reputation of taking no guff—this wouldn't change over the years—quickly kicking players out of the game for strenuous arguing. On August 20, Kansas City's Jimmy Callahan used language a bit too salty for Caruthers' taste, and he was ejected and removed from the ballpark. Blues owner, manager, and second baseman Jim Manning sided with the umpire over his own player. "I like to see an umpire who is the boss of the field. That's one thing I like about Caruthers," Manning said. "He may sometimes be a little hasty in putting players off the field, but if one of my men kicks too hard, or uses language which is [not] innocent, I will be the last man to object to him being put out of the game."[11]

While he gained good notice from locales such as St. Paul ("his work was strictly first-class. ... His work on balls and strikes was particularly good and neither pitcher had any just cause for complaint"[12]), Kansas City newspapers were not as kind. "When in the dim and distant future the record of utterly ignorant and miserably incompetent umpires shall be made up, lo! Bob Caruthers' name will head all the rest,[13]" said the *Kansas City Daily Journal.* "As an umpire Bob Carruthers is a dismal failure," chastised the *Kansas City Times.* "He had better return to dealing faro." The papers regularly accused Caruthers of conspiring against the Blues. "Caruthers Does Not Intend to Let Them Win,"[14] intoned one subheadline in the *Daily Journal*, which accused him of "deliberately"[15] making bad calls to cost Kansas City a pair of games in a doubleheader.

As Caruthers entered the Kansas City ballpark on September 6 for a doubleheader between Detroit and Kansas City, "he was greeted by a furious storm of hisses."[16] One fan yelled out to him, "We've got a rope for you if you are dishonest today."[17] It wasn't the home team which Caruthers had to worry about that day but the visitors. In the first inning, Detroit's Lew Whistler argued a called strike—the partisan *Kansas City Daily Journal* claimed the "ball was over his head"[18]—and was fined $5 by Caruthers, which turned to $10 and an ejection from the grounds with a police escort. The mood was set. In the fourth, Hunkey Hines, the same player Caruthers recommended to Brooklyn a year earlier, objected to being called out on a close play at first, as did his Tigers teammates, who rushed onto the field, surrounding, yelling at, and cursing Caruthers.

That was enough for Caruthers. He quit on the spot, didn't umpire the second game (players from each team took his place), and sent his resignation to Johnson, who tried to get Caruthers to stay on, but his five telegrams went unanswered. Caruthers returned to Burlington, now settled with his family, and played some semi-pro baseball the remainder of the fall.

After enduring a tough off-season—Caruthers broke his ankle on Christmas and in March saw Dave Foutz succumb to tuberculosis at age 40, the third teammate from his Browns heyday to die, joining Yank Robinson (1894) and Curt Welch (1896); "Bob says Foutz always looked as if he had consumption."[19]—before resuming his coaching duties at Indiana and signing on to umpire in the Western Association for "$125 a month plus mileage."[20] This time Caruthers made it through the entire season, but it wasn't without its bumps.

On May 20, Quincy pitcher Dan Monroe, unhappy over some ball-strike calls, challenged Caruthers to a fight right there on the Peoria field. "If you want to fight I will accommodate you," Caruthers told the player. "Just come back of the stables here where no one can see us."[21] With the prospect of being away from an audience, Monroe backed down. The next day, Peoria catcher-manager Dan Dugdale, after a call went against his team to end the game, tackled the umpire from behind, but Caruthers quickly took control, getting on top of Dugdale and

Jim Manning, who owned, managed and played for the Kansas City Blues in 1896, praised Bob Caruthers as an umpire, saying he liked someone who was "the boss of the field."

pummeling him before being torn away. An irate crowd flowed onto the field, shouting "Lynch him!"[22] with Peoria third baseman Jimmy Burke helping Caruthers escape the mob. Caruthers sent in his resignation to league president T.J. Hickey, who instead just shifted his assignment to Cedar Rapids, with Caruthers complying.

Keeping Caruthers was something of a coup. Umpires resigned—or were fired—often. Later in the year, fellow Western Association umpire Gus Alberts quit for fear of his life in St. Joseph. "It is absolutely impossible to officiate fairly. The crowds are frightfully partisan and between them and the players the umpire's life is actually in danger," Alberts said of his experience officiating in that city. "Although it is my home, and my family are there, I do not care to work at that place. ... I firmly decline to offici-ate in a city where an umpire must openly rob the visitors, as is the case at St. Joe. That's why I'm out of business."[23]

Caruthers was "afraid of the crowd"[24] in Dubuque and refused to accept any assign-ments there, and in turn that team asked Hickey not to have Caruthers officiate any of its games. Later in the summer, Caruthers did end up in that city, and things went bet-ter than expected, with the fans and players treating him in fine fashion. "His work here since the home series opened has been unequaled,"[25] commented the *Dubuque Daily Times*.

He was also well-regarded in Rockford—the *Rockford Star* said he was the top arbi-ter in the Western Association—and St. Joseph, where the *St. Joseph Herald* said, "His decisions are impartial and as near perfect as possible."[26] The *Sporting Life's* St. Joseph correspondent, one N. Edwards, claimed, "Bobby Caruthers is without any possibility of a doubt the best umpire in the Western Association. He handles the men in excellent shape, and does not allow any back talk."[27]

Caruthers also was complimented in Cedar Rapids, although that took a turn quickly after a 4–3 loss by the hometown Rabbits to St. Joseph on July 14. In the ninth inning, he ruled that the Saints' Billy Kinlock was hit by a pitch instead of, as the locals insisted, it being strike three with the batter offering at the ball (St. Joseph pulled off a three-run rally to win). The Cedar Rapids papers blamed Caruthers for the loss, even though another hit batter, a throwing error, walk, and single followed, and went as far as to accuse the umpire of being intoxicated. "Whether Mr. Carruthers ... tarried too long at certain First avenue bar on Tuesday evening The Gazette does not presume to say," said the *Cedar Rapids Gazette*, "but certainly Bobby was about as far from right as New York is from San Francisco. ... Bob should cease the elbow bending operations and pay strict attention to his official duties."[28]

Another resignation followed, although Caruthers again did not follow through. "I am sorry such a thing happened. I never made a mistake before and am not entirely con-vinced I have done so yet," he told the *Cedar Rapids Times*. "I did the best I could and decided as I saw the play. If the man struck at the ball he was out, but I don't think he did. I have resigned, but Hickey has taken no action as yet. ... I don't blame Cedar Rap-ids, for it was hard luck to lose yesterday's game after it was won."[29]

The comment didn't placate the Cedar Rapids newspapers. After a July 26 contest in which the Rabbits beat Burlington, 12–6, the *Gazette* said it was "a game as full of fea-tures as Bob was of beer"[30] while the *Cedar Rapids Republican's* game story mentions "a drunken umpire."[31]

"Just why President Hickey will keep such a soak on the pay roll is a mystery to the patrons of the game in Cedar Rapids," the *Gazette* pontificated, adding "in all candor and honesty, that the sooner he gives Bob Carruthers his release the better it will be for every team in the association, financially and in every other way. He is a disgrace to the profession, an incubus on the association and the last man whom Mr. Hickey can afford to support."[32] In September, the paper took another dig when Cedar Rapids was play-ing in Peoria: "the fact that Bob Carruthers is umpiring the Peoria games and is within almost hailing distance of the world's greatest distilleries, lent much interest to yester-day's contest."[33] After Caruthers forfeited a game to Rockford in which Cedar Rapids led, 3–2, the *Gazette* noted, "Manager Hill did not stop to argue with the drunken tool of the Rockford team, but loaded his men into a hack and left the grounds."[34]

While the Cedar Rapids fans and press weren't sad to see Caruthers leave town, Burlington welcomed him with open arms. Caruthers hadn't officiated a game in that city since early May when he returned for the final week of the season. He wasn't the most notable name in town—boxer Gentleman Jim Corbett was on a Midwest tour, playing baseball with Western Association teams. Corbett's share of the gate for a September 17 game in which he played first base for Burlington, which lost to Des Moines, 6–5, and went 1-for-5 with 11 putouts and two errors, netted Corbett more money than Caruthers made in a month umpiring (Caruthers also umped a game with Corbett at Rockford a few days earlier). However, it was Caruthers who received a loud ovation when he took the field, whereas the reaction to Corbett, who suffered his first loss as well as the heavyweight title back in March, was tepid.

While it might have been interesting to see what Caruthers would have done if Corbett argued a call, the game, played in front of over 1,200 spectators, went off without a hitch. Unlike those games in Cedar Rapids, Caruthers was praised in Burlington. "The talent were glad to see Bobby Carruthers again, as undoubtedly he is by far the best judge of base ball in the league," opined the *Burlington Evening Gazette*. "It was plainly seen that no kicking or wrangling took place, as Bobby will not stand any such work."[35] Perhaps Caruthers played to the crowd and wiped away home plate with a whisk broom, something he'd taken to using that year (at the time, and early into the 20th century, umpires usually used full-sized brooms).

Having Corbett in town did the trick for Burlington in drawing a nice crowd. But with the boxer moving on to his next stop, the last-place team drew few fans over its final few games. On September 20, only a reported 14 turned out. About the only thing Caruthers didn't do was join Corbett in the field or at the bat. But his playing days weren't over, not just yet.

24

Arbiter Adventures

After the 1897 baseball season, Joe Cantillon and a few of his Dubuque teammates, including future major leaguers Gus Dundon and Billy Sullivan, set sail down the Mississippi River, doing the occasional fishing and hunting while stopping at various towns along the way. One of those was Burlington, Iowa, where Bob Caruthers now decided to reside.

Acting as the gracious host to the group, Caruthers stayed by their side constantly, showing them the town and even serving as a waiter when the ballplayers had a feast with Burlington newspapermen. While Caruthers delivered Cantillon dinner, in the end it was Cantillon who took food off Caruthers' plate.

It was reported in late 1897 and in early 1898 that Caruthers was to be an umpire, once again, in Ban Johnson's Western League. In March, the *Chicago Tribune* reported that the circuit was to have five umpires—Caruthers, Jack Haskell, Al Manassau, Jack Sheridan … and Cantillon. However, with eight teams and a one-umpire system, only four officials were needed. Johnson announced that Haskell, Manassau, and Sheridan were signed. "The selection for the remaining place lies between Cantillion and 'Parisian Bob' Carruthers,"[1] Johnson said.

Johnson chose Cantillon. A look into his decision-making process could be gleaned from a $100 bonus Johnson offered to any of his umpires who didn't miss a game. Caruthers had a history of, on occasion, not showing up. The fact that Johnson considered Caruthers and that Caruthers wanted to rejoin the league after the way he parted in 1896 speaks to Caruthers' ability, the lack of quality umpires, and/or the Western League providing a decent salary compared to other circuits.

While Caruthers did umpire an exhibition game between Burlington and a team from Jacksonville, he was without a job. After the Western League gig fell through, he applied to be an umpire in the Western Association, but it was too near the start of the season, and the staff was already set. However, league president T.J. Hickey said he would find a spot for Caruthers if an opening occurred.

Looking for work, Caruthers was thrown a lifeline by the Burlington team, which was having some employment problems of its own. Second baseman Pete Healey had an issue with the management of the Hawkeyes, as they were now dubbed. Healey played for Burlington the previous season, but that didn't curry him any favors. The team sent him a train ticket, but upon getting his first paycheck, Healey discovered that the fare had been deducted from his salary. Healey objected, refused to play, and was subsequently released.

Burlington looked in its own backyard and signed Caruthers to play right field, with Perry Coons, who had been stationed there, moving to second base. "'Bob's' arm has regained its strength. He can now throw quite well," reported the *Burlington Hawk Eye*. "His batting and fielding was [sic] always good."[2]

Caruthers traveled with the team to Quincy, and in his first game on May 17, he went 0-for-3 with a walk and a stolen base in a 4–2 loss. The next day, he had three hits with a run scored and a steal, and on May 20 in Rockford, he added another hit and walk. Then, just like that, he was gone.

On May 21, Hickey lived up to his promise, hiring Caruthers to be an umpire in the Western Association—yes, the same league in which he had just played three games. Caruthers was replacing Teddy Ready—who had been the umpire when Burlington played in Quincy (the *Quincy Daily Whig* wasn't thrilled with his work, saying, "Umpire Ready's work showed a streak of yellow all the way through."[3])—although Ready returned a little over a week later when another umpire was dismissed.

It turned out to be a smart move by Caruthers. If he had remained a player, he would shortly have been out of a job. On June 6, Burlington folded, with Cedar Rapids following suit. Of course, this also meant that with two fewer clubs—one fewer game per day—one umpire was out of a job as well. Caruthers was concerned that he was the odd man out, but he remained.

On June 18, Caruthers umpired a game in Peoria in which the hometown starter tossed a one-hit shutout. That pitcher was Joe McGinnity, whom Caruthers touted to major league teams, saying, "his delivery is very much like [New York fireballer Amos] Rusie's in speed and variety of curves."[4] McGinnity signed with Baltimore in 1899 as he began his eventual Hall of Fame career.

While McGinnity wasn't on the move until the following year, Caruthers was packing his bags again, leaving the Western Association for another opportunity to umpire in the Western League. However, this job didn't last long either.

Caruthers' latest tenure in the circuit began in Detroit, which was managed by George Stallings, who in his major league debut in 1890 happened to be the catcher with Caruthers pitching. A friendship was certainly not born that day. When Caruthers arrived at Bennett Park, he was greeted by Tigers outfielder Jack Sharrott. The two were longtime friends, and Sharrott warned the umpire, as Caruthers recalled years later, "that Stallings had given his players the tip to go as far as they liked and browbeat me as much as they could. From the first inning of the first game I had my troubles. Each afternoon during my week's stay in that town a crowd of ruffians followed me out of the park and stoned me while I was being driven to my hotel. Oh, but it was exciting, but I stuck through the week without being hurt."[5]

After Detroit lost to St. Joseph, 6–5, on July 19, Caruthers had to duck into a barber shop to avoid the hostile fans who chased him out of the ballpark. The next day, arguments between Detroit players and Caruthers were the norm—it was the worst "'chewing' match of the year,"[6] said the *Detroit Tribune*—as the Tigers lost again. One player, Pat Dillard, eventually was suspended three games by Ban Johnson for incessant swearing at Caruthers. After a big tussle in the seventh inning, Caruthers kicked out Detroit's feisty Kid Elberfeld (and fined him $25). "Say, Bob, how much are you insured for?" one irate spectator threatened. "That barber shop racket won't go tonight."[7] A few policemen had to help Caruthers make it to a streetcar without being beat up.

The arguing didn't end in Detroit. On July 24 in St. Joseph, Caruthers ejected Indianapolis' George Hogreiver in a game which featured "much wrangling."[8] Two days later, Milwaukee's Tom Daly—a teammate of Caruthers' in Brooklyn in 1890 and

1891—already given a warning due to incessant arguing, started cursing out Caruthers after he ruled George Shoch picked off third base. Caruthers fined Daly $25, but that didn't stop the player from continuing his tirade, which got him kicked out of the game and the ballpark. This angered manager Connie Mack, who, after quickly engaging in an argument, found himself also $25 lighter in the wallet and ejected. "Any man that would make a decision like that is a thief,"[9] Mack grumbled as he left the field.

The Detroit papers had already complained about Caruthers—"[his] wretched work has disgusted patrons of the game here,"[10] said the *Detroit Free-Press*—and the St. Joseph scribes quickly followed suit. "Carruthers did some very rank work,"[11] said the *St. Joseph Gazette,* while the *Herald* proclaimed, "Unless Mr. Carruthers does better work as an umpire a petition will be sent to President Johnson asking for his removal from this city. A mistake once in a while is excusable, but when he makes bum decisions all the time then is the time to call a halt."[12]

In a series between, ironically, Detroit and St. Joseph, the newspapers got their wish: Ban Johnson fired Caruthers. The *Free-Press* rejoiced over the news with the sub-headline: "THE INCOMPETENT CARUTHERS HAS AT LAST BEEN DROPPED."[13] The move was made so quickly there was no replacement in town, and players from each team officiated the August 4 game between the two clubs.

Caruthers' time as an umpire was over in 1898, but he was back at the job in 1899. After playing briefly with the semipro Chicago Marquettes—this prompted rumors that he had quit umpiring—Caruthers was back officiating in the Western Association. However, that league didn't even survive two months, disbanding on June 16. Fortunately for Caruthers, the Interstate League had an opening after Eddie Zinram resigned, and on June 24 he presided over his first game in Youngstown, Ohio.

"I believe the Interstate league is a pretty fast minor league organization," said Caruthers, who was to make $160 a month umpiring in the outfit. He was getting good notice around the league. "Bobby Caruthers … is the best umpire that ever set foot in this town," wrote the Wheeling, West Virginia, correspondent for *Sporting Life.* "He means exactly what he says, as more than one player has found to his sorrow, and his decisions are correct as well as impartial."[14] The *Wheeling Daily Intelligencer* thought a promotion to the highest level was in order. "'Bobby' Carruthers is umpiring better ball than has been seen before this season in Wheeling, and when there is a vacancy on 'Uncle Nick's' [Nick Young] staff the National league could get a first class man in the former great pitcher," the paper told its readers. "'Parisian Bob' is a gentleman as well as a good umpire."[15]

Fort Wayne manager Jack Glasscock, a teammate on the 1892 St. Louis Browns, went on record that Caruthers was the most outstanding umpire in the league. "Carruthers' umpiring is relished by the crowds which now attend the games," reported the *Fort Wayne Evening Sentinel.* "He makes mistakes, it is true, but he doesn't allow a half dozen players to congregate about him and kick on the decisions. Neither does he permit the continual coaching from the bench. Carruthers should be retained by (Interstate League) President Power next season."[16]

Caruthers had an interesting experience occur on July 24. Not only did he call a no-hitter thrown by Dayton's Charles "Doc" Watkins, who was a teammate of Caruthers with Grand Rapids in 1894, but also he wasn't the only officiator—at least for a few innings. Boxer James J. Jeffries, who won the heavyweight title a month and a half earlier with an 11th-round knockout of Bob Fitzsimmons, umpired on the bases for three

President of the National League Nick Young (seated middle) did not acquiesce to Bob Caruthers' desire—not to mention others around baseball—for Caruthers to umpire in his league. Seated on the far right is Brooklyn owner Charles Byrne, while St. Louis owner Chris Von der Ahe is standing second from left.

innings—it was estimated that he made five calls—and midgame, he and his brother, Jack, staged a four-round bout. The exhibition was tame compared to the game. "Watkins' performance had it beaten a mile,"[17] noted the *Dayton Herald*.

Not everything was rosy, however. On August 4 in Toledo—a game the home team *won*—he was chased out of the park by fans, who threw projectiles at Caruthers (some of which landed). On August 22 in Fort Wayne, Toledo pitcher Eli Cates took exception to a number of called balls and let Caruthers know about it. Caruthers retorted that Cates was a "rotten pitcher," which naturally didn't sit well with the Mud Hens hurler. The argument continued later in front of the hotel where the players and umpire were staying. Cates demanded an apology which Caruthers refused, saying he called two pitches strikes for Cates which could have been balls. Cates insisted that Caruthers missed 18 pitches, Caruthers called Cates a liar, whereupon the Toledo pitcher hurled obscenities at Caruthers, and just like that a fight commenced. Caruthers swung at Cates, who deflected the punch, then struck back. The two combatants tangled like two wrestlers meeting at the center of the ring.

The conflict drew a crowd, consisting of both Toledo players and people who happened to be milling about. With the two bodies ensnared, Cates' teammates went in to separate the two—or perhaps get in some shots on Caruthers themselves or even grab hold of him so Cates could have undefended hits. Shortstop Steve Griffin was one of those players who approached the grapplers. Bystander Al Wolf (or Wolfe) thought Griffin was up to no good and threw a haymaker at Griffin, who partially deflected the punch. However, it was enough to send Griffin through the plate glass window of the hotel bar, leaving the Toledo shortstop with a ripped shirt and a nice three-inch cut. That broke things up, and everyone dispersed. Griffin played the next day—now dubbed "Glass Front" Griffin—and the Fort Wayne crowd let him have it all game, booing him loudly throughout. "Carruthers has umpired better ball than any umpire sent here this season by President Power,"[18] insisted the Fort Wayne News-Gazette, which noted that the hometown team had more bad calls against it than Toledo in the series.

A few weeks later, Caruthers umpired a game in New Castle with Cates once more pitching. No incident was reported between pitcher and official, but Griffin was ejected for "abusing the umpire."[19] The New Castle Courant-Guardian liked what it saw in Caruthers, commenting that he "is one of the best umpires in the league, and he will not permit any monkey business. In this New Castle is fortunate in one way, while we lose in another. All the club can ask for is fair treatment, yet that is just the thing we could never get away from home, yet no team can feel afraid of getting the worst of it here with Caruthers handling the indicator." That feeling wasn't necessarily shared by the New Castle fans.

On September 4 in the ninth inning of a game against Fort Wayne, Caruthers called New Castle's Frank "Kohly" Miller out at the plate on a close play. An irate Miller slugged Caruthers and was ejected. Fort Wayne won the game in the bottom of the ninth (the home team still did not necessarily bat last) on what was deemed a "questionable decision"[20] by Caruthers. With the game over, fans of New Castle, ironically known as the Quakers, were upset with how things unfolded and took it out on the umpire. It was a decent-size crowd of 1,500, and many of those entered the playing field, surrounded Caruthers, and attacked him. Fort Wayne pitcher John Swaim got in the way of one punch and took it on the chin. Caruthers was able to make it safely to the locker room but "was a badly scared man, and he was lucky to escape with his life."[21]

Days later in Fort Wayne, Mansfield player/manager Dennis Lowney constantly argued with Caruthers during his team's 4–3 win, once even claiming he was going to take his team off the field. Afterwards, he said Caruthers wasn't going to umpire in Mansfield, where the same two teams were playing the next day. Undeterred, Caruthers made the trip, although admitted to the Fort Wayne Sentinel that "he wasn't afraid of any one man that ever lived, but he did fear a crowd such as Lowney said would get after him in Mansfield."[22] After a 0–0, 10-inning tie, Caruthers' worry became a reality as he was assaulted, but he managed to escape unscathed. Caruthers finished out the season with no more incidents, and in the final game on September 17 at Fort Wayne, in the sixth inning he said he was sick and could no longer perform his duties. Whether he was just using that as an excuse for being hung over, drunk, or wanting to drink or actually ill wasn't reported, even after the fact.

After the season, Caruthers retreated to Chicago, where he once again based his family. He made it back in time to see a son, Harry, born on October 9. However, like Caruthers' daughter, Dorothy, who was born in 1893, Harry's life was a short one. He died before the year was out. Sadly, none of Caruthers' four children would reach the age of 30.

Professionally, Caruthers' mind was concentrating solely on umpiring—and he was setting his sights high. Local minor league newspapers weren't the only ones who thought Caruthers deserved a shot in the big time. He did, too. Caruthers wrote to National League president Nick Young, expressing his desire to work in that circuit.

Alas, his letter went unanswered (ironically, later that season Young hired another former Brooklyn pitcher as an umpire—Adonis Terry).

Upon return home from the 1899 season, Caruthers had umpired some games between the Chicago Unions and Columbia Giants in the so-called western championship of African American teams. With his dream of umpiring in the big leagues on hold, Caruthers took to officiating Unions games, which were played on Sundays. By mid–May, he found regular work, once again hired by the Interstate League after another umpire quit following the death of his father.

The trip around the Interstate League in 1900 was better than the previous year, with no reported fan attacks. The *Fort Wayne Sentinel* crowed, "Caruthers is an excellent umpire and his work was about the most satisfactory in the league."[23] There were, of course, issues with managers, players, newspapermen, and cranks—par for the course for any arbiter—with the prevailing attitude depending on how the call went against the favored team. For example, in an August 16 game between Wheeling and Fort Wayne, Caruthers called Frank Hemphill of the latter (and home) team safe at third on a stolen-base attempt. The *Wheeling Daily Intelligencer* claimed Hemphill was "out by three feet,"[24] while the *Fort Wayne Sentinel* reported he was safe "on a close decision."[25]

There were times, however, when Caruthers created his own enmity. Twice he left games early. On July 26 in Wheeling, Dayton won the game in 15 innings on a play at first in which the losing team claimed there was runner interference. The hometown fans cried foul and made vocal threats—although no one jumped onto the field or physically confronted Caruthers, nevertheless Caruthers had enough and said he wasn't going to umpire the second game of the scheduled doubleheader. He even requested police protection on his walk to the trolley even though—according to the Wheeling papers—there was no imminent violence. On August 12 in Dayton, after arguments ensued following a couple of calls on walks in the seventh inning, with a triple scoring both runs, Caruthers decided he'd gotten enough of a roasting from the fans and players that he handed over the game balls and left the park.

There was also the issue of drinking. In mid–July, Toledo manager Charles Strobel declared that his team would rather forfeit than participate in a game umped by Caruthers because "whisky and baseball do not go together."[26] Alcohol was perhaps a factor in Caruthers not showing up for various games—August 13 in Dayton (although that was after the above incident), then August 29, again in Dayton (after umpiring the previous two games). He wouldn't return to the field until September 10.

It's conceivable that Caruthers' thirst for liquor could be a reason the Interstate League wouldn't have had him back in 1901, but the league ended up folding, so he was in search of work regardless. He once again umpired games between the Chicago Unions and Columbia Giants, played at Chicago's West Side Park, home of the National League Cubs, in mid–October "for the colored championship."[27] In early February, he was appointed to the staff of the Western League.

This wasn't Ban Johnson's Western League, where Caruthers had served a couple of stints previously. That circuit was now called the American League and in 1901 was classified as a major league. This new Western League began in 1900 and featured teams in Colorado Springs, Denver, Des Moines, Grand Rapids, Kansas City, Minneapolis, Omaha, St. Joseph, and St. Paul.

There were no incidents of Caruthers drinking—at least none reported—and his season as a whole was an umpiring success. Not that there weren't conflicts as teams got used to Caruthers' brand of umpiring—he left no doubt as to who was in charge, quickly fining and/or ejecting players who argued too vociferously and sticking by the rule book. For example, in a May 8 Des Moines at Denver game, he called a ball on Des Moines' Michael Steffani for not pitching within a 20-second time limit (Caruthers was well ahead of the 21st-century pace-of-play curve).

Overall, the notices on his umpiring were positive. "Bob Carruthers' umpiring was the best ever seen here,"[28] posited one notice from Denver. The *Minneapolis Star Tribune* noted, "Mr. Carruthers, touted as the best one of Mr. Hickey's selections, has been winning praise even from the rooters, who refuse to believe that an umpire can be good."[29] The *Omaha Daily Bee* chimed in as well, saying, "Popular 'Bob' Carruthers was there to umpire and he gave great satisfaction. ... 'Bob' is a real umpire."[30]

Writing about issues with other league umpires and their turmoil with players and fans, the *Denver Post* remarked that wasn't something seen when Caruthers was calling a game. "The fact is that Carruthers umpires the game as he sees it," relayed the paper. "He does not favor the home team in order to win approval from the spectators. The visiting team gets just as much chance to win as the local team. That and that alone is the reason that Carruthers is the success he is. And yet Carruthers probably gets no more salary than Hickey's other umpires, and he is worth the whole bunch put together."[31] The *St. Joseph Gazette-Herald* backed up the Post's assertion, claiming, "Bob Carruthers has got every ball player in the league afraid of him. No one dares to dispute his decisions."[32]

Jack Crooks, briefly a teammate of Caruthers in St. Louis in 1892, played a handful of games with St. Paul and Minneapolis in 1901. A veteran of eight major-league seasons plus a few more in the minors, Crooks declared ,"Bobby Carruthers is the best umpire I ever saw. ... His judgment on balls and strikes is fine, his base decisions always correct and the players behave when he is around. Carruthers has gone every one of [National League president] 'Nick' Young's umpires beaten thirteen ways from the ace, and why he has never got a big league appointment is more than I can understood."[33]

While Caruthers was stuck in the Western League and not the National League in 1901, as it turned out, he got an opportunity to officiate games with major league players that year.

Back in the Majors

New Mexico started holding a territorial fair in 1881. Twenty years later, one of the event's purposes, which was held annually in Albuquerque, was to stump for statehood. Baseball had been a feature of the fair for years, with the local Blues taking on various competition. But in 1901, organizers took it to another level.

It was announced that Albuquerque would play El Paso at the fair in mid–October—but both clubs were to be significantly strengthened. Many players from the Western League champion Kansas City Blues would join El Paso—enough that it was dubbed the Blues—along with some other minor league players as well as pitchers Dale Gear and Wyatt Lee from the American League's Washington team. Albuquerque had a veritable National League All-Star squad, which included outfielders Topsy Hartsel of the Chicago Cubs and the New York Giants' George Van Haltren, both of whom hit .335 in 1901, Cubs outfielder Danny Green (.313), St. Louis Cardinals first baseman Dan McGann (.272), Cards pitcher Jack Powell, and two players at the beginning of Hall of Fame careers—Cubs catcher/outfielder Frank Chance (he became a full-time first baseman a couple of years later) and Giants pitcher Christy Mathewson, who was coming off his first full major-league season, in which he went 20–17 with a 2.41 ERA.

Such a matchup—which came with a $1,000 prize for the winner of the series—needed a big-time umpire. In late August, C.C. "Lum" Hall, the vice president of the Albuquerque Fair Association, locked down Bob Caruthers for that role, "which is a guarantee that the best team will win."[1] The fair featured exhibits from surrounding counties, Navajo Indians showing off their goods, such as blankets and trinkets, basketball games, harness racing, and a cattle-roping contest with a $200 prize. But the baseball games were the feature.

Nearly 6,000 turned out to witness the third game in the series, which Mathewson pitched and ended in a 9–8 victory for Albuquerque, its third straight win. Before the fifth and final game on October 19, New Mexico congressman Bernard Rodey was set to give his speech calling, once again, for statehood when it was realized that the contest was set to begin. The meeting was hurriedly discontinued with Rodey's moment lost in favor of watching Mathewson pitch. Albuquerque squeaked out a 12–11 win with Van Haltren and El Paso shortstop Kid Lewee (one of the Kansas City contingent) hitting home runs to earn a $25 prize. Albuquerque won four of the five games to win the $1,000 purse—each game was close, with each victory by the major leaguers by just one run and El Paso winning its lone tilt, 8–6.

Despite getting some guff from National League players, especially those from Chicago, there were no complaints about the job Caruthers, dubbed "the king of umpires"[2] by the *Albuquerque Citizen*, did, and he was brought along for a three-game series between the two teams in El Paso. Rain delayed the playing of those games for a few days, and the players, and Caruthers, took advantage of some of the local gambling houses (including Mathewson, who newspaper writers in later years held up as a virtuous All-American male). Caruthers apparently didn't fare well in his card playing, having to borrow $25 from Hartsel, which he never paid back and eventually became a point of contention.

In the first game, played on October 24, Albuquerque led, 4–1, in the ninth inning when Caruthers told Powell he had to use a fresh baseball—no reason being given in the local reporting of the contest. The pitcher at first rebuffed the umpire, but when told it was either use that ball or forfeit, Powell decided on the former. El Paso scored four runs in that inning, much to the delight of the raucous crowd, and held off Albuquerque in the bottom half to win, 5–4. A 5–0 Albuquerque win on October 26 set up a winner-take-all—in this case $2,000, the money put up by the players—and in front of a packed house at Athletic Park, El Paso won, 14–8.

The fall's baseball playing finally over, Caruthers headed back to Albuquerque—along with players Tom Hughes, Patsy Flaherty, and Powell—before traveling home to Chicago. He brought with him some news: He was offered a job to be an umpire in the American League in 1902, once again in business with Ban Johnson. Caruthers' hiring wasn't official until late January—perhaps there was some negotiating going on. Joe Cantillon, Tom Connolly, and Jack Sheridan were all holding out for more money (reportedly in the $1,800–$2,000 range), with Cantillon eventually signing with the National League. Caruthers was joined in the AL by Connolly, Sheridan, and another newcomer, Silk O'Laughlin, who had previously umpired in the Eastern League. "I do not anticipate any trouble from inefficient umpires," Johnson said in March. "If the men I hire cannot do satisfactory work, then I will get somebody else. However, I am sure that the men who perform in the American League will not cause any trouble."[3]

Caruthers' first assignment, ironically, was in St. Louis, where he received a nice ovation despite looking nothing like the pitcher who toiled there so many years ago. "Caruthers has changed greatly," reported the *St. Louis Republic*. "He is thin and a huge mustache almost obliterates any resemblance to the young pitcher, who, a dozen years ago, was pitching the Browns to victory."[4]

Umpiring, as usual, behind the pitcher, Caruthers drew some criticism for some of his ball/strike and foul calls. But the big complaint, one which festered for years, came in the fourth game of the season, on April 26, with the Browns hosting Cleveland. Future Hall of Fame pitcher Addie Joss made his major league debut that day. In the seventh inning, Joss smote a pitch deep to left field and off the fence for a double. Or, at least, it *seemed* to go off the fence. Joss later said it went over the wall and back onto the field, and he should have had a home run (he'd have just one career homer, coming in 1909).

But Joss' real issue occurred in the sixth inning. St. Louis' Jesse Burkett led off with a blooper to right field, with Cleveland outfielder ZaZa Harvey racing in and attempting the catch. Caruthers declared that the ball bounced into Harvey's mitt, the right fielder strenuously objecting to the call. It was the only hit allowed by Joss, who won 3–0 but was denied tossing a no-hitter in his first American League start. "I'll never forgive Caruthers for that,"[5] Joss said six years later in recalling the incident. His tune did change slightly after throwing a perfect game in 1908. Later that off-season, while still holding out that "All the St. Louis players afterward admitted that Carruthers made a mistake," Joss added, "I have always had it in for Carruthers, but I'll have to forgive him, as I put a no-hit game in my 1908 record at the expense of the White Sox."[6]

Joss wasn't the only player to take issue with Caruthers in 1902. One end-of-the-season report had American League umpires ejecting 68 players, with Caruthers leading the way with 22—and that total might be conservative. On April 29, he ejected three players—Detroit catcher Fred Buelow for arguing a fair call on a line drive down the third-base line, and St. Louis' Dick Padden and Jesse Burkett, the former for protesting a called strike and the latter for defending his teammate. According to newspaper reports, in a letter to Ban Johnson, Caruthers told the AL president that "in his long career as a professional he never heard such profane language in his life as Burkett, Padden and Buelow directed at him Tuesday."[7] Buelow was suspended five games and fined $10, but the Browns players, who denied cursing out Caruthers, were exonerated. "In every instance the umpire was applauded for exercising his authority," said *The Sporting News*. "Public sentiment is against rowdyism and it is growing stronger every season."[8]

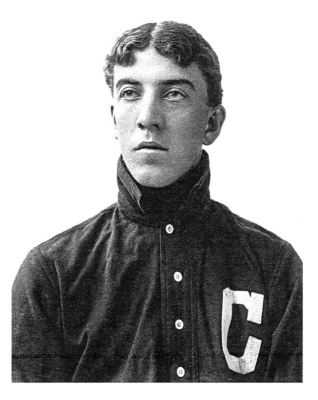

Pitcher Addie Joss held a grudge against Bob Caruthers for years, claiming the umpire cost him a no-hitter in his first major league game by ruling an out a hit.

Calls for a two-umpire system intensified, and beginning May 11, Caruthers was matched with another arbiter for much—but not all—of the remainder of the season. He was umpiring solo in Boston on May 16 when he called the home team's Hobe Ferris out on strikes in the fourth inning. The Boston second baseman argued, to no avail, of course, then took it up again with Caruthers in the fifth inning and was promptly ejected. Former pitcher turned *Boston Globe* sportswriter Tim Murnane praised Caruthers' actions.

> Taking the game as a whole Mr. Carruthers did well. He was lively on his feet and prompt giving decisions. If Ferris or the crowd imagined that Carruthers would weaken they could not have known their man, for Bobby is simply full of sand and has gone through the baseball game as an artist. He looked a bit older than when he was here last, and promises to make a good umpire. The players can well afford to help him instead of wrangling with him.[9]

Even manager Jimmy Collins was satisfied with Caruthers, although his tune would change soon enough.In Washington on June 24, Collins was displeased with some calls on balls and strikes as well as two plays in which Caruthers called Senators safe on close plays on the bases. On the second instance, Washington's Wyatt Lee was ruled safe at third base—Collins' position. An argument ensued and, as Caruthers was quick to do, he ejected Collins. Boston lost, 7–6, and Johnson suspended Collins three games. "It is pretty tough business to have to suffer for the utter incapacity of Mr. Johnson's umpires," Collins—of whom the *Washington Post* wrote, "there is no more gentlemanly fellow in the game"[10]—remarked a week later. "Mr. Carruthers gave two outrageous decisions that lost us the game, as all the Washington players and press did testify, and for this blunder I called Carruthers' attention to the fact that he was four-flushing by remaining in the game. I used no vile language, and will use just as vigorous when he does like work again. I did not deserve to be laid off."[11] The Boston fan club, known as the Royal Rooters, wrote to Johnson, asking that Caruthers not umpire any of their team's games, no matter the venue (alas, he did, but only twice—in St. Louis in early August and Chicago in early September).

Chicago pitcher-manager Clark Griffith called Caruthers "a home umpire"[12] back in May and was kicked out of at least five games which Caruthers officiated. The largest brouhaha occurred September 7 in Chicago in the second game of a doubleheader. The White Sox were tied at 3, with Washington heading into the 14th inning. The Senators' George Carey rocketed a Griffith pitch into center field, to the deepest part of the ballpark, where fans had congregated to watch. Chicago hurried the ball back in, and Carey was held to a double. However, the ground rules at South Side Park called for an automatic triple if the ball went into the crowd or was touched by a fan, so Caruthers pointed Carey to third base. Chicago players insisted the ball wasn't touched or hit into the band of spectators and quickly surrounded Caruthers, arguing their case with Griffith taking hold of the umpire and violently shaking him.

The White Sox fans weren't happy, either. Roughly 6,000 of them, according to one report, took the field (or just over one-third of those in attendance), showing their anger by throwing various objects at Caruthers. Billy-club-armed policemen helped hold back the crowd. Things finally began to quiet down, and the game was almost ready to continue, when Griffith and shortstop George Davis, who appeared ready to fight Caruthers, found out they had been ejected. Caruthers took out his watch—signaling the game would be forfeited if the field wasn't cleared posthaste—but this only further enflamed the players and fans, figuratively and literally. With darkness having descended, Washington's Ed Delahanty decided to light some matches. Fans followed suit, both those on the field and in the bleachers, lighting whatever paper was around to create de facto torches. While it was probably quite a sight to behold, the situation was a mess, and the game was declared a tie.

"An umpire's lot is not a happy one," Caruthers ruminated earlier in the year, "but I am off well this season and think that I will give satisfaction all around. I have figured it out that in the average game of ball an umpire has 300 plays to decide. So we must make our blunders, just as the most brilliant fielders do. Baseball, perfectly played, wouldn't be a game. It is the uncertainties that make it so popular."[13]

Caruthers made it through the season, however, and was kept on by the American League for 1903. His finances were another story. In November, it was reported by the *Chicago Tribune* that he sold property—using a quitclaim deed, usually reserved for transactions with family—on South Clark Street (311–315 and 323) to Benjamin Arnheim—for $1. If the *Tribune* was correct on the sale price, perhaps it was related to gambling losses or maybe he was to get a share of any proceeds if it were to be sold. For Caruthers' sake, hopefully it was the latter. Weeks later, Arnheim sold the property at 323 S. Clark St.—a 25ft × 105ft lot being rented by the Hip Lung company—to A.M. Barnhart for $43,000.

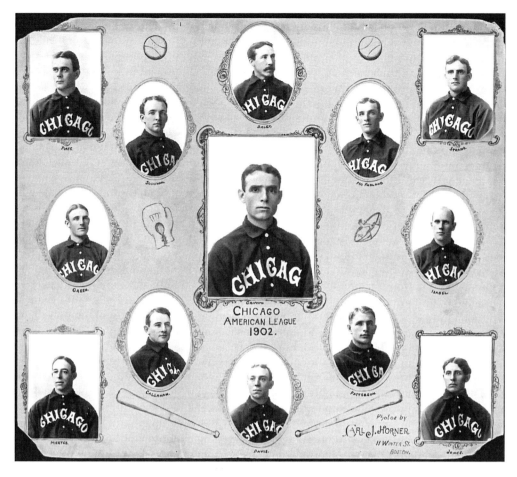

CHICAGO
AMERICAN LEAGUE
1902.

Photos by
CARL J. HORNER
11 WINTER ST.
BOSTON.

Bob Caruthers led American League umpires in ejections in 1902. Chicago pitcher-manager Clark Griffith (middle) was the recipient of at least five of those (Michael T. "Nuf Ced" McGreevy Collection, Boston Public Library).

The 1903 season started out in a prestigious manner for Caruthers. On Opening Day in Philadelphia on April 22, he was on the receiving end of the ceremonial throwing out of the first ball made by newly elected mayor John Weaver. The rest of the year, however, wasn't as glorious.

The ejections continued—and Ban Johnson was handing out more and more suspensions. In a May 5 game at Boston, which eventually was wiped out due to rain, Collins got thrown out and was given a three-game hiatus from the AL president. Four days later in the same city, with New York (now managed by Griffith, but he was already suspended for his actions against another umpire) in town, Highlanders pitcher Jesse Tannehill and second baseman Jimmy Williams got ejected and, after continuing to harangue Caruthers from the bench, were ordered to leave the park altogether. They, too, were handed three-game suspensions.

Caruthers was umpiring in the field on June 1 in Detroit when his partner, Big Jim Hassett, called St. Louis' Barry McCormick out on strikes to end the seventh inning with two men on base. McCormick and teammate Dick Padden took exception and let Hassett know. When outfielder Emmet Heidrick jogged out to his position, he turned

The May 10, 1903, *Boston Post* depicted Bob Caruthers' ejections of New York's Jesse Tannehill and Jimmy Williams (*Boston Post*).

and said something to Caruthers regarding his fellow umpire—certainly not flattering—and was promptly ejected. That caused players to rush at Caruthers, and Browns manager Jimmy McAleer ran onto the field to cool off his players while getting in some words of his own. When play resumed, pitcher Jack Powell turned to Caruthers, tipped his cap, and said some complimentary—albeit sarcastic—words about the quality of his work. Like Heidrick, Powell was summarily kicked out of the game. Johnson suspended McAleer five games and Heidrick and Powell three each.

Murnane was no longer in Caruthers' corner. "I have no sympathy with the kickers in baseball, but I can understand how hard it is to control one's temper when the work of the umpire is very bad, such, for instance, as I have seen at the American grounds here this season by Carruthers and Hassett,"[14] he wrote.

During a June 25 game in Detroit, Caruthers ejected Philadelphia's Topsy Hartsel after he argued a called third strike. On his way to the bench, Hartsel exclaimed for all to hear that Caruthers should pay up the $25 borrowed from him back in El Paso in 1901. Not only did Hartsel not get his money, but he also ended up being fined $10. "Lave Cross says Caruthers owes money to almost every ball player in the country," reported the *Philadelphia Record*, "and after taking their money he has the nerve to put them out of the game."[15]

While Caruthers' season started on the unofficial holiday of Opening Day, it all but came to an end on another day of celebration—July 4. In the first inning in Cleveland, Washington's Kip Selbach stole second base, with second baseman (and manager) Nap Lajoie raising a stink over the safe call. Caruthers, as usual, ejected Lajoie, who refused to leave the field. A police officer had to be called to escort Lajoie to the bench. (Lajoie was suspended indefinitely by Ban Johnson, but he later dismissed it.) In the fifth inning, Caruthers retired from the game, overcome, it was said, by the heat. He didn't appear at the park for the next game two days later and claimed to still be sick on July 8, at which time Johnson sent Silk O'Laughlin to Philadelphia and fired Caruthers (Hassett was let go as well in August).

Caruthers retreated to Chicago and found work at a yeast factory—likely the William H. Bunge Vinegar and Compressed Yeast Company located on Racine Ave. in the Fulton Market district—before signing on to replace Lou Mahaffey as an umpire in the Pacific National League. He officiated his first game in Tacoma on August 7 and was praised by the *Associated Press* for his "high-class umpiring."[16]

He took a line drive to the ribs in Butte on August 18, and 11 days later he was reportedly stricken with pneumonia, not returning to umpiring until September 5 in Seattle. He was to finish up the season in Spokane—the locals were looking forward to his appearances, with the *Spokesman-Review* noting, "The arrival of the once famous pitcher will be an event in the local baseball world."[17] However, he didn't show up for any more games—no explanation was given—and needless to say was not rehired for 1904.

The Western League, though, was happy to take him back—and make him the chief umpire, at that.

26

Tragedy

Baseball became something of a family affair for the Caruthers in 1904. With his return to the Western League as an umpire, Bob Caruthers moved his clan to Des Moines, which housed one of the six teams in the circuit. His youngest son, 13-year-old David, who suffered from what was described as "chronic valvular heart disease hypertrophy,"[1] served as the mascot and bat boy for the Prohibitionists—an ironic team name considering Bob Caruthers' drinking issues—and the following year sold peanuts at the ballpark, at times put in charge of running the stand.

Caruthers' latest foray in the Western League went largely without incident, with the exception coming, funnily enough, in Des Moines, where the fans and local papers groused about his officiating. In one late July game, in which the home team lost, 4–3, Des Moines patrons threw cushions at Caruthers, who needed help from a policeman to leave the park safely. "Really, the fans have no right to say that he has shown favoritism against the local team, for his poor decisions seem to be more the result of incompetency and lack of judgment than of any desire to favor the visiting team," the *Des Moines Register* said after a Prohibitionists 8–1 victory. "Yesterday his distinction between balls and strikes was a unique performance, and he kept the audience in a state of expectant admiration through the easy nonchalance he displayed in calling these by the wrong names."[2]

Objections, though, were not as prevalent as in years—and leagues—past. "Carruthers is about the best minor league umpire in the business," offered the *Denver Post*. "He makes few mistakes, and gives the decisions as he sees them. In a word, he knows the game, and the players don't fool him."[3] In the end, even the *Des Moines Register* came around. "Of all the umpires tried out by the managements, Carruthers was the only satisfactory one,"[4] the paper asserted.

With ejections on the decline, players found other ways to challenge Caruthers. In Sioux City during the final days of the season, Caruthers got into a friendly argument with Denver outfielder William Hayes (actually Bill McGivray, who was playing under an assumed name). The result was that the 21-year-old challenged the nearly 40-year-old umpire to a race. Caruthers got a slight head start—10 feet—but showed he still had some quickness left in his legs, winning the 100-yard dash by roughly the lead he was given. He also pocketed $10, thanks to a wager on the sprint.

That money probably didn't stay in Caruthers' wallet long, perhaps spent on drink or gambling. The latter is how he passed his off-season, spending his time at the racetrack and checking results from other horse races plus earning a bit on the side as a bookie.

But that was merely a way to keep busy in the winter. It was back to umpiring in 1905, and there was competition for his services. Michael Sexton, who had been president of the Western League, was no longer in that position but was putting together the schedule for the Central League. He recommended Caruthers to that league's president, Dr. F.R. Carson—who reportedly had a prior relationship with Caruthers. Carson went to Chicago to discuss employment—the Central League was in the Midwest and filled with cities familiar to Caruthers, such as Fort Wayne, Grand Rapids, and Springfield. However, the Western League was a higher classification (A compared to B for the Central) and still had a team in Des Moines, where Caruthers was living. Plus, new league president Norris O'Neill set up the circuit's office in Chicago. It was easy to keep Caruthers' ear all off-season. The Western League won out.

He was welcomed back. "There is less kicking about Bob Caruthers' umpiring than there is about any other arbitrator in the league,"[5] noted the *Des Moines Register*. St. Joseph outfielder Abel Lizotte said of Caruthers: "There's an umpire that is all wool and a yard wide. He's the best in the business. Square as a die and won't stand for any monkeying. That's the kind of an umpire for me. If he makes a mistake he isn't going to try and make a standoff on the next decision. He gives the decisions as he sees the plays and I don't believe that there is a player in the league who doesn't respect Bobby and his work."[6]

Not everyone was enamored with Caruthers, however. Specifically, Des Moines secretary Mike Cantillon (brother of Joe, the former player, manager, and umpire whom Caruthers entertained back in 1897 in Burlington) disagreed. It started in front of a small crowd of 350 in Des Moines on April 17, when the Underwriters, as they were now known, lost an exhibition to Keokuk, 12–11 in which Caruthers umpired. "Bob Caruthers has given us the worst of it in every one of the six or eight close decisions that he has been called on to make in the exhibition games," Mike Cantillon said after that game. "If he keeps that gait up, there's going to be trouble for a certain Bob Carruthers."[7] True to his word, Cantillon feuded with Caruthers all season.

Caruthers still umpired from behind the pitcher, leaving him open to more than the usual criticism on his decisions on balls and strikes. In the first game of a home doubleheader on May 30 against St. Joseph, Cantillon continually squawked over too many of these calls, and Caruthers ejected him. Things really heated up between the pair in August.

The exact details are a tad sketchy—it happened during the first game on August 5 between Des Moines and Sioux City or between games of the doubleheader; Cantillon was on the Des Moines bench or, he came down onto the field. Either way, at some point after Bob Ganley stole home but was ordered back to third base because Caruthers said the ball hit the bat of Howard Wakefield for a foul, the two got into a heated argument, and it looked like a fight was going to start, but it was broken up before any punches were thrown. Instead of taking his place on the field for the second game, an angry and upset Caruthers retreated to the stands and refused to umpire. "I will not work under such abuse as that. I'll get out and handle a pick and shovel first,"[8] he reportedly said. Sioux City manager Jack Carney pleaded with him to return. Fans yelled, "Put Cantillon out and Carruthers in"[9] to no avail. Finally, realizing there would be no game without him, Caruthers relented—but he wasn't at the following day's game, with Harry Mace sent by the league to officiate. Caruthers sent a letter to O'Neill, threatening to resign. "If the president will allow his umpires to stand the abuse from managers and players which I stood to-day then the game had better be abandoned. I am done with it unless something is done with Cantillon."[10]

Caruthers continued umpiring, however, and didn't officiate a Des Moines game again until the end of August in Omaha. During the opener of an August 27 double-header, Cantillon let Caruthers have it during the first six innings, constantly hurling insults and profanity at the umpire. Caruthers tried to quell the situation with warnings, which Cantillon ignored, so finally in the seventh inning, he ejected the Des Moines secretary. Cantillon flew off the bench and, with 6,000 Omaha fans booing him, argued even more. Caruthers sat on the Omaha bench and told manager Billy Rourke, "I positively will not umpire in a league where a manager can talk to an umpire like that."[11] Caruthers again said he wouldn't umpire the second game, and this time he meant it, with a player from each team filling his roles. The local papers backed Caruthers. "Cantillon is the only man in the league who cannot get along with the popular little umpire,"[12] said the *Omaha Daily News,* while the *Omaha Daily Bee* declared, "The Western League is fortunate to have such a gentleman as Bobby Caruthers to umpire, but it is decidedly unfortunate to tolerate a foul-mouthers [sic] ruffian as a manager."[13]

Both Cantillon and Caruthers were back at the park the next day, and once again the Des Moines official cursed out the umpire. Another ejection ensued, and Cantillon had to be dragged away by two policemen after making overtures that he'd beat up Caruthers right there and then.

No punishment of Cantillon was forthcoming—it was noted that O'Neill likely got his job thanks to the help of the Cantillon brothers—which only further angered Caruthers. There was a later report that Caruthers had offers from other leagues, but O'Neill wouldn't let him out of his contract. "What am I going to do about it? I have reported the state of affairs to President 'Tip' O'Neil and he pays no attention to it. What am I going to do about it?" Caruthers wondered before answering his own question. "It is the worst I have ever experienced. And I'll tell you right now I won't stand it another season. The abuse which I have been called upon to take has been something fearful. And it has come from the bench. The players have treated me nicely."[14]

Cantillon, however, didn't give Caruthers any more difficulty that season (ironically, Des Moines won all four games against Omaha), but Caruthers still had troubles—self-inflicted ones. His drinking was apparently getting worse.

In early May, it was announced that Caruthers "had been taken suddenly ill"[15] and was pulled from the umpiring rotation, returning two weeks later. Perhaps Caruthers actually was sick. But that wasn't the case a month later.

Caruthers was scheduled to umpire a game in Omaha on June 10 but never appeared. At first, it was reported that he was ill again, but in reality O'Neill suspended him for two weeks for excess drinking, or as the *St. Joseph News-Press* put it, "looking upon the wine when it was red."[16] He also missed a game in Sioux City on July 13 and three games late in the season in Omaha—after having umpired there the previous few days. He did, however, make his way back to the field in Omaha and closed out the season umpiring in Des Moines without incident.

More serious matters were afoot in November. It was reported that Caruthers was near death due to heart disease. Evangelist Billy Sunday—the former ballplayer who played against Caruthers in a World Series as a member of the Chicago White Sox and also raced Arlie Latham, which caused a rift between the two Browns players—learned of Caruthers' condition while eating dinner in Burlington, Iowa. Upon hearing the news, he immediately penned a letter: "To Bob Caruthers, Des Moines, Iowa: I hear you have about reached home base. Do you need any help? I am praying for you and am ready to add works to faith. W.A. SUNDAY."[17]

However, it wasn't Bob Caruthers who was seriously ill but rather his son, David. The younger of the two Caruthers boys, David Caruthers already had health issues—when the number of steps at school was too difficult for him to ascend, he was transferred to another, the Crocker School. One day in early November, after he and his class went through some exercises—his teachers, fearful of David's condition, wished he would skip these, but both his parents insisted—David was, according to an investigation conducted by the superintendent, "out of breath, pale and … lips blue."[18] Something then occurred—it was never disclosed what—which caused David Caruthers' teacher, Paul Dietrichson, to punish him. This involved shaking the 14-year-old boy. David went into shock, was bedridden, and in critical condition. Someone from the Humane Society suggested to the Caruthers that they file charges against Dietrichson.

"I have nothing to say in defense of Dietrichson's act," Des Moines superintendent W.O. Riddell said.

> Corporal punishment is forbidden in this district except in the presence of the principal, away from the other pupils and an hour or more after the offense. This is to ensure that the punishment shall not be inflicted in anger. I think it very likely that Mr. Dietrichson, who is a new teacher, was not aware of this rule. … Another thing, Mr. Dietrichson of course knew nothing of the boy's constitutional weakness.[19]
>
> "I cannot express how sorry I am over this," Dietrichson said. "It is hard for me to believe that the trivial punishment I administered could have caused the boy's serious illness. I did not shake him vigorously, and when I had finished he laughed in my face. I know I wished then I had made the punishment more severe, but the statement I afterward made a threatening move toward him is absolutely false."[20]

David Caruthers died on December 7 at 9:30 a.m. The subsequent investigation by Riddell found no fault with Dietrichson, who was not disciplined. "Mr. Dietrichson is complexly broken up over the occurrence and I am grieved that such a thing happened, but I think it is unfair to say that the boy's death was due to the shaking he received," Riddell said. "He has been a sufferer from valvular heart trouble all his life, and his mother herself said that she was constantly in fear for his life." Dr. George Hanawalt—who has an elementary school named after him in Des Moines—agreed that the heart condition was the likely cause of death but made no conjecture on the role the shaking, or the boy's nervousness (it was reported that David "continually called in his delirium for protection against the man he thought was his murderer."[21]), had in his demise.

There is no record of Bob and Mamie Caruthers taking any legal action. One local paper advised them against it. Two days after David Caruthers' death, the *Marshalltown Evening Times* lectured:

> Discipline in school is an essential. There are few families where corporal punishment is not at times considered salutary and a school is only a family multiplied. Few teachers are cruel or inflict pain needlessly. It might be argued that a child so seriously afflicted as the one in question appears to have been, was hardly a fit member of a public school. Unless the circumstances are different than appears on the surface of the report, it is hard to see how the teacher is to be held legally or morally culpable. If Des Moines is to investigate it should be done without feeling and with the utmost caution, and the bereaved parents should inquire carefully into the case and question themselves for contributory negligence before they demand punishment for a teacher who perhaps was simply doing his duty.[22]

(If you believe in karma, in 1907, Dietrichson, now teaching at North High School in Logan, Iowa, was badly beaten up by the town's mayor, C.A. Bolter, who was also on the school board, in an argument over the poor play of the school's football team.)

The funeral, held at the same place where David died—the Caruthers' home on 703 7th Street, located roughly a mile from the state capitol—was something of a local affair. Floral arrangements were sent from businesses all around town and officials from the baseball world; the local newsboys presented the family with a wreath and a pillow decorated with flowers and the boys' names, a gift from various businessmen and former ballplayers. Several Des Moines players traveled from their off-season homes for the funeral, and two, "Big Bill" Chappelle and Ganley (who hadn't played for the team since August after being purchased by Pittsburgh and clearly showed no grudge from the steal of home incident), were pallbearers.

The funeral perhaps helped thaw the frosty relationship between Bob Caruthers and Mike Cantillon. In October 1906, Caruthers traveled with the Des Moines team—owned by the Cantillon brothers—to Burlington to umpire a state championship between those two clubs. It wasn't enough, however, to get Caruthers to return to the Western League.

Caruthers made his intentions quite clear during the season. His issue was not only with Cantillon but also league president O'Neill. There was also a report, years later, that O'Neill fired Caruthers due to his excessive drinking. Either way—or even if was a mutual decision—Caruthers wasn't going to umpire in the Western League in 1906.

Uncertain of his future, Caruthers started working at the Agar Packing Company. Getting yelled at by players, managers, and baseball officials was still probably more appealing than toiling in a meat factory, and Caruthers applied to be an umpire in various leagues. In March, an opening occurred in the Three-I League—shorthand for Illinois-Iowa-Indiana—when one of their officials, Stephen Cusak, left for the New York State League. Caruthers also had an offer from the Pacific Coast League and, despite the Three-I being in a lower class than the PCL (and Western League), the locale had to have been a selling point. He would make $150 a month. Not everyone was pleased. When the *Omaha Bee* found out Caruthers was out of the Western League and replaced by "Slats" Davis, it lamented, "And to think that Bobby Carruthers has been released to make room for this freak."[23]

Others were overjoyed. He received good notice from local newspapers in Davenport, Dubuque, Peoria, and Rock Island from the start. Visiting Minneapolis manager Mike Kelley remarked that Caruthers was better than any umpire in the American Association, where he skippered and regularly tangled with officiators. By August, Caruthers was the only umpire to start the season in the Three-I League who had not been replaced. All was going well, but things changed in mid–August.

In a game in Peoria on August 11, Caruthers, umpiring behind the mound as usual, was hit in the head by a ball thrown in from the outfield. It knocked him out for 10 minutes. He finished the game and umpired the next eight days in Peoria, although at night in his hotel, he complained of being dizzy and one time even fainted. Caruthers' next assignment was Rock Island—but he didn't show up and sent no word to the league of his whereabouts.

The *Bloomington Pantagraph* reported three days later that Caruthers sent a telegram to Three-I president Edward Holland that he was over a sickness and ready to umpire again. However, his days of officiating in that circuit were over. Caruthers' next public appearance came on September 21 in Chicago as a guest of Charles Comiskey, who brought in over 100 19th-century ballplayers—including Caruthers' and Comiskey's former St. Louis Browns teammates Sam Barkley, Nat Hudson, and Arlie Latham—for a doubleheader between the White Sox, which he owned, and the New York Highlanders.

Caruthers returned to Des Moines, where he took the field in a benefit game for the Western League club which once again won the league title. The game itself was something of a farce, but he did pitch a couple of innings for the Benevolent and Protective Order of Elks and struck out three Des Moines players. The subject of pitching came up in June the following year in conversation after a game was rained out. "I think I could pitch now, with a little practice, for I have done nothing of the kind for a long time, but I passed my forty-second birthday and I suppose that means that I am out of it so far as any active work on the ball field is concerned," Caruthers responded. "I think I can get more money umpiring than any team would be willing to give me for pitching ball now."[24]

Umpiring was indeed his lot now, and he was looking to make more money in that employment. To do that, he had to leave the Midwest. For the first time, at least to begin a season, he was ready to do just that.

Reminiscences

Despite Caruthers being missing for the final weeks of the 1906 season, Three-I League president Edward Holland was ready to take him back. However, Caruthers had his eye on a new locale and larger salary. Early in the off-season, between his shifts at the Agar Packing Company, he applied to the Southern League.

The Southern League was one of the top circuits in the country, Class A, and its president, W.M. Kavanaugh, was in search of the best umpires for his crew. That, of course, meant handing out nice salaries, likely in the range of $200 a month. Kavanaugh also had an affinity for former players. All five umpires Kavanaugh hired played professionally, and two, Caruthers and Charles "Chief" Zimmer, had been major leaguers.

Caruthers' first assignment was, of all places, in Memphis, his home before moving to Chicago at age 12. After officiating the first two games between the hometown Egyptians and Little Rock, with a rainout in between, Caruthers didn't show up for the third game, scheduled for April 13. In a familiar storyline, Kavanaugh hadn't heard from Caruthers and had no clue as to why he missed the contest.

This time, though, it wasn't a drinking bender. Caruthers had gotten severely ill and, according to one report, lost 35 pounds. Kavanaugh allowed Caruthers to return, which he did April 29 in Little Rock. He umpired along with Zimmer—and ejected New Orleans second baseman Frank Gatins on April 30—but on May 1 he was once again a no-show.

Still not over the effects of his sickness, Caruthers abruptly resigned and returned home. His spring and summer would not be spent at a meat plant, however, as one of the Three-I umpires left to manage a team at a lower level, and Holland hired Caruthers to fill the void. The *Decatur Daily Review*, for one, was glad Caruthers was back in the league. "This is a great umpire—this Caruthers," the paper declared in mid–June.

> He keeps the game going, is fair in his decisions, is one of the best judges of balls and strikes in the business, and his decisions generally go unquestioned. He was an old pitcher and he knows. He understands all the stunts of slab artists who deliver a ball too high or too low, but yet over the pan, and these don't go for strikes with him. When we think of some of the others it makes us say of Caruthers "Take him for all in all, we shall not look on his like again."[1]

There wasn't much trouble for Caruthers in the Three-I in 1907, but when there was, Holland had his back—which was probably nice to know after the difficulties he had in the Western League with Norris O'Neill. The most notable example of this occurred on July 13 with Springfield visiting Decatur, in a game won, 1–0, by the home squad. There was a lot of arguing from Springfield during the game, and at one point Senators shortstop and manager Henry Scharnweber was fined, then ejected, then tossed from the ballpark by Caruthers (the play in question, as it turned out, had no effect on the final score). Springfield president Dick Kinsella, who weeks earlier slapped an umpire, didn't assault Caruthers but filed a protest to Holland and threatened to not have his team play if Caruthers umpired the following day. The *Herald and Review* reached Holland on the telephone to get his reaction, and he told the paper, "You may state in the Herald that I am running this league and not Mr. Kinsella. Springfield will play ball in Decatur tomorrow and the game will be played with Mr. Carruthers umpiring."[2]

It rained the following day, thus not allowing fans to see if Kinsella's promise would be fulfilled. However, the Springfield team did show up before the contest was called off. When asked if the Senators would have taken the field, Kinsella offered a boorish response: "Well, since the rain has knocked things out, anyway, I am not saying whether I would have permitted the boys to play or not."[3]

In fact, outside of Kinsella, Caruthers was well regarded and respected. When Rock Island, in fourth place, hosted two of the better teams in the circuit—Springfield and Peoria—Holland made sure Caruthers was umping. He also added a new umpire, Dan Daub, a rare two-umpire setup for that league, but he wanted to fortify the officiating for those two key series. Daub didn't last long, fired after making what were generally accepted as bad decisions in Peoria's 4–2 win on August 23.

Caruthers was back to umpiring solo—although Jocko "Crazy" Schmit, his teammate, briefly, with Grand Rapids in 1894, joined him for three Springfield at Decatur games (yes, Springfield played with Caruthers umpiring) before he, too, departed. "I am inclined to believe that the sending of an extra umpire here was ill advised, especially where one of them is as good a man as Carruthers," said former Western League president Michael Sexton, who was living in Rock Island. "Bobby is capable of alone handling any critical developments in a game, and when he on the field another official is merely a supernumerary."[4]

Despite the mostly good feelings towards his umpiring in the Three-I League, Caruthers wasn't intent on returning. He had taken the job though the salary ($150 a month) was not to his liking because he needed it after having to leave the Southern League. He wasn't inclined to work for the same amount in 1908. Caruthers did have a little more umpiring to do in 1907. The board of directors for the Iowa and Wisconsin Leagues—of which Sexton was president of the board of control—hired him to umpire a series between the two winners of their outfits, Waterloo and Freeport. "Umpire Caruthers is giving universal satisfaction,"[5] reported the *Freeport Daily Journal* after the fourth game.

Caruthers headed back to Des Moines—he got in one more officiating job, umpiring a local semi-pro game. With the World Series about to get under way, Caruthers was asked by a local paper who he thought would win. He picked the Chicago Cubs to beat the Detroit Tigers, a prediction which came true (and perhaps one on which he won a few dollars). Caruthers' name often came up when the World Series was being played, thanks to his performances in the 1880s version of a championship series.

He was often brought up when someone bemoaned the lack of pitchers who could hit. In 1910, future Hall of Fame pitcher Mordecai "Three Finger" Brown griped:

The batting helplessness of pitchers has been a rich joke for thirty years, and no doubt will continue to be so as long as the old game is played. ... Of course, a pitcher who can bat has a big advantage over the fellows who are unable to swat the leather. It means a lot of difference when a team sends nine sluggers into action, or eight batters and a sure out for the ninth man.

Some of the good batting pitchers of the past—Luby, Caruthers, Radbourn, Gumbert, for example—won many of their best games by slamming the ball themselves.[6]

Brown went on to wish that he could hit .300 because then he'd win 85 percent of his games (at the time he was a .183 career hitter with a .681 winning percentage).

Cincinnati manager Clark Griffith, who had his run-ins with Caruthers, in 1911 also noted the importance of having a pitcher who could hit. "Wish we had a ... Caruthers with the team,"[7] he sighed.

The same year as Brown's lament, writer John B. Foster groused about the new era of hurlers who were being babied because they sat out if they felt sick, knowing there were plenty of other pitchers on the staff who could take the mound instead. "One wonders some times what the present-day pitchers would think if they had been asked to do what a celebrated pair could do in the past—'Bobby' Carruthers and 'Dave' Foutz," wrote Foster.

On one day one of them would play right field and the other would pitch, and on the following day the second man would pitch and the relief would play right field. Have we got any athletes of that kind nowadays in professional base ball? If "Bobby" Carruthers had the stomach ache in the morning, do you suppose that he would come around in the afternoon and plead for relief on the ground that he taken a dose of bromo seltzer before 12 o'clock noon? As a matter of fact, I have seen him pitch, and seen him play right field when he looked as if he would far rather be in bed, but he was out there working, and it was a little difficult to figure that his work was any the less effective for the reason that he might have preferred to remain in quiet. He had grit and pluck, and so had a lot more of the men who were in base ball at the time that he was.[8]

Caruthers was always happy to discuss baseball but generally avoided talking about himself unless he was asked. "I am not sermonizing, not given to boasting about what I did, and I answer these inquiries only because you ask and because a great many fans may have forgotten dates, as you suggest," he told a Decatur reporter in 1907.

He was, however, contradictory. In 1901, he defended his contemporaries:

I don't see that the pitchers of the present day have anything on the stars of fourteen and fifteen years ago. The best men of the later 80's would, in my opinion, be as fully effective under the rules of today as they were under those under which they did the work that made them famous. It is true that the present day slab artists are handicapped to a certain degree by the fact that the pitching distance is five feet greater than it was then, but in those days fouls did not count as strikes as they do now, and this difference more than offsets the other. What would John Clarkson, Tom Ramsey, Dave Foutz and Charlie Nichols have done under the rules which makes the first two fouls strikes? Mind you, I am not saying anything against the ability of the present day artists, but only upholding the reputations of the men who were the stars at the time when I was actively in the game.[9]

When it came to hitters, however, he sang a different tune in 1905.

Oh the game has changed. They tell you about the good old days when some famous ball players lived, and a fan once in a while will say that there are no players any longer like Jack McCormick, Harry Stovey, Buffinton, Sam Wise, Burdock, John Hornung and other well known men of the past. But that is a mistake. The old ball players could not be mentioned in the same breath with those of today. There is absolutely no coupling the name of Fred Dunlap or Fred Pfeffer with that of [Nap] Lajoie. Why, the Cleveland man has forgotten more about the fine points of the game than Pfeffer ever dreamed. And Dicky Johnston or Jimmy Fogarty have no right to range alongside of Willie Keeler or Jack McCarthy. You can tell me all you want about the old days when the great heroes of the game cavorted about, but I'll tell you the truth, and that is that the game is so much faster today than it was fifteen or twenty years ago. If one of the old time stars should get into the game today he would look like a bush leaguer.[10]

Caruthers might not toot his own horn, but others stuck up for him. In 1901, Charles Comiskey commented, "Give me a couple of men like Caruthers and Foutz again and I could win any pennant in the country. Those were the game fellows. They played baseball because they liked it and they liked to win."[11] In 1909, the *Boston Post* reported, "Evangelist Billy Sunday says modern baseball is a better game than the old-time variety, but he qualifies his praise by naming Buck Ewing, Mike Kelly, Bennett, Carruthers, Foutz and Orr as being the peers of anyone playing ball today."[12]

One possibility for why Caruthers didn't like discussing himself was because he saw himself as an umpire and no longer a ballplayer. He probably wished he were a magnate—he tried and failed in Cedar Rapids and had

World's Series Proves That the Pitcher is the Big Man in the Game.

BOBBY CARRUTHERS,

Who, in His Time, Won Many Laurels as a Pitcher, Once Being Instrumental in Bringing the Championship to St Louis.

During the early days of the modern World Series, Bob Caruthers was a popular subject. This is from the *Boston Globe* in 1903 (*Boston Globe*).

an idea for a barnstorming series between major league and Western League all-stars which went nowhere—or maybe even a manager, but he was done in by financial undoings (both of his own accord and things out of his control) and his penchant for alcohol. "I have made mistakes like many another ball player has," he said in that 1907 Decatur interview. "If I hadn't perhaps I would not be umpiring here now. But that is another story—and I said I was not going to sermonize."[13]

Umpiring was indeed his lot in life, and a reported return to the Three-I League was inaccurate. Instead, he headed west and signed on with the Northwestern League. His reputation—both good and bad—preceded him. "Caruthers is said to be as good [as umpire Ralph Frary] when riding the water cart,"[14] stated the *Anaconda Standard*, using a euphemism for someone who stopped drinking. The paper added, "Bobby Caruthers … is touted as the classiest indicator holder that ever held this whip hand in this territory."[15]

The players quickly learned that Caruthers took little guff. In his first game umpiring in the league—Butte at Seattle on April 19—Caruthers, now sporting a thick, bushy moustache, ejected a player who was on the bench for arguing that an opposing player didn't try to get out of the way after being hit by a pitch.

They also got to see his style of umpiring—standing behind the pitcher instead of the plate. The *Oregon Daily Journal* talked to him about his reasoning, which it paraphrased in a June article, saying:

> [Caruthers] gives reasons for his contention that the proper place for an umpire is in the center of the diamond, asserting that the plate is always in full view, whereas, if the umpire is behind the catcher he is likely to have the view obstructed by the catcher and has to dodge foul tips and passed balls, all of which affects an umpire's judgment more or less. Again, by being the in middle of the diamond an umpire can always be right on the spot and tell positively whether or not the baseman touched the base runner. If behind the catcher it is often guesswork with an umpire, as it is with the spectators. It has been noticed that Carruthers gives his decisions very quickly. He can do this, he says, because he can see all the signals the catcher gives, and cannot only tell the kind of a ball the pitcher is to deliver, but can anticipate the play to be pulled off. The only drawback from umpiring behind the pitcher is the likelihood of misjudging a ball batted near the foul line, but if the first and third basemen or the fielders are alert and go after a foul ball with energy and haste, as spectators have a right to expect them to do, their location on fair or foul ground will tell an umpire the nature of the hit at a glance, argues Carruthers. Occasionally batters assert that the dark uniform of an umpire prevents them from seeing a ball well. If the middle of the diamond becomes the location of all umpires, as Mr. Carruthers thinks it will I time, this objection will probably be overcome by the umpire wearing a lighter uniform.[16]

Bob Caruthers' mustache grew bushier in his later years (*The Inter Ocean*).

Portus Baxter of the *Seattle Post-Intelligencer* was extremely impressed by what he saw. In late April, he wrote that Caruthers was "umpiring almost perfect ball."[17] A couple of weeks later, he piled on the platitudes, writing, "Carruthers is the best umpire ever seen on this park. He is on top of every play, allows no foolishness, and is unusually good on balls and strikes. To err is human, of course, but it may be truthfully said of Carruthers than he minimizes errors."[18]

The Spokane papers were dazzled by how Caruthers stayed with the play by racing around the bases to follow runners as they circled the bags, even with the fastest of runners. The Spokane fans even took to cheering him (partly due to his skill but also their frustration with other umpires) so much that "his head will be turned if the applause goes on much longer."[19] "Carruthers is right on top of every play, his judgment in most cases is good and everything is run off without any waiting or friction,"[20] declared the *Spokane Chronicle*.

The *Spokesman-Review* gushed over Caruthers:

Long experience with the game makes it come natural for Carruthers to anticipate every possible play in advance, so that he can almost always beat the ball to a spot where close play is liable to occur. A pitcher for 15 years—and one of the best the game ever knew—he has splendid judgment on balls and strikes. It is actually a treat to sit behind him. No quick break, wide drop, no high fast one escapes him. He calls them all and seldom misses any by the closest, where his judgment is apt to be better than that of one in the grandstand. Above all, Carruthers, while an absolute master of the players, has such a quiet way of handling the game that one almost overlooks his tremendous influence in hustling the play through. Tuesday's, his first game on the Spokane grounds, was played in 1:25, the fastest game so far of the season. Yet the fans did not realize the speed of the game, so smoothly did it run. Carruthers pays no attention to the stands, and consequently he is overlooked by them in turn. Which, in a nutshell, is the correct idea in umpiring. The less an umpire listens to the raucous rooter the less the rooter directs his spleen at the official. Carruthers has a quiet way of calling down a player who is inclined to want to raise a protest, and does not antagonize the men under him, thus making less trouble for himself. When the end of the Northwestern league season of 1908 is over it will not be surprising if President Lucas' records show that Carruthers has fined fewer players than any other umpire in the league, at the same time having probably less complain from players and patrons.[21]

On September 27, Caruthers umpired every game of a Spokane at Tacoma tripleheader by himself—yes, a *tripleheader*—a total of 26 innings, with the finale ending after the eighth. There were no reports of any issues with his officiating.

Not everyone was infatuated with Caruthers—of course, can't that be said about any umpire in the history of the game? One fan penned a letter to Vancouver manager Richard Dickson which stated: "If you are going to stand the class of umpiring that was in evidence at to-day's ball game, I for one, will be an absentee at all future games."[22] At least it was just words. One Northwestern umpire, Robert Black, was bombarded with lemons by an angry Vancouver crowd.

28

The Umpire Is Called Out

After a successful 1908 campaign as an umpire in the Northwestern League, it was a no-brainer to bring Bob Caruthers back in 1909, which is just what circuit president William H. Lucas did. The year wouldn't go as smoothly for Caruthers, however.

After officiating some exhibitions in Des Moines, Caruthers headed west to Spokane for his first assignment, which delighted one local newspaper. "President Lucas has made a hit by assigning Bobby Carruthers here for the first games," said the *Spokane Press*. "He's the most popular umpire on the circuit and most satisfactory to everybody concerned."[1]

Caruthers lasted a week before not showing up at the ballpark. He was sent to Seattle, which was his home base while working in the Northwestern League, with Mamie Caruthers—who had been visiting Lucas' wife in Portland—joining him to nurse him back to health. If he was sick, that is. This was likely a case of alcohol getting the better of him and being sent home to dry out under the guise of being ill.

He returned to the field in Vancouver on May 3. While there were no reports of him being derelict in his duties the rest of the spring or summer, he did miss some time after taking a line drive to the sternum during an August 11 game in Seattle. Despite taking that hard shot to the chest, he umpired the next day before being sidelined. The *Spokesman-Review* reported that Caruthers was "said to be in critical condition," but this was an overstatement. He did miss 10 days, however, returning August 23. His absences weren't forgotten by the *Spokesman-Review*'s J. Newton Culver, who in March 1910 wrote that Caruthers "practically 'blew up' under the high pressure last season in this league between infirmity and booze."[2]

Nevertheless, the Northwestern League was interested in bringing him back for the next season, but with the league dwindling to four teams, only two umpires were needed, and those jobs went to Ralph Frary and Rasty Wright (not his former Grand Rapids teammate). Once again, though, Caruthers had options.

The Western League—and a reunion with Norris "Tip" O'Neill, which didn't exactly end on the friendliest of terms—appeared to be his next destination, with multiple reports in February saying he'd been hired. However, it's likely that Caruthers was going to be slotted as a fifth extra umpire, and instead he signed back with the Three-I League.

Interestingly, in all the announcements of his hiring—real or otherwise—it was noted that Caruthers would have to control his drinking, and that he swore to abide. His use of alcohol was hardly a secret anymore. The *Davenport Daily Times*, upon the news that Caruthers was officially joining the Three-I staff, said, "If he will only be able to control his habits this summer, he ought to make one of the best men on [league president Al] Tearney's staff."[3]

To that end, Caruthers had some help to keep him sober: His wife, Mamie, was going to travel with him throughout the season. The presence of his missus appeared to be working. Early reports around the league were glowing. "The work of Umpire Bobby Caruthers was all that could be desired," said the *Bloomington Pantagraph* after the local team fell to Peoria, 3–1, on May 1. "He was impartial and fair to both and there were no kicks of consequence. He promises to prove one of President Tearney's best men this season."[4]

During a late May series in Davenport, it was written that Caruthers "is getting away in his customary swell form. Not a violent objection or one that gave any indication of physical manifestation was made against his decrees during the game he officiated in Davenport by either the visiting or the local players. This prehistoric baseball character has an eye as keen as in the by-gone days, his judgment never falters and his nerve holds all the trouble makers in leash."[5] On his next assignment in Rock Island, the *Argus* opined, "Bobby Caruthers umpired two nice games yesterday and we are glad to have him in our midst."[6] Next up was Waterloo, which also approved. "Speaking of umpires it is only fair to say that Mr. Caruthers has given satisfaction in these parts," said the *Waterloo Courier*. "He has made, no doubt, a few mistakes, but it is the opinion that he is the best in the business working in minor league base ball."[7] The *Argus* called for the other three umpires in the league to be fired, but not Caruthers, who was "the only indicator holder against whom there is no kick to make. He is fair and impartial, knows the game and his judgment is good."[8]

It wasn't just the newspapers who respected Caruthers. When the Rock Island Islanders, champions of 1909, were going to have a ceremony for the raising of their pennant, team president Warren H. Reck requested that Caruthers be assigned. Reck wanted Caruthers because this contest was against another top team, Waterloo, and a good umpire was needed. Plus, "it will please the fans to have a competent man like Caruthers on the job."[9] The request, however, was denied.

Things soured for Caruthers in Waterloo, which was playing a big three-game series against first-place Springfield. In the opening game on August 10, he got on the bad side of the fans by ejecting manager Frank Boyle, the first time he had been ejected at home all season (which perhaps speaks to the fairness of Caruthers, as many umpires were wary of upsetting home crowds). Waterloo lost that game as well as the next day. On August 12, Caruthers made a couple of out calls on the bases which went against Waterloo, which lost, 1–0. The 516 fans at the game were "incensed"[10] and yelled all sort of invectives at Caruthers during the game, including robber, rotten and thief—just in case you were wondering what they thought of his officiating.

After the game, Waterloo fans—perhaps 20 or so—followed Caruthers and continued to yell at him. Caruthers returned fire, cursing out what was later described as a "young man slight of build."[11] Caruthers had his wife send Tearney a report saying he was attacked by the mob, which caused Tearney to chastise Waterloo. Team president P.J. Martin responded that "There was no rowdyism at yesterday's game, and none afterwards. Caruthers and a young man had an argument—both to blame. Wait for written report. There has been or will not be any trouble for Carruthers or any umpire in Waterloo."[12] J.J. Dunnwald, a ticket manager for Waterloo, backed up Martin's story, saying he witnessed the event. "There was no trouble at the park, of that I am positive, for I remained until the umpire and all the crowd had left the grounds," he told the *Waterloo Times Tribune*. "Carruthers engaged in an altercation with a crowd of young men and picked out one of the smallest for his personal physical attention."[13] "As to 'Bobby' Caruthers," said the *Waterloo Courier*, "hero of the diamond in years gone by, he has hidden himself behind his wife's skirt and will be forgotten as speedily as possible."[14]

Caruthers had more excitement in the waning months. On August 18, he called a perfect game thrown by Davenport's Red Faber at Dubuque and a no-hitter by Davenport's Frank Bates Archer, on September 7, against Danville. The latter city was also a site of the opposite kind of excitement for Caruthers. On September 14 in Davenport, Caruthers called a game between that team and Rock Island at about 5:30 p.m., even though it was light enough to play, with the teams tied at 3 after 11 innings. Around 50 people rushed out of the stands to confront Caruthers, who was struck by at least one. Rock Island players came to Caruthers' rescue, armed with bats to fend off the crowd, while manager Jack Tighe grabbed the umpire and threw him into one of the Islanders' cars. The reason Caruthers stopped the game? He had to catch a train to Danville, where he was umpiring the next day.

Caruthers might have wanted to leave early, but he did make it to Danville for the next series. In fact, unlike previous years, he didn't miss one game all season. The presence of his wife likely assured that.

But things weren't all rosy for Caruthers. The family fortune was gone—he and Mamie moved into her parents' house in Peoria in 1910 while Flora Caruthers, who once owned expensive Chicago property, was living with her daughter, Elizabeth, now a widow who ran a boarding house. Bob Caruthers supplemented his umpiring income in the off-season by working at a cigar store, which was owned by Dave Rowan, the manager of the Peoria Distillers—the nickname of the team perhaps representing why this city might not have been the best place for Caruthers to reside.

In February, it was announced that Caruthers was signed to return to the Three-I League, the third umpire under contract for the 1911 season. This time, however, Mamie Caruthers didn't go around the circuit with her husband. We don't know why this decision was made—perhaps she thought he could handle himself after the previous year, or maybe he insisted that she not be with him—but whatever the reason, it was a poor one.

After umpiring the first week in Peoria with no issues, Caruthers didn't show up in Danville. He returned five days later in Rock Island and, claimed the *Rock Island Argus*, "as usual filled the bill."[15] After umpiring by himself in Rock Island and a couple of games in Dubuque, he was joined by Bill Guthrie for a Decoration Day doubleheader on May 30. Guthrie manned home plate, while Caruthers handled the bases and by all accounts was energetic in his approach. "Bobby Carruthers delighted the fans by sprinting around the sacks, getting down on his hands and knees, twisting his neck, and waving his hands aloft," reported the *Dubuque Telegraph Herald*, "but outside of that nobody was hurt."[16]

He officiated with Guthrie again the next day, but on June 1 he was nowhere to be found—perhaps to the dismay of Guthrie, who had a rough time of it and was assaulted by fans in the clubhouse after Dubuque's 6–5 loss.

Caruthers turned up in Davenport on June 6, ostensibly to umpire, but was in such bad shape that he found some trees to lie under to take cover from the sun. Three-I president Tearney had no choice but to relieve Caruthers of his duties. "Bobby has not been in proper condition to work this season," reported the *Davenport Daily Times*, which added, "Bobby has been one of the best umpires this league has ever known, and his departure to his own recklessness will be regretted."[17]

Caruthers wasn't going away that quickly, however. He showed up at Peoria's ballpark on June 15 and, after talking with umpire Steve Cusack and Peoria manager Charlie Stis (who had taken over during the year for Rowan) he convinced them to let him umpire, they perhaps thinking he had been reinstated. While the *Peoria Star* thought "Carruthers showed yesterday that he was in form again,"[18] he had in fact not been restored to his position by Tearney, who made it clear days later that Caruthers was no longer an umpire in his league.

Already with a drinking problem combined with living with his in-laws, all but one of his children dead and now with no job, Caruthers went on a bender. On July 15, he stumbled into a Peoria courthouse. Once dressed to the height of fashion, Caruthers was now at the opposite end of the spectrum. Looking pale and rail-thin, likely not having much nutrition the past few weeks, dressed shabbily and covered in dirt and grime, a drunk Caruthers turned himself in and requested to be sent to a workhouse, also known as a poorhouse, where those with no financial means were sent to help get them back on their feet. "The spectacle was sickening," reported the *Peoria Star*. "Not only were the ravages of intemperance shockingly visible in the face, form and gait of the unhappy man, but he was unspeakably filthy."[19] Caruthers was sentenced to 20 days in the workhouse. Peoria chief of police W.W. Rhoads took it upon himself to try to sober up the one-time baseball star. Tearney provided some additional motivation, saying there'd be a job in the Three-I League for Caruthers once he got himself straightened out.

Caruthers lasted only a few days at the workhouse. The effects of abstaining from alcohol got the better of him. While some outlets reported Caruthers as having a nervous breakdown, he was having the usual symptoms—delirium, the shakes, etc.—for those trying to detox and was sent to St. Francis hospital. Reports alternated over the next couple of weeks. Caruthers was in critical condition and about to die, only for it to be written that he was making a recovery.

But things went back to worse, and on August 5 at 7:45 a.m., Bob Caruthers died at the age of 46 with his wife, two brothers, and sister at his side. Doctors blamed diseases brought on by alcoholism. The *St. Louis Star*, chronicler of Caruthers' baseball heyday, ran both an Extra edition to get notice of his death on the top of its sports page and in the final edition had it on page 1, albeit at the bottom of the page.

After a viewing at the Boland Mortuary in Peoria, Caruthers' remains were sent to Chicago, the pine box ordained with numerous floral arrangements, expression of the respect from the people of Peoria. A small funeral service was held at the home of Caruthers' brother, John, in Chicago before he was buried at Graceland Cemetery, where he remains to this day.

It had been nearly 20 years since Caruthers last played in a major league game, but the news of his death made newspapers all over the country. "He was invincible on the ball field, but left his reputation and renown in the bar room," said the *Lincoln Daily Star* in one of the many obituaries to reference his alcoholism. "Immoderate drinking dragged him down."[20]

Many of his former Browns colleagues were already dead—Doc Bushong (1908), Dave Foutz (1897), Rudy Kemmler (1909), Yank Robinson (1894) and Curt Welch (1896)—and it's not like he got along with all of his teammates. Thus, the tributes upon his death from those he played with were few.

"It makes me sick to hear of poor Bobby Carruthers' fate. You know a quarter of a century ago he and I were teammates on what I believe without boasting was the fastest ball club ever put on the field," said former Browns outfielder Hugh Nicol, who was then serving as a scout for Cincinnati as well as physical director at Purdue University.

> We owed our long string of victories mainly to the wonderful work of our twirlers. It was generally conceded that Carruthers was the best of them and more was the greatest of any pitcher in any of the leagues of his day. He was the idol of St. Louis fans and in fact wherever baseball was played the name of Carruthers stood for the highest ability in pitching. ... A more gentlemanly honorable ball player than Bobby Carruthers never lived. Many a ball player of the past and many more of the present will shed a tear for him.[21]

Said George Pinkney, who played with Caruthers in Brooklyn, St. Louis, and Grand Rapids:

> I "bunked" with Bobby for four years when both of us were members of the Brooklyn team in the late eighties. He was an exceptionally fine "pal" and the best sportsman to ever don a player's uniform in the history of baseball. Bob knew no enemies on or off the field. He was respected by all the players, while in each city he visited he was received with an ovation foreign to his team. Many an old time baseball player, as well as all of the present day who knew him, will shed a tear hearing of his death.[22]

As the years went on and modern baseball flourished—Ty Cobb hit .400 for the first time the year of Caruthers' death, and the coming of Babe Ruth would see the game take off in popularity—19th-century players, with a few exceptions, became more and more forgotten. Caruthers' name was bandied about usually in October in the early 20th century when the World Series was under way, his exploits for the St. Louis Browns in their postseason play touted and remembered. But soon the modern World Series, organized by the leagues and only played at the sites of the two participating teams, broke with the ones from the 1880s, which were set up by club owners and often used as a traveling show in other cities, and with it references to the old days—and Caruthers—went away.

Once in a while, Caruthers' name would come up in articles—brief mentions perhaps touting him for the Hall of Fame, notes on his winning percentage, his two-way play, and other such statistics. In 1935, for example, Lady Baldwin, who pitched for Detroit against the Browns in the 1887 World Series, brought up Caruthers, as well as Charles Comiskey, Silver King, and Curt Welch. "I'd like to see some of those fellows go after the Cardinals."[23]

But those mentions were far and few between, especially as the years went by and those who played in the 19th century passed on. Caruthers' nickname—"Parisian Bob"—might be his longest-standing connection to the baseball world. The Society of American Baseball Research (SABR) helped keep his name and memory in 21st-century minds by producing a grave marker at Caruthers' resting place in Graceland Cemetery. "Most versatile major league player prior to Babe Ruth," reads the plaque, which, however, lists his birth year incorrectly as 1864.

That sentiment isn't just a product of SABR. The impact of Caruthers is perhaps best left to those who played with, were acquainted with, and/or covered him. Charles Comiskey, who probably knew Caruthers best, having been his captain and manager in St. Louis and Cincinnati, not to mention his dealings as a team owner when Caruthers managed and umpired, said of Caruthers following his death: "Bobby Caruthers was one of the greatest pitchers ever known. ... Caruthers was one of the greatest batting pitchers I ever saw."[24]

There was, of course, much more to Caruthers' existence than his baseball playing

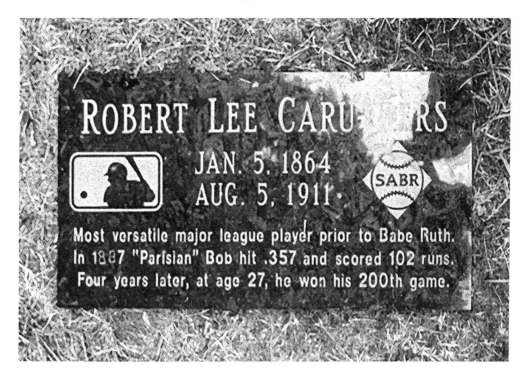

Bob Caruthers' gravestone marker at Graceland Cemetery in Chicago, with incorrect birth-date, was dedicated in September 2018 (SABR).

days. "He was great as a pitcher and great as an umpire," said the *Bloomington Pantagraph*. "It is a mockery of fate that his death should carry with it so many elements of pathos. The transformation wrought by the flying years will bring regret to all who knew him."[25] The *Pantagraph* ended its epitaph with six words which perhaps best summed up Caruthers' life, once filled with wealth and promise but which disintegrated into desperation and anguish: "He had but one enemy, himself."[26]

Chapter Notes

Chapter 1

1. *Logansport Chronicle*, Dec. 3. 1887.
2. "Veteran Player A Star Umpire," *Spokesman-Review*, June 7, 1908, 36.
3. https://digital.la84.org/digital/collection/p17103coll3/id/17119/rec/5.
4. A Brief [Life] of John Caruthers, A Pioneer: His Descendants and Collateral Kin by E.M. Wright, 1944 by E.M. Wright, Springfield, Mo., 35.
5. https://sparedshared4.wordpress.com/letters/1848-elizabeth-rivers-mcneill-caruthers-to-martha-rivers-mcneill/.
6. Cases argued and determined in the Supreme Court of Tennessee, during the year 1868. By Thomas H. Coldwell, State Reporter, Volume 5 (Nashville, SC: Mercer, 1869).
7. https://memphislibrary.contentdm.oclc.org/digital/collection/p13039coll1/id/51/.
8. http://reigelridge.com/roots/index.htm?ssmain=p2149.htm.
9. https://twitter.com/thorn_john/status/1439285162290909187.

Chapter 2

1. *Cases at Law and in Chancery Argued and Determined in the Supreme Court of Illinois*, Vol. 245, Isaac Newton Phillips, Bloomington, IL, 1910; 627.
2. *Ibid.*
3. *Ibid.*
4. *Ibid.*
5. *Ibid.*
6. "Memphis Protestant Collegiate Institute," *Memphis Daily Appeal*, June 28, 1877, 4.
7. Baseball Hall of Fame clip file.
8. *Logansport Chronicle*, Dec. 3. 1887.
9. "Diamond Dust," *St. Louis Post-Dispatch*, July 2, 1885, 5.
10. "Cincinnati Chat," *Sporting Life*, Feb. 29, 1888, 2.
11. Boddie and Allied Families, 137.
12. http://physics.bu.edu/~redner/projects/population/cities/chicago.html.
13. "The Court Record," *Inter Ocean*, Feb. 24, 1879, 6.
14. "Personal," *Memphis Daily Appeal*, Sept. 2, 1877, 4.

15. "Caruthers," *St. Louis Post-Dispatch*, March 21, 1887, 4.
16. Pruter, Robert. "Youth Baseball in Chicago, 1868–1890: Not Always Sandlot Ball." *Journal of Sport History*, 26, no. 1 (1999), 21.
17. "Caruthers' Career," *Moline Dispatch*, May 13, 1908, 6.
18. Pruter, Robert. "Youth Baseball in Chicago, 1868–1890: Not Always Sandlot Ball." *Journal of Sport History*, 26, no. 1, 1999, 7.

Chapter 3

1. *Grand Rapids Daily Democrat*, June 3, 1883.
2. *Ibid.*
3. *Grand Rapids Daily Democrat*, June 9, 1883.
4. "Base-Ball Notes," *Quincy Daily Whig*, June 10, 1883, 2.
5. *Spalding's Base Ball Guide and Official League Book for 1884* (Chicago: A.G. Spalding & Bros, 1884), 44.
6. "Morning Menu," *Quincy Daily Whig*, July 12, 1883, 1.
7. *Grand Rapids Evening Ledger*, July 13, 1883.
8. *Ibid.*
9. *Grand Rapids Daily Times*, June 13, 1883.
10. *Grand Rapids Daily Democrat*, June 13, 1883.
11. *Grand Rapids Evening News*, June 21, 1883.
12. *Grand Rapids Daily Eagle*, July 19, 1883.
13. *Ibid.*
14. *Grand Rapids Daily Times*, July 21, 1883.
15. *Grand Rapids Daily Eagle*, July 24, 1883.
16. *Grand Rapids Daily Democrat*, August 1, 1883.
17. *Grand Rapids Daily Eagle*, August 6, 1883.
18. *Grand Rapids Daily Eagle*, August 10, 1883.
19. *Grand Rapids Daily Democrat*, Sept. 26, 1883.
20. *Grand Rapids Daily Democrat*, August 25, 1883.
21. *Grand Rapids Daily Times*, Oct. 20, 1883.

Chapter 4

1. "Base Ball Biffs Back," *Fort Wayne Daily Gazette*, Jan. 13, 1884, 8.

2. "The Men Minneapolis Backs," *Daily Minnesota Tribune*, Feb. 8, 1884, 7.

3. "The Sports," *St. Paul Daily Globe*, April 22, 1884, 7.

4. https://www.thevintagenews.com/2016/10/11/king-dudes-berry-wall-fashion-leader-gilded-age-changed-clothes-40-times-breakfast-dinner-2.

5. *Cincinnati Commercial Gazette*, April 21, 1884.

6. "A Good Pitcher," *The Sedalia Weekly Bazoo*, March 11, 1890, 6.

7. *Springfield Daily Rebulic*, Nov. 29, 1886.

8. "Diamond Chips," *St. Louis Post-Dispatch*, April 16, 1884, 5.

9. "A Good Pitcher," *The Sedalia Weekly Bazoo*, March 11, 1890, 6.

10. "Notes," *Quincy Daily Whig*, May 4, 1884, 3.

11. "The Dudes Downed," *St. Paul Daily Globe*, July 4, 1884, 1.

12. "First of the Season," *St. Paul Daily Globe*, June 10, 1884, 2.

13. "Minneapolis Notes," *St. Paul Daily Globe*, June 13, 1884, 5.

14. *Ibid.*

15. "Minneapolis vs. Quincy," *St. Paul Daily Globe*, June 14, 1884, 5.

16. *Ibid.*

17. *Spalding's Base Ball Guide and Official League Book for 1884* (Chicago: A.G. Spalding & Bros, 1884), 32.

18. *Grand Rapids Daily Eagle*, May 21, 1884.

19. "Minneapolis vs. Milwaukee," *St. Paul Daily Globe*, June 18, 1884, 4.

20. "Nine Times 0 Equals 0," *Minneapolis Daily Tribune*, August 3, 1884, 4.

21. "Notes and Comments," *Sporting Life*, Sept. 10, 1884, 5.

22. "Caruthers Not Suspended," *St. Paul Daily Globe*, August 30, 1884, 4.

23. "Chicago Gossip," *Sporting Life*, Feb. 22, 1888, 8.

24. *Ibid.*

25. *Ibid.*

26. *Ibid.*

27. *Ibid.*

28. http://research.sabr.org/journals/chris-von-der-ahe-baseballs-pioneering-huckster.

29. "Ex-Manager Williams Is Disgusted," *St. Louis Globe-Democrat*, Sept. 7, 1884, 8.

30. "Notes and Comments," *Sporting Life*, Oct. 29, 1884, 5.

31. "They Did Win," *St. Louis Post-Dispatch*, Sept. 8, 1884, 5.

32. "St. Louis, 6; Athletics, 2," *St. Louis Globe-Democrat*, Sept. 8, 1884, 3.

33. "Baltimore, 2; St. Louis, 1," *St. Louis Globe-Democrat*, Sept. 10, 1884, 8.

34. "St. Louis vs. Baltimore," *St. Louis Post-Dispatch*, Sept. 10, 1884, 7.

35. "The Browns-Mets Series," *St. Louis Post-Dispatch*, Sept. 12, 1884, 5.

36. "St. Louis vs. Brooklyn," *St. Louis Post-Dispatch*, Sept. 24, 1884, 2.

37. *Baltimore Sun*, Oct. 16, 1884.

Chapter 5

1. "A Four-Base Hit," *St. Louis Post-Dispatch*, Oct. 27, 1884, 7.

2. "The Arbitration Meet," *Sporting Life*, Nov. 12, 1884, 3.

3. "A Base-Ball Sensation," *Richmond Dispatch*, Jan. 7, 1885, 4.

4. "The Champion Browns," *St. Louis Globe-Democrat*, Oct. 8, 1885, 8.

5. "Ixion's Letter," *St. Louis Post-Dispatch*, Sept. 13, 1884, 13.

6. "The Local Series," *St. Louis Post-Dispatch*, Feb. 6, 1885, 5.

7. "Sporting," *St. Louis Globe-Democrat*, April 20, 1885, 6.

8. "The Browns' Welcome," *Sporting Life*, Oct. 14, 1885, 2.

9. "St. Louis, 6; Cincinnatis, 0," *St. Louis Globe-Democrat*, April 30, 1885, 8.

10. "Diamond Dust," *St. Louis Globe-Democrat*, May 3, 1885, 8.

11. "Sporting," *St. Louis Globe-Democrat*, April 27, 1885, 8.

12. "A Poor Way to Play," *Baltimore American*, June 2, 1885, 4.

13. "The Ball Field," *Philadelphia Inquirer*, June 5, 1885, 2.

14. *Cincinnati Commercial Gazette*, June 29, 1885.

15. "Browns 6; Cincinnatis 1," *St. Louis Globe-Democrat*, August 24, 1885, 6.

16. *Cincinnati Commercial Gazette*, August 24, 1885.

17. "King Hecker's Defeat," *St. Louis Post-Dispatch*, Sept. 4, 1885, 3.

18. *Ibid.*

19. "Browns, 2; Louisvilles, 1," *St. Louis Globe-Democrat*, Sept. 7, 1885, 3.

20. "The Champion Browns," *St. Louis Globe-Democrat*, Oct. 8, 1885, 8.

21. "Cincinnatis, 18; Browns, 3," *St. Louis Globe-Democrat*, Oct. 12, 1885, 10.

22. "The Championship of America," *NY Clipper*, Oct. 24, 1885, 505.

23. "Sporting Sundries," *St. Louis Post-Dispatch*, Oct. 16, 1885, 8.

24. "Diamond Dust," *St. Louis Globe-Democrat*, Oct. 17, 1885, 7.

25. "Sporting," *St. Louis Globe-Democrat*, Oct. 18, 1885, 9.

26. *Ibid.*

27. "Sporting," *St. Louis Globe-Democrat*, Oct. 19, 1885, 6.

28. "St. Louis Browns-Chicago Game," *St. Louis Globe-Democrat*, Oct. 25, 1885, 25.

29. "The Browns And Chicagos," *St. Louis Post-Dispatch*, Sept. 18, 1886, 12.

30. "Sporting," *St. Louis Globe-Democrat*, Oct. 26, 1885, 6.

31. "A Double Surprise," *St. Louis Globe-Democrat*, Nov. 2, 1885, 8.

32. "The Championship," *St. Louis Post-Dispatch*, June 15, 1886, 5.

Chapter 6

1. "Sporting," *St. Louis Globe-Democrat*, Oct. 25, 1885, 9.

2. "Sporting Sundries," *St. Louis Post-Dispatch*, Oct. 26, 1885, 6.

3. "Diamond Dust," *St. Louis Globe-Democrat*, August 2, 1885, 9.

4. *Ibid.*

5. "'Bobbie' Carruthers 'Fans' A Little," *Sioux City Journal*, June 12, 1905, 3.

6. "Caruthers and the Browns," *Omaha Daily Bee*, July 24, 1904, 11.

7. "'Bobbie' Carruthers 'Fans' a Little," *Sioux City Journal*, June 12, 1905, 3.

8. "Chat of the Diamond," *Philadelphia Inquirer*, August 24, 1891, 3.

9. *Ibid.*

10. *Chicago Tribune*, Dec. 20, 1885.

11. https://chicagology.com/goldenage/golden age127/.

12. *Chicago Tribune*, Dec. 20, 1885.

13. https://www.officialdata.org/.

14. "Carruthers Will Sign," *St. Louis Post-Dispatch*, Jan. 12, 1886, 8.

15. "Sporting Sundries," *St. Louis Post-Dispatch*, Jan. 18, 1886, 3.

16. "Minneapolis Personals," *St. Paul Daily Globe*, June 20, 1884, 5.

17. "Diamond Dust," *St. Louis Globe-Democrat*, April 16, 1886, 10.

18. "The Caruthers Case," *St. Louis Globe-Democrat*, Jan. 31, 1886, 9.

19. *Ibid.*

20. *Ibid.*

21. "Marquard's Threat Reminds of One Other Hold Out," *Mansfield Shield*, Jan. 14, 1913, 6.

22. http://daytoninmanhattan.blogspot.com/2012/11/the-lost-windsor-hotel-5th-avenue-and.html.

23. "Streetscapes: The Windsor Hotel Fire," New York Times website, Jan. 7, 2010.

24. "Caruthers Has Sailed," *St. Louis Globe-Democrat*, Feb. 14, 1886, 10.

25. *Ibid.*

26. *Ibid.*

27. http://www.norwayheritage.com/p_ship.asp?sh=auran.

28. "Overshot the Mark," *Sporting Life*, Feb. 24, 1886, 2.

29. *Ibid.*

30. "Tales of the Diamond," *Philadelphia Inquirer*, Feb. 3, 1900, 10.

31. "Caruthers," *St. Louis Post-Dispatch*, March 13, 1886, 11.

32. "Caruthers Replies," *St. Louis Post-Dispatch*, March 15, 1886, 5.

33. "Caruthers Coming," *The Sporting News*, March 17, 1886, 1.

34. "Dickering Dave," *St. Louis Post-Dispatch*, Feb. 25, 1887, 10.

35. "Caruthers' Return," *St. Louis Globe-Democrat*, April 2, 1886, 8.

36. *Ibid.*

37. *Ibid.*

38. *Oshkosh Daily Northwestern*, August 19, 1911.

39. "Caught on the Fly," *The Sporting News*, Nov. 27, 1886, 5.

40. "St. Louis Siftings," *Sporting Life*, Feb. 11, 1893, 4.

41. "Bobby Carruthers Was One of Characters Of Baseball," *Butte Daily Post*, August 5, 1911, 8.

42. "Caruthers' Return," *St. Louis Globe-Democrat*, April 2, 1886, 8.

43. *Ibid.*

44. *Boston Post*, April 9, 1886.

Chapter 7

1. "Changes in the Playing Rules," *St. Louis Post-Dispatch*, March 3, 1886, 8.

2. "Styles in Sliding," *St. Louis Post-Dispatch*, July 31, 1886, 12.

3. "Pfeffer on Sliding," *St. Louis Post-Dispatch*, Oct. 23, 1886, 8.

4. "Caught on the Fly," *The Sporting News*, March 17, 1886, 3.

5. "Gossip of the Game," *St. Louis Post-Dispatch*, April 8, 1886, 5.

6. "From the Mound City," *Sporting Life*, April 14, 1886, 4.

7. "From the Mound City," *Sporting Life*, April 21, 1886, 3.

8. "Diamond Dust," *St. Louis Globe-Democrat*, April 18, 1886, 9.

9. "From the Mound City," *Sporting Life*, April 28, 1886, 4.

10. "St. Louis, 14; Cincinnati, 12," *St. Louis Globe-Democrat*, April 27, 1886, 5.

11. *Ibid.*

12. "St. Louis, 5; Kansas Citys, 3," *St. Louis Globe-Democrat*, May 11, 1886, 5.

13. "Caught on the Fly," *The Sporting News*, June 7, 1886, 5.

14. "Bushong Slugs Latham," *Baltimore American*, June 4, 1886, 4.

15. *Ibid.*

16. "George Munson Visits Quincy," *Quincy Daily Journal*, August 22, 1895.

17. "From St. Louis," *Sporting Life*, June 16, 1886.

18. *Racine Daily Journal*, July 13, 1907.

19. "Played Ball 32 Years," *Berkshire Eagle*, Feb. 16, 1905.

20. "The Reds Not in Condition," *St. Louis Post-Dispatch*, June 19, 1886, 12.

21. "Anson Talks," *St. Louis Post-Dispatch*, July 12, 1886, 7.

22. "The Browns the Champions," *St. Louis Globe-Democrat*, July 14, 1886, 8.

23. "Caruthers and Foutz Call the Chicagoan's Bluff," *The Sporting News*, July 19, 1886, 4.

24. *Ibid.*

25. "Anson's Big Buff," *St. Louis Post-Dispatch*, July 14, 1886, 7.

Chapter 8

1. "Gossip of the Game," *St. Louis Post-Dispatch*, July 19, 1886.

2. "The New Rules," *St. Louis Post-Dispatch*, Nov. 19, 1886, 7.

3. "Brooklyns, 11; Browns, 9," *St. Louis Globe-Democrat*, August 17, 1886, 8.

4. "From St. Louis," *Sporting Life*, August 25, 1886, 5.

5. "An Umpire in Danger," *Baltimore American*, Sept. 19, 1886, 7.

6. *Ibid.*

7. *Ibid.*

8. "His Own Figures," *St. Louis Post-Dispatch*, August 18, 1886, 5.

9. "From St. Louis," *Sporting Life*, Sept. 29, 1886, 4.

10. "Diamond Dust." *St. Louis Globe-Democrat*, August 16, 1886, 8.

11. *Ibid.*

12. "Caruthers Quits," *St. Louis Post-Dispatch*, Sept. 28, 1886, 9.

13. "Bob Caruthers' Mother Speaks," *St. Louis Globe-Democrat*, Dec. 4, 1887, 11.

14. "Caruthers Quits," *St. Louis Post-Dispatch*, Sept. 28, 1886, 9.

15. *Ibid.*

16. *Ibid.*

17. "Caruthers' Trouble," *St. Louis Post-Dispatch*, August 4, 1887, 5.

18. "As to Caruthers," *St. Louis Post-Dispatch*, Oct. 7, 1886, 10.

19. *Ibid.*

20. "From St. Louis," *Sporting Life*, Oct. 6, 1886, 4.

21. *Ibid.*

22. *Ibid.*

23. *Ibid.*

24. "Caruthers and the Browns," *Omaha Daily Bee*, July 24, 1904, 11.

25. "Diamond Dust," *St. Louis Globe-Democrat*, March 28, 1886, 7.

26. "The Wiman Trophy," *The Sporting News*, Oct. 18, 1886, 5.

Chapter 9

1. "Chadwick on the Browns," *St. Louis Post-Dispatch*, Sept. 21, 1886, 11.

2. "The World's Champions," *St. Louis Globe-Democrat*, Oct. 18, 1886, 6.

3. *Ibid.*

4. *Ibid.*

5. *Ibid.*

6. "The Browns-Chicagos Series," *St. Louis Globe-Democrat*, Oct. 17, 1886, 11.

7. *Ibid.*

8. "Stray Bits," *Inter Ocean*, Oct. 21, 1886, 3.

9. "Stray Bits," *Inter Ocean*, Oct. 19, 1886, 3.

10. "Even Money," *St. Louis Post-Dispatch*, Oct. 18, 1886, 7.

11. "Chicagos, 6; Browns, 0," *St. Louis Globe-Democrat*, Oct. 19, 1886, 5.

12. "'Doc's' Dictum," *St. Louis Post-Dispatch*, Oct. 19, 1886, 7.

13. "Carruthers' World's Pitching Feat," *Wapanucka Press*, August 29, 1912, 7.

14. "Chicago Chats," *St. Louis Post-Dispatch*, April 11, 1887, 5.

15. "Beer Beats Them," *The Inter Ocean*, Oct. 20, 1886, 2.

16. "Betting in Chicago," *St. Louis Globe-Democrat*, Oct. 20, 1886, 8.

17. *Decatur Herald and Review*, August 15, 1901.

18. "Chicagos 11, Browns 4," *St. Louis Globe-Democrat*, Oct. 21, 1886, 8.

19. "Home Again," *St. Louis Post-Dispatch*, Oct. 21, 1886, 8.

20. *Ibid.*

21. "'That's the Way!'" *St. Louis Post-Dispatch*, Oct. 22, 1886, 7.

22. "Pitching Stars Past and Present," *St. Joseph Gazette-Herald*, June 12, 1901, 3.

23. "'That's the Way!'" *St. Louis Post-Dispatch*, Oct. 22, 1886, 7.

24. *The Cardinals Encyclopedia*, 423.

25. "A Big Stake," *St. Louis Post-Dispatch*, Oct. 23, 1886, 8.

26. *Ibid.*

27. "Tebeau Talks of Brashear," *St. Joseph News-Press*, Jan. 28, 1902, 4.

28. "St. Louis' Great Victory," *Inter Ocean*, Oct. 24, 1886, 4.

29. "A Chicago Account of Chicago's Defeat," *St. Louis Globe-Democrat*, Oct. 26, 1886, 5.

30. "St. Louis' Great Victory," *Inter Ocean*, Oct. 24, 1886, 4.

31. "Base Ball Notes," *St. Louis Post-Dispatch*, Oct. 25, 1886, 5.

32. "President Stearns' Opinion of the Browns," *St. Louis Globe-Democrat*, Oct. 29, 1886, 5.

33. "Chris Von der Ahe, the Most Picturesque Figure in Baseball History," *St. Louis Post-Dispatch*, April 17, 1904, 40.

34. "How the Game Was Won," *St. Louis Post-Dispatch*, Oct. 25, 1886, 5.

35. "Day St. Louis Won," *St. Louis Post-Dispatch*, Dec. 29, 1899, 5.

36. "Tales of the Diamond," *Philadelphia Inquirer*, Feb. 3, 1900, 10.

37. "St. Louis, 4; Chicagos, 3," *St. Louis Globe-Democrat*, Oct. 24, 1886, 11.

38. "Results of the Series," *St. Louis Globe-Democrat*, Oct. 24, 1886, 11. *Ibid.*
39. "Chicago Conquered," *Inter Ocean*, Oct. 24, 1886, 4.

Chapter 10

1. "Caruthers and the Browns," *Omaha Daily Bee*, July 24, 1904, 11.
2. "A Reception on 'Change," *The Sporting News*, Oct. 30, 1886, 3.
3. *Ibid.*
4. *Arkansas Democrat*, Oct. 29, 1886.
5. https://www2.census.gov/library/publications/decennial/1950/population-volume-2/18310273v2p4ch1.pdf.
6. "Hyde's Opera House" advertisement, *Daily Arkansas Gazette*, Oct. 29, 1886, 6.
7. *Ibid.*
8. "Base Ball," *Daily Arkansas Gazette*, Oct. 30, 1886, 6.
9. *Ibid.*
10. "Maroons, 2; Browns, 1," *St. Louis Globe-Democrat*, Nov. 1, 1886, 6.
11. "Caught on the Fly," *The Sporting News*, Nov. 20, 1886, 5.
12. "The Browns' Medals," *St. Louis Post-Dispatch*, Nov. 8, 1886, 7.
13. "The St. Louis Browns," *The Sporting News*, Nov. 13, 1886, 5.
14. "Base Ball," *The Sporting News*, Nov. 27, 1886, 2.
15. "I Won't Play," *St. Louis Post-Dispatch*, Nov. 25, 1886, 8.
16. "Base Ball," *The Sporting News*, Dec. 4, 1886, 2.
17. "I Won't Play," *St. Louis Post-Dispatch*, Nov. 25, 1886, 8.
18. *Ibid.*
19. https://www2.census.gov/prod2/decennial/documents/13982433v3ch02.pdf.
20. "Caruthers and the Browns," *St. Louis Globe-Democrat*, Jan. 19, 1887, 5.
21. https://insight.ieeeusa.org/articles/your-engineering-heritage-electromagnetic-quackery-and-bizarre-medical-devices/.
22. "Caruthers and the Browns," *St. Louis Globe-Democrat*, Jan. 19, 1887, 5.
23. "Caruthers," *St. Louis Post-Dispatch*, March 21, 1887, 3.
24. "Spalding to Blame," *St. Louis Post-Dispatch*, Jan. 27, 1887, 5.
25. *Ibid.*
26. "Bobby Is Better," *St. Louis Post-Dispatch*, Feb. 3, 1887, 8.
27. *Ibid.*
28. "Dickering Dave," *St. Louis Post-Dispatch*, Feb. 25, 1887, 10.
29. "Will Buy Ramsey," *St. Louis Post-Dispatch*, Feb. 9, 1887, 5.
30. "The Browns Meet To-Day," *St. Louis Globe-Democrat*, March 10, 1887, 5.

31. "Blacklisting Ball-Players," *St. Louis Globe-Democrat*, March 15, 1887, 8.
32. "A Ballplayers' Rights," *Philadelphia Times*, March 20, 1887, 11.
33. "Caruthers," *St. Louis Post-Dispatch*, March 21, 1887, 3.

Chapter 11

1. "Eaten By 'The Tiger,'" *Chicago News* via *Savannah Morning News*, April 13, 1887, 3.
2. *Ibid.*
3. "'Old Reliable,'" *St. Louis Post-Dispatch*, April 2, 1887, 10.
4. "The Court Record," *Inter Ocean*, April 28, 1887, 9.
5. "In General," *Inter Ocean*, April 20, 1888, 10.
6. "The New Rules," *St. Louis Post-Dispatch*, Nov. 19, 1886, 7.
7. "Chat with Comiskey," *St. Louis Post-Dispatch*, March 19, 1887, 10.
8. "Sporting," *Louisville Courier-Journal* via *St. Louis Globe-Democrat*, April 19, 1887, 3.
9. *St. Louis Post-Dispatch*, April 4, 1887.
10. "Diamond Dust," *St. Louis Globe-Democrat*, April 4, 1887, 8.
11. "Base Ball Briefs," *St. Louis Post-Dispatch*, April 6, 1887, 8.
12. *Chicago Tribune*, Dec. 23, 1886.
13. "Chicago Arrives," *St. Louis Post-Dispatch*, April 6, 1887, 8.
14. "Diamond Dust," *St. Louis Globe-Democrat*, April 9, 1887, 7.
15. "Chicago Chats," *St. Louis Post-Dispatch*, April 11, 1887, 5.
16. "What They Think," *St. Louis Post-Dispatch*, April 11, 1887, 5.
17. *Ibid.*
18. "Nicknames for Ball Players," *St. Louis Globe-Democrat*, April 14, 1887, 5.
19. "A Terrific Batting Game," *Indianapolis Journal*, April 15. 1887, 7.
20. "Sporting," *St. Louis Globe-Democrat*, April 19, 1887, 3.

Chapter 12

1. "Diamond Sparks," *St. Louis Post-Dispatch*, May 26, 1887, 5.
2. "The Browns to Be Weakened," *St. Louis Globe-Democrat*, May 23, 1887, 10.
3. "Diamond Sparks," *St. Louis Post-Dispatch*, May 14, 1887, 12.
4. Advertisement, *The Sporting News*, July 30, 1887, 7.
5. "The Official Charges," *St. Louis Post-Dispatch*, June 18, 1887, 12.
6. *St. Louis Post-Dispatch*, June 21, 1887.
7. *Baltimore American*, June 18, 1887.
8. "The Baltimore Outrage," *St. Louis Globe-Democrat*, June 29, 1887, 4.

9. *Ibid.*

10. "From St. Louis," *Sporting Life,* July 6, 1887, 5.

11. "Going Into Business," *St. Louis Post-Dispatch,* June 29, 1887, 11.

12. "No Bluff," *St. Louis Post-Dispatch*, August 4, 1887, 5.

13. *Ibid.*

14. "Metropolitans 10; St. Louis 6," *St. Louis Globe-Democrat,* July 21, 1887, 8.

15. "No Bluff," *St. Louis Post-Dispatch*, August 4, 1887, 5.

16. *Ibid.*

17. *Ibid.*

18. "Caruthers Arrives," *St. Louis Post-Dispatch,* August 18, 1887, 8.

19. "Browns 22; Athletics 8," *St. Louis Globe-Democrat,* August 20, 1887, 7.

20. "Caruthers Wins Medal," *St. Louis Globe-Democrat,* August 28, 1887, 9.

21. *Ibid.*

22. "Browns 10; Metropolitans 1," *St. Louis Globe-Democrat,* August 28, 1887, 9.

23. "Caruthers and the Browns," *Omaha Daily Bee,* July 24, 1904, 11.

24. "Notes and Comments," *Sporting Life,* Oct. 7, 1885, 3.

25. "Tim Murnane's Pointers," *Boston Globe,* May 29, 1888, 5.

26. "Caruthers Wins Medal," *St. Louis Globe-Democrat,* August 28, 1887, 9.

27. "Sporting," *St. Louis Globe-Democrat*, Sept. 5, 1887, 8.

28. "Comiskey Still Swears by the Old St. Louis Browns," *St. Louis Republic*, Nov. 24, 1901, 17.

29. "Color Line in Base Ball," *Philadelphia Times*, Sept. 12, 1887, 1.

30. "The Color Line on the Base Ball Diamond," *Decatur Saturday Herald*, Sept. 17, 1887, 6.

31. "Color Line in Base Ball," *Philadelphia Times*, Sept. 12, 1887, 1.

32. "Diamond Points," *Boston Globe*, Sept. 17, 1887, 3.

33. "Color Line in Base Ball," *Philadelphia Times*, Sept. 12, 1887, 1.

34. "The Browns' Color Line," *St. Louis Globe-Democrat,* Sept. 13, 1887, 8.

35. Green Cathedrals, 227–228.

36. "They Beat the Champions," *Philadelphia Times,* Sept. 13, 1887, 2.

37. "The Browns' Color Line," *St. Louis Globe-Democrat,* Sept. 13, 1887, 8.

38. *Ibid.*

39. *Billings Gazette,* Jan. 11, 1928.

40. "Trouble in the Browns," *Philadelphia Times,* Oct. 2, 1887, 14.

Chapter 13

1. "'Der Prown's' President," *The Inter Ocean,* Sept. 5, 1887, 2.

2. "Detroit's Arrival," *St. Louis Post-Dispatch,* Oct. 10, 1887, 8.

3. "'A Good Club,'" *St. Louis Post-Dispatch*, Oct. 11, 1887, 5.

4. *Ibid.*

5. *Chicago Examiner,* Feb. 19, 1911.

6. "Comiskey's Carelessness," *St. Louis Globe-Democrat,* Oct. 13, 1887, 8.

7. *Ibid.*

8. "A Sorry Confession," *St. Louis Globe-Democrat,* Oct. 22, 1887, 7.

9. "'We Are Chumps,'" *St. Louis Post-Dispatch,* Oct. 19, 1887, 5.

10. "Chadwick's Chat," *Sporting Life,* Oct. 26, 1887, 5.

11. "Caruthers the Star," *St. Louis Post-Dispatch,* Oct. 16, 1887, 6.

12. *Ibid.*

13. *Ibid.*

14. "Bobby's Big Head," *St. Louis Post-Dispatch,* Oct. 16, 1887, 6.

15. "Will Lay Gleason Off," *St. Louis Post-Dispatch,* Oct. 16, 1887, 6.

16. "Defeated Again," *St. Louis Globe-Democrat,* Oct. 18, 1887, 8.

17. *St. Louis Post-Dispatch,* Oct. 18, 1887.

18. *Ibid.*

19. "'We Are Chumps,'" *St. Louis Post-Dispatch,* Oct. 19, 1887, 5.

20. *St. Louis Post-Dispatch,* Oct. 18, 1887.

21. "'We Are Chumps,'" *St. Louis Post-Dispatch,* Oct. 19, 1887, 5.

22. "No One But 'Bob,'" *St. Louis Post-Dispatch,* Oct. 20, 1887, 8.

23. "Baseball," *NY Clipper,* Nov. 12, 1887, 558.

24. "St. Louis Settings," *Sporting Life,* Nov. 16, 1887, 4.

25. "Chicago Gossip," *Sporting Life,* Feb. 22, 1888, 3.

26. "Caruthers Was Notified," *St. Louis Globe-Democrat,* Nov. 6, 1887, 11.

27. "Bob Caruthers' Mother Speaks," *St. Louis Globe-Democrat,* Dec. 4, 1887, 4.

28. "Caruthers' Bluff," *St. Louis Globe-Democrat,* Nov. 2, 1887, 8.

Chapter 14

1. "The Brooklyn Club," *The Sporting News,* Dec. 10, 1887, 5.

2. "'Bob' and 'Doc,'" *St. Louis Post-Dispatch,* Oct. 2, 1887, 10.

3. *Ibid.*

4. "Bobby's Big Head," *St. Louis Post-Dispatch,* Oct. 16, 1887, 6.

5. "Caruthers Will Quit," *St. Louis Post-Dispatch,* Nov. 4, 1887, 8.

6. "Von der Ahe's New Club," *Philadelphia Times,* Nov. 6, 1887, 14.

7. *Ibid.*

8. "Bob Caruthers' Mother Speaks," *Chicago Tribune* via *St. Louis Globe-Democrat,* Dec. 4, 1887, 11.

9. "Trying to Get Players," *Philadelphia Times*, Nov. 13, 1887, 2.

10. "Ball Players Engaged," *NY Times*, Nov. 23, 1887, 3.

11. "The Case of Caruthers," *The Sporting News*, Nov. 19, 1887, 5.

12. "That Big Sale," *St. Louis Post-Dispatch*, Nov. 21, 1887, 8.

13. "Our New Browns," *The Sporting News*, Dec. 3, 1887, 1.

14. "Releasing Players," *San Francisco Examiner*, Nov. 25, 1887, 2.

15. "Von der Ahe Goes Home," *Philadelphia Times*, Nov. 24, 1887, 1.

16. "'Bob' Wants $5,000," *St. Louis Post-Dispatch*, Nov. 23, 1887, 8.

17. *Cincinnati Commercial Gazette*, April 3, 1892.

18. "Base Ball Interests," *Brooklyn Daily Eagle*, Dec. 11, 1887, 7.

19. "Ball Players for Brooklyn," *NY Times*, Nov. 26, 1887, 3.

20. "Schmelz Gives Up," *St. Louis Post-Dispatch*, Nov. 25, 1887, 8.

21. "Von der Ahe on the Changes," *St. Louis Globe-Democrat*, Nov. 26, 1887, 7.

22. *Ibid.*

23. "The Deal Finished," *St. Louis Post-Dispatch*, Nov. 27, 1887, 6.

24. *Ibid.*

25. "Caruthers Goes Back on Brooklyn," *NY Sun*, Nov. 28, 1887, 5.

26. *Ibid.*

27. "Foutz Secured," *Brooklyn Daily Eagle*, Nov. 30, 1887, 6.

28. "Caruthers Declines Five Thousand," *St. Louis Globe-Democrat*, Nov. 29, 1887, 8.

29. "Caruthers' Final Refusal," *St. Louis Post-Dispatch*, Nov. 29, 1887, 8.

30. "Our New Browns," *The Sporting News*, Dec. 3, 1887, 1.

31. "Caruthers Threatens," *St. Louis Post-Dispatch*, Nov. 30, 1887, 8.

32. "Cincinnati Chips," *Sporting Life*, Dec. 7, 1887, 3.

33. *Cincinnati Enquirer*, Dec. 4, 1887.

34. *Ibid.*

35. "A Talk with the 'Boss Manager,'" *St. Louis Globe-Democrat*, Dec. 4, 1887, 11.

36. *Chicago Tribune*, Dec. 6, 1887.

37. "A Rich Mother," *Brooklyn Daily Eagle*, Dec. 16, 1887, 8.

38. "Beats the Kelly Deal," *St. Louis Post-Dispatch*, Dec. 15, 1887, 8.

39. https://babel.hathitrust.org/cgi/pt?id=mdp. 39015059385339&view=1up&seq=375.

40. "The Big Deal," *Sporting Life*, Dec. 21, 1887, 1.

41. "Crippled Browns," *St. Louis Post-Dispatch*, July 7, 1894, 2.

42. "Caruthers and the Browns," *Omaha Daily Bee*, July 24, 1904, 11.

Chapter 15

1. "Good-Bye Caruthers," *St. Louis Post-Dispatch*, Dec. 14, 1887, 8.

2. "A Talk with the 'Boss Manager,'" *St. Louis Globe-Democrat*, Dec. 4, 1887, 11.

3. "The Big Deal," *Sporting Life*, Dec. 21, 1887, 1.

4. "Chicago Gossip," *Sporting Life*, Feb. 22, 1888, 3.

5. "Diamond Dust," *Inter Ocean*, March 4, 1888, 12.

6. "Signed for Life," *San Francisco Examiner*, March 9, 1888, 1.

7. "Stray Sparks from the Diamond," *New York Clipper*, March 17, 1888, 11.

8. "News of the Ball Players," *NY Sun*, March 20, 1888, 5.

9. "Notes and Comments," *Sporting Life*, April 11, 1888, 6.

10. "Much In Little," *Buffalo Commercial*, April 4, 1888, 3.

11. "Scattering Bits," *Memphis Avalanche*, April 1, 1888, 15.

12. "The First Game," *Brooklyn Daily Eagle*, April 2, 1888, 2.

13. https://www.seamheads.com/ballparks/ballpark.php?parkID=NYC05.

14. https://www.census.gov/history/www/through_the_decades/fast_facts/1890_fast_facts.html.

15. "On the Diamond Field," *Brooklyn Standard Union*, April 23, 1888, 2.

16. "The American Games," *Brooklyn Daily Eagle*, April 26, 1888, 1.

17. "No One Blamed," *Brooklyn Daily Eagle*, April 27, 1888, 1.

18. https://ourgame.mlblogs.com/news-from-the-plus-%C3%A7a-change-department-7d70a9786610a.

19. *Ibid.*

20. "Fair Play for the Strangers," *Brooklyn Daily Eagle*, May 14, 1888, 1.

21. *Ibid.*

22. "'A Base Ball Crank,'" *Brooklyn Daily Eagle*, May 19, 1888, 1.

23. "The Brooklyn Base Ball Club," *Brooklyn Daily Eagle*, May 29, 1888, 4.

24. "Baseball Gossip," *Brooklyn Citizen*, June 5, 1888, 3.

25. "Caruthers' Big Day," *Brooklyn Standard Union*, June 13, 1888, 4.

26. "Bobby's Home Runs," *NY Evening World*, June 12, 1888, 1.

27. "Notes and Comments," *Sporting Life*, June 27, 1888, 7.

28. *Ibid.*

29. "Brooklyn's Revenge," *Brooklyn Citizen*, June 29, 1888, 3.

30. Logansport Chronicle, Dec. 3. 1887.

31. "Cincinnati Chat," *Sporting Life*, Feb. 29, 1888, 2.

32. Advertisement, *St. Louis Globe-Democrat*, July 6, 1888, 7.

33. *Ibid.*
34. "Diamond Dust," *St. Louis Globe-Democrat*, July 11, 1888, 8.

Chapter 16

1. "Base Ball Day," *St. Louis Post-Dispatch*, July 6, 1888, 8.
2. "Wants to Come Back," *St. Louis Post-Dispatch*, July 2, 1888, 5.
3. "They're on Top," *Brooklyn Daily Eagle*, July 7, 1888, 2.
4. *Indianapolis Sun*, August 13, 1888.
5. "They're on Top," *Brooklyn Daily Eagle*, July 7, 1888, 2.
6. "Won in Ten Innings," *Brooklyn Citizen*, July 11, 1888, 3.
7. *Sporting Life*, August 22, 1888.
8. "Still Losing," *Brooklyn Daily Eagle*, August 27, 1888, 2.
9. "Grand Stand Chat," *St. Louis Post-Dispatch*, Sept. 4, 1888, 8.
10. "Base Ball Notes," *Sporting Life*, June 1, 1887, 10.
11. "A Game Lost by Errors," *Philadelphia Times*, Sept. 16, 1888, 2.
12. "It Will End To-Day," *Brooklyn Standard Union*, Oct. 16, 1888, 4.
13. "Caruthers Talks," *St. Louis Post-Dispatch*, Feb. 11, 1889, 8.
14. "The Great Trip," *Sporting Life*, Oct. 17, 1888, 4.
15. "Gossip of the Ball Field," *NY Sun*, Dec. 30, 1888, 9.
16. "Little Hughes Kicks," *Pittsburgh Dispatch*, Jan. 7, 1889, 6.
17. "Sports with the Ball," *NY Sun*, Jan. 8, 1889, 3.

Chapter 17

1. "Chicago Sentiment," *Sporting Life*, Dec. 5, 1888, 1.
2. "Chicago Gleanings," *Sporting Life*, Jan. 23, 1889, 3.
3. "Baseball," *Buffalo Courier*, Jan. 24, 1889, 3.
4. *Chicago Tribune*, Jan. 20, 1889.
5. *The Sporting News*, Feb. 16, 1889 via "In and Out Door Sports," *NY Sun*, Feb. 20, 1889, 1.
6. "A Royal Feast," *Brooklyn Daily Eagle*, March 11, 1889, 1.
7. "Still Losing," *Brooklyn Daily Eagle*, April 23, 1889, 2.
8. "Notes," *Brooklyn Standard Union*, July 24, 1889, 4.
9. "Psychic Force," *Brooklyn Daily Eagle*, July 25, 1889, 6.
10. *Ibid.*
11. *Ibid.*
12. "Team Talkers," *Brooklyn Daily Eagle*, July 26, 1889, 4.

13. "By Four Points," *Brooklyn Daily Eagle*, August 5, 1889, 2.
14. "The Sporting World," *Brooklyn Citizen*, August 26, 1889, 3.
15. "Baseball Gossip," *Brooklyn Citizen*, Sept. 1, 1889, 3.
16. "Baseball Gossip," *Brooklyn Citizen*, Sept. 5, 1889, 3.
17. "Black-Guards Play," *Brooklyn Citizen*, Sept. 8, 1889, 2.
18. *Ibid.*
19. "He Is Now Sane," *Brooklyn Daily Eagle*, Sept. 11, 1889, 2.
20. "Von der Ahe's Kick," *Brooklyn Citizen*, Sept. 9. 1889, 3.
21. "Von der Ahe Weakens," *Brooklyn Standard Union*, Sept. 10, 1889, 4.
22. "Notes," *Brooklyn Standard Union*, Sept. 14, 1889, 6.
23. "Would Not Go," *Brooklyn Daily Eagle*, Oct. 10, 1889, 1.
24. "Return of the Conquered Heroes," *St. Louis Post-Dispatch*, Oct. 18, 1889, 6.
25. "Baseball Gossip," *Brooklyn Citizen*, Oct. 20, 1889, 3.
26. "By a Single Run," *Brooklyn Daily Eagle*, Oct. 23, 1889, 1.

Chapter 18

1. "Diamond Dust," *St. Louis Globe-Democrat*, Oct. 16, 1889, 8.
2. "Now They Legislate," *Brooklyn Citizen*, Nov. 1, 1889, 1.
3. *Ibid.*
4. "Already Deserting," *NY Sun*, Nov. 10, 1889, 5.
5. *Cincinnati Commercial Gazette*, Dec. 29, 1889.
6. "Athletic Sports in Burlesque," *Brooklyn Citizen*, Nov. 29, 1889, 3.
7. *Ibid.*
8. "The Sporting World," *Brooklyn Citizen*, March 1, 1890, 3.
9. "The Colts Won," *Brooklyn Daily Eagle*, March 13, 1890, 1.
10. "At Home Again," *Brooklyn Daily Eagle*, April 1, 1890, 1.
11. "A Ladies' Day," *Brooklyn Daily Eagle*, April 4, 1890, 2.
12. "Caruthers' Mistake," *Sporting Life*, April 26, 1890, 6.
13. "Again Delayed," *Brooklyn Daily Eagle*, April 26, 1890, 1.
14. "Brooklyn to the Front," *Brooklyn Times Union*, April 29, 1890, 4.
15. "Brooklyn Boys Winners," *Brooklyn Times Union*, May 20, 1890, 2.
16. "Notes," *Brooklyn Standard Union*, June 3, 1890, 4.
17. "Notes and Comments," *Sporting Life*, Sept. 1, 1886, 5.

18. *Lexington Herald-Leader*, Oct. 29, 1889.

19. "Clubs Had Few Pitchers," *Sioux City Journal*, March 21, 1918, 10.

20. "How to Hit a Ball," *Buffalo Sunday Morning News*, Oct. 7, 1888, 6.

21. "Bridegrooms Win at Boston," *Brooklyn Citizen*, August 16, 1890, 3.

22. "Notes" *Brooklyn Standard Union*, Sept. 3, 1890, 3.

23. *The Sporting News*, Sept. 27, 1890.

24. "Championship Season Closes," *Brooklyn Citizen*, Oct. 5, 1890, 3.

25. *The Sporting News*, Oct. 18, 1890, 4.

26. "Brooklyn Budget," *Sporting Life*, Nov. 1, 1890, 5.

Chapter 19

1. "The Sporting World," *Brooklyn Citizen*, Dec. 4, 1890, 6.

2. *Ibid.*

3. "McGunnigle's Case," *Sporting Life*, Jan. 3, 1891, 7.

4. "In the Metropolis," *The Sporting News*, March 21, 1891, 5.

5. *Ibid.*

6. "Brooklyn Budget," *Sporting Life*, April 4, 1891, 7.

7. "In a Leading Position," *Brooklyn Daily Eagle*, April 12, 1891, 2.

8. "Open the Fight," *Brooklyn Daily Eagle*, April 23, 1891, 1.

9. "Capt. Ward Injured," *Brooklyn Citizen*, April 24, 1891, 3.

10. "Base Ball Notes," *Boston Globe*, May 7, 1891, 5.

11. "In Sixth Place," *Brooklyn Daily Eagle*, June 10, 1891, 2.

12. "Baseball Gossip," *Brooklyn Citizen*, June 6, 1891, 3.

13. "East and West," *Brooklyn Daily Eagle*, June 8, 1891, 2.

14. "Another Good Spurt," *Brooklyn Citizen*, June 10, 1891, 6.

15. "Brooklyn Budget," *Sporting Life*, June 20, 1891, 9.

16. "Caruthers' Curves," *St. Paul Globe*, March 7, 1888, 5.

17. "An Essay on Ball-Pitching," *Philadelphia Press* via *St. Louis Globe-Democrat*, May 12, 1886, 5.

18. "Brooklyn Club Notes," *Sporting Life*, August 14, 1889, 5.

19. *Washington Evening Star*, Feb. 23, 1928.

20. "The Game Has Changed," *Wilkes-Barre Record*, Jan. 19, 1899, 3.

21. "Bob Carruthers, Old Pitcher, Not Likely to Die," *New York Evening World*, July 20, 1911, 12.

22. "Giants Couldn't Win," *Brooklyn Citizen*, June 25, 1891, 8.

23. "Rusie and Buckley," *The Sporting News*, July 25, 1891, 1.

24. "Down Again," *Brooklyn Daily Eagle*, August 11, 1891, 1.

25. *Cincinnati Commercial Gazette*, August 17, 1891.

26. "A Jolly for Pittsburgh," *Pittsburgh Press*, April 3, 1892, 5.

27. *Cincinnati Commercial Gazette*, April 3, 1892.

28. "A Jolly for Pittsburgh," *Pittsburgh Press*, April 3, 1892, 5.

29. *Ibid.*

30. "Many Changes," *Brooklyn Standard Union*, Sept. 7, 1891, 1.

31. "Next Year's Ball Team," *Brooklyn Daily Eagle*, Sept. 27, 1891, 8.

32. "Caruthers and the Browns," *Omaha Daily Bee*, July 24, 1904, 11.

33. "Umpire Robert Caruthers," *Daily Review Decatur*, June 23, 1907, 5.

Chapter 20

1. "Chat of the Diamond," *Philadelphia Inquirer*, Jan. 10, 1892, 3.

2. "A Month in the South," *Brooklyn Daily Eagle*, Feb. 14, 1892, 20.

3. "Base Ball Notes," *Washington Evening Star*, Feb. 29, 1892, 6.

4. *Chicago Tribune*, Feb. 27, 1892.

5. "Pinkney at Caruthers Will Play with the Browns," *St. Louis Globe-Democrat*, March 2, 1892, 9.

6. *Ibid.*

7. *Cincinnati Commercial Gazette*, April 3, 1892.

8. "Manager Cushman Red-Hot," *St. Louis Globe-Democrat*, April 6, 1892, 4.

9. "Base Ball Briefs," *St. Louis Post-Dispatch*, April 9, 1892, 8.

10. "Caught on the Fly," *The Sporting News*, March 19, 1892, 3.

11. "Base Ball Gossip," *St. Louis Post-Dispatch*, May 3, 1892, 10.

12. "Brooklyn's Last Game," *St. Louis Post-Dispatch*, May 6, 1892, 9.

13. "Caruthers' Success as an Outfielder," *St. Louis Post-Dispatch*, May 7, 1892, 10.

14. "Base Ball Notes," *Brooklyn Daily Eagle*, May 27, 1892, 1.

15. "For Hub Collins' Family," *St. Louis Globe-Democrat*, May 30, 1892, 7.

16. "Von der Ahe's Pets," *St. Louis Post-Dispatch*, June 16, 1892, 12.

17. "Made His Pay-Roll Smaller," *St. Louis Globe-Democrat*, July 9, 1892, 7.

18. "These Browns Are Quitters," *St. Louis Globe-Democrat*, August 3, 1892, 5.

19. *Ibid.*

20. *Ibid.*

21. "Will Be Retained," *St. Louis Post-Dispatch*, August 3, 1892, 8.

22. *St. Louis Globe-Democrat*, August 17, 1892.

23. "Those Browns," *St. Louis Globe-Democrat,* August 18, 1892, 11.

24. "Comedy of Errors," *St. Louis Post-Dispatch,* August 18, 1892, 12.

25. "Base Ball," *St. Louis Post-Dispatch,* August 20, 1892, 8.

26. "Base Ball Notes," *Brooklyn Daily Eagle,* August 23, 1892, 2.

27. "Base Ball Comments," *Brooklyn Daily Eagle,* Sept. 9, 1892, 7.

28. "Hawley's Friends Were There," *St. Louis Globe-Democrat,* August 30, 1892, 9.

29. *Ibid.*

30. "Runs Came in Blocks of Five," *St. Louis Globe-Democrat,* August 31, 1892, 5.

31. "Von der Ahe's Pets," *St. Louis Post-Dispatch,* Sept. 3, 1892, 8.

32. "Caruthers' Little Say," *St. Louis Post-Dispatch,* Sept. 24, 1892, 8.

33. "Beat the Champions Again," *St. Louis Globe-Democrat,* Oct. 2, 1892, 8.

34. "Very Ragged Fielding," *St. Louis Globe-Democrat,* Oct. 14, 1892, 9.

Chapter 21

1. "St. Louis Siftings," *Sporting Life,* Feb. 11, 1893, 4.

2. *Ibid.*

3. "Base Ball," *St. Louis Post-Dispatch,* March 23, 1893, 7.

4. "Base Ball," *St. Louis Post-Dispatch,* April 14, 1893, 10.

5. *Cincinnati Commercial Gazette,* April 29, 1893.

6. "Chicago Gleanings," *Sporting Life,* May 13, 1893, 2.

7. *Chicago Tribune,* May 2, 1893.

8. *Cincinnati Enquirer,* May 1, 1893.

9. *Cincinnati Enquirer,* May 6, 1893.

10. *Cincinnati Enquirer,* May 6, 1893.

11. *Cincinnati Enquirer,* May 14, 1893.

12. *Chicago Tribune,* July 10, 1893.

13. "Chicago Gleanings," *Sporting Life,* March 25, 1893, 14.

14. "Editorial Views, News, Comment," *Sporting Life,* August 26, 1893, 4.

15. "Days of Long Ago," *Sporting Life,* Sept. 16, 1893, 11.

Chapter 22

1. http://reigelridge.com/roots/index.htm?ssmain=p2149.htm.

2. *Chicago Tribune,* Sept. 7, 1895.

3. "The World of Sport," *Minneapolis Star Tribune,* Feb. 4, 1894, 3.

4. "Comers," *Dayton Daily News,* April 7, 1899, 3.

5. *Bloomington Evening World,* May 9, 1922.

6. *Grand Rapids Herald,* June 30, 1894.

7. *Grand Rapids Democrat,* May 2, 1894.

8. *Milwaukee Journal,* Jan. 23, 1895.

9. *Grand Rapids Herald,* June 14, 1894.

10. *Grand Rapids Democrat,* June 13, 1894.

11. *Grand Rapids Herald,* July 13, 1894.

12. *Grand Rapids Herald,* June 24, 1894.

13. *Grand Rapids Herald,* Sept. 12, 1894.

14. "News, Gossip and General Comment," *Sporting Life,* Dec. 8, 1894, 2.

15. "All About Base Ball," *Philadelphia Inquirer,* Jan. 27, 1895, 24.

16. *Philadelphia Times,* Feb. 10, 1895.

17. "Diamond Dust," *Quincy Daily Herald,* June 1, 1895, 1.

18. *Quincy Daily Whig,* June 1, 1895.

19. *Jacksonville Daily Journal,* August 7, 1895.

20. "Connie Mack Talks of St. Louis," *St. Louis Globe-Democrat,* July 12, 1895, 5.

21. *Indianapolis Sun,* June 4, 1895.

22. *Burlington Gazette,* Sept. 4, 1895.

23. *Dubuque Daily Times,* Sept. 12, 1895.

24. "Sporting News," *Buffalo Enquirer,* Nov. 12, 1895, 8.

25. "Local gossip," *St. Louis Globe-Democrat,* July 7, 1889, 6.

26. *Ibid.*

Chapter 23

1. *Burlington Hawk Eye,* May 9, 1896.

2. *Burlington Gazette,* May 23, 1896.

3. *Ibid.*

4. *Burlington Gazette,* May 27, 1896.

5. *Burlington Hawk Eye,* June 21, 1896.

6. "Caruther's Brave Act." *St. Joseph Gazette,* June 24, 1896, 5.

7. "Local Brevities," *St. Joseph News-Press,* June 24, 1896, 6.

8. "Caruther's Brave Act," *St. Joseph Gazette,* June 24, 1896, 5.

9. "Burlington Bits," *Sporting Life,* July 18, 1896, 13.

10. *Burlington Evening Gazette,* August 5, 1896.

11. *Burlington Hawk Eye,* August 27, 1896.

12. "Eight Big Errors," *St. Paul Globe,* August 8, 1896, 5.

13. *Kansas City Daily Journal,* Sept. 1, 1896.

14. *Kansas City Daily Journal,* Sept. 6, 1896.

15. *Ibid.*

16. "Between the Bases," *Washington Evening Times,* Sept. 10, 1896, 3.

17. *Ibid.*

18. *Kansas City Daily Journal,* Sept. 7, 1896.

19. *Burlington Hawk Eye,* March 9, 1897.

20. "The Poor Umpire," *Quincy Daily Journal,* May 29, 1897, 6.

21. "Notes," Peoria Transcript via *Quincy Daily Journal,* May 22, 1897, 3.

22. *Burlington Hawk-Eye,* May 23, 1897.

23. *Burlington Evening Gazette,* Sept. 11, 1897.

24. *Dubuque Daily Times,* August 31, 1897.

25. *Dubuque Daily Times,* August 28, 1897.

26. "Notes," *St. Joseph Herald,* July 2, 1897, 6.

27. "St. Joseph Jottings," *Sporting Life,* July 17, 1897, 8.

28. "Were Robbed," *Cedar Rapids Gazette*, July 15, 1897, 5.

29. *Burlington Evening Gazette*, July 17, 1897.

30. "The Diamond," *Cedar Rapids Gazette*, July 27, 1897, 5.

31. *Quincy Daily Whig*, July 29, 1897.

32. "The Diamond," *Cedar Rapids Gazette*, July 27, 1897, 5.

33. "Still Lead," *Cedar Rapids Gazette*, Sept. 8, 1897, 5.

34. "It Is Cinched," *Cedar Rapids Gazette*, Sept. 13, 1897, 5.

35. *Burlington Evening Gazette*, Sept. 18, 1897.

Chapter 24

1. "Season Will Soon Open," *Minneapolis Daily Times*, March 13, 1898, 13.

2. *Burlington Hawk Eye*, May 17, 1898.

3. *Quincy Daily Whig*, May 19, 1898.

4. "Baseball," *Ottawa Citizen*, March 15, 1899, 6.

5. "Carruthers' Little Talk," *Buffalo Courier*, May 5, 1902, 9.

6. "The Game of Ball," *Detroit Tribune* via *Windsor Star*, July 21, 1898, 3.

7. *Ibid.*

8. *Indianapolis Sun*, July 25, 1898.

9. *St. Joseph Herald*, July 27, 1898.

10. *St. Paul Globe*, July 24, 1898.

11. "Baseball Notes," *St. Joseph Gazette*, July 29, 1898, 3.

12. *St. Joseph Herald*, July 30, 1898.

13. *Detroit Free Press*, August 5, 1898.

14. "Wheeling's Way," *Sporting Life*, July 15, 1899, 1.

15. "Base Ball Comment," *Wheeling Daily Intelligencer*, August 2, 1899, 3.

16. "Notes of the Game," *Fort Wayne Sentinel*, August 21, 1899, 2.

17. "Which?," *Dayton Herald*, July 25, 1899, 6.

18. "Notes of the Game," *Fort Wayne Sentinel*, August 25, 1899, 2.

19. "At New Castle," *Dayton Daily News*, August 29, 1899, 3.

20. "Cy Swain Hit on the Chin," *Ft. Wayne News*, Sept. 5, 1899, 4.

21. *Ibid.*

22. "Notes of the Game," *Ft. Wayne Sentinel*, Sept. 12, 1899, 2.

23. "Base Ball Notes," *Ft. Wayne Sentinel*, Feb. 12, 1901, 6.

24. "Inter State League," *Wheeling Daily Intelligencer*, August 17, 1900, 3.

25. "Hemphill Showed Up Well," *Ft. Wayne Sentinel*, August 17, 1900, 6.

26. "To Be Revised," *Dayton Daily News*, July 17, 1900, 2.

27. *Chicago Tribune*, Oct. 13, 1900.

28. "Omaha Tries Hard in Vain," *Omaha Daily Bee*, May 4, 1901, 2.

29. "Millers and Saints Play Double Header Today," *Minneapolis Star Tribune*, July 7, 1901, 6.

30. "More Glory for Omaha," *Omaha Daily Bee*, July 10, 1901, 4.

31. "Western League Notes," Denver Post via *Minneapolis Star Tribune*, August 23, 1901, 3.

32. "Fodder for the Fans," *St. Joseph Gazette*-Herald, Sept. 13, 1901, 2.

33. "Sports and Pastimes," *St. Louis Globe-Democrat*, July 21, 1901, 32

Chapter 25

1. "The Weekly News," *Williams (AZ) News*, August 31, 1901, 4.

2. "Four to Three," *Albuquerque Citizen*, Oct. 26, 1901, 1.

3. "Johnson's Umpires," *Buffalo Courier*, March 17, 1902, 9.

4. *St. Louis Republic*, April 24, 1902.

5. "Robs Joss of No Hit Game," *Inter Ocean*, July 29, 1907, 8.

6. *Decatur Daily Review*, Nov. 20, 1908.

7. "Jesse Burkett Shocks Umpire," *Pittsburgh Press*, May 2, 1902, 16.

8. *The Sporting News*, May 10, 1902, 4.

9. "Carruthers as Umpire," *Boston Globe*, May 17, 1902, 5.

10. *Washington Post*, July 7, 1902.

11. "Jimmy Collins Is Suspended 3 Days," *Buffalo Times*, July 3, 1902, 8.

12. "Bobby Carruthers Won't Do," *Buffalo Enquirer*, May 13, 1902, 4.

13. "Carruthers' Little Talk," *Buffalo Courier*, May 5, 1902, 9.

14. *Boston Globe*, May 17, 1903.

15. "American League Notes," *Sporting Life*, July 4, 1903, 9.

16. "Tigers Beat Los Angeles," *San Francisco Examiner*, August 8, 1903, 9.

17. "Carruthers to Umpire," *Spokesman-Review*, Sept. 27, 1903, 3.

Chapter 26

1. David Caruthers death certificate.

2. "Locals Climb to Half Way Mark," *Des Moines Register*, August 1, 1904.

3. *Washington Post*, August 7, 1904.

4. "Will Hire Better Umpires," *Des Moines Register*, Oct. 19, 1904, 5.

5. "Baseball Gossip," *Des Moines Register*, May 21, 1905, 23.

6. "Players Do Some Fanning," *Sioux City Journal*, June 4, 1905, 9.

7. *Des Moines Capital*, April 18, 1905.

8. *Burlington Evening Gazette*, August 7, 1 905.

9. *Ibid.*

10. *Burlington Evening Gazette*, August 7, 1905.

11. *Indianapolis Sun*, Dec. 21, 1905.

12. "Notes of the Game," *Omaha Daily News*, August 28, 1905, 5.

13. "Sporting Brevities," *Omaha Daily Bee*, August 29, 1905, 9.

14. "Is O'Neill a Weakling?," *Sioux City Journal*, August 30, 1905, 7.

15. "Carruthers Ordered Home," *Des Moines Register*, May 8, 1905, 5.

16. "Could Not Hit Ball," *St. Joseph News-Press*, July 1, 1905, 3.

17. "Billy Sunday Sent a Wire," *Quincy Daily Journal*, Nov. 18, 1905, 1.

18. "School Board Will Take No Action," *Des Moines Register*, Dec. 9, 1905, 6.

19. *Burlington Evening Gazette*, Dec. 5, 1906.

20. *Ibid.*

21. "Carruthers' Young Son Dies," *Quincy Daily Herald*, Dec. 9, 1905, 6.

22. "The Case of David Carruthers," *Marshalltown Evening Times*, Dec. 9, 1905, 4.

23. "Carruthers Gets a Berth," *Sioux City Journal*, March 21, 1906, 7.

24. *Decatur Daily Review*, June 23, 1907.

Chapter 27

1. *Decatur Daily Review*, June 18, 1907.

2. "New Umpire or No Game—Kinsella," *Decatur Herald*, July 14, 1907, 5.

3. "Kinsella's Bluff Was Called," *Decatur Herald and Review*, July 15, 1907, 3.

4. "Two Umpire System Not Needed Here," *Rock Island Argus*, August 24, 1907, 3.

5. "Notes of the Game," *Freeport Daily Journal*, Sept. 30, 1907, 2.

6. "Sporting Gossip," *Los Angeles Herald*, Dec. 7, 1910, 10.

7. "Old-Time Twirlers Were Better Batters Than Present Day Crop," *Escanaba Morning Press*, May 19, 1911, 16.

8. "Brooklyn Budget," *Sporting Life*, July 30, 1910, 6.

9. "Pitching Stars Past and Present," *St. Joseph Gazette*-Herald, June 12, 1901, 3.

10. "Baseball Now at Its Best," *Sioux City Journal*, May 25, 1905, 8.

11. "Baseball Gossip," *Decatur Herald*, August 15, 1901, 2.

12. *Boston Post*, August 2, 1909.

13. *Decatur Daily Review*, June 23, 1907.

14. "Good Umpires Signed for Northwest League," *Anaconda Standard*, March 2, 1908, 8.

15. "Current Northwest Comment," *Anaconda Standard*, April 20, 1908, 8.

16. "Carruthers and Umpiring Style," *Oregon Daily Journal*, June 2, 1909, 10.

17. "Fast Race Is Now Assured," *Butte Miner*, April 27, 1908, 2.

18. "Pertinent Paragraphs Pertaining to Players," *Seattle Post-Intelligencer* via *Vancouver Daily World*, May 20, 1908, 12.

19. "Altman Is Here," *Spokane Chronicle*, August 13, 1908, 6.

20. "Harry Rush Whole Game," *Spokane Chronicle*, June 5, 1908, 6.

21. "Veteran Player a Star Umpire," *Spokesman-Review*, June 7, 1908, 36.

22. "Fan Kicks Against Umpire Carruthers," *Vancouver Province*, April 30, 1908, 10.

Chapter 28

1. *Spokane Press*, April 16, 1909.

2. "City Leaguers Are Lobbying," *Spokesman-Review*, March 10, 1910, 9.

3. "Bob Carruthers Will Umpire Here," *Davenport Daily Times*, March 11, 1910, 8.

4. "Normal Notes," *Bloomington Pantagraph*, May 2, 1910, 9.

5. "Boots and Boosts," *Quad City Times*, May 29, 1910, 7.

6. "Notes of the Game," *Rock Island Argus*, May 31, 1910, 3.

7. "Grounders," *Waterloo Courier*, June 6, 1910, 2.

8. "Zephyrs from the Diamond," *Rock Island Argus*, June 14, 1910, 3.

9. "Expect Big Crowd," *Rock Island Argus*, June 21, 1910, 3.

10. *Waterloo Times Tribune*, August 13, 1910.

11. "President Tearney Slaps Waterloo Base Ball Lovers," *Waterloo Courier*, August 15, 1910, 2.

12. *Ibid.*

13. *Waterloo Times Tribune*, August 14, 1910.

14. "President Tearney Slaps Waterloo Base Ball Lovers," *Waterloo Courier*, August 15, 1910, 2.

15. "Notes of the Game," *Rock Island Argus*, May 25, 1911, 3.

16. *Dubuque Telegraph Herald*, May 31, 1911.

17. "Baseball Notes," *Davenport Daily Times*, June 7, 1911, 6.

18. "Bobby Not Yet Reinstated," *Peoria Star* via *Davenport Daily Times*, June 17, 1911, 8.

19. "Exit Bob Carruthers," *Peoria Star* via *Moline Dispatch*, July 15, 1911, 8.

20. *Lincoln Daily Star*, August 5, 1911.

21. "Pays a Tribute to Bob Carruthers," *Rock Island Argus*, July 29, 1911, 3.

22. "Old Player Called Out," *Quincy Daily Herald*, August 9, 1911, 9.

23. "Detroit Hopes Chicago Will Capture Flag," *Glen Falls Times*, Sept. 26, 1935, 8.

24. *Waterloo Times Tribune*, August 6, 1911.

25. "Glints from the Diamond," *Bloomington Pantagraph*, August 7, 1911, 9.

26. *Ibid.*

Bibliography

Books

Boddie, John Thomas, and John Bennett Boddie. *Boddie and Allied Families*. Privately published, 1918.

Coldwell, Thomas H. *Cases Argued and Determined in the Supreme Court of Tennessee, During the Year 1868–9*. Nashville: Jones, Purvis, 1870.

Eisenbath, Mike. *The Cardinals Encyclopedia*. Philadelphia: Temple University Press, 1999.

Lowry, Philip J. *Green Cathedrals: The Ultimate Celebration of All Major League and Negro League Ballparks*. 10th edition. Phoenix: Society for American Baseball Research, 2019.

Phillips, Isaac Newton. *Cases at Law and in Chancery Argued and Determined in the Supreme Court of Illinois, Vol. 245*. Bloomington, IL: Pantagraph, 1910.

Spalding's Base Ball Guide and Official League Book for 1884. Chicago: A. G. Spalding & Bros., 1884.

Spalding's Base Ball Guide and Official League Book for 1885. Chicago: A.G. Spalding & Bros., 1885.

Wright, Edward Monroe. *A Brief of John Caruthers, a Pioneer: His Descendants and Collateral Kin*. Springfield, MO: E.M. Wright, 1944.

Articles

Bauer, Robert Allan. "Outside the Lines of Gilded Age Origins of the Brotherhood War." PhD diss., University of Arkansas, Fayetteville, July 2015. Accessible at https://scholarworks.uark.edu/etd/1215/.

Egenriether, Richard. "Chris Von der Ahe: Baseball's Pioneering Huckster." *Baseball Research Journal* 18 (1989): 27–31.

Pruter, Robert. "Youth Baseball in Chicago, 1868–1890: Not Always Sandlot Ball." *Journal of Sport History* 26, no. 1 (1999): 1–28.

Thorn, John. "News from the *Plus ça Change* Department." Our Game (blog), Jan. 26, 2018.

_____. "Why Is the National Association Not a Major League … and Other Records Issues." *Our Game* (blog), May 4, 2015. https://ourgame.mlblogs.com/why-is-the-national-association-not-a-major-league-and-other-records-issues-7507e1683b66.

"Wages of Unskilled Labor in the United States 1850–1900. *The Journal of Political Economy* 13 (September 1904–September 1905).

Newspapers

Albuquerque Citizen
Anaconda Standard
Arkansas Democrat
Baltimore American
Baltimore Sun
Berkshire Eagle
Billings Gazette
Bloomington (IL) Pantagraph
Bloomington (IN) Evening World
Boston Globe
Boston Post
Brooklyn Citizen
Brooklyn Daily Eagle
Brooklyn Standard Union
Brooklyn Times Union
Buffalo Commercial
Buffalo Courier
Buffalo Enquirer
Buffalo Sunday Morning News
Buffalo Times
Burlington (IA) Evening Gazette
Burlington (IA) Gazette
Burlington (IA) Hawk Eye
Butte Daily Post
Butte Miner
Cedar Rapids Gazette
Chicago Examiner
Chicago Tribune
Cincinnati Commercial Gazette
Cincinnati Enquirer

Daily Arkansas Gazette
Daily Minnesota Tribune
Davenport Daily Times
Dayton Daily News
Dayton Herald
Decatur Daily Review
Decatur Herald and Review
Decatur Saturday Herald
Des Moines Capital
Des Moines Register
Detroit Free-Press
Dubuque Daily Times
Dubuque Telegraph Herald
Escanaba Morning Press
Fort Wayne Daily Gazette
Fort Wayne News
Fort Wayne Sentinel
Freeport (IL) Daily Journal
Glen Falls Times
Grand Rapids Daily Democrat
Grand Rapids Daily Eagle
Grand Rapids Daily Times
Grand Rapids Democrat
Grand Rapids Evening Ledger
Grand Rapids Evening News
Grand Rapids Herald
Indianapolis Journal
Indianapolis Sun
Inter Ocean
Jacksonville Daily Journal
Kansas City Daily Journal
Lexington (KY) Herald-Leader
Lincoln Daily Star
Logansport (IN) Chronicle
Los Angeles Herald
Mansfield Shield
Marshalltown (IA) Evening Times
Memphis Avalanche
Memphis Daily Appeal
Milwaukee Journal
Minneapolis Daily Times
Minneapolis Daily Tribune
Minneapolis Star Tribune
Moline Dispatch
New York Clipper
New York Evening World
New York Sun
New York Times
Omaha Daily Bee
Omaha Daily News
Oregon Daily Journal
Oshkosh Daily Northwestern
Ottawa Citizen
Philadelphia Inquirer
Philadelphia Times
Pittsburgh Dispatch
Pittsburgh Press
Quad City Times
Quincy Daily Herald
Quincy Daily Journal
Quincy Daily Whig
Racine Daily Journal
Richmond Dispatch

Rock Island Argus
St. Joseph Gazette
St. Joseph Gazette-Herald
St. Joseph Herald
St. Joseph News-Press
St. Louis Globe-Democrat
St. Louis Post-Dispatch
St. Louis Republic
St. Paul Daily Globe
San Francisco Examiner
Savannah Morning News
Sedalia Weekly Bazoo
Sioux City Journal
Spokane Chronicle
Spokane Press
Spokesman-Review
Springfield Daily Republic
Vancouver Daily World
Vancouver Province
Wapanucka (OK) Press
Washington (DC) Evening Star
Washington (DC) Evening Times
Washington Post
Waterloo (IA) Courier
Waterloo (IA) Times Tribune
Wheeling Daily Intelligencer
Wilkes-Barre Record
Williams (AZ) News
Windsor Star

Periodicals

Baseball Magazine
Sporting Life
The Sporting News

Collections

Bob Caruthers clippings file, National Baseball
    Hall of Fame

Correspondence

Bradley D. Cook, Curator of Photographs, Editor
    of Manuscripts Indiana University, Jan. 12–20,
    2022

Online Resources

Ancestry.com
Available City Population Data (https://physics.
    bu.edu/~redner/projects/population/)
ballparks.com
baseballalmanac.com
Baseball History Daily
baseball-reference.com
Cedar Rapids Public Library community history
    archive
censusrecords.com
Chicagology

chroniclingamerica.loc.gov
Daytonian in Manhattan
Des Moines Public Library ProQuest
Dig Memphis: The Digital Archives of Memphis
  Public Libraries
FindaGrave.com
Gale News Vault
The Game of Games
Google Books
Google Newspaper Archive
Grand Rapids Public Library digital collections
IEEE-USA InSight
Illinois Digital Newspaper Collections
LA84 Foundation digital library
Minnesota Digital Newspaper Hub
New York Public Library Spalding collection
New York Times archive
Newspaperarchive.com
newspapers.com

Norway Heritage
NYS Historic Newspapers
officialdata.org
paperofrecord.com
Quincy Public Library community history archive
retrosheet.org
SABR Bio Project
Seamheads.com ballpark database
Spared & Shared: Saving history one letter at a
  time…
Sporting News Player Contract Cards
Terry & Nancy's Ancestors (reigelridge.com)
Threads of Our Game: 19th century baseball uni-
  form database
United State Census Bureau
The Vintage News
Washington Digital Newspapers
Wikipedia

Index

Numbers in **bold italics** indicate pages with illustrations